Shot on Location

▦ TECHNIQUES of the MOVING IMAGE

Volumes in the Techniques of the Moving Image series explore the relationship between what we see onscreen and the technical achievements undertaken in filmmaking to make this possible. Books explore some defined aspect of cinema—work from a particular era, work in a particular genre, work by a particular filmmaker or team, work from a particular studio, or work on a particular theme—in light of some technique and/or technical achievement, such as cinematography, direction, acting, lighting, costuming, set design, legal arrangements, agenting, scripting, sound design and recording, and sound or picture editing. Historical and social background contextualize the subject of each volume.

Murray Pomerance
Series Editor

Shot on Location

Postwar American Cinema and the Exploration of Real Place

R. BARTON PALMER

RUTGERS UNIVERSITY PRESS

NEW BRUNSWICK, NEW JERSEY, AND LONDON

LIBRARY OF CONGRESS CATALOGING-IN-PUBLICATION DATA

Palmer, R. Barton, 1946–
    Shot on location : postwar American cinema and the exploration of real place /
R. Barton Palmer.
        pages cm. — (Techniques of the moving image)
    Includes bibliographical references and index.
    ISBN 978–0–8135–6409–8 (hardcover : alk. paper) — ISBN 978–0–8135–6408–1
(pbk. : alk. paper) — ISBN 978–0–8135–6410–4 (e-book (web pdf)) — ISBN 978–0–8135–
7549–0 (e-book (epub))
    1. Motion pictures—United States—History—20th century. 2. Motion pictures—
Production and direction—United States—History—20th century. 3. Motion pictures—
Setting and scenery. I. Title.
    PN1993.5.U6P28 2016
    791.430973—DC23

                                                                    ,   2015012453

        A British Cataloging-in-Publication record for this book is available
                        from the British Library.

            Visit our website: http://rutgerspress.rutgers.edu

            Manufactured in the United States of America

CONTENTS

PREFACE

Shot on Location focuses on those Hollywood productions of the initial postwar era, roughly 1945–1965, in which the already existing real (geographical, human, and cultural) is featured in important ways as itself. Thus the world outside the studio is incorporated within the film in ways that exceed its usefulness for and subordination to the narrative, most often through the growing fashion for location shooting, but also through a weakening of the formal boundaries between the fictional and the journalistic, between the use of realia to stand for those things that function strictly in some fiction (such as an actor playing a role) and as unfictionalized, that is, partaking of what identity they possess before becoming textualized. This is an era of American film practice in which the cinema was often involved in the telling (or, perhaps better, re-creation) of "true stories" in ways that emulated the reportorial accuracy required in the nonfictional media, a rhetorical aim that is arguably just as culturally significant as when, which is not seldom the case, the actual truth value of the story is more than a little questionable. One of the cinema's technical capacities (of immense usefulness to those pursuing certain forms of realist aesthetics) is that actuality or documentary footage can easily, and more or less seamlessly if so desired, be joined to representations that are the product of the usual commercial forms of staging and dramatization, a marrying of modalities not so available, if at all, to storytellers in other media. Such footage corresponds aesthetically to the modernist notion of *objets trouvés*, those things that came to have the form they possess before the process of artistic creation (or assemblage) began, but, once existing, can be made a part of the resulting work of art, which is both "made" and "found," as it were, reflecting gestures of incorporation as well as manufacture. Actuality footage, of course, is as much "shot on location" as are post facto dramatizations or re-creations that access existing places as the settings for stories, either those in which the action re-created on the screen actually occurred or others that are plausible, authentic substitutes.

A number of the films considered in this book are usually said to be semi-documentary, an interesting and revealing classification whose full meaning requires substantial further discussion and exemplification. Semi-documentary filmmaking, we might observe at the outset, describes traditions that complexly intersect the categories of "fictional" and "actual," a dialectic whose mediating term might be "re-creation," the faithfully imitating reproduction of the real or particular. The notion of a "story" that is "true" neatly captures the referential instability of such a creation, as the film medium, with actuality footage and restagings providing fidelity, can be used to dramatize historical events, including recent ones, in a particularly forceful and persuasive manner. The accuracy of such representations, as well as what kind of rhetorical force they are permitted to wield, becomes as heavily controversial as the events themselves, in the precise manner of traditional historical writing.

A film that depicts a historical or cultural event becomes such an event in its own right, with the accuracy or appropriateness of its representations and style a matter for heated debate. The filmmakers whose work is discussed in this book are the predecessors in one way or another of contemporary directors like Oliver Stone. In his favorable assessment of Stone's oeuvre, Robert Rosenstone writes, "The historical film will always include images that are at once invented and, at best, true; true in that they symbolize, condense, or summarize larger amounts of data; true in that they impart an overall meaning of the past."[1] This may strike many as a too-expansive definition of what truth might be said to be, but it does take into account the peculiarities of filmic representation, a presence fully evident to the senses signifying an ultimate absence, as Rosenstone suggests: "This apparently most literal of media never delivers a literal representation of the past. It speaks about the past, it comments on it, its raises the issues of the past and tells us what these issues (can) mean. But it cannot show the past to us."[2] It would be a mistake, Rosenstone concludes, to judge what were sometimes called "films of fact" in postwar Hollywood in terms of their "detail," but rather "at the level of argument, metaphor, symbol."[3]

This heightened presence of the actual and particular is, to be sure, not the only significant aspect of the evolving realism of the period's filmmaking. It can also be glimpsed in the way in which the representational reach of the industry's productions was expanded, with more of the truths, often uncomfortable ones, of how people actually live their lives becoming available for the sort of cinematic re-presentation that Rosenstone describes, especially as films found themselves provided with First Amendment protection after a key Supreme Court decision in the *Miracle* case (1951). That films should tell more of the truth about contemporary American life was a trend that had begun before the war, as part of the aesthetic Saverio Giovacchini usefully terms "Hollywood democratic modernism." As he points out, "The artists gathering in Southern California carried with them a concern for radical politics . . . [and were] inclined to attune the Hollywood screen to the political reality of the day" and "open up its message to the masses insofar [as they were] . . . increasingly aware that the work of the previous generation of modernists had been hampered by the narrowness, elitism, and overall fragmentation of its audience."[4] The growing political engagement, and so cultural relevance, of what Hollywood produced was accelerated by the war. The enormity of the national commitment to global hostilities at first prompted morale-building productions to mask the dark reality of military setbacks in the Pacific, North Africa, and the Atlantic, but these were followed by a series of more realistic, and so disturbing, tributes to the terrified heroism of the ordinary citizen soldier (several of which are discussed in the introduction). It is possible, as film historian Nick Smedley argues, to see the postwar period "as one of declining optimism in America, a time when the idealism and moral certainty of the 1930s appeared to have evaporated." This view might in some sense be seen as confirmed by the advent of film noir, with its first productions, most directed by talented émigrés, released in the closing years of the war, a cinematic tradition that Smedley sees as limning "the moral emptiness at the heart of American life in the 1940s."[5]

The tradition explored in this book connects interestingly if at times obliquely to the noir aesthetic, which is itself hardly unitary, even as it suggests a more complex, even contradictory national mood, one that can with equal justice be described as an "age of doubt" or "an American high."[6] However, it is not the intention here to anatomize the intellectual, social, political, and institutional complexities of postwar Hollywood as a site of the production of films that went far beyond the straightforwardly simpler forms of celluloid entertainment that dominated an earlier era. This important task has already been ably advanced by the writings of Giovacchini, Smedley, Drew Casper, Peter Stanfield, Frank Krutnik, and others.[7] *Shot on Location* concerns itself with the analysis of key texts in a particular tradition of Hollywood realism that we might term *locative*, in which journalistic authenticity is a (sometimes obtrusive) focus for the filmmakers involved. Only in chapter 2 is a theoretical issue raised about film semiotics, and nothing original is claimed for the argument presented there.

My principal intention here is to offer readings of how place, which might also be designated as real space, figures in representative films of this tradition. Place is more aesthetically and culturally interesting than film historians acknowledged until somewhat recently. For the last decade or so, there has been a growing interest in the various questions, aesthetic and ideological, raised by the notion of place, a category of description whose essence and importance have been an issue of philosophical speculation since the ancient Greeks, reflecting the opposition within theoretical speculation between the universal (potential) and the particular (actual). It is particularity that has, of course, suffered from modes of thought that move from the individual to the categorical, from which the individual is customarily considered, as in Plato's thought, to draw its essence and importance. As Edward S. Casey points out, "At work in the obscuration of place is the universalism inherent in Western culture from the beginning . . . in the search for ideas, usually labelled 'essences,' that obtain *everywhere* and for which a particular *somewhere*, a given place, is irrelevant . . . is considered merely parochial in scope."[8]

This long-established and vexed dialectic between space and place finds a reflex of sorts in cinematic practice as the distinction between the (at least potential) universality of the soundstage that can and does stand for anyplace, anywhere as needed and the ineradicable particularity of locations (including their human dimension) that always already reference themselves in addition to whatever fictional guise they can be made to assume. The particular, of course, can be generalized, if not universalized, emptied of itself in order to represent a geographical or historical category that is more abstract, which is what happens in John Ford's reconstruction of Monument Valley, Utah, as this site is accommodated over a series of texts to the notion of "westernness." Many projects that escaped the studio soundstage, then as now, utilized existing locations as nonparticularized background or context for narratives that either ignore or reduce to vague generalities the influence of environment on human experience. The filmmaker interested in a locative aesthetic, by way of contrast, commits to exploring the preexisting truth of the places his camera finds and records, and in some cases re-creating real events, often by utilizing the concept of typicality at the heart of the social realist tradition. This filmmaking tradition explores how place shapes experiential possibilities, establishing, as in Italian Neorealism, a direct, mutually informative connection between character and locale, as human beings give meaning to those places that confine and define them, and vice versa.

Another aim of this book is to memorialize, if only briefly in many cases, some of the considerable number of realist fictional films produced during the period that have fallen into critical and historical oblivion, most, if not all, of which make extensive use of actual place. Consider, for example, the extended cycle of productions devoted to the exploration of contemporary social groups or institutions. These include Fred Zinnemann's exploration of postwar New York and rural Italy, *Teresa* (1951), as well as Alfred L. Werker's *The Young Don't Cry* (1957), filmed, save for a few studio-based interiors, in its entirety at the Bethesda School for Boys in Savannah, Georgia. *The Young Don't Cry* is, on one level, a teen pic in which the innocent protagonist, played by Sal Mineo, predictably finds himself in conflict with the gang of inmates who, with the connivance of some adult staff members, run the institution. But the plot, and the thoroughly typical characters around whom it revolves, more importantly serves to record and illuminate the workings of the home, expressing (in ways that are both disturbing and reassuring) the nature of what sociologist Erving Goffman at the time appropriately termed "asylums."[9] If, as Goffman says, "every institution captures something of the time and interest of its members and provides something of a world for them," then Werker's film may be appreciated as an extended exploration of that something.[10]

A similar intent to cinematize a world captured in its unique microcosmicness is apparent in many other films of the postwar realist tradition that focus on social institutions. Zinnemann's *The Men* (1950) explores the difficult recovery of paraplegic veterans; location work for the film was completed at the Birmingham Army Hospital in Van Nuys, California, near Los Angeles, and forty-five of the patients there constituted the cast, along with professional actors in the principal roles, including Marlon Brando, Teresa Wright, and Everett Sloane. Producer Stanley Kramer's controversial study of mentally ill children, *A Child Is Waiting* (John Cassavetes, 1963), was shot in part at the Pacific Coast Hospital, utilizing a number of patients and staff in minor roles. Hall Bartlett's *Unchained* (1955) takes a similar approach to documenting prison life, with principal photography done at the Chino penitentiary in California and inmates, including well-known jazz musician Dexter Gordon, appearing as themselves. Though it focuses on a jailbreak and thus is more obviously fictional, engaging a long-established Hollywood sub-genre, Crane Wilbur's *Canon City* (1948) also aims to depict a world by chronicling the *moyen de vivre* of its inhabitants; this low-budget production, with some second-rank Hollywood performers in lead roles (Scott Brady, Jeff Corey, and Whit Bissell), was shot almost entirely at the Colorado State Penitentiary, of which it provides an impressive documentary record. Wilbur's *Inside the Walls of Folsom Prison* (1951), with most scenes shot at the institution named in the title, offers a similar mix of fictional and documentary techniques, with once again an accurate portrayal of this real place constituting its chief appeal to audiences. Don Siegel's *Riot in Cell Block 11* (1954) is staged in the same prison and also makes use of guards and prisoners in minor roles; here, too, is a film that engages with a social problem then very much on the national agenda (increasingly deplorable conditions in a system of decaying lock-ups that provoked inmates into the hopeless gesture of rioting), even as it provides no easy answers. An only minimally optimistic conclusion, in keeping with the stark realism of the film's grim evocation of a notorious pit of misery, refuses the reassurance of the traditional Hollywood ending, with its full endorsement of the status quo and the social institutions that are its most obvious expression.

Much recent work on place/space in film studies has emphasized the various ways in which the histories of modernity, epitomized by the city, and the cinema, the modern city's most characteristic art form, are mutually imbricated. As Jean Baudrillard has famously remarked, "The American city seems to have stepped right out of the movies," which, for Baudrillard, implies that the "cityscape" should be approached as a "screenscape," collapsing in effect the disciplinary boundaries between sociology and film studies.[11] For David B. Clarke, the connection between the cinema and the city means, among other truths, that "the spectacle of the cinema both drew upon and contributed to the increased pace of modern city life, while also helping to normalize and cathect the frantic, disadjusted rhythms of city life."[12] Clarke and others make the case that film studies should take part in what some have called the "spatial turn" in social and cultural theory, which involves, as Mark Shiel puts it, the "growing recognition of the usefulness of space as an organizing category." Because it is a "peculiarly spatial form," the cinema, in Shiel's view, "operates and is best understood in terms of the organization of space," particularly in the analysis of "space in films" through the "mapping of a lived environment."[13] As far as the analysis of real locations is concerned, this mapping process has two intimately connected aspects: first, in terms of material production, the research and selection of locations, and second, in formal terms, the use made of these representations in the signifying patterns that constitute the finished filmic text.

There seems no good reason to restrict this inquiry to films that represent cityscapes, an approach that, to be sure, has yielded impressive results, as in Edward Dimendberg's *Film Noir and the Spaces of Modernity*.[14] Rural and natural locales, defined by local rather than cosmopolitan cultures, also constitute a potentially fruitful field of inquiry. In this book, the two aspects of the mapping process are equally emphasized, with a view toward delineating for these locations (and their representations) the "sense of place," which, in John Agnew's view, must take account of the cultural semiotics that establishes the human meanings of an environment. The local social worlds that figure in cinematic texts cannot, for Agnew, "be understood apart from the macro-order of location and the subjective territorial identity of sense of place," social meanings that postwar American realist films are heavily invested in evoking and critiquing.[15] It is also appropriate to acknowledge the importance of the following studies to the emerging field of place studies in film, key works by Deborah Carmichael, John Brinckerhoff Jackson, Imogen Sara Smith, Martin Lefebvre, John David Rhodes and Elena Gorfinkel, Graeme Harper and Jonathan Rayner, and W.J.T. Mitchell.[16]

A key element of the analyses offered here is reading out (from both production histories and the finished filmic texts) the senses of place that determined/conditioned the choice of locations in both general and particular terms. These locations become key narrative or thematic elements, sometimes even the main character of a film (e.g., producer Mark Hellinger's *The Naked City* [1948], in which characters "tell" the story of New York City through the ventriloquizing voice of the film's omniscient, omnipresent narrator). American postwar realism is enough of a submerged cinematic tradition to require, as a preliminary to other kinds of critical analysis, some gestures at taxonomic survey, however necessarily sketchy and incomplete, which the following chapters attempt, in addition to exploring a number of critical issues. The introduction examines a cycle of postwar productions in which the European war and its aftermath, including key events of the Allied occupation of Germany, figure as subjects; the aim here is to show something of the interconnection between current events and their representation. Chapters 1 and 2 attempt to unpack the several meanings of "setting" as a category of cinematic narrative, while chapter 3 draws a distinction between real locations used as backdrop and those that are given narrative focus as place. Chapter 4 argues that American postwar realism is paralleled by, but quite distinct from, Italian Neorealism, even as a main source of the Hollywood movement is to be found in the evolution of feature-length newsreels and their concern with "true stories." Here a key focus is on the work of Louis de Rochemont and his 1940 production, *The Ramparts We Watch*, the first of a series of films that can appropriately be termed "pictorial journalism." Chapter 5 offers an outline of the development of the "factual drama," largely under the influence of Fox's Darryl F. Zanuck, and its connection to film noir. The various legacies of *Ramparts* are examined in chapter 6, including André de Toth's *None Shall Escape* (1944) and *Judgment at Nuremberg* (1961), the first Hollywood films to deal with what has become known

as the Holocaust, as well as the cycle of noir semi-documentaries, the most interesting of which is Phil Karlson's *The Phenix City Story* (1955). Focusing on three
films, *Gentleman's Agreement* (1947), *Lost Boundaries* (1949), and *Whistle at Eaton
Falls* (1951), the conclusion evaluates the nature and value of pictorial journalism,
too easily dismissed as authentic banality.

ACKNOWLEDGMENTS

Any work of film criticism that, like this one, depends heavily on an uncovering of production history owes a huge debt to the archives that provide access to primary documents. The writing of this book would simply have been impossible without the patient, competent, and thorough assistance provided by the staffs at the American Motion Picture Arts and Sciences Library in Beverly Hills (the Margaret Herrick), the American Humanities Research Center in Laramie, Wyoming, the Louis de Rochemont Center at Keene State College in New Hampshire, and the American Film Institute Library in Los Angeles. I am mindful as well that these repositories are supported by those who are dedicated to the advancement of knowledge; I am very grateful for their generosity. Murray Pomerance has been a loyal friend and tireless colleague, and I count myself lucky to share many scholarly interests with him. Tom Doherty, Leslie Mitchner, and Mark Shiel are also owed thanks and appreciation for their substantial help with this project. The Calhoun Lemon Foundation at Clemson provided me with travel funds and released time to complete the research and writing of this book. Valuing scholarly productivity and excellence, Clemson University has been generous in providing both financial support and flexibility with my teaching schedule. Dean Richard Goodstein and Dr. Lee Morrissey, chair of the English department, have been continually supportive and helpful. I owe a huge debt as well to Robert Sklar—teacher, mentor, colleague, and friend. Bob, many times in writing this book I thought of what you might have to say about it, and I often found myself correcting bad thinking and inept style.

Shot on Location

Introduction

Real History, Real Cinema

Headlines for Grabbing

World War II in Europe ended in early May 1945 with the surrender of the German armed forces; by the following summer and in accordance with previous agreements, the victors had divided the territory of the defeated enemy into four occupation zones. The first three of these corresponded to the western parts of the country overrun by American and British armies (with some token participation from de Gaulle's Free French forces), while the fourth covered the more extensive eastern reaches taken at much greater cost by the Red Army. The apocalyptic battle for Berlin had cost the Soviets more than 360,000 dead and wounded. Though the price paid for the enemy capital had been extraordinarily high and the broad metropolis was more or less in the center of the Russian zone, the Soviets agreed to its division, with the French, British, and Americans administering the western portions and the Russian the eastern. Stalin, it would later come to light, was committed to persuading his erstwhile allies from the city by making it inconvenient for them to continue to support a capitalist island in the middle of a communist sea, but at first he did not think West Berlin was worth a major confrontation. It was only a matter of time, he calculated, before Western Europe collapsed further into economic distress and political turmoil, paving the way for a more or less bloodless communist takeover of the entire continent.

Economically, West Berlin was at the mercy of Soviet goodwill since it was completely dependent on the importation of food and other supplies delivered by rail, autobahn, air, and canal from the western zones through Soviet-held territory. That lifeline could at any moment have been subjected to a thoroughgoing blockade if the Soviets simply refused to keep the borders open. But for three years, the soldiers and bureaucrats of the four powers administered their separate areas of the former enemy's homeland without major disputes. Continuing cooperation had been formalized by the protocols that emerged from the Potsdam conference (16 July–2 August 1945), during which the "Big Three" (France did not

1

have a seat at the negotiating table) agreed on a basic framework for the occupation: demilitarization, denazification, democratization, decentralization, and decartelization. Thorny issues connected to the future of the country, however, were postponed indefinitely. When should occupation end? When it did, should Germany be reunited? If so, should the country constitute part of the democratic West or a Soviet-dominated East? Or would a suitably defanged former enemy become a neutral buffer state between the two superpowers, which were now increasingly divided by conflicting ideologies and incompatible systems?

Dire economic circumstances soon forced a solution to the issue, as the unusually harsh winter of 1947–48 emphasized the inadequacy of the meager rations and limited coal for heating supplied to the Germans even though these were all the Allies could afford to provide. The country was reduced in large part to bartering and the black market in order to obtain scarce necessities, even as the Germans faced the monumental tasks of clearing away the thousands of square miles of urban rubble and restoring the devastated transportation infrastructure. Lacking a reconstructed political system and a modern economy, Germany could neither govern nor feed itself, while its moribund manufacturing sector and wrecked banking system meant that there were no means to pay for the substantial imports necessary to sustain collective life on even the most marginal level. The burden of provisioning their zone was especially onerous for the British, who were then enduring a series of severe crises of their own, including the failure of the wheat crop in 1946, which forced them for the first time since the outbreak of the war to ration bread.

During that harsh winter, the Western allies, not consulting their erstwhile Soviet counterparts, agreed to merge resources as well as liabilities, creating a "trizone" that would move quickly toward status as a separate nation, eventually designated the Federal Republic of Germany. The FRG would not be neutral, but integrated into the Western system; only in this way could it contract for the loans necessary for rebuilding and redevelopment from the Marshall Plan, which had been drafted the previous summer (Stalin had rejected Eastern Bloc participation in U.S.-financed reconstruction). Economic recovery, so officials from the three governments concluded, would follow only from a stable financial system, and this necessitated the creation of a new currency. Backed by a newly constituted federal bank (Bank Deutscher Länder), the Deutschmark went into circulation on 20 June 1948, replacing the Reichsmark, a relic from the previous regime that the four powers had agreed to use pending final negotiations on the status of the country, a question that at this point was preempted by the rapid succession of events and never to be resolved by agreement between the former allies until events on the ground nearly four decades later paved the way for German reunification.

Because they had not been consulted, the Soviets regarded the reorganization of the western zones as a violation of the Potsdam protocols, and it also seems that they feared the creation of a viable political entity that promised expanding economic prosperity in the midst of their sector, where conditions were even more desperate than in the western zones. They determined then to force the Allies from West Berlin in response, cutting off all ground and canal transportation to the city four days after the new currency went into circulation. Rather than abandon their zones, the Western allies conceived a plan to resupply the civilian population through a massive air operation that lasted until the Soviets relented on 12 May 1949, totaling an amazing 270,000 flights by Allied (three-quarters of which were American) transport aircraft. By the time that the land, rail, and canal routes were reopened, more than two million tons of supplies had been delivered to the beleaguered citizens.

The Truman administration counted the Berlin Airlift as a major victory in the continuing East/West rivalry soon to be known as the Cold War; the U.S. public was encouraged to view it as a triumph of American organization and determination that enabled the effective deployment of the country's seemingly unlimited material resources. Most important, the airmen had demonstrated the commitment of the Western allies to preventing any further expansion of the Soviets into German territory. The successful resistance to the attempt to starve out the city solidified relations between the newly emergent FRG and its U.S. patron, clarifying for many Germans what were the best prospects for their shattered country. Meanwhile, the currency reform that had been the *casus belli* motored a rapidly expanding economy, within a few years bringing the West Germans a prosperity scarcely conceivable when their new country was founded.

Hollywood Responds

Even before the Soviets restored the status quo and handed their rivals a propaganda triumph, Twentieth Century–Fox planned a cinematic tribute to what the U.S. Air Force had called "Operation Vittles." The story could have been told by dramatizing those who had planned and managed the operation, whom historian Andrei Cherny calls "misfits, the leftovers, history's second-stringers," men who, offered an opportunity to make their mark, "stumbled their way into inventing a uniquely American approach to the world that married the nation's military and moral might."[1] It is only a slight exaggeration to proclaim, as does Cherny, that "never before—or since—would America be so admired around the world and stand so solidly on the side of light."[2] With no distortion of the facts needed, such a film could have featured the kind of triumphal character arcs and patriotic conclusion favored by the industry. But production head Darryl F. Zanuck was not interested in heroicizing the efforts of the political and military leaders involved, including General Lucius D. Clay (who was instrumental in persuading an ambivalent Truman to make a stand) and War Department planner Bill Tunner, not to mention their British counterparts, who were equally intrepid and resourceful. To understand why the film project took the particular shape that it did, we need to explore in more depth Hollywood's approach during the late 1940s to films about the global war concluded only a few years earlier, a multi-theater conflict to be succeeded by a rivalry that was, at least directly, more political than military.

Zanuck indeed had another idea about how to capitalize on this uplifting story that was front-page news month after month. Studio director George Seaton embraced the task of creating an engaging script in accord with his vision, which was to dramatize the events of the airlift from the viewpoint of the enlisted personnel directly involved, with a particular focus on the experiences of the thoroughly fictional T/Sgt Danny MacCullough (Montgomery Clift). In important ways, the film would be journalistic, that is, intended to document, dramatize, and memorialize; but its main characters would be typical, not based on actual individuals; the focus on "ordinary" soldiers would be relentlessly populist. The blockade had just been lifted when script construction began; so the important details could be handled summarily for filmgoers who were presumed to be more or less informed. To the consternation of some, the film dealt more substantially with the important cultural issues raised by the American occupation, which, with the recent establishment of the FRG, had begun to shift dramatically. Film critic Bosley Crowther, for example, complained that the film was hampered by its portrayal of the "limited experience of one soldier" (which was not really the case) and that in consequence it "lacks cohesion, clarity or magnitude."[3] The usually perspicacious Crowther in this instance missed how the social realist focus on ordinary airmen caught up in these events made it possible for The Big Lift to personalize the complicated relationship between the FRG and the United States, while exploring that most difficult to cinematize of intrasubjective phenomena—a collective state of mind.

Seaton uses the developing relationship between MacCullough and an attractive, somewhat older German widow, Frederica Burkhardt (Cornell Borchers), to give his camera access to different parts of the city (all the principal exteriors and some interiors were shot on location in a Berlin still very much in ruins), recording the lives of its inhabitants living life as themselves.[4] The Berliners are shown struggling with the destruction caused by the war as they attempt to create a new culture under the watchful eyes of the occupiers, who have taken responsibility for their welfare. Pursued at one point by the military police because Danny is out of uniform and has no civilian papers, the couple manage to melt away into the crowd when they enter a traffic circle over which all four occupying powers claim limited, if hard to fix precisely, sovereignty. The police become too concerned with the question of who has jurisdiction there to pay proper attention to the fugitives, a humorous development that speaks volumes about the fate of ordinary people in a postwar Europe increasingly dominated by petty rivalries among the victors.

The young soldier has for the time being been forced to abandon his uniform, and so, dressed in the same shabby work clothes as the other inhabitants, he is forced on this odyssey to experience something of what it must be like to be them. In trouble with the authorities instead of at the moment being one of them, MacCullough must draw on his own resources in order to escape capture by American MPs. In one humorous scene at a night club, in order to avoid having his papers checked by a patrol, he joins a quartet singing Glenn Miller's "Chattanooga Choo-Choo," with which he has no difficulty until his fellow singers switch from English to German. On a tram, the couple merges with a group of fellow passengers, most of whom are involved in black market shopping or buying, as revealed after a security check that once again threatens Danny with exposure. Visiting Frederica's apartment in a badly damaged building, he meets up there with one of her neighbors, Herr Stieber (O. E. Hasse), an aged German working as self-confessed Russian spy counting the airlift flights arriving at nearby Tempelhof. Why do the Russians need an agent with binoculars to tell them what anyone can confirm by reading the newspaper, which prints the actual figures involved? The answer is that they do not trust the accuracy of information supplied that readily within a free society; it simply must be false. The spy, as he tells Danny, is in any case not much of one since the Americans know about his mission, of which they thoroughly approve. So much for the strident us-versus-them politics of the Cold War; here the somewhat farcical rivalry predictably puts a bemused and world-weary German in the middle, who is accorded a secure income for simply reporting the obvious.

While providing an attractive dramatic center, the international romance thus provides a vehicle for the film's exploration of the politics of postwar reconstruction and reconciliation, especially as Danny and Frederica plan to get married and move to the United States. What should Americans think of the Germans, who were now important allies to be sure, but whose hard-to-shake allegiance to an aggressive National Socialism had just a few years earlier made them formidable enemies who abjured surrender until the bitter end? Had they now begun to embrace democracy and the benefits of an alliance with the West, justifying the vast effort that had just been made to prevent one of their major cities from falling under Soviet domination? What we might sum up as "the German question" offered more possibilities for dramatization, and for journalistic portrayal in the larger sense of the term, than chronicling in detail what essentially was a round-the-clock delivery operation.

The Big Lift concludes triumphally with a burst of military music and a series of thank-you cameos identifying the principal air force personnel who took part in the production as "themselves," an interesting use of nonprofessionals, of which more below. But the film's politics, both dramatic and representational, are more nuanced than such a chauvinistic finale might suggest; what the characters say and do, and what images Seaton provides viewers of the strange world of a still-ruined Berlin, matter more than this de rigueur acknowledgment of the assistance of the U.S. military in making the film. To be sure, the access to actual military operations, facilities, and personnel that the filmmakers were furnished was crucial to its strictly documentary intentions, which are considerable. Its depictions constitute an invaluable record of a key moment in the history of the city and of the occupation of Germany, as reviewers noted approvingly. Consider the account of the film provided by the *Hollywood Reporter*:

> William Perlberg's production of "The Big Lift" appears to allow the factual story of the air shuttle over blockaded Berlin to tell itself; there are some fictional embellishments but nothing suggesting artificiality. And by staying largely with the basic facts in a situation where the injection of glamor and heroics might have been a temptation, the film has succeeded in mirroring the taut drama and excitement inherent in an episode of post-war history which stirred unrest throughout the world. . . . For authenticity, "The Big Lift" could be surpassed only by a documentary.[5]

A specially modified transport plane enabled the filmmakers to shoot wide-angle panoramas from above a city whose near complete ruin at that time could only have been glimpsed from the air, and these completed the portrait of the current situation begun briefly in the opening sequence (footage that came from an actual Fox Movietone issue). With its unstaged sequences depicting flight operations on the ground and in the air (including a detailed demonstration of how radar allowed the continuing stream of planes to land safely in conditions of zero ceiling), *The Big Lift* illustrates how the round-the-clock flights enabled a population already suffering from the aftereffects of the war in a city that had experienced near total destruction, as chronicled in two of the most important early postwar European productions, Wolfgang Staudte's *Die Mörder sind unter uns* (The Murderers Are among Us) (Germany, 1946) and the last entrant in Roberto Rossellini's postwar trilogy, *Germania Anno Zero* (Germany Year Zero) (Italy, 1948).[6] These two films were also filmed largely on location in Berlin, but without the cooperation of occupation authorities; in fact, they more or less ignore the widespread presence of Allied soldiers and administrators.

Given its production history and projected market, it is hardly surprising if *The Big Lift* adopts throughout the viewpoint of the occupiers, who inevitably see Berlin, like the western zones in general, as posing a series of problems for which they have the only solutions. The Berliners come into focus only insofar as they connect with the airmen involved; this story belongs more to their rescuers. Uninterested in detailing in depth the extent of continuing deprivation and uncertainty in the civilian population, Seaton paints a perhaps distorted positive picture of the half-completed process of reconstruction, one that soft-pedals the deprivation afflicting the population. The film has little to say about the founding of the FRG, the currency change that angered the Soviets, their now-complete domination of Eastern Europe, the economic and political differences between the eastern and western zones of the country and its former capital, or the cobbled-together strategy of the Western allies to circumvent the blockade by relying on air resupply. German political authorities appear only briefly in the film during a ceremony at Tempelhof to honor the men, including MacCullough and his

FIGURE 1 A U.S. Air Force cargo plane, passing over the bombed-out wasteland of Berlin, delivers supplies to sustain the beleaguered population in *The Big Lift* (frame enlargement).

flying partner, Hank Kowalski (Paul Douglas), who have just completed the 1,000th flight of the operation.

The film opens with a newsreel-style sequence briefly mentioning some of these political issues, though nothing is said of Soviet reasons for cutting off the western zones of the city. But this journalistic perspective, replete with an omniscient voiceover narrator, is immediately abandoned once it is revealed that this opening is in fact a newsreel being shown to the airmen of the 19th Troop Carrier Squadron who are stationed at Schofield Barracks in Hawaii, a place that might seem worlds away from the events depicted on the screen. The fictional narrative that begins at this point sets itself the task of demonstrating how the distance between Oahu and Berlin can be traversed with surprising ease and speed; even before the evening's celluloid entertainment is finished, the squadron is ordered into the air to join up with other units ferrying food, fuel, and medicine into Berlin. The film identifies a massive movement of men, machines, and equipment that neatly exemplifies the global nature of the American commitment to preserving international order, then taking shape as an element of national policy in the wake of the initial promulgation of the Truman Doctrine in 1947.

Seaton traces the journey of the transport squadron across two oceans and a continent in a sequence of insert shots of a world map that illustrate a relentless progress, faithfully documented with a number of in-flight sequences (including one devoted to a brief refueling stop in the Azores that, as records show, was actually shot on location in a further gesture toward authenticity).[7] In their desire to present the United States as a major power, the filmmakers naturally ignore the fact that the crisis erupted just as the country was continuing to make cuts in its military, demobilizing a huge wartime force; planning for the defense of Europe came to increasingly depend on the atomic threat, which was undermined by the Soviet development of nuclear weapons, with the first successful test of such devices taking place in August 1949 while the blockade of Berlin was in full force. The more prescient among the initial audience would have understood that, given Soviet belligerence, the American military presence in Germany had no foreseeable end even after the lifting of the blockade and the assumption of political power by an elected German government in the new capital of Bonn. The successors to the film's airmen would be doing more than helping out with the Marshall Plan's implementation.

The Big Lift, to be sure, offers a hymn of praise to national virtue that was intended to cheer the hearts of the moviegoing public. Like its European predecessors, however, the film draws a somewhat disturbing portrait of the war's aftermath, in this instance focusing on a new form of international rivalry that threatens further political, economic, and perhaps armed struggle. Both Rossellini and Staudte deploy the bombed-out ruins of Berlin as symbolically appropriate backdrops for the dramatization of the psychological and moral damage done to German society by National Socialism and the war that was fought to end it. These films exemplify the often-forgotten truth about the postwar era that, as historian Keith Lowe reminds us, "the moral landscape of Europe had become every bit as unrecognizable as the physical landscape. . . . Even a *perceived* threat to one's survival seemed to be enough for some to justify the abandonment of virtue."[8] Staudte's disoriented, dismayed survivor of Wehrmacht service, Dr. Hans Mertens (Ernst Wilhelm Borchert), becomes obsessed with taking vengeance on his erstwhile commander, who returns, apparently with his conscience untroubled, to his still-intact prewar life as a prosperous businessman after ordering the slaughter of numerous civilians on the Eastern Front. Only when Hans realizes that the killing must now end can this deeply scarred veteran abandon a suicidal descent into alcoholism; he releases his intended victim to rejoin, unpunished, the same society he himself has returned to, where the murderers truly are "among us," a chilling thought that he must learn to dismiss from his consciousness if he is to regain his equilibrium. Staudte's film ends with Hans accepting love and companionship from another survivor. She is a just-released former political prisoner of the Nazi regime, who also must forgive the wrongs done her and forgo any quest for retribution; tellingly, the two meet after separately laying claim to the same wrecked flat, indexing the disruption to ordinary life (including property rights) caused by the war, but, more hopefully, illustrating how the disparate, formerly unconnected survivors must join forces to create a new German society. Rossellini's vision is grimmer, tracing the efforts of a family to survive the near-starvation of postwar rationing. Their collective desire to stay together and alive ends tragically as the younger son, influenced by the cruel ethos of Nazi collectivism, poisons his sick father so that the family will have enough to eat. Guilt-ridden, at film's end this energetic and thoughtful adolescent, frustrated in his search for proper adult guidance, kills himself in a gesture that suggests Germany has no viable future, that it is truly stuck in its "zero hour."

In part because conditions in the country had improved as the forties came to an end, *The Big Lift* does not draw as distressing a portrait of a still-recovering German society as do its two European-produced predecessors. And yet this American entrant in the international postwar Berlin cycle also probes the moral discontents of the postwar era, providing dramatizations that are likewise deeply and disturbingly realistic. Seaton, in fact, pursues the same themes as Staudte and Rossellini: the overwhelming desire for the settling of moral accounts that obsessed those who survived the war, as well as the continuing damage wrought by a National Socialism that is no longer a political force, but has yet to be ripped out of the hearts and minds of those it once enraptured. A country deliberately severed from its Enlightenment heritage of respect for individual rights is shown having entered a postwar era in which deprivation and dislocation promote a deadly me-first anticommunalism. As Lowe suggests, in such circumstances individual survival inevitably became for most the paramount interest, with the "abandonment of virtue" of every kind a sad consequence.

Affected by the gratitude expressed by young and old for his efforts on their behalf, Danny feels a growing sympathy for the Germans that contrasts sharply with the hatred directed against the former enemy by Kowalski. Danny at first rejects as unreasonable Hank's mistrust of the Germans, but the former B-17 navigator is proven correct in his suspicions, if only in part. Shot down during a bombing mission over Germany, Hank had spent time in a POW camp, where he had been treated harshly by captors delighting in the power they wielded over a now helpless enemy. When the airlift begins and his unit is ordered to a Germany he has no wish to ever see again, Hank tries and fails to secure a transfer from his unsympathetic and frankly puzzled commanding officer, who does not realize the depth of Hank's enmity for those he now must save from starving. One day walking through the city, Hank comes across and confronts the guard who had made a special point of tormenting him. His immediate thought is to kill the man, whom he tracks to a bombsite where he might do so undetected. But, like Hans Mertens, he discovers that his bitterness has its limits; revenge, in the course of its being exacted, loses its appeal in a movement not toward forgiveness and mutual understanding but, more simply, away from an entrapping past. Kowalski lets the frightened man go after roughing him up. There is no meeting of ideological and political differences, no confession expressed or forgiveness offered. Denazification means simply a useful, self-serving amnesia, an important lesson about the postwar situation in general that the film exemplifies in microcosm. Interestingly, this sequence does play out in a less disturbing fashion than that originally intended by Seaton, as Joseph Breen at the Production Code Administration found this part of the script objectionable:

> Care will be needed to avoid undue brutality in the scenes of Hank beating Gunther. Specifically, on this page, we suggest omitting the action of Hank picking up the marble fragment to beat him with, and also his line "this is about the size of a gun butt, I guess."
>
> This back and forth slapping of Gunther by Hank must not be carried to excess. As now written it seems excessive.[9]

What might that audience reaction have been if Seaton had been able to go ahead with the script as first written and show Kowalski pummel his victim with a substantial chunk of rubble, then slap him "back and forth"? In any event, satisfied by this more limited cathartic violence, Kowalski was never intended to complete the vengeance he had long contemplated. One way or another, he was going to walk away.

In raising the issue of German mistreatment of American prisoners, this episode connects obliquely to what was still in the news: the ongoing controversy over the SS massacres of U.S. POWs during the Battle of the Bulge, war crimes for which a number of the perpetrators were convicted at Nuremberg, with most getting early release in the late 1940s and early 1950s as the American interest in righteous vengeance weakened, a softening of demands for retribution that became even more apparent during the so-called secondary series of trials of Nazi officials, including the justices in charge of the country's legal system. This important event is effectively dramatized in Stanley Kramer's *Judgment at Nuremberg* (1958), discussed in chapter 6.[10] In line with this developing consensus, *The Big Lift* suggests that any continuing push for retribution on the part of the victors is perhaps misguided. Despite (or perhaps in some dark sense because of) his anti-German feelings, Kowalski also develops a relationship with one of the city's numerous schatzies, an unattached young woman he somehow meets named Gerda (Bruni Löbel). She confesses herself eager to go to America one day and is shown spending all her free time studying the American system of government, intrigued that it is so different from the way National Socialist Germany had been governed. In ways whose questionable morality the film does not shrink from dramatizing, this relationship is dependent on the fact that the occupiers have access to provisions unavailable otherwise to civilians surviving on a bare minimum of calories every day. It is, in fact, a form of informal prostitution that allows American servicemen a power over desirable women that in different circumstances might have no interest in them. This concubinage (what else to call it?) makes it possible to get sexual favors and other benefits (Gerda does Hank's laundry and provides the occasional home-cooked meal) the soldiers would otherwise have to pursue in other ways.

As with Kowalski's planned pummeling of Gunther, the all-too-obvious nature of the relationships between the G.I.'s and their German girlfriends caused some consternation at the PCA. The Code did not countenance what its officials characteristically dismissed as "sex affairs": in his letter to the studio Breen objected to much of the dialogue between Danny and Frederica, arguing that it was "excessively sex suggestive" and "inevitably suggests an illicit sex affair." He also did not like the frank byplay between the two men about their chosen companions. Breen ordered removed from the script Danny's response to Hank's warning about Frederica: "Don't be silly. She's not Kudam, you can tell that in five minutes." After all, what would a nice clean American boy know about Berlin's most famous red light district? Though the erotic byplay between Danny and Frederica was also considerably cut, filmgoers could hardly fail to understand the particular social and cultural aspects of Danny's meeting with the woman, especially after Kowalski's frank description of the practical advantages entailed in his "contract" with Gerda. What is shocking is that a serious romantic connection apparently develops on both their parts.

The relationship between the other "lovers" is in many ways more interesting. Part of Hank's frustration with Gerda, toward whom he often acts dismissively and coldly, counting on her difficult circumstances to keep her compliant, is that she challenges him to explain the principles of democracy. Hank shows himself embarrassed by his inability to demonstrate why a system whose foundation is individual rights is superior to the collectivism of National Socialism. Embracing a Jeffersonian sense of natural entitlement, she starts to stand up to his attempts to lord it over her despite the risk of losing his much-needed support. Hank subsequently treats her with grudging respect. Her demand to be his equal in a free society can be seen as a shot fired in the transnational war between the sexes. Once again, this was a topic of current international interest as the UN Declaration of Human Rights, promulgated less than two years before the film's release, had made a special point of emphasizing the rights of women, which prevented the UNDHR from being ratified in countries such as Saudi Arabia, which operated under Sharia principles.[11] But Gerda's insistence on universal, inalienable rights also recalls the ideological struggle between the Third Reich and an America committed to Enlightenment political values and thought. Her forceful rejection of Hank's imperiousness (at one point she chases him out of her apartment with a barrage of china) also asks to be read as a microcosm of sorts of a postwar German political transformation, with the reconstructed nation fully embracing American principles in order to maintain its independence within a democratizing West. Gerda's Americanized conviction about self-determination, of course, is not without its ironic message to those in the West who might be eager to turn Germany into little more than a client state; Americanism offers, at least theoretically, a political model whose most attractive prospect might be a defiant independence.[12] With her earnestness and energy, Gerda seems to represent the newly constituted country's best hope to avoid the mistakes of its past and get as far as possible from the hopelessness of the "zero hour" mentality, that collective failure to acknowledge a way ahead into some kind of different future that had prevailed in the first years after the end of hostilities.

The film's treatment of its "sympathetic" Germans, however, is by no means simple. As Hank discovers and then tells Danny, it turns out that Frederica has lied about her past when they had first met and she was eager to make a good impression. Her father was not a professor imprisoned for speaking out against National Socialism, as she had boasted, and thus she has no connections to any resistance to Hitler, which is to say she is no different from the vast majority of her countrymen, a reminder of the deep popularity of the regime. Participation in some form of "resistance" to the continent-wide domination of National Socialism was, of course, one of the most common lies that Europeans, both collectively and individually, told about their experience during war and occupation, as Hank wearily observes at one point. On the contrary, her husband had served in the Waffen SS and was a party member, as was her father. Believing that it is not fair to judge her by the politics of her family, Danny is eager that they should be married in any case, but Frederica is soon exposed as concealing from him even more damaging information.

She is, in fact, not at all what she seems, a young woman eager to make a new life for herself with an American soldier, but an opportunist who schemes to exploit marriage to Danny in order to gain U.S. citizenship. Her intention is to divorce Danny once they have entered the country and then rejoin her German lover, who is already living in the States. There is no doubt that this is the case. Suspicious of his neighbor, Stieber has intercepted a letter from her lover in which these plans are discussed and turns it over to Danny, whom he has grown to like. It is just at this moment that the Russian blockade ends and Danny's unit returns home. Hank decides to stay on and help with the Marshall Plan reconstruction of the country, exemplifying the change in heart toward the Germans that, in part because of the Cold War and the stirrings of an emergent democratic culture, had become official U.S. policy. Gerda says that she intends to use what she has learned about democratic government in order to help reconstruct a society that had brought ruin upon itself through political malfeasance. These somewhat improbable finales perhaps make little sense in terms of psychological realism. They ask to be read ideologically, as outlining a certain *mentalité*.

The Big Lift refuses the too easily optimistic conclusion of a pair of intermarriages in which conflicting national histories and interests might somehow be understood as reconciled, with two German women, shown to be worthy, delivered to Americanizing futures. Instead, Seaton establishes how the German past of aggressive militarism and crimes against humanity cannot easily be shaken off completely even through creative self-refashioning. Denazification, it seems, is no easy project, dependent as it is on internalized ways of thinking and living not always amenable to identification and uprooting. Though hurt by her perfidy, Danny simply walks away from an unmasked Frederica; he lacks the resources or will to change her, and in any case his connection to the country where she will remain is transitory, offering yet another way of imagining the (dis)connection of the United States to its now-rehabilitated and, hopefully, more or less self-supporting former enemy. As Saverio Giovacchini points out about Billy Wilder's more darkly humorous view of postwar Berlin in *A Foreign Affair* (1948), discussed further in chapter 5, "The American people, as represented by American servicemen, are not up to the task of reeducating Germans. . . . Rather than civilizing the Germans, American soldiers imitate their captors' moral debauchery: American soldiers trade cigarettes and chocolates for a date with a German girl."[13] If only barely, Danny and Hank do get beyond exploiting the young women with whom they connect, but they otherwise do little to advance the national *mission civilisatrice*; they fail at schooling ex-Nazis in the foundational values of participatory democracy, including respect for others. The film thus offers a not altogether flattering portrait of both sides even while celebrating their inevitable interdependence.

Furthermore, Seaton intends what the ironist Wilder never allows: that the viewer, expecting a conventional happy ending, be frustrated by an unexpected revelation. There is no hint until Stieber opens the letter from her inamorato that Frederica is anything but the pleasant, intelligent, and hardworking woman she appears to be. Borchers is encouraged to exude warmth and friendliness in her portrayal of Frederica. Lacking a husband or family to help support her, the widow seems to have accepted without bitterness her temporary lot working as a *Trümmerfrau*, a "rubble woman" whose job is to salvage reusable bricks from the city's seemingly limitless bombed-out buildings. She enjoys the admiration of her fellow citizens, as evidenced by her selection to represent the grateful citizens of Berlin in the ceremony at Tempelhof where she meets Danny for the first time. She is not presented in any way as "on the make." Danny is the one who seeks out a relationship, which she agrees to in an agreeable, not overly eager way, and Frederica, accepting her role as a schatzie, is not the one who pushes marriage. Coming just moments before the film ends, the revelation of her intended betrayal is thus not only shocking but disappointing, a violation of viewer expectations barely compensated by Hank's sudden conversion and the determination of Gerda to assist in the making of a better Germany.

With the founding of the FRG as part of the western sphere, increasingly grim Cold War realities fostered a more positive view of a former deadly enemy. Americans were worried by a succession of disturbing events that could be understood as indicating that world communism was on the march, including the victory of the People's Liberation Army in the Chinese Civil War, with the establishment of a new government proclaimed by Mao Tse-tung on 1 October 1949. Not long after *The Big Lift* was released in April 1950, North Korea, backed by both the Soviet Union and China, invaded its southern counterpart, sparking a war that would last for three years before lurching into enduring inconclusiveness. By 1950, Eastern Europe was entirely "red," and so were two of the world's largest and most populous countries. And, as the FRG became established as part of the Western Bloc, many West Germans began to show increased interest in and enthusiasm for democracy and the economic benefits that would flow from an embrace of

FIGURE 2 Frederika (Cornell Borchers) hard at work as a "rubble woman" clearing
bomb damage in *The Big Lift* (frame enlargement).

American-style capitalism. Yet, like many in Europe, there were some Americans
who continued to distrust the apparently uniform good intentions and easy (too
easy?) friendship extended to them by the Germans. Seaton suggests that this
hesitation was well grounded, even though he offers no solution to further the
necessary project of denazification.

The Big Lift dramatizes the complex state of mind of a German public still
recovering from its National Socialist past and from the near-anarchic social
conditions of the early postwar era, but it also explores something of the range
of American opinion. Danny did not serve during the war and thus, unlike Hank,
he feels no bitterness toward a former enemy of whom he knows nothing before
arriving to serve in the airlift effort. In his portrait of Gerda, Seaton shows how
a democratic tradition might take hold in the country, as those with eyes on the
future explore what is of interest and value in the American system, with its
key emphasis on individual rights rather than the presumed collective will of
the *Volk*. And yet, determined to stand up for herself, Gerda decides to devote
herself to the communal problem of making a new Germany, in stark contrast to
the deceptively selfish Frederica, whose plan is to desert her country despite its
evident need of her considerable talents and energies. Gerda plausibly explains,
although she does not excuse, the woman's betrayal of Danny. Hank, she affirms,
must remember that long years of war and the bitter peace that followed had

encouraged everyone in the country to adopt poisonous forms of amorality, whose effects were not so easily alleviated even by healthy doses of good will from a naïve American boy eager to offer her a life free from the entanglements of the past.

Realism, Not Heroics

As was his usual practice, Zanuck's interest in and approach to this project was deeply affected by his reading of the marketplace. *The Big Lift* was to be one of Fox's ripostes to a rival's signal success in returning to the subject of the war and its aftermath. MGM's *Battleground* had been one of the big box office successes of the previous year, earning close to $5 million. It was the studio's most financially successful release in five years, playing a significant role in a momentous change at the highest levels of management as producer Dore Schary (who brought the project with him from his time at RKO) eventually replaced Louis B. Mayer, who had not favored *Battleground*, as head of production. Directed with grit and authenticity by World War I veteran William Wellman, *Battleground* (1949) memorializes American victory in the late 1944 European offensive that had come to be known as the Battle of the Bulge. With a focus on the experience of a platoon of riflemen caught up in immense operations that lasted for six weeks and involved more than a million men, the film had been one of the most profitable of Hollywood's releases that year, proving the appeal of positive war stories that looked at the global struggle from the perspective of ordinary soldiers. Robert Pirosh had been a screenwriter at MGM before enlisting in the army and serving as a noncommissioned officer, and, returning to his job after the war, he talked with fellow veterans (including his erstwhile commander General McAuliffe) as well as with studio executives about transforming Pirosh's wartime experiences in the 35th Division into an appealing feature. "The time has come to make a war picture," Schary is said to have proclaimed when greenlighting the project.[14] Concerned that rival studio production heads would realize that making such a film might be exploiting a latent trend, Schary gave the project a deceptive working title (*Prelude to Love*) and made sure, as historian Steven Jay Rubin reports, that all "preproduction planning [remained] secretive."[15]

   Battleground celebrates the Allied repulse of a forceful German counterattack that threatened for a time to force the Allied offensive into stalemate. Yet the immense strategic importance of victory, achieved at appalling cost, is only briefly evoked in the film. As McAuliffe himself observed after reading the script, "Who cares about generals, except other generals and their families?"[16] Schary agreed. The subject of this film would be the experience of enlisted men. In its unglamorous and low-key depiction of a grim struggle in difficult circumstances, *Battleground* was substantially different from the patriotic films that Hollywood had turned out during the war, with the exception of two late entrants: Wellman's own *The Story of G.I. Joe* (1945), based on the reporting of the Italian campaign by famed journalist Ernie Pyle, and Lewis Milestone's *A Walk in the Sun* (1945), produced for Fox and adapted from army journalist Sgt. Harry Brown's novel about the same campaign. Unlike *Battleground*, these films find no victory to celebrate, but they were similarly invested in offering realistic and to some extent authentic representations of battle, which are seen from the perspective of the ordinary soldier.

Production for *Battleground* drew on the considerable resources of studio filmmaking, especially the ability of American filmmakers to re-create the setting for the dramatization of a historical event. The frozen Ardennes forest where the film's combat sequences were dramatized was reproduced on MGM soundstages, where "a total of 528 trees were shipped . . . from Northern California. These included giant pines, identical to the Bastogne species,"[17] a considerable feat of reconstruction. The actors, including stars Van Johnson, John Hodiak, and Ricardo Montalban, were put through something like a rapid course of basic infantry training in order to lend their performances the requisite sense of authenticity. Focusing on the stubborn defense of the key town of Bastogne, *Battleground* scrupulously avoided casting aspersions on a leadership that unwisely discounted intelligence that showed the Germans were massing for an offensive. That the enemy came dangerously close to a tremendous victory that might well have turned the tide of the conflict was not mentioned. If partial, *Battleground*'s dramatization of history was accurate enough, almost startlingly so in the light of the morale-boosting Hollywood war films that had preceded it; Schary correctly calculated that the project's entertainment value would be closely tied to its being perceived as true to life. He was smart to depend on Pirosh's first-hand knowledge and scriptwriting talents to confect a plausible account of the European war viewed from up close. Mayer thought a presumably war-weary public wanted to be entertained, not reminded of the horrors of a global conflict, but recent studio releases made according to his reading of the marketplace had been embarrassingly unsuccessful, especially the ill-starred *Desire Me* (1947), an improbable and unengaging World War II romance set in France that starred Greer Garson and Robert Mitchum. That film's watchword, unfortunately, was an at-times laughable inauthenticity, typified best perhaps by MGM's decision to build a "French village" on the studio back lot to serve as the setting for a drama that did not seem European in the least, despite being based on the Expressionist writer Leonhard Frank's sensational novel *Karl und Anna* (1926), which had been successfully adapted for the stage and for two previous film versions.

Filmgoers, Schary saw correctly, were interested in more gripping forms of realism, and this was a view that Zanuck shared, as evidenced by his sponsorship of Louis de Rochemont's *House on 92nd Street* (1945), the first of what have come to be called noir semi-documentaries (discussed further in chapters 5 and 6). In *Battleground*, glamor and derring-do were both out; extended sequences of hand-to-hand fighting seemed terrifyingly brutal and thoroughly plausible, never cartoonish like the too-easy slaughter of hapless buck-toothed Japanese troopers in Raoul Walsh's *Objective, Burma!* (1945), a film that was as much an Errol

Flynn swashbuckler as a reenactment of the considerable exploits of a special army unit, Merrill's Marauders. The script for *Battleground* required none of the "grunts" to make impassioned speeches about the defense of democracy. There was no demonization of the enemy, who are allowed their humanity; there was no cheap sentimentalism. The film avoided scenes where a lonely rifleman reads to his equally homesick fellows a frothy letter from the girl back home or where grief-stricken soldiers conduct an informal funeral for a beloved comrade. Wellman even accepted Pirosh's advice that the actors should wear their increasingly dirty uniforms day after day and cultivate a ragged appearance. *Battleground* ends with no sense of victory, but with the worn survivors happy to be alive and showing their pride in a mission seen to its end through quiet bravery. As we have seen, *The Big Lift* would take a similar "everyman" approach to the dramatization of the oddest of military operations, but a crucial difference is that Seaton's film focuses more on the exploration of a complex physical and social place. Even the film's intertwined romantic plots, the most common of Hollywood entertainment conventions, are subordinated to that locative intention. It is true enough, as Rubin suggests, that "as propaganda and glory were left behind, realism became a prime element in the American combat film."[18] But some forms of realism can be counted more authentic, perhaps more cinematically true than others.

The Fox War Series

The Big Lift is the third entrant in a successful and long-running series at Fox that explored various aspects of World War II and its political aftermath, especially the outbreak of the Cold War. As Schary had predicted, in the closing years of the decade American filmgoers were indeed ready to return to history, both recent and current, providing that the films in question offered substantial entertainment value. This trend would end with the epic production *The Longest Day* (1962). Establishing the popularity and profitability of the Fox war series had been Henry King's *Twelve O'Clock High* (1949), which chronicles air force operations of a very different kind from the life-saving but decidedly unglamorous resupply missions of the transport fliers celebrated in *The Big Lift*. Because the two films, though made at the same time and at the same studio, offer quite differently inflected forms of cinematic realism, *Twelve O'Clock High* is worth a further look.

King's gritty and downbeat (but also very popular) film explored the crisis that plagued the U.S. Air Force bomber squadrons stationed in Britain after massive raids on German industry in the supposedly invulnerable B-17 "Flying Fortress" had resulted in horrendous rates of loss of planes and men, prompting something of a crisis in morale.[19] It was the second Hollywood film that addressed the troubling costs and dubious accomplishments of the "precision bombing" of German war industry and infrastructure, a campaign that came to an end not because it achieved the goal set for it but because the progress of the land campaign made further operations unnecessary. MGM's *Command Decision* was intended as a dramatic vehicle for the studio's star leading man, Clark Gable, who joined the Army Air Force in 1942, receiving the rank of lieutenant, and was eventually assigned to the 8th Air Force, where he flew on a number of combat missions over Germany. The project was thus meant to be vaguely autobiographical, recalling as well the commitment of the Hollywood community to the war effort. *Command Decision* and *Twelve O'Clock High* are not true stories as such because the names of the principals involved are lightly fictionalized, as are the events of the campaign, whose difficulties and frustrations are somewhat soft-pedaled. But, like *The Big Lift*, they were intended to memorialize and anatomize important military operations and so, in general terms, are meant to signify in some fashion, even as they comment on, historical truth.

Based on the best-selling and brutally honest memoir of a surviving veteran, *Twelve O'Clock High* is impressively authentic in some ways, marking a significant change from the carefully guarded representations of combat in *Battleground*, in which agonizing death, mutilation, and unimaginable suffering, both physical and mental, play only limited, bloodless, and momentary roles. In *Twelve O'Clock High*, the horrors of war are not hinted at but unflinchingly dramatized, though not visualized in gruesome detail. In an initial sequence, a B-17 with extensive battle damage lands through the efforts of its copilot, forced to fly the plane by reaching over the pilot, who, jammed in his seat with half his skull shot away and his brain exposed, has been reduced to screaming incoherence. After the wounded are evacuated, a further distressing duty must be performed. Wounded by flak, the waist gunner has lost his arm; because he was bleeding to death, he was parachuted out over France in hopes that he might receive immediate medical attention. What to do with the severed limb, still in the plane? One of the unit's senior commanders wraps it up in his coat and, hesitant about what to do next, stows it somewhat pointlessly in the ambulance.

The film makes it clear from the outset how the brutality of the fight explains the growing reluctance of air crews to continue with the strategic bombing campaign. Their incipient mutiny is in the end dampened only by the stern discipline imposed by a new commander, Gen. Frank Savage (Gregory Peck). Savage manages to imbue the group with a renewed sense of pride and dedication, but does not in the least solve the problem of keeping more of his men alive. He feels increasingly burdened by the responsibility of ordering them out on missions from which substantial numbers do not return; simple calculations make it clear to one and all that the chances of surviving the required number of missions are slim or none. Faced with this hopeless mathematics, Savage "cheers" the men by telling them before one flight that they should all think of themselves as already dead; this seems appropriate advice in the circumstances. Flying himself on several of these operations, the general eventually succumbs to what was then called "battle fatigue," precisely the problem he had been called up to solve. The film's unflinching depiction of the mute immobility to which the incredible stresses of the air war has reduced the very tough Savage is a first for any Hollywood film, and

FIGURE 3 The opening scene of the flashback narrative in *Twelve O'Clock High* depicts the removal of a wounded crewman's arm from a B-17 just returned from a bombing run over Germany (frame enlargement).

his breakdown is surely one of the most distressing sequences in any American film of the period.

Twelve O'Clock High, in Bosley Crowther's measured evaluation for the *New York Times*, is a "tremendously vivid fictional story," with "conspicuous dramatic integrity."[20] No doubt it broke new ground for the industry in terms of its narrative and themes, providing a more truthful account of a bombing campaign that in the end yielded only debatable results, never forcing the Germans to surrender as its advocates in the USAAF and the RAF vigorously argued it would, while costing the lives of many thousands of air crew (160,000 killed for the three air forces involved). The film has no victory to celebrate, but it has much to say about the price paid in the effort to obtain one; it is startlingly realistic in its breaking of hitherto strict representational taboos, including the depiction of air combat, whose brutality is enhanced by the use of U.S. Army Air Force and Luftwaffe gun camera footage, an impressive gesture that the filmmakers proudly ballyhoo in the opening credits. The film's representations are real in the sense that they are eminently plausible, an effect created by carefully researched art design, the use of an actual B-17 in some sequences, and skillful impersonations by experienced studio performers. Viewers are encouraged to understand the events depicted in the film as if they are historically accurate, which in general terms they certainly are. The actuality footage incorporated into the film is, of course, more than plausible. These sequences connect directly to the actual events to which the film makes reference. Such footage is thus authentic in a way that the reenactments in *Twelve O'Clock High* staged at an abandoned airbase in the southern United States are simply not, however much they plausibly connected to historical events known to most of the film's original audience. Avoiding industry clichés such as a romantic subplot (the film has an all-male cast), King's film promotes the high seriousness of the democratic modernism that developed in the industry during the 1930s and whose exploration of contentious political issues offered a model for filmmakers well into the next decade.

As do all Hollywood films that aim to create an engaging and vivid story world, *The Big Lift* also offers its viewers plausible drama, engaging in this case with the meanings that can reasonably be derived from a historical event and the places where it occurred. They were meant to be intrigued by Kowalski's path to empathetic conversion and the ups and downs of Danny's bittersweet romance, aspects of the film that offer what we might call complementary ideological lessons. The Germans are not all bad, as Kowalski discovers, and some might in fact be eager to embrace democracy after years of suffering under a totalitarian regime, providing hope for the FRG just then coming into existence. And yet, the American soldiers stationed in Germany should be careful about violating the seldom-observed official injunction against fraternization with their former enemies. Otherwise, perhaps with no little poetic justice, they risk becoming exploited exploiters, with the schatzies, their affections obtained at first by food from the PX or a pack of cigarettes, now looking for a quick exit from the country by exacting a promise of marriage from naïve G.I.'s impressed by continental sophistication. In their newly found role as world conquerors, Americans, so the film suggests, should be careful about having their natural openness and honesty exploited by those eager to leave behind a devastated and starving Europe. But if the film had truths to convey, aligning it with the usual aims of social realist representation, it also had an important event to chronicle, with the cinema in this instance called upon to memorialize a national triumph in the manner of historical writing, in addition to providing, like journalism, important information about pressing current issues.

Forms of Postwar Realism

Twelve O'Clock High and *The Big Lift* are equally realist in the sense that they tell stories that deal more or less accurately with the very recent past; both offer convincing reconstructions of slightly different kinds. With an interest in conveying and embodying the particularities of place, Seaton's film, however, aims for a greater sense of authenticity in terms of style and production values. The setting in *Twelve O'Clock High* is realistic enough, but not authentic. It has a locative realism that is nearly completely lacking in King's film, in which Eglin Air Force Base and other locations in the Fort Walton Beach area of Florida are substituted for the southern England bases used by the strategic bombers (some background photography was done at an abandoned RAF location). Seaton's approach was quite different. As a title card proudly proclaims, *The Big Lift* was not only "made in occupied Germany," but "all scenes were photographed in the exact locale associated with the story, including episodes in the American, French, British, and Russian sections of Berlin." King's film is a slickly made, thoroughly professional production, dependent on the talents of a cast of professional performers, including one of the era's A-list players, Gregory Peck, in the lead role. Though it does feature some exterior sequences, including, most notably, the crash landing of a B-17 (daringly performed by well-known stunt pilot Paul Mantz), the heart of the film is a series of dramatic encounters featuring experienced actors that were filmed on a soundstage. The film is theatrical in significant ways; interestingly, the very similar *Command Decision*, at first a novel by William Wister Haines, was produced as a play before being adapted for the screen, and *Twelve O'Clock High* could certainly be staged without losing what is essential about the film's more or less faithful dramatization of an important issue, as well as its exemplification of the terrible stresses endured by the airmen involved because of the peculiarly deadly conditions of the bomber campaign. It proved easy enough to convert the film into a successful and long-running American television series of the same name, also produced by Fox (ABC TV, 1964–1967). And the script became the basis for a radio play performed by the Screen Guild Players (with Peck repeating his role) that was broadcast in 1950, capitalizing on the success of the film, which earned more than $3 million in its initial U.S. release.[21]

FIGURE 4 Making use of only limited exteriors, *Command Decision* offers a spectacular re-creation of London's Bomber Command headquarters (frame enlargement).

Stage, radio, or serial TV versions of *The Big Lift*, in contrast, are simply inconceivable; the film's dramatic encounters draw out and express the meanings of the real place in which they are set, which is presented at a particular moment in its history, without which the story it has to tell would be reduced to banality, if not incoherence. The film's realism is fundamentally locative, particular rather than universal. To be sure, Seaton elicits a fine performance from newcomer Montgomery Clift in the lead, with known (but not A-list) actors in the supporting roles, including two Germans, Cornell Borchers and Bruni Löbel, who would not have been familiar to American filmgoers. These performers expertly create the typical characters that the script called for. More importantly, however, the bulk of the cast, including many with hardly insignificant speaking roles, are not Hollywood performers, but actual participants in the events just recently concluded, yet another fact noted with pride in the opening credits: "With the exception of Montgomery Clift and Paul Douglas, all military personnel appearing in this film are actual members of the U.S. Armed Forces on duty in Germany." Their presence can only be documented in the film. The producers might have noted that these "real" soldiers and airmen were encouraged to improvise their lines and performances, turning the film into something rather like journalism as they reenact the roles just played in the success of Operation Vittles. As George Seaton recalled, shooting on location and using nonprofessionals made production something of an adventure, with Soviet authorities doing their best to obstruct the scenes photographed in their sector of the city.[22] In complete contrast to *Twelve O'Clock High*, the film was to some degree a guerilla production, as the crew had to adapt to changing conditions on the ground rather than busy themselves creating an artificial space in which the story they were interested in telling might unfold.

Getting outside the studio and using actual locations (rather than accessible and convenient substitutes) involved more than a little trouble, but the filmmakers and Zanuck felt it was worthwhile, as by this time, having made several of what he called "factual films," the studio head knew from experience (this Fox production trend is explored further in chapter 5). Transported to the actual location depicted in the film, Seaton's camera could take advantage of realia that no studio-based production could include. Most strikingly, perhaps, the film includes a kind of reality effect completely disconnected from any narrative importance, such as the extended performance of a crack army drill team that Seaton captured by chance and that he used to swell a scene that unfolds, if somewhat implausibly, at Tempelhof. Similarly, the presence of large numbers of American servicemen in the city provided the human material for the accidental encounter the director could readily stage between a truckload of airmen and another of soldiers that sets off a verbal explosion of intra-service rivalry, replete with obviously unscripted, and quite extravagant, wisecracks and insults. Once again, this strikingly un-Hollywoodian sequence is a reality effect, part of Seaton's attempt to capture the besieged city's atmosphere. If the film gives an impression of being unscripted in part, this is because it was. *The Big Lift* is, in fact, every bit as much a documentary as a fiction film, an effective portrayal of place and the important events for which it served as a setting. Here, the film says, is where history was just made. And here, playing themselves, are some of those who made that history, which we have also determined to tell in a more traditional way through dramatic fiction. However, this is a story that belongs less to the actors performing the script confected for them and more to those who can only figure here as something like human setting.

In one way, *The Big Lift* is less realistic than King's drama, which was designed to shock at least as much as celebrate. Seaton does not follow him in expanding the boundaries of what can be represented in a Hollywood film; his film offers no equivalent to the gruesomely authentic elements of *Twelve O'Clock High*, with its disturbing dramatization of horrific wounds both physical and psychological. King's film is more realistic in that sense. But it is Seaton, not King, who finds himself able to take advantage of the special capacity of the cinema to deliver up the actual, particular real through a deployment of setting that knows no equivalent in either fiction or the theater, a theoretical issue to which we now turn in the next two chapters.

1

Filming the Transitory
World We Live In

Settings, Literary and Cinematic

Of the three elements usually said to be constitutive of narrative in both its literary and cinematic forms—action, character, and setting—criticism has routinely seen the place where the action unfolds, where characters do and are, as little more than backdrop or frame. Setting is most important, perhaps, when context is considered to be in some significant sense determinative of character or a limiting factor on action, as for example in the somewhat special case of naturalism, with its tendency to underplay free will and promote environment, broadly considered, as the driving force of the plot. But even in naturalist texts, setting is usually not what stories are about. In traditional filmmaking, of course, settings in a material sense are also the "where" in which principal photography takes place. They are indispensable in the sense that they make themselves available for the staging of the action to be recorded by the camera, without which there is no film, at least in the conventional sense.

The ontology of the literary text is somewhat different. Setting in a work of fiction can be crucial, with the evocation of lived space an important concern of the novelist. In Lawrence Durrell's *Alexandria Quartet* (1957–1960), for example, the city named in the title becomes a kind of composite character brought to life by a gallery of diverse inhabitants featured in a linked series of fictional sketches. But a literary setting can also be so lightly drawn, or even elided (as in Philip Roth's *Deception* [1990], which is all dialogue), as to become virtually invisible, save for the minimal filling-in provided by cooperative readers, who must imagine a world in some sense as the place where the characters are and on which the action achieves some kind of existential purchase. This seems true enough even if this "where" is a mental landscape whose events can in some sense be narrated. An extreme example would be Joyce's *Finnegan's Wake* (1939). Consider also the stage of sorts on which thought assumes verbal form through the device of interior monologue, a convention that assumes a speaking self in some sense and thus

24

an intra-mental place for speaking; Faulkner's *As I Lay Dying* (1930) exemplifies a variety of different ways in which such monologues can be presented. Even when it is not mostly dramatic interchange, a literary text can foreground character and voice. This remains true for the contemporary novel even though pictorialism and visuality have been strongly valued at least since Joseph Conrad affirmed, in the preface he wrote for *The Nigger of the "Narcissus"* (1897), that "My task, which I am trying to achieve is, by the power of the written word, to make you hear, to make you feel—it is, before all, to make you see."[1] Conrad, of course, was simply assenting to a general aesthetic tendency in Victorian fiction writing, what was often called word painting, a desire for the engaging image that first photography and then the motion pictures came into existence in order to satisfy.[2]

Despite the influence that pictorialism has exerted on modern fiction (reinforced by the occulting of the narrator's presence favored by Henry James), not every novelist would agree to the visual imperative Conrad promotes, at least not as a general rule. In Kazuo Ishiguro's *The Remains of the Day* (1989), for example, the principal action unfolds in what is only vaguely designated as a huge, presumably ancient country house called Darlington Hall. Despite its importance to the tale told by Mr. Stevens, its head butler, Darlington Hall is never accorded even a short paragraph of rudimentary description, a neglect that indexes Stevens's inability to objectify and analyze the surroundings, physical and social, in which his narrowly circumscribed life has unfolded, so inevitable, and right, do they appear to him. The butler's silence about the physical environment in which his life plays out becomes a key element of self-characterization. Its particularities are so strongly present to him that they do not need to be communicated to those who do not share this domestic space. His psychological state is overdetermined by the sheer weight of a seemingly endless sameness that is insulated from the immense changes endured by the nation he inhabits, which has barely survived the Pyrrhic victory of World War II. His tale thus begins with the first of many inventories of his own state of mind, without more than the slightest gesture toward setting a scene: "It seems increasingly likely that I really will undertake the expedition that has been preoccupying my imagination now for some days . . . [that] may keep me away from Darlington Hall for as much as five or six days."[3]

Though they listen *in extenso* to what Stevens has to say about himself, readers are not invited to share the perceptual or sensorial aspects of his experience in the setting that most perfectly defines and explains him. In order to visualize his world in even the haziest fashion, we are forced to deploy our inferential powers to broaden and particularize the selective accounts and musings his narrative makes available, conjuring up what is at best a vague image of Darlington Hall from our repertoire of cultural knowledge, especially our sightings of other oversized residences of an English aristocracy doomed to class extinction in an ever-leveling modern world. Stevens provides no self-portrait, nor indeed any description at all of the others who figure in the account he offers of his life in Darlington Hall. They are named for us and come to possess recognizable qualities of mind and self as Stevens recounts his interaction with them. But, failing even the most rudimentary of physical accounts, we cannot imagine them as individuals of a certain stature, look, or presence.

Assigning himself a mission that takes him by stages far from Darlington Hall, in the course of the narrative Stevens finds himself simultaneously tracing a vigorous arc of inner development, one that returns him, albeit transformed, to his long-time home. In the end, he possesses his experiences as objects of a troubled consciousness and perplexed moral analysis, even as he ruminates about the place that had hitherto completely contained him. Unexpectedly, Stevens discovers on his travels the significance that place can possess, as each day's journey is defined by the particularities of the countryside and villages he passes through. The excited presentism of his observations of this, for him, brave new world beyond his employer's country house is communicated by increasingly detailed diary entries. We see that he has now learned to look. Preventing the reader from imagining Darlington Hall in a comparable fashion reveals itself as a key element of characterization in this modernist tale of introspection, moral doubt, and eventual, resigned embrace of the unavoidable costs of "being," of persisting, no matter what, in a *moyen de vivre* that can be defended, if not unhesitantly, as of supreme value. Stevens comes eventually to understand life as a zero-sum proposition in which the choice of one form of living precludes others, but this spiritual turning occurs only after his monologue deploys what might be considered an anti-setting that fails to evoke what F. R. Leavis would call any thick sense of lived experience, underpinned by freedom and choice. Stevens does not think to limn the contours of a world that the reader, too, might be able to find a place to live vicariously within.

In the Merchant/Ivory film adaptation (1993) of the same title, however, Darlington Hall comes to life in full particularity, its image, which dominates the beginning and ending of the film, indicating the objective immensity of its atavistic opulence. An impressive seventeenth-century manor, Dyrham Park, Chippenham, was commandeered for the impressive opening shot of the film, and a nearby Georgian property was used for the closing, "helicopter-out" sequence, while the house's interiors were shot in a number of places. Thus the film's "Darlington Hall" is assembled from different real locations in a process that admirably suits its typicality. The history of the house immediately emerges as the film's proper subject. Its endurance and renewal provides the requisite plot, replete with happy ending, as even the moral failings of its aristocratic owner, as well as the changing mores of a postwar society newly committed to the welfare state, do not prevent its being reclaimed as the home of yet another wealthy gentleman who will carry on the self-indulgent lifestyle of his predecessor, who has died in disgrace, leaving no issue to perpetuate family tradition.

Tellingly, the film's establishing shot locates Darlington Hall as its furnishings are being auctioned off, and a voiceover (a passage from a letter read by Miss Kenton [Emma Thompson], the former housekeeper) reveals that the now dilapidated and presumably culturally irrelevant property had been scheduled

FIGURE 5 The camera swoops in to focus on Darlington Hall in transition as its contents are auctioned off in the opening of *The Remains of the Day* (frame enlargement).

for demolition. The film thus does not begin, as the novel does, with a *crise de conscience* striking the most compliant representative of the serving class, but with the distinct possibility, viewed with alarm, that Darlington Hall, and the Edwardian social relations sustaining it, might be swallowed up in a postlapsarian modernity devoted to the parasitical dismemberment of the once-glorious. But this possibility becomes less likely as the narrative admits immediately of a gesture toward restoration. Persisting in the auction battle for the house's furnishings, the new owner buys one of the ancient family portraits, preventing its removal and establishing himself as a legitimate, if self-adopting, heir.

Appropriately, as it is soon revealed, this is a movement back to the future. Darlington Hall has been purchased by a former guest, a rich American politician, Trent Lewis (Christopher Reeve), who wishes to relive the pleasant, and momentous, time he spent there during an international conference more than a decade earlier. Mr. Lewis has decided that to make this happen he must retain the services of the aged head butler, Mr. Stevens (Anthony Hopkins). Both the property and the man who has long overseen its functioning figure in the narrative of regeneration and reconciliation that the film traces. First captured performing his duties (opening the long-closed dining room shutters in a gesture not void of symbolism), Stevens is only barely a main character, rarely seen in close-up, and only intermittently the source of voiceover that reveals the content of the letters he writes. He is not present in every dramatic scene, including and especially those that detail the unfortunate political flirtation of his previous employer, Lord Darlington (James Fox), with Hitler's foreign minister, Joachim von Ribbentrop (Wolf Kahler), and a thinly disguised version of Sir Oswald Mosley (Rupert Vansittart), the leader of the British Fascist Union. Von Ribbentrop, entering Darlington Hall, remarks to a subordinate that this residence, and others like it, are going to be among the prizes of a successful German invasion, defining one aspect of what might be at stake in the war then only being contemplated.

Thus the past that the film traces is not in the least limited to Steven's remi-
niscences. In contrast to the subjective approach of the novel, Stevens is conjured
up by the impersonal narrator not as the source of meditations about the various
questions, some profoundly ethical, that occupy his reflections in his novel, but as a
laboring presence within Darlington Hall, as a human figure who expresses in part
what the house means as a lived space where domesticity regularly becomes transformed into political theater. In effect, Stevens makes Darlington Hall "be" through
the ways in which he helps it function, and his life is presented as subordinate to
the continuing fact of its persistence. The house dominates the film, evoked as a
social environment in constant motion, dependent on the complex orchestration
of a considerable number of different tasks. Many of these are accorded reverential
visual attention (the polishing of antique brasses, the sweeping of stone floors, the
careful laying out of banquet tables, the keeping of account books, the carrying of
heavily laden trays of food, the preparation of huge meals in a cavernous kitchen,
and the careful stationing of impassive footmen at dinner). Darlington Hall is a
location meant to convey power and wealth, a domestic site within which a mul-
titude of human beings enact complex forms of hierarchy that connect it through
informal statecraft to the governmental function of the ruling class. The house is
animated by figures who are almost always glimpsed in purposive motion.

The narrative of their activity, devoted to "service," reveals a series of more
or less connected interior spaces that are eloquently expressive of the always
connectable separation between the rooms set aside for the use of residents and
those in which the huge staff work and find homes of sorts. These spaces also of
course serve as platforms for the performance of the film's actors, who actualize the book's minimal evocation of character in full ontological particularity,
becoming present, visible, and knowable individuals (their historicity expressed
through period dress and manner) rather than briefly evoked memories conjured into brief existence only by and in the butler's troubled consciousness. In
the novel, the only shape the other characters are permitted to take is filtered
through a restless memory searching for answers to existential and ethical questions it labors to frame. In the film, like the house in which they live and work,
Stevens and fellow residents simply *are*, existing in and for themselves, even as
their presence and labor define the complex social environment contained within
Darlington Hall while obscuring the nature of the wealth and inherited privilege
that sustain this community.

A novel like *The Remains of the Day* may avoid setting (and description in general) in order to focus the reader's attention on voice or, more broadly in this case,
on ideas and the mental geography of an individual's limited interrogation of self.
However, such abstraction, such a suppressive representation of setting (or of
human figures) is less likely, or desirable, in a medium that confronts more readily
the semiotic immensity of the seen and so is less likely to ignore the opportunity
to provide striking, readable images of what the novel's protagonist passes over in
silence. Stevens becomes one more object for the camera rather than the source

of a knowledge imparted through all-encompassing monologue whose rhetorical exclusions and inclusions prove crucial. The viewer comes to know the butler and his world with a perceptual fullness denied the novel's reader, but this objectivist approach comes at a representational price. It means that the erstwhile main character's *état mental* cannot be accorded the depth it comes to possess for readers. Only the silent monologue of his musings could afford Stevens, whose public face is all helpful abnegation, a roundness of character, an inner depth that belies the carefully contrived shallowness of his public self, with manner, accent, and bearing all in conformity to long-established professional protocols. In the film, what he thinks or feels is only rarely capable of restaging in dialogue. It briefly burbles to the surface in slippages of one kind or another, often in facial expressions pointing toward something left unsaid, but this hardly matters since the focus of the fiction has decisively shifted from character to setting. Perhaps better, we might say that the film details the multilayered interdependence of character and setting, portraying a location of built and occupied space *as lived.*

Lavish, eye-satisfying pictorialism is a key element in the genre of literary adaptation Andrew Higson and others have termed "heritage cinema," a popular and acclaimed form of British filmmaking for which *The Remains of the Day* was enthusiastically claimed by Merchant/Ivory Productions. In heritage films, settings like Darlington Hall index the social standing of a class that thinks itself as propertied:

> Most of the costume dramas seem fascinated by the private property, the culture, and the values of a very limited class fraction in each period depicted, those with inherited or accumulated wealth and cultural capital. . . . The national past and national identity emerge in these films as very much bound to the upper and upper middle classes, while the nation itself is often reduced to the soft pastoral landscape of southern England, rarely tainted by the modernity of urbanization or industrialization.[4]

The filmmakers report being drawn to Ishiguro's novel because of the opportunity it offered for being turned into a heritage film, making prominent a sense of spectacular, unusual place that might be easily construed as the object of pleasurable, if hardly unconflicted, nostalgia. Conceived as a sequel to the same production team's spectacularly successful *Howard's End* (1992), the screen version of *Remains* not only repeats the critically acclaimed romantic pairing of Emma Thompson and Anthony Hopkins, but, with no little success, attempts to reconfigure Darlington Hall as a symbolic space equivalent in terms of its social significance to the less grand but still impressive eponymous country house that figures so centrally in the earlier production.[5] Viewed as the residential center of a rich farm whose fields are improbably but appropriately displayed as being worked by horse-drawn equipment, Howard's End represents one of heritage cinema's most memorable tableaux, with what seems a deliberate evocation of Jean-François Millet's rural landscapes and the nostalgia for an agricultural past that they so movingly evoke.

In the two Merchant/Ivory productions, a dwelling configures, or makes
manifest, the interrelationship of the characters who inhabit it; ownership is
contested and finally resolved even as the property, if transformed, endures tri-
umphantly, providing an image of solidity in the face of thoroughgoing historical
change. Because camera-style in this form of filmmaking is pictorialist, Higson
writes, the effect of visualization is often to transform "narrative space into heritage space, a space for the display of heritage properties."[6] The rhetoric of such
films, in short, is directed toward the appropriate spectacularization of a location
that the viewer is coaxed to reverence. The narrative, as Higson suggests, discovers its conclusion less in the working out of mutually imbricated character arcs
and more in the reestablishment of a symbolically valuable building, whose persistence is for a time in doubt. Character-driven stories often end with a projected
closure that outlines a future for its focused personages; because it is generally
banal and predictable, this future can be safely and briefly summarized. In these
two films, by way of contrast, it is the two houses whose ongoing, domestic everydayness is suggested by final, metonymic scenes. Howard's End and Darlington
Hall will continue to be occupied and thus "live," or so the viewer is reassured,
and this means that what will also endure in the wake of narrative endings are
the values they represent and enact (benevolent aristocratic amateurism in the
one case and bourgeois high-mindedness in the other). In fact, that there *were*
such residences still standing in the England where the films were made testifies
to the valuing of heritage in the midst of thoroughgoing social transformations
promoted within both story worlds. The real endures in order to be made the
appropriate subject of its memorializing representation, and the film itself is the
down payment on the contentious preservationist politics its narrative reverently
endorses.

The connection between story and setting is conveyed powerfully by the pro-
motional icons for the two films, with the *Remains* image particularly revealing in
the appeal it issues to prospective viewers. Mr. Stevens and Miss Kenton, in full
formal costume, are posed standing in what can only be a public room of some
kind, just to the side of a long curtained window, his stiffly professional demeanor
in slight contrast to her indecorous refusal to keep eyes front, as her face is
turned toward his, unsmiling but with a look too personal to signify anything but
amorous interest. The main focus of the image, however, is the open window,
through which, carefully composed in depth through painterly perspective, can
be glimpsed formal gardens of considerable extent, dominated by a gushing foun-
tain. To be sure, the images of the two stars, Hopkins and Thompson, are larger in
scale, with their grouping suggesting both a genre (romance) and the problem the
narrative will set itself to resolving (the self-denial of his über-professionalism).
Yet the dynamics of the composition mean that the eye is drawn from them to the
opulent decorativeness of the estate, which is established as more than a simple
setting by this metonymic revelation of its *démodé* embodiment of class privilege.
Characters, in the final analysis, are but decoration or framing.

Sets and Setting

Though digital magic can these days substitute for the realia (persons, places, and things) that for decades were the only source of a film's setting, traditionally there is an interesting relationship between the concepts of setting (a function of narrative, in which it is designated and, as it were, inhabited) and set (the physical platform where the so-called pro-filmic events ready for the camera are staged). Where a film is shot is conventionally called its "set," a term that recalls the process of staging or mise-en-scène that is the necessary prelude to principal photography and which can be either a simulacrum (often of most complicated constructive complexity) or a place that is always already there in some sense, presencing itself, as it were, to the filmmaker's shaping intention, providing it with, in the poetic phrase of director Cesare Zavattini, the most eloquent spokesman for Italian Neorealism, "the power and faculty of communication, the radiance, which, up until the moment of neo-realism, we did not know it could possess."[7] Place perceived in all its particularity can become the subject of a film, can be transformed from that which seemed banal into that which, according to Zavattini, is "extremely rich," anthropomorphized insofar as it is revealed by the filmmaker as possessing the power to communicate its essence through a reversal of narrative and representational priorities. Characters can even be reduced to a series of expressive signs of their world from a more novelistic complexity that, at least in literary modernism, figures them as possessing an interest because of their postulated uniqueness, which is energized by an inner life recounted in detail.

Such a transformation, it could be argued, is at the heart of the film adaptation of *The Remains of the Day*, whose spectacular opening sequence depicts the house in all its ancient splendor before the characters who constitute its life are introduced. Is it an accident that the narrative first focuses on the auctioning off of the contents of Darlington Hall, which are nothing other than the portraits of its former aristocratic inhabitants? The human selves from an honored past are now threatened by the consequences of the biological expiration of their lineage, even if hitherto memorialized by an assumed never-ending afterlife within, and on, the very walls that contained them while living. Thus the film begins with a bravura image of Darlington Hall that is quickly revealed as a shelter of identity, both individual and collective; the house's uncertain fate, so the film seems to suggest, is thus of foundational concern.

But neorealism, at least in Zavattini's theorizing, goes even further than the heritage cinema practiced by Merchant/Ivory, understanding character as "discovered" in the real, as proceeding from a setting actualized by human activity. As Zavattini affirms, it means "getting to the bottom of things . . . showing the relationships between the situations and the process through which the situations come into being."[8] This process begins with place, represented in its natural and human dimensions, in its real and actual, essentially unreconstructed form. Another way of putting this would be to say that it is impossible to conceive a true literary equivalent of neorealism, for in a verbal text *ekphrasis* (literally, a "calling out" or "naming" of the world of objects), while a rhetorical turn insofar as fiction is concerned, is the visual *sine qua non* in some sense of cinematic representation. What is shown to be there is *ipso facto* named. The camera's capturing of a world is thus easily theorized as the foundation from which other movements of form, particularly narrative, might be thought to flow. For Zavattini, the "radiance" of the real is in the world properly captured and revealed by the camera, not an effect achieved in such fullness by verbal stylization, however much an order of words might by analogy be able to elicit in the reader something of an appreciation for the thereness of the place, real or imagined, to which they refer.

The neorealist character, if we follow the logic of Zavattini's view, thus lacks the roundness (to invoke the modernist terminology promoted by novelist E. M. Forster) that follows from contradictory traits and elaborate personal histories, whose meaning is revealed through the narrator's analysis and whatever action unfolds in a setting, including and especially the interior space of consciousness. The neorealist character, of course, is by no means two-dimensional in the sense that Forster postulates of the flat literary character, that is, defined by one signal quality and incapable of either revelation or change. Flat characters are, Forster opines, "little luminous disks of a pre-arranged size, pushed hither and thither like counters across the void or between the stars." Round characters, in contrast, reveal themselves as "capable of surprising in a convincing way"; they have about them something of the "incalculability of life."[9] The neorealist character, while hardly "of pre-arranged size," is round in a different sense; such a character is a place that is made to speak its human truth, in the process limning "a complex and vast world, rich in scope and possibilities, rich in practical, social, economic, and psychological detail," as Zavattini writes. Such characters, to be sure, cannot be conceived as unique individuals; they are not "incalculable" in the sense that Forster means, continually unknowable until revealed by some key word or deed. Inevitably neorealist characters (and here we must extend this honor to the characters who inhabit Darlington Hall in *The Remains of the Day*) are types, and in this way they conform to Forster's notion of novelistic flatness. "I am against exceptional persons, heroes," Zavattini proclaims, following the logic of according primacy to place, whose "vastness" for him is necessarily social, capable of being exemplified by an individual, but hardly suited to expressing individuality in the neoliberal sense popularized by literary modernism and so usefully exemplified in Ishiguro's novel.[10] Forster remarks that Moll Flanders, in the novel by Daniel Defoe that bears her name, "stands in an open space like a tree, and having said that she seems absolutely real from every point of view, we must ask ourselves whether we should recognize her if we met her in daily life"; in that novel "*nothing* matters but the heroine" (emphasis mine), which is, to paraphrase Zavattini, precisely the reason why such a being would be unrecognizable on the street where we actually live.[11]

In Vittorio de Sica's *Bicycle Thieves* (1948), whose script was written by Zavattini, the father, Antonio Ricci (Lamberto Maggiorani), does not exist in depth (with

a backstory "explaining" who he is). His desires and anxieties, his responsibilities—
all of which are typical and existentially simple—express the desperation and
deprivation that dominate postwar Rome, meanings that emerge in subtle, if
essentially impersonal ways, as he moves through this stressed urban space,
accompanied by his son, Bruno (Enzo Staiola), whose uncertain dependence on
his father suggests the fragile contingency of a future that seems as unpredictable as the journey the two must take to preserve the family, in effect taking the
law into their own hands in the absence of any effective and enforcing authority.
It is the journey through social and built space in *Bicycle Thieves* that reveals the
world of now through movement and action. In the film, postwar Rome takes
shape as a place through the interconnected activities of those who live there.
The characters are instruments of that discovery, not its focus. They are not trees
standing in open spaces. They are instead, to put a finer point on it, the agents of
their world's moral portraiture, in which thievery, at first a crime only shallowly
understood since the malefactor's motives are unknown and undepicted, subsequently is revealed as necessary in the war of all against all. The film's narrative
thus turns on a dispiriting paradox. In this Rome, the responsible are threatened
by the criminal, even as they must themselves become criminal in order to
remain responsible, making a poignantly unforgettable point about the moral
destruction suffered by Italian culture as a result of the war and its impoverishing
aftermath.[12]

To be sure, the title trains viewer attention on the moral complexities besetting the would-be law-abiding, who are seeking only the remunerative work they
need to perform in order to sustain their lives but find themselves reduced to the
same petty violation with which others plague them. The fall into thievery that
is the film's surprising and troubling conclusion, however, is less the last stroke
in a developed character arc and more the crucial revelation about the perilous
environment in which father and son find themselves. Because the film was shot
on location, using the entire city as a series of places to be explored through a
picaresque narrative, the implied world that exists beyond the frame in that final
sequence (the place as lived that is directly and indelibly therein represented)
cannot help but also come into focus in its shockingly crowded human immensity, embroiled by peril.

The focus on Rome overwhelms any sense of meaningful individuality that
the underplayed drama here proposes as also worthy of the viewer's emotional
involvement and intellection. Possessed of such representational intentions, the
filmmakers would have had no use for a studio soundstage dressed to stand in for
rather than "be" a street in one of Rome's poorer quarters. In such an artificial
conception, there would be no real. The connection between place and its human
reflexes could not emerge to be seen if place were simply an abstraction or simulacrum. The place that preexists its filmic exploitation exerts a strong appeal for
filmmakers interested in the kind of realism to which de Sica and Zavattini were
committed. Such an artistic engagement with the real is hardly inevitable. And yet

FIGURE 6 The act of thievery that sets the narrative into motion in *Bicycle Thieves* is glimpsed as part of the hurly-burly of street life in postwar Rome (frame enlargement).

the pictorial reconfiguration of Ishiguro's novel in the startlingly visual Merchant/ Ivory film adaptation suggests the strong affinity for the cinema between what reality "presences" in terms of setting and the stories that might be set there, their form and themes reoriented to reflect a quite different representational priority in which even character becomes a key element in the locative heritage whose per-durable value the film celebrates through the cinema's memorializing capacity.

Of Soundstages and City Streets

The history of the cinema, of course, is more complicated than the straight-forward commitment to camera discovery that Zavattini postulates and that Merchant/Ivory, looking for a real to correspond to an already written story, approach in their different fashions. As a commercial/artistic practice, the American cinema has also been defined by two kinds of sites—real locations and purpose-built constructions—where the films destined for exhibition in national theaters have usually been shot, especially since the evolution of increasingly elaborate multi-shot narrative films in the first decade or so of the twentieth cen-tury. Dependent on motion picture photography and cameras that have always been more or less mobile, movies can be filmed anywhere that the technical requirements of the recording process permit (including even underwater— think of Esther Williams in such aquatic classics as *Dangerous When Wet* [1953], sequences of which were photographed from within specially designed pools or tanks on studio lots). Films can be, and often have been, shot "on location," that is, in preexisting spaces, either natural or built, that are thought for different reasons to suit the story or themes and where shooting proves conveniently practical, economically feasible, or aesthetically desirable.

Location shooting was a common practice during the early decades of the silent era. Consider, for example, Charlie Chaplin's second film, *Kid Auto Races at Venice* (1914), which was shot during, and actually "in," the running of the Junior Vanderbilt Cup competition, with the comedian and the other performers ad-libbing gags of various kinds for the camera against the backdrop of an actual event, providing an interesting mixture of performance, fictionality, and what would later be called documentary. Similarly, the two-reelers that D. W. Griffith made for Biograph from 1908 to 1914 were filmed not just in the Biograph studio in Manhattan, but in locations that the director/scriptwriter scouted out in the greater New York metropolitan area for his stock company to use as they pursued a rapid production schedule that often saw them turn out a film or two every week. And Griffith and Chaplin were hardly the only early filmmakers who took full (and then cost-saving) advantage of the real.

At a time when filmmaking did not dispose of the more complicated, and less easily portable, technology that would later emerge, especially after the conversion to sound, the real location offered cheap, available, and appropriately varied settings for the exteriors required in the melodramas, comedies, and costume dramas of the era. Griffith's first film for Biograph, *The Adventures of Dollie* (1908), for example, was filmed at an outdoor location that historians have identified as Sound Beach, Connecticut (probably in the municipality of Old Greenwich). It was only the first of many other Griffith melodramas that used particular locations that figured in the narrative not as themselves, so to speak, but in a more abstract or general fashion. These locations are either not named in the narrative, remaining unspecified, or, more commonly, they function as performance platforms whose meaning, geographical and cultural, can readily be co-opted into some other locative identity, like the California fields upon which the siege of Petersburg in part unfolds on full epic scale in Griffith's famous feature film *The Birth of a Nation* (1915). *Kid Auto Races at Venice*, as the film's quite particular title suggests, offers a different model, one in which a particular location as lived space becomes the focus of the narrative, even as the fictionalizing that transforms it displaces spectatorial attention onto a comically colonized foreground.

In these three cases, however, the locations are real or, perhaps better, authentic in the ontological sense. They are spaces that exist beyond the filmmakers' intentions; they are *in* the film, not *for* the film. They are not simulacra. They will endure after their use as performance platforms. Such locations are, to quote Siegfried Kracauer, one of film realism's most articulate spokesmen in the postwar era, "actually existing reality—the transitory world we live in."[13] But, with its co-optational rhetoric, Chaplin's film is in many ways an outlier, a powerfully metafictional exercise in which performance and performers intrude upon an event that otherwise feeds off its own, pre-cinematized energies. *Dollie* and *Birth* are much more typical of industry practice at the time since their settings do not function as forms of realia, imparting a significant trace of extra-filmic particularity to the film. Instead the real is reoriented or recontextualized through the kind of artistic stipulation familiar from theatrical production. A West Coast meadow becomes a Virginia battlefield in much the same way that the stage in Shakespeare's *Henry V* is imagined successively as a ship in harbor, the Agincourt battlefield, the court of that country's defeated king, and other sites relevant to the drama's historical sweep, as the spectator follows the suggestions of the onstage master of ceremonies, the character named Chorus, who unsuccessfully calls upon "a Muse of fire" to produce "a kingdom for a stage." The play's original audience would have to have been satisfied with the more abstract facilities of the then newly opened Globe, whose ever-empty stage could be transformed into a series of requisitely individualized settings only through the workings of their collective imagination, anticipating what film viewers have most often been asked to do as well when presented a setting that is demonstrably stagey or, most subtly, a simulacrum in which the spectator is encouraged to invest a limited amount of belief. If not so designated for the simple reason that any sense of particularity is thought irrelevant, the location is simply subsumed into some more general category. The stream down which the kidnapped child floats in *Dollie*, removed from its particular geographical and cultural contexts, becomes a stream somewhere or perhaps anywhere in a vaguely evoked contemporary America. Griffith's narrative of danger and rescue requires no sense of particular place; it is a tale in which what are important are the exciting contours of the plot, as well as the affect aroused through suspense about the victim's safety and a predictable happy reunion between child and parents. The stream's thereness is provided with no aesthetic importance. Reduced to a generality (a briskly flowing rivulet, nothing more), it might as well have been constructed for the purpose. It has no meaning to communicate, shapes none of the characters involved in the dramatic events that play around and on it, though it facilitates what they do, in effect calling them to take action in order to save Dollie from a watery grave.

Chiefly for economic reasons, however, as the industry capitalized on its success and expanded during the next decade, it became more common for the principal photography that is the primary material of filmmakers to be staged and then completed in purpose-built or suitably converted interior or exterior spaces, not in the midst of a public event or in some location that the filmmakers, traveling from their Manhattan base, might locate in the not-far-distant countryside then accessible by automobile. Such facilities are of course most familiar in the developed form of what came to be called the soundstage (an enclosed space resembling the theatrical stage, but generally much larger), which, as the industry expanded in the early years of the twentieth century, became the principal facility of a production complex usually called a studio. In terms of their scale, soundstages were designed to permit the building of vast sets—the simulacra of an urban neighborhood, a small village, or a seemingly unlimited expanse of ostensibly open country, over which a gentle rain might begin to fall from overhead sprinklers. Such a manufactured storm arrived only on cue; filmmakers were neither held captive to local weather conditions that made outdoor production impossible nor frustrated by the failure of the meteorological conditions required by the film's narrative and visual programs to manifest themselves.

A filmmaker, it goes without saying, must work harder to capture the real; the soundstage or constructed interior offers great convenience. Eager to shoot crucial sequences of *Fargo* (1996) in a Minnesota of snow-covered town and country scenes that are made difficult to see by white-out snowstorm conditions, the filmmakers, Joel and Ethan Coen, were forced to shift from one location to another (including some located in nearby North Dakota) as the winter of 1995 proved much milder than expected; obtaining the desired "real" effect proved time-consuming and expensive as the crew was forced to wait upon an only reluctantly provident Nature. In a film that complexly engages questions of truthfulness and *vraisemblance*, however, this careful, authentic evocation of place proves crucial.[14] In *Fargo*, Minnesota and environs are signified as themselves in a manner that is powerfully authentic; the film's reference to the cultural and geographical real is reinforced by its photographic incorporation of locations. For filmmakers less interested in such effects, however, the studio soundstage obviates the kinds of difficulties the *Fargo* crew was forced to surmount, providing a more convenient, more easily workable solution to the necessary provision of setting and performance platform.

The perhaps surprising adaptability of the soundstage is easily illustrated by a production discussed in the introduction. Though it features a few exterior sequences filmed on West Coast locations, *Battleground* was shot largely on an MGM soundstage, which was constructed to resemble a stretch of frozen Ardennes forest, complete with foxholes, pine trees of considerable height, and a thick blanket of artificial snow; studio lighting easily reproduced the conditions of cloudiness and ground-clinging haze, the plane-grounding zero visibility that played a crucial part in the battle. The inability of the actors to somehow fake misty exhalations of frozen air gives the simulacrum game away, but this is perhaps not a fatal flaw in the film's effect. Some might agree with Kracauer that "the important thing is that studio-built facilities convey the impression of actuality, so that the spectator feels he is watching events that might have occurred in real life and have been photographed on the spot."[15] And yet the photographic invocation of a real place lends quite a different force to events conceived in the subjunctive ("might have occurred"), with their fictionality, however typical or illustrative, grounded in a space firmly anchored in the indicative mood and lacking any sense that it is some form of purpose-built construction.

In the case of *Battleground*, the real in a general sense (a wintry forest) and in particular terms (the Ardennes) are equally absent from the film, whose historically required setting is gestured at by an illusionism viewers might find convincing, but which is also quite evidently not the real thing, though the competence of the artistic design eases our investment of belief in this world as if it were real. In other words, the viewer is invited to construe "as real" what is manifestly (but not too manifestly) not real. An inevitable element of the viewing experience is the double consciousness that all is in some sense artifice even as we consider ourselves to be witnessing something that has occurred "as itself." For we always know that what we see on the screen has its origin in a stream of light passing through celluloid (or its digital equivalent). Place is absent from *Battleground* in two senses: the constructed set is only a simulacrum of a snow-covered pine forest; and it also fails to make any authentic reference to, or provide an appropriately real substitute for, the embattled Belgian countryside around Bastogne. Only because its battle sequences were actually shot outdoors can *A Walk in the Sun* make a somewhat greater, though still weak, claim on authenticity. For the Italian countryside a few miles inland from the landing beaches at Salerno, director Lewis Milestone substituted the rolling hills and meadows of the Twentieth Century–Fox Ranch (also known as Malibu Creek Park), a site first used for the 1941 production of *How Green Was My Valley*, which once included a ritzy country club and the nearby homes of several members. So enamored of the property were Fox executives that they considered moving their production facilities there. The farmhouse that the platoon of G.I.'s assaulted at the film's climax was purpose-built for the production, not far from where studio engineers and workers constructed the family residence featured in *Mr. Blandings Builds His Dream House* (1948), a building that in an interesting twist on the connection between fiction and real life has been since transformed into the administrative center for the park.[16] More expansive in its geographical reach than *Battleground, The Story of G.I. Joe* is also a strictly U.S.-bound production, with many sequences shot on interiors and exteriors at Selznick studios and others at the Iverson Movie Ranch in Chatsworth, the California-Arizona Army Maneuver Area, Camp Carson near Colorado Springs, and California's Camp Cooke.

Inevitably, there is a difference in authenticity between appropriately real substitutes (the exteriors in *The Story of G.I. Joe* are truly exteriors) and (re)constructed settings, no matter how convincing, as the faux Belgian pine forest interior set certainly is in *Battleground*. Consider the example of David Lean's heavily atmospheric epic film *Dr. Zhivago* (1965), whose story, carried by a gallery of socially differentiated and interestingly connected characters (none of whom was portrayed by a Russian), is nothing less than the history of the Russian Revolution and the early, difficult, if successful growth of the Soviet state, as detailed in the film's source, the internationally acclaimed novel by Boris Pasternak. In his earlier film epic, *Lawrence of Arabia* (1962), Lean had astounded filmgoers with the spectacular, hitherto unexampled cinematographic effects, convincingly realistic, achieved by his insistence on filming many of the action sequences in the Middle East, with sites in Jordan (including most spectacularly Wadi Rumm) standing in for what is now

FIGURE 7 The seemingly endless expanse of desert in *Lawrence of Arabia* is the ground for a continuing drama of human conflict and connection (frame enlargement).

Saudi Arabia. The desert that appeared in the film was not just a desert; it was also *almost* the actual desert in which the events depicted in the film occurred, rather than being some place far distant, say in Arizona or Morocco, sites that would have yielded a plausible, if hardly authentic, substitute.

In the 1960s, Cold War tensions, among other problems, prevented Lean from filming *Zhivago* in the still-existing places, including several in St. Petersburg (Leningrad), where it was set and where the larger events referred to in the narrative took place. Were the alternatives he settled on true to the high standard he had set in *Lawrence*? One might say that it was quite a different matter in this regard for period buildings in Helsinki, Finland, constructed while that country was part of the czarist empire, to substitute in some sequences for the similar public spaces of a not-far St. Petersburg than it was for the filmmakers in other sequences to shoot in the faux exteriors of a ten-acre version of early twentieth-century Moscow purpose-built in a Madrid suburb. Between those two extremes, we might place Lean's use of a frozen farmhouse in Alberta, Canada, for yet another set of exterior shots, which are real but not even close to being *the* real (matched, in the truly cinematic fashion of creative pastiche, with interiors confected on a suitably dressed soundstage set up a continent away).

But *Lawrence* itself had, of course, already admitted of such compromises. The film's opening sequence devoted to the great man's funeral at Saint Paul's Cathedral makes use of the steps outside the actual building, while the interior was reconstructed on a soundstage in Spain. The town of Aqaba assaulted by Lawrence and his Arab allies did not "exist," or, more accurately, no longer existed in the form that the film required. This stirring action sequence was filmed on a specially constructed "town" on a beach near Almeira, Spain. The civic buildings of Lawrence's Jerusalem were "real," but found in Seville, not Palestine. These locations were chosen because they would, in terms of architecture, seem real enough, matching up to the cultural expectations of viewers. With the exception of the Jordanian desert, which, brilliantly photographed, yielded up its inherent meanings to the camera, the film's settings were selected as plausible, photographically suitable backgrounds for a tale that was self-avowedly character-driven. *Lawrence*'s focus on the exceptional European subject, of course, narrowed its exploration of the Middle Eastern desert, which is presented to the viewer strictly through Lawrence's experience of it, providing an additional layer of irony to Lean's conscious deconstruction of Eurocentrism, of the hero's projection of alien ideas (the least exploitative of which might be ethnic nationalism) onto the resisting ground of a real whose post facto evocation, however authentic to some degree, in no way facilitated getting to the bottom of things, at least in the sense promoted by Zavattini. Much the same must be said of *Zhivago*, whose principal virtue may be said to be its effective dramatization of historical events, conceived largely as a series of impressive spectacles staged in eminently plausible, if often only problematically real, backgrounds, some much more authentic than others, in the sense that they already existed and were closely analogical to the particular locations in which the reconstructed events—some particularly true, most only generally so—had taken place.

Matters are slightly different, of course, when the setting in question is not the unique place where events are now to be reconstructed, dramatized, and photographed, but rather a fiction, like Darlington Hall in *Remains*, with only a few scenes being in any sense reconstructions of actual events. In this case, there is no question of referential truth in any particular sense, but of authenticity pure and simple. The confected nature of this film's principal exterior reflects the dedication of the project's location team to find appropriate period sites, places where the events the film traces might plausibly have occurred. Most of the interiors were shot in Badminton House, then the home of the Duke and Duchess of Beaufort (near Chipping Sudbury, Avon, and some distance—geographical if not architectural—from Dyrham Park in the West Country, source of the hall's impressive façade). Other interior sequences were staged in Powderham Castle (near Exeter) and Corsham Court, which was the home of Lord Methuen in Wiltshire. Preproduction planning, as John Pym recounts it, admirably suited the film's concern with the life of the country gentry: "When the Duke of Beaufort showed members of the production team round Badminton House, he unlocked one room which had been closed for many years. Inside was a cabinet filled with scores of glasses. 'I wish I'd known about these,' he said, 'I'm forever being sent out to buy new glasses.'"[17] For the film crew, the house held numerous unanticipated treasures. The room in question was turned into Miss Kenton's parlor, an irony that suits the film's concern with the demise of the once-absolute separation between the servant class and a somewhat feckless gentry, of which the present owner, the duke who possesses more glassware than he can keep track of, seems an excellent example. This provocative exploration of built space, unfortunately, *Remains* could scarcely tolerate. Badminton House yields a meaning here that can only be appreciated extratextually, as a deconstruction of the nostalgic preservationism (with its supposedly "natural" class order) at the heart of heritage cinema, a value that the film strives mightily to express. The film, in contrast, ends not with a critical but a reverential evocation of a category of place, as (the image of) Darlington Hall still stands despite the potent threat of irrelevance. The house's refunctioned magnificence fills the screen, its occupation by a rich American striving desperately to look and act the part of a British lord signifying that not much has really changed. Of course, the eagerness of the Anglophilic Mr. Lewis to change cultures makes a mockery of the period's cultural, economic, and political realities, as an embrace of aristocratic country living transforms the erstwhile New World democrat's distrust of Old Europe. *The Remains of the Day* is a useful reminder that cinematic realism in which the exploration of lived space is an aesthetic priority need not be committed to populist concerns with ordinary people.

During the classic studio period, the soundstage interior could and often was turned into a narrative exterior of sorts, but studio complexes came to incorporate as well standing built exteriors, most notably streets of various architectural and historical types, consisting largely of propped-up false fronts. Though its several rural outdoor sequences were filmed in such California locations as Lake Arrowhead, which, with its mountainous terrain and pine forest, could convincingly stand in for Norway, *The Moon Is Down* (Irving Pichel, 1943), for example, was shot otherwise entirely at Fox's Hollywood studio complex, where an exterior "European street" was suitably modified and dressed to suggest the small Norwegian village where this wartime drama unfolds. Studio exteriors were convenient for outdoor settings that, for whatever reason, were not found suitable for shooting on some suitably constructed soundstage interior. In this case, the sequences staged on the studio lot, though palpably not real, are marked by an obvious outdoor look that makes them similar to those filmed on analogous locations, providing some sense of authenticity, however limited, which must have seemed desirable, even necessary to the narrative's evocation of recent historical events.

Standing facilities, of course, can be even more exotic than the soundstage, which is basically just a large enclosed space with an interior platform. The final, fatal moments of the fishing ship caught in *The Perfect Storm* (2000) were staged in a vast studio water tank, enabling director Wolfgang Petersen to simulate the kind of extreme weather that nature thankfully does not often provide; the tank was large enough to serve as an aquatic stage for the various forms of large-scale action set there, which were supplemented by location filming in and around Gloucester, Massachusetts. At least according to its website, the Louisiana Wave Studio, which rents its sophisticated facility to producers in need of a watery setting, offers even more advantages than those Petersen disposed of:

> Originally built by the Aquatic Development Group for Walt Disney Pictures' "The Guardian" in 2005, the Louisiana Wave Studio, in Sealy Slack Industrial Park, Shreveport, Louisiana, is the only computer-controlled precision wave-making facility designed for and dedicated to the making

of motion pictures in the world. The tank and its built-in wavemakers is
a state-of-the-art facility capable of generating up to 13 different types of
2 foot to 8 foot waves, and a variety of water effects that can be customized
to meet the needs of the motion picture director. . . . It is five times larger
than the one used to shoot effects for "The Perfect Storm."[18]

Capable of holding 750,000 gallons of water, and measuring 100 feet by 80 feet,
this impressive "stage," animated by a wave-making machine capable of producing many different kinds of seas, is nevertheless admittedly itself outclassed by
the facilities available at Fox's Baja Studio, where, most famously, *Titanic* (1997)
was largely filmed. In addition to several other kinds of prepared sites, this studio
disposes of four large-scale tanks, one of which—located indoors, so to speak—has
a 4.3 million-gallon capacity, with dimensions of 200 feet by 100 feet.[19]

The prepared location designed for substantial reuse and reconfiguration,
which remains indispensable today, became a vital element of commercial filmmaking by the beginning of the studio era in America in the early 1920s. The
industry then determined on an economic model that depended on a constant
flow of feature-length films whose multi-stage production required the ministra-
tions of an ever-increasing number of specialized workers. Gone were the days
when Griffith could set out from Manhattan for the surrounding country with
cameraman Billy Bitzer and a small cast of performers. This flow of constantly
"coming attractions" enabled regular and relatively rapid program changes at
theaters, which could in this way ensure regular attendance on the part of their
steady customers. For reasons of economies of scale and convenience (with production enjoying a central physical location ensuring the proper use of all available resources, technical and human), what would soon become known as the
soundstage, supplemented by standing exteriors, became the default site for principal photography, with crews only occasionally dispatched to real locations in
order to film background footage for local color or to shoot particular sequences.
The real often figures only as disposable background. Ubiquitous in films of the
early sound era are medium shots of a conversing couple seated in an automobile
as an urban trafficscape "rolls by" through the rear window. Here the real has
been marginalized and made abstract in its reduction to something close to set
dressing, a photographed backdrop that is back projected on a stage-mounted
screen and thus rendered no more semiotically significant than the Sound Beach
location in *The Adventures of Dollie*.

In the United States, reflecting the centrality of shooting on prepared sites,
film producing companies themselves came to be called studios, including both
the so-called five majors that emerged by the 1920s (Warner Bros., Twentieth
Century–Fox, Paramount, MGM, and RKO) and the Poverty Row production companies (such as Columbia, Republic, and Monogram). All were dependent on
purpose-built facilities of one kind or another. Monogram Studios, for example,
specializing in B-westerns, maintained in addition to a quite large Los Angeles

studio complex its own continuing "location" at the Monogram Ranch near Placerito Canyon in Newhall, California, not far from the San Gabriel range. There the horses used in innumerable films were stabled and cared for, while the canyon property on the ranch served as the setting for the large-group pursuits and shootouts that had become narrative staples of the studio's series westerns, including those featuring stock companies known as the Rough Riders, the Range Riders, and the Trail Blazers. (These performance collectivities are themselves continuing, preexisting resources, something like human "sets," if you will.)

During the first decades of the classic studio era in the United States (approximately 1920–1945), the vast majority of commercial films were shot on studio soundstages dressed or constructed to suit narrative needs. Filmmaking came indoors. Few productions of this period can be said to have been shot largely on location, that is, on sites, exterior and interior, that were neither constructed nor remade to suit the filmmakers. Locations that functioned in some sense as themselves—that is, as bearers of the real outside the default staginess of Hollywood filmmaking—were few and far between. This was often true even when the setting was real in some particular sense (and not just generic, such as a sandy beach, a small town, or an abandoned lot). Though the production featured a good deal of location shooting at such sites as Owens Lake, California, Boulder Dam in Nevada, and New York's Radio City Music Hall, the dramatic ending of Alfred Hitchcock's *Saboteur* (1942) plays out on, can in fact only play out on, a simulacrum of the Statue of Liberty. Some footage was shot on Liberty Island, but the climactic struggle took place on a studio soundstage. Later, in *North by Northwest* (1959), Hitchcock did much the same, with a studio-constructed version of part of Mount Rushmore filling in for the real thing (previously evoked by some location-filmed footage). The obviously stagey playscape for the latter film's thrilling climax is the perfect platform for a drama performed for that most relevant of audiences, the villain whose fate will be decided by the outcome and who is its severest critic. Watching from a safe distance, Philip Vandamm (James Mason) wryly contests the justice of the struggle being decided by real bullets, a judgment that the frank artificiality of the proceedings renders almost acceptable. The film thus adopts a metadramatic perspective that perhaps suits perfectly the theatricality that is a persistent strain in Hitchcock's approach to filmmaking. In its unabashed staginess, the climactic sequence contrasts interestingly with *North by Northwest*'s otherwise interesting location-shot sequences— filmed in a number of places, including, most notably, Glen Cove, Long Island; Midway Airport, Chicago; Grand Central Station; and New York's Fifth Avenue. And yet, though real and authentic, these locations are deployed only as backdrops for a story that, as Zavattini might comment, is merely a superimposition, a dramatic intention seeking a stage of some appropriately useful kind. Hitchcock, as is well known, was interested at times in a more profound exploration of real locations, and these projects are discussed in the next chapter.

2

The Postwar Turn toward the Real

Beyond the Theatrical Model

The most notable of early "studios" was undoubtedly Thomas Edison's so-called Black Maria, a tarpaper-covered outbuilding (some might say shack) with a retractable roof that permitted the use of natural light; the building, whose interior consisted of a platform like a theater stage, was sited on a turntable so that it could be rotated to catch the sun at different times of the day. Built in 1893 on the grounds of the inventor's West Orange, New Jersey, laboratory, the Black Maria was put into service early in 1894. Like the increasingly sophisticated forms of purpose-built production sites that have since emerged around the world, the Black Maria was in essence an extension of the theatrical stage. Both the studio and the stage offer play spaces of infinite adaptability because they are blank and bare, designed to have no fixed meaning beyond the necessary architectural minimum until they are dressed or otherwise prepared. The virtues of such soundstages are fundamentally ontological. Studios, that is, partake of the general qualities of the "built" (covered, capable of being illuminated by artificial light, disconnected from irrelevant surroundings); they convey the sense of being inside necessary to many forms of drama staged for the camera. But they are also, and not insignificantly, economical (reusable, fixed on site, as well as transferable and depreciable like all commercial property).

It has often been said, in fact, that the studio, though deriving from the theatrical stage, also offers in some ways an interesting variant of the modern factory. Like the factory, the studio can provide flexible platforms for the different forms of interrelated work that, in addition to principal photography, go into the filmmaking process. The term "studio," borrowed from Italian in the early nineteenth century, was first used in English, and still is, to describe the interior workplace of a painter or sculptor. In a familiar and revealing metaphor, the Hollywood studio system has often been referred to as a "dream factory"; and this way of imagining the industry, emphasizing as it does the several commercial, psychological, and creative aspects of filmmaking, offers some cultural hints as to why such a commercial workspace has nevertheless claimed a name that instead links it to the individual or small group practice of the plastic arts, which depend on forms of creativity often summed up in the interestingly cinematic and thoroughly neoromantic concept of "imagination."[1]

The studio, of course, differs from the traditional theatrical stage in a fundamental way. Reflecting the nature of the practice it is designed to serve, the studio is a site only for filmmaking *tout court*. A studio does not include the social space in which, as a performance art of a particular kind, the resulting film is exhibited for spectators. The peculiar commercial advantage of filmmaking as an art form is that it reifies performance, turns it into an object (the photographic negative) that constitutes the basis for unlimited, precise mechanical reproduction. The reification of performance is one of the medium's most important links to what cultural critics such as Walter Benjamin have taught us to see as a defining feature of modernity: that art has been freed from the unique particularity that was hitherto of its essence and is now rendered at least potentially universally accessible through its copies, even though these might lack the "aura" of an original. In the case of the cinema, of course, these copies (unlimited in their potential number) depend for their cultural power on the scope of their exhibition, where yet another mechanical reproduction of the art object takes place, one that multiplies the reach of each of these copies, and, especially now with digital transmission of various modalities, in a fashion that seems absolutely without necessary limits.

What these characteristics of the medium/institution emphasize is that the cinema is thoroughly modern in its profitable exploitation of a flexible asymmetry between exhibition and performance. Film has been liberated thereby from the spatial and temporal limitations under which the theater had always been compelled to operate. True enough, the early development of the studio as a production space as a kind of stage does seem something of an inevitability, one of the several genetic links of filmmaking to the theater that were unlikely to be ignored and have not been (another would be the division of labor employed in the staging aspects of both arts, including such "functions" as director, actor, set designer, and so forth). Evidence of this is that the studio with its fixed sets has persisted and seems likely to endure as long as performance remains at the heart of the medium, even if this becomes merely some annex to motion capture technology or some other such method that enhances or transforms live action into computer-generated imagery, which has, of course, the potential of eliminating photography altogether as the source of cinema's material. What is completely untheatrical, however, is that spectator and performer inhabit absolutely distinct existential spaces in the cinema and, as many have observed about the evolution of writing as a means of materializing speech, the consumption of performance, frozen in photographic objectness, is infinitely deferrable. One of the signal pleasures of filmmaking is that we may enjoy the performances of those who long ago shuffled off this mortal coil, but who, through the technological magic of photography and sound recording, have been rendered in some sense eternal, partaking of the unending presentness (or, perhaps better, atemporality) that the medium bestows on what would otherwise be their fleeting physical actions and presence, which can now, as it were, appear to unfold anywhere, anytime. And the same is true for the places in which cinematic action unfolds, whose ontological particularities are likewise memorialized.

The cinema, as Robert Knopf has suggested, may well be the "youthful off-spring . . . of an ancient mother, the theatre," but Knopf's exploration of the homology between the two art forms ignores the radical break effected by the cinema, in which performance has been existentially separated from exhibition.[2] To be sure, the essential formal elements of dramatic presentation, and the traditional terms used to designate them, are retained in what has been termed the seventh art since the 1950s, but this creates something of a false sense of continuity between the two media. Film theaters most closely resemble their traditional counterparts in being seat-filled auditoria designed to accommodate spectators. In a successful push to attract customers accustomed to theatrical presentation, from the 1910s onward the American film industry took over from legitimate stage production not only the serried row design of the hall, but the built-up, and often curtained, proscenium or stage at its front, the theater's performance space. When the program offered there included live acts, the stage was used for non-cinematic performance.

Since the beginning of the sound era, however, such stages have for the most part become vestigial, serving only as the platforms above which recorded performances that have taken place elsewhere play back for assembled viewers. The essence of the medium reveals itself in what Gilberto Perez terms its "material ghosts," the glimmeringly present screen traces of what is now absent.[3] In such a realm of poignant, perceptual lack, an untrodden stage is perhaps a revealing memento. Above the stage, or replacing it altogether in more modern constructions, is the screen, which is filled with images of human figures rather than the figures themselves. Plays are always staged. For the cinema, however, "staging" is often, if not always, only a metaphor, connected in any case to production rather than exhibition. The cinema, in other words, still knows a functional reflex of theatrical play space, but this is no longer located in a theater. The interestingly named sound "stage" faces no rows of seats and what happens there plays to no one present save those involved in the various tasks of production. Such performance is intended to be witnessed elsewhere and at another time, with such deferral a central feature of film form (which is based on recording) and of the cinema's institutional functioning, which, as the industry evolved, came to depend on a locative freedom from some limited number of designated venues.

The cinema knows nothing that corresponds to a center for public performances that as an ensemble cannot be duplicated elsewhere such as the New York "theater district," offering instead a theatricality that, once reified by photography, is made available for infinite duplication and dispersal. Filmic materiality thus facilitates modes of consumption quite different from those of the theater, as well as a distinct business model for their management, which includes a key activity—distribution—that intervenes between production and exhibition and is enabled by how films can, in the famous Benjaminian formula, be the objects of "mechanical reproduction." Forms of distribution are useful reminders that the deferral upon which the cinema depends promotes a paradoxically atopic universalism. Divorcing performance from constraints of both space and time, the cinema makes it possible for that performance to be screened anytime, anywhere.

It is easy enough to explain the homologies between the cinema and the theater as produced by the history of their interaction, symbiosis, and competition, which is far too complex even to be summarized here. Suffice it to say that within two decades of its emergence, the film business had determined for sound commercial reasons that buildings designed to imitate rather precisely the venues of the legitimate theater would be where exhibition would occur. But as a medium the cinema is not restricted by such an industry decision. Times change, and what constitutes the cinema has been able to change with them, a fact that is perhaps the most important reflex of the medium's modernity. For some time now traditional theatrical exhibition or "four-walling" has figured as only the usual, if not required, form of initial release, with an increasing number of other forms (VHS, DVD, narrow/broad casting, and so forth) providing additional "runs." Bound by unbreakable restraints of time and space, the theater can know no similar development, with its present form *mutatis mutandis* still that of the archaic ritual drama of ancient Greece.

A freedom from place also characterizes the cinematic modes of production and exhibition. The recording of the "pro-filmic events" that in their various forms constitute the material from which all films are eventually assembled can also take place anytime, anywhere. But the medium, as its recent history reveals, possesses an even more radical freedom from actual space. The advent of computer-generated imagery demonstrates clearly that filmic events themselves can be simulacra that never take place (in the literal sense of the term). Films so produced may therefore dispense with staging in any traditional sense. This complete divorce between what only seem to be events (now composed of data and not necessarily based on performance) and their witnessing marks the outer limits of the cinema's transcendence of the ontology of the theater. If production need not be performance witnessed *in vivo*, need not be dependent on events in the normal sense, then digital wizardry may serve as a perfectly useful substitute. Similarly, recent technological developments have shown that playback of any film can be managed on any appropriately designed device, the forms of which seem at the moment to be in a continual state of evolution, from huge screens upon which images are projected to much tinier, multi-purposed versions mounted in those personal computers we somewhat misleadingly label smart phones. Films can be shot anywhere, and they may be seen, not only anytime and anywhere, but, to exaggerate only slightly, anyhow.

Despite their utility and convenience, from the beginning of the film business purpose-built or dressed sets, located inside, could not claim priority as shooting sites. Though the soundstage is unlikely to be completely bypassed by the medium's evolution, it remains absolutely dispensable. Many films have been made without any part of the production taking place on a stage as such. Like Chaplin in the case of *Kid Auto Races at Venice*, filmmakers have sometimes found it convenient, useful, economically advantageous, or artistically appropriate to shoot films in spaces that assumed their essential shape before any determination to use them as settings for fictional performances had been made. Such settings are the stuff of life itself (to reanimate a cliché) rather than reflections of theatrical design. Here again theatrical production, at least in the accepted sense, is inflexibly different; it takes place only in and on a physical location purposed for it. This space may be left undressed and localized only through the dialogue of the performers (as in Elizabethan/Jacobean theater). The stage may also be particularized as a set. In the "missing fourth wall" tradition that came to prominence in the nineteenth century, the stage is designed to appear as a room replete with furnishings and walls, the fourth of which, facing the audience, is imagined conventionally as somehow transparent. In either case, the theater spectator must be aware that the stage is a stage, no matter what the drama that unfolds there suggests it somehow stands for.

The dramatic stage, in other words, is always strictly theatrical, in the sense of being *of* the theater in every sense. In contrast, filmmakers can and do dispose of actual locations that lack artistic intentionality except insofar as cinematic production shapes them for its own purposes. Aesthetically speaking, such locations are chosen to be *in* the film precisely because they are not *for* it. What has been found for the camera is "real," to use the misleading but conventional term. A carefully dressed missing fourth wall set does not lack for ontological objectness; it is as "real" as any location. What is crucial is that such a set can be nothing but inauthentic, always and ever purposed, not purposeless, always located in the theater, not in the larger world of which the theater is a small part and to whose living reality the drama that unfolds thereupon can only make indirect and generalizing reference. Its mode is imitation or *mimesis*, a mode with the secondary process of substitution at its center. The most important freedom that filmmakers dispose of is that they may completely eschew the "putting into the scene" upon which theatrical design without exception depends. Limiting production to the soundstage, films may be thoroughly theatrical. But cineastes may take their artistic practice into the world and through the resources of the cinema there capture and textualize its singularity in representations that are thoroughly iconic, that is, always with the mirrored real as signifiers.

The thereness that inheres in such locations comes already replete with meanings that can be shaped in different ways to suit the filmmaker's vision. But these places chosen for inclusion continue to reference the world beyond the texts in which they now appear. Transformed into signposts, shadows of the materiality that lies beyond the frame, indications that what we are now allowed to see is part of a larger, also potentially visible reality. This is not the case with studio platforms, which are uninhabited, unhumanized, and uncultured, coming into being only for the reflexive gesture of their own representation and thus defined by a malleable abstractness that suits the industry's dedication to offering a continual flow of product. The film business came early to depend on maximizing the advantages of economies of scale in which repetitiveness plays a crucial role. In essential ways, the films produced had to be all the same, even as, in order to entice the desire of paying customers for the yet-unseen and utterly new, they are also *sui generis*. Fixed in space but capable of "becoming" almost anything, the studio soundstage perfectly suits this dialectic of sameness and difference. Its semiotic blankness yet unlimited potential for signification are important advantages for the serial but hand-made production of a never-ending series of films.

The authenticity conferred upon a film by real locations evoked in their particular cultural and geographical reality points the medium in another direction, one in which money-saving reusability is no longer a key value. In some cases, location shooting, to be sure, could be economical, but it imposed considerable practical difficulties as well as the necessarily limited signifying possibilities of any one place, requiring filmmakers to decamp to a series of sites so that the locative imaginary designated in the screenplay might be assembled piece by piece. It seems that the most insistent reasons for this change in production strategy were aesthetic, a result of shifting values on the part of both filmmakers and filmgoers.

Reflecting this changed atmosphere in the postwar era, Siegfried Kracauer enthusiastically opined that "films come into their own when they reveal physical reality . . . [they have] a marked affinity for the visible world around us . . . animated by a desire to picture transient material life . . . [and] penetrate the world before our eyes."[4] Kracauer's statement is an affirmation of his hope that somehow the medium, so dependent on science and technology, could play a role in the great trajectory of progress unleashed by the Enlightenment. He perhaps overreaches in proclaiming that the cinema can "redeem" reality (even if this redemption is psychological, a transformation effected intrasubjectively and transsubjectively), but he does not go against the received wisdom of the era in limning the phenomenological potentials of the medium. Few at the time would have been inclined to fundamentally disagree. Consider, for example, French theorist André Bazin's point that its basis in photography confers on the filmic image "a quality of credibility absent from all other picture-making. . . . We are forced to accept as real the existence of the object reproduced, actually *re*-presented." Moreover, in filmic images the illusion of motion (which is real because it is "in" what is re-presented, not just a technological effect) is "likewise the image of their duration, change mummified as it were."[5] If it is true, as Dudley Andrew argues, following Bazin's lead, that "the object photographed haunts the photo from which it is absent in both space and time," then it matters deeply whether this "object" is authentic or some contrivance.[6] Insofar as location is concerned, it matters whether the place where the action unfolds (in its natural, built, and human dimensions) preexists the filmmaker's representational gestures. Authenticity either "haunts" the film, deepening its engagement with the human condition, or staginess reinforces the fictionality of narrative and performance, weakening their direct connection to the world outside the frame. As Andrew writes, "In the great volume of a dark theater the spectator gazes at and reflects upon images that relay a world that is both elsewhere and present in its visual trace."[7] Concerned with the moral and psychological aspects of this perceptual condition, Andrew, however, ignores a key point. For the cinema's connection with the real is absolutely dependent upon the precise nature of that "elsewhere" toward which the cinematic spectacle directs our imagination and spirit. The film image either refers us back to a stage of one kind or another, or points us toward a world that might move and intrigue us in ways of which the stage in itself is fundamentally incapable.

Exploring the semiotic possibility of the location, of natural and built spaces that lie outside the hermeticism of the enclosed soundstage or the faux city streets of the back lot, means altering but not necessarily abandoning the model of the entertainment film developed during the classic studio era. It involves some gesturing toward a particularity that cannot be compassed by what otherwise seems the filmmaker's God-like ability to construct, shape, and animate some form of fabulation. To put this in the terms of modern artistic practice, represented locations (including their human dimensions) can be made to function as forms of the *objet trouvé*, challenges to the otherwise purposefully created nature of art, liminal presences that are in the text even as, existing referentially outside it, they point toward the constructiveness of representation, emphasizing its unbreakable material connections to the world. In the words of art historian Matthew Gale, the found object "comments on the relationship between reality, representation and illusion," violating and yet respecting (by rejecting the totalizing reach of authorial construction) the ontological barrier customarily observed between *realia*, on the one hand, and art objects, on the other.[8] The notion of the *objet trouvé* takes us beyond the emphasis by theorists like Kracauer and Bazin on the cinema's photographic powers and the motion it can restore to a sequence of still images. The film medium is also materially incorporative, not only in the sense in which it, for example, can include in recorded form natural sound and music. Its realia can, and often do, include sequences of film from other sources whose authenticity extends beyond object-haunted representations. Beyond what it represents, a sequence of actuality footage is a real object whose authenticity is its most important quality. In two different but related ways, the cinema thus finds itself with the capability to escape the theatricality with which the transitions to assembly-line production of a sort and then the conversion to sound for some time threatened it, reinforcing the need for a stage.

The studio as an infinitely adaptable industrial workspace devoted to the fabrication of a substantial flow of product tended to confine filmmaking to an abstractness and generality that were dramatically engaging, to be sure, but phenomenologically empty, real enough after a fashion, but always already inauthentic, more art than world. The conditions of the marketplace meant that the conveniently enclosed pseudo-world of the soundstage would be abandoned only if audience tastes changed, making the limited realism of theatrical filmmaking no longer sufficiently engaging, or if, for a variety of reasons, it became financially possible as well as artistically desirable to move back, if only in part, to real places. Literary critic William Gerhardie asserts that the naturalist impulse is animated by the desire "to resurrect the *complete* illusion of real life, *using the things characteristic of real life*" (emphasis mine).[9] Such a desire is shared by most forms of realism, and, as Kracauer reminds us, because of the "intrinsic nature of photographic film," can be more startlingly realized in the cinema than in literary fiction.[10] It is hardly surprising that American commercial filmmakers have sometimes found it impossible to resist deploying those things "characteristic of real life," which can not only be referenced (a capacity of literary representation as well) but through the iconic wizardry of photography and sound recording in some sense incorporated within the cinematic text.

In the early 1940s, but more especially in the long decade after the end of World War II in 1945, American filmmakers rediscovered a practice that, while prevalent through the early feature film era, had become rather rare during the studio era. No doubt, technical advances in cameras (which became lighter and more portable) and sound recording equipment made such a rediscovery and renewed exploitation of the world outside soundstage walls and back lots increasingly practical. And the growing popularity during the era of semi-independent production, based on the so-called "package-unit system," made real location shooting desirable economically, as urban and open country settings could be cost effective, even relatively inexpensive for filmmakers who would otherwise have to rent facilities. Location research, scouting, acquisition, and management became important aspects of the production design of many postwar films, and not just those produced in Hollywood, a trend that has continued to the present day, as the examples of *The Big Lift*, *Fargo*, and *The Remains of the Day* suggest. But in the 1940s, 1950s, and 1960s, this rediscovery of the usefulness, and the signifying potential of real space, was not a shift determined only by the constantly evolving economics of commercial film production. In the early postwar period, as historian Aubrey Solomon explains:

> Studios could no longer get away with placing actors on a sound stage with a rear-projection screen behind them showing exotic locations. Audiences were beginning to tire of such artificiality. Much more costly location shooting was becoming not only common, but a necessity. . . . The one obvious drawback of a great amount of location work was that it further cut the need for huge, expensive sound stages. It also reduced the need for contracted set designers, carpenters, art directors, and it meant that the studio's great backlog of standing sets were no longer as useful.[11]

Business practices, as always, had to adapt to rapidly changing popular tastes. The aesthetic contract between Hollywood and its customers had altered somewhat by the time peace came in 1945. Millions of Americans had seen more of the world than had their parents, while those who remained stateside to play different roles in fighting a total war had been informed of its global progress by newsreel coverage that was unprecedented in its thoroughness and, often if not always, in its commitment to portraying disturbing truths (an issue explored further in chapter 4).

As discussed in the introduction, the war films made during the closing years of the conflict and in the immediate postwar period expanded significantly the range of political and social issues that could be raised in what remained essentially an entertainment cinema, demonstrating that, as Saverio Giovacchini remarks, despite the collapse of the fruitful collaboration of Hollywood intellectuals of different background during the 1930s, "cinematic realism did not disappear" in the postwar period. Giovacchini refers mainly to production trends, such as the anticommunist cycle, that offered filmmakers with a progressive bent the opportunity to "maintain at the level of esthetics a sense of moral consistency endangered by their political choices."[12] To be sure, the public issues raised in *Command Decision* and *Twelve O'Clock High* have little to do with a progressive or, more radical, an agit-prop agenda, but they call into serious question the strategic policy followed by both the British and Americans during the war, especially the decision by the latter air force to continue daylight bombing in the face of horrendous losses. During the war years, American filmgoers were given a taste for the eventful, the authentic, and sometimes the controversial by the newsreels and documentaries that were either supported or approved by the Office of War Information, mostly famously the *Why We Fight* series overseen by Frank Capra. But other prominent Hollywood directors, including John Huston, John Ford, and William Wyler, also produced feature-length documentaries meant to further the war effort, including Ford's *The Battle of Midway* (1942), chosen by the Academy as Best Documentary Picture; Wyler's *Memphis Belle* (1944); and Huston's *The Battle of San Pietro* (1945). A documentary stylization, along with the casting of a veteran in a key role, marks the industry's moving melodramatic tribute to the nation's military, William Wyler's *The Best Years of Our Lives* (1946). One of the film's most effective scenes was shot at the Ontario Army Air field in Ontario, California. A former bombardier, Fred Derry (Dana Andrews), desperately seeking his own future, wanders among acres of B-17s awaiting scrapping, an image whose metaphor draws its power from the overwhelming presence of these swords awaiting transformation into ploughshares. No set could substitute for these realia that testify to the facticity of the war that had just been won, requiring an immensity of effort otherwise impossible to convey. One of the most profitable entertainment films of the decade, *Best Years* in some sense completes the portrait of the high cost of victory begun in *Memphis Belle: A Story of a Flying Fortress* (1944), a morale-building documentary directed by Wyler when he was Maj. William Wyler, USAAF, that probably served as a model for Seaton's *The Big Lift* just a few years later.

Not surprisingly, a development we shall have cause to trace in some detail is the formative influence of wartime newsreels and documentaries on the evolution and sustained success during the early postwar period of feature films that can be justly described as pictorial journalism. These semi-documentaries interestingly straddle the line between reportage on the one hand and social realist fictionalizing on the other. The semi-documentaries depend on two quite different but complementary approaches to cinematic realism: the incorporation of already-shot actuality footage into dramatizations that were usually staged, at least in part, in real locations, where typical and authentic characters figure in fictional narratives that focus on important events, issues, or trends. Such films, and *The Big Lift* usefully exemplifies the type, often feature the re-creation of "true stories" or "actual events," with their realism dependent on carefully documented recourse to particular places and objects.

The change in audience taste and expectations that occurred during the war meant that half-hearted gestures toward anatomizing the social/geographical real often did not pay off. An interesting case in point is Hitchcock's *The Trouble with Harry* (1955), filmed in part on real exteriors in small-town Vermont (Morrisville, Barre, and Craftsbury), but, because of persistent rain, also on palpably artificial exteriors set up in a local gymnasium and at Paramount Studios. For Hitchcock, the New England fall peaked too early, and when the filmmakers showed up in the last week of September, too many of the trees were already bare. The director's solution was to glue leaves on the naked limbs. In the finished film, the combination of palpably real sequences with others that were either staged or "enhanced" is jarring. A script from John Michael Hayes that was only occasionally darkly humorous might be held responsible in large measure for the film's failure to find an audience upon initial release (though it is highly valued by many Hitchcockians today). Nonetheless, it also seems clear that the film's too evident staginess was an aesthetic lapse, making less interesting Hayes's gentle satirizing of a gallery of New England country types whose two-dimensionality is not firmly grounded in a deep exploration of place.

The Trouble with Harry fails to exploit the signifying possibilities of the already existing real with as much effectiveness as do the director's other on-location productions of the period: *The Wrong Man* (1956), with extensive sequences filmed in New York's Jackson Heights and City Prison (in Queens); and *Vertigo* (1958), so dependent upon its portrayal of a San Francisco trapped between modernity and its discontents, with the commercial center of a contemporary city revealing the traces of a still powerful and ethnically distinct past, marked by religious zeal and colonial grandeur. It is in that center that *Vertigo* opens, with a pursuit across and then a fatal fall from a nondescript high-rise, a type of action sequence that by 1958 had become a standard feature of urban noir (see, for example, the more elaborate versions that provide with energetic conclusions both *The Naked City* [Jules Dassin, 1948] and *Panic in the Streets* [Elia Kazan, 1950]). But then *Vertigo*, its narrative abandoning the city, closes with a sequence staged in an ancient mission miles distant,

FIGURE 8 Hitchcock's *The Trouble with Harry* aestheticizes the real Vermont landscape, transforming it into something like a natural stage (frame enlargement).

built before California was annexed by the United States, where a similar involuntary and fatal plunge unexpectedly endorses a bygone era's supernatural hold on the present. This fall completes returns to both the cultural and also the narrative past, powerfully rejecting the contemporaneity of the story's presentness in which the tragic climax of the lovers' reunion is marked by that most ancient of funereal gestures: the tolling of a church bell. *Vertigo*'s ending, we might say, is constructed as location-specific through the effective recontextualization of the source novel (which is set in France). In *The Trouble with Harry* the running gag concerning the guilt passers-by feel about a dead body, whose demise they talk themselves into feeling responsible for, is not location-specific. These macabre encounters could be staged anywhere, not just on a Vermont hillside whose almost preternatural sunniness, enhanced by Technicolor cinematography, ironically contrasts with a corpse whose inconvenient presence seems to demand explanation on a universally existential level. The unpleasant and disturbing anomaly of death obtrusively present in the midst of vibrant life might have seemed less harmlessly theatrical in a setting firmly grounded in the particular real. Despite its wittiness and striking visuals, however, *The Trouble with Harry* demonstrates that on-location shooting, with the reality of place somehow preserved in the story world (Vermont does appear as Vermont), need not necessarily be deployed in the service of cinematic realism in any more than a superficial sense.

Like that of a number of other directors of the period who had started in the business before the war, Hitchcock's commitment to the locative realism that came into greater fashion in the 1950s varies from one project to another, with his never-extinguished attraction to theatricality often dominant over his desire to communicate the meaning of place, a referential gesturing at which he shows

FIGURE 9 The Mission Dolores is one of the well-known sites in San Francisco used as a setting for various events traced by *Vertigo*'s narrative (frame enlargement).

considerable talent.[13] Though ostensibly set in Greenwich Village, *Rear Window* (1954), for example, makes no attempt to either disguise or escape from its sound-stage set, precisely the type of elaborate indoor simulacrum that became popular in German films of the 1920s shot at the UFA studios such as *Der letzte Mann* (The Last Laugh) (F. W. Murnau, 1925), a production strategy that was subsequently imitated by Hollywood, most notably in King Vidor's *The Crowd* (1928). In spite of its announced setting, *Rear Window* is not place-specific, beyond requiring an urban apartment complex that permits the curious to spy, however benignly, on neighbors with whom they are not acquainted; Hitchcock even avoids deploying stock footage of the city, including its signature skyline, to ground the complex in a depicted urban real. In contrast, *The Wrong Man* is in many ways about New York, which is evoked, according to its meaning for the national culture, as a metropolis with an enormous population of those who are strangers to one another, making not only possible, but even plausible, the sort of unintentional (mis)identifications on which the plot depends.

The impersonality of the city's social fabric is most poignantly evoked in those sequences set in the Queens City Prison, where the main character, with the tellingly generic name Manny (Henry Fonda), undergoes a kind of assembly-line processing along with a seemingly unending chain of equally anonymous others, actualizing the contradiction of a lonely crowd. The gritty realism of this dehumanization is aptly expressed by the filmmakers' use of a low-contrast black-and-white film stock and avoidance for the most part of expressive lighting effects; but it is surely the real location that provides the deep affect here, making clear for one and all the possibility of being tragically misidentified, with the standardized procedures of the bureaucratic state answering perfectly to the generalized unknownness of the people it serves. Manny is freed, ironically enough, not because he is recognized as himself, but because another seems a truer, fitter match to the fleeting and demonstrably unreliable impressions of witnesses to the crime. The randomness of his victimization answers to the fortunate happenstance of his delivery from accusation; both depend on the serial encounters with strangers that are characteristic of modern metropolitan existence, a truth whose most terrifying aspects become clear in the prison sequences, as Manny becomes an unwilling member of another kind of mass public in which individual identity becomes increasingly irrelevant.

Similarly, *Vertigo* depends on the referentially correct placeness and particular cultural history of San Francisco, of which the film's narrative at various points provides an interesting tour (one that visitors to the city can even now enjoy).[14] The film's thematizing of anachronistic romantic obsession depends on contrasting love interests for the protagonist, Scottie (James Stewart)—Midge Wood (Barbara Bel Geddes) and Madeleine Elster (Kim Novak), who embody, respectively, a solid, self-sufficient practicality rooted firmly in the present and an elegant, aristocratic weakness that seemingly falls easy prey to a malevolent spirit from the familial past. These different women seem to represent San Francisco's unreconciled forms of built space—a contemporary, undistinctive, and thus thoroughly American modernity, alongside the surviving structures from a past that is more Spanish than American, more elegant and exotic, better suited to the gothicness and aura of religiosity (or at least the belief that human life might go on beyond the grave) on which the plot so heavily depends. *Vertigo*, like all Hitchcock films, disposes of its fair share of evident narrative implausibilities, but these are easily ignored and do nothing to mar its unforgettable evocation of San Francisco as what cultural critic Nathaniel Rich calls the nation's most haunted place.[15] With its focus on the romance that develops between its two charismatic stars, Stewart and Novak, *Vertigo* to be sure conforms to time-honored conventions of the American commercial cinema. And yet, for all the soundstage and special effects wizardry that Hitchcock famously deployed in crafting, among other sequences, the famous vertigo subjective shots, the film differs substantially from the studio-bound past in offering through the use of real locations a city portrait of intriguing depth and complexity.

In the postwar era, filmgoers did not find themselves less interested than their counterparts from earlier decades in traditional forms of Hollywood entertainment, including genres that were devoted to pleasurable fantasy like musicals and comedies. But the national audience that emerged at that time also displayed consistent interests in engaged, realist forms of cinema. And this was true for many in Hollywood as well, especially those who had served overseas. Consider, for example, how director Frank Capra felt upon his return to Hollywood:

> The cataclysmic aftermaths of war—hunger, disease, despair—would breed gnawing doubts in Man. Why? Why? Why did my wife and children have to be blown to bits? Where is God now? Why must I starve? Why must whole

villages starve while fat American soldiers offer us chewing gum and ravish our women? Why? Why? . . . As a filmmaker I will champion man—plead his causes, protest the degradation of his dignity, spirit, divinity. . . . I will deal with the little man's doubts, his curses, his loss of faith in himself, in his neighbor, in his God.[16]

Capra reminds us that only in retrospect does the first decade of peace appear as the inevitable prelude to a period of unprecedented prosperity and social stability. Historian William Graebner, for example, sees the end of the war as ushering in an "age of doubt." This was a time that was strongly colored by "the anxiety of the lonely, fragmented individual," of which *Vertigo*'s Scottie is a striking example.[17] The postwar era thus became, in Graebner's formulation, a "culture of contingency."[18] The causes, he argues, are clear enough. By the end of the 1940s, unpredictable and destructive international events had succeeded one another for more than two decades with bewildering rapidity. And so Americans had come to sense that chance, not the iron laws of economics or the inevitability of human progress, was now ruling individual and collective experience. A shooting war in which perhaps 50 million, even more, had perished raised, in Graebner's view, "the possibility of sudden, undeserved death" for one and all.[19] And, even before the Russians developed nuclear weapons of their own in 1949, a perhaps unwinnable Cold War had broken out, threatening slaughter on a scale never before imagined in human history. Americans had discovered, as theologian Reinhold Niebuhr told his fellow countrymen in 1952, that they were "the custodians of the ultimate weapon which perfectly embodies and symbolizes the moral ambiguity of physical warfare." Once invented, "the bomb" could not be renounced because no nation can justly dispense with the means to forestall a threatened destruction. And yet, if forced to use it, Niebuhr predicted, "we might insure our survival in a world in which it might be better not to be alive."[20]

But the national mood was not dominated simply by nuclear dread and terror. Many commentators at the time also lamented the failure or abandonment of traditional notions about human purpose and virtue, prompting what Graebner terms a moral crisis, for "the seminal events of the forties seemed to confirm that humanity had, indeed, been set adrift from its ethical moorings."[21] For Niebuhr, the defeat of European fascism and Asian militarism was deeply ironic, calling into question the conventional pieties of the national creed. He opined that "we are the poorer for the global responsibilities which we bear. And the fulfillments of our desires are mixed with frustrations and vexations." Most frustrating, and morally puzzling, was the fact that "the paradise of our domestic security is suspended in a hell of global insecurity," undermining the "conviction of the perfect compatibility of virtue and prosperity which we have inherited from both our Calvinist and our Jeffersonian ancestors."[22]

Though beginning to enjoy an unprecedented, broadly based prosperity, Americans were thus beset by daunting problems, both domestic and international, whose nature they were disposed to contemplate, at least during their time at the local movie theater, the primary purpose which, of course, remained the providing of entertainment (a concept, of course, not divorced from confrontation of a kind with the real). The cessation of hostilities in 1945 between the major warring states did not mark a definitive end to the crises that had begun in the 1930s; Europeans and Asians continued to kill each other well into the next decade, with another large-scale conflict emerging in June 1950 when the North Koreans invaded their southern neighbors. The determining ground of both the Italian and American forms of postwar realism is clearly the development during the war of realist or semi-documentary forms, not only in these national traditions but also in the British and German cinemas, of which more in chapter 4. In the United States, realism in its different forms still seemed to filmmakers and filmgoers alike an appropriate aesthetic response to the times and their various challenges during the tumultuous first years of the postwar era. As historian Thomas Schatz notes, "In a sense, the war had presented Hollywood with a massive 'social problem' which utterly consumed the industry from 1942 through 1945 and demanded a more overtly social, political, and realistic approach to filmmaking than ever before. Filmmakers continued to refine this approach after the war, despite the phasing out of the war film itself, and audiences (and critics) clearly responded."[23] A number of American filmmakers such as Louis de Rochemont, George Seaton, Jules Dassin, Stanley Kramer, Elia Kazan, Alfred E. Werker, and Fred Zinnemann agreed with Zavattini that "the most urgent need of our times is social contact, social awareness."[24] And, as noted in the introduction, a major studio, Twentieth Century–Fox, where Darryl F. Zanuck was in charge of production, while certainly not neglecting more traditional forms of celluloid entertainment, committed itself as well to an impressive series of realist films, many of which, in addition to chronicling various aspects of the recent war, explored social problems: antisemitism in *Gentleman's Agreement* (Elia Kazan, 1947), racial boundaries in *Pinky* (Elia Kazan, 1949), the treatment of the mentally ill in *The Snake Pit* (Anatole Litvak, 1948), and race prejudice in *No Way Out* (Joseph L. Mankiewicz, 1950). Under Harry Cohn, Columbia Pictures also turned out an impressive number of films that engaged deeply and meaningfully with contemporary social issues, such as *From Here to Eternity* (Fred Zinnemann, 1953), *On the Waterfront* (Elia Kazan, 1954), and *The Bridge on the River Kwai* (David Lean, 1957), all of which featured extensive real location sequences and were honored by the Best Picture Academy Award, which speaks to the respect paid to this filmmaking trend by those in the industry. Another important series of realist films released by Columbia was produced by Stanley Kramer, perhaps the period's most forceful advocate for an engaged filmmaking.

Even a studio as thoroughly and profitably committed as was MGM to the turning out of classy entertainment vehicles showcasing the talents and glamour of its numerous stars sponsored the making of a film, *Intruder in the Dust* (Clarence Brown, 1949), that resolutely avoided glitzy fantasy to engage instead one of the most troubling and divisive issues then facing the nation. Based on a novel by William Faulkner that addresses the cultural intricacies of Southern race relations, the film was shot on the streets of Oxford, Mississippi, the home of the novelist and the presumed model for the setting of his fictional tale. The townspeople (for the most part, those white citizens who agreed to participate) provide a seemingly omnipresent and often troubled or angry public who judge the official investigation of the murder of a white farmer. The prime suspect in the crime is the community's most uppity "colored" man, who, because he is related by blood to a prominent white family, does not respect the informal rules meant to govern Negro behavior. *Intruder in the Dust*, to say the least, evidences a quite different approach to commercial filmmaking than the rest of the studio's more profitable releases that year, such as *In the Good Old Summertime*, a musical starring Judy Garland and Van Johnson that grossed nearly three times the only $800,000 that Brown's film disappointingly earned, putting it substantially in the red. But there were other rewards for filmmakers who, like Brown, pursued a politically engaged realism even if only occasionally. His work on *Intruder* earned him the British Academy's award for Best Director. Brown's subsequent projects for the studio marked a reversion to usual commercial form; these included the romantic comedy *To Please a Lady* (1950), starring Clark Gable and Barbara Stanwyck, and the very fluffy sports fantasy film *Angels in the Outfield* (1951), about a gruff baseball manager who is persuaded to change his abusive ways when he starts hearing a heavenly voice. *Intruder* was a completely different project. Bosley Crowther, reviewing *Intruder* for the *New York Times*, enthusiastically proclaimed it as "one of the great cinema dramas of our times . . . for here, at last, is a picture that slashes right down to the core of the complex of racial resentments and social divisions in the South—which cosmically mocks the hollow pretense of 'white supremacy'— and does it in terms of visual action and realistic drama at its best."[25] That a resolutely mainstream Hollywood director like Clarence Brown would have engaged so deeply with this project testifies to the power within postwar cinema culture of the realist aesthetic, as well as a growing preference for both location shooting and the extensive use of non-actors in minor roles and as human scenery.

The American directors active in postwar realist production would have understood why Zavattini saw his brand of filmmaking as "an army prepared to march . . . [who] must lead the assault . . . it is the only way the war can be won."[26] The war of which Zavattini speaks, however, is not the war that Italy lost and, after switching sides in 1943, eventually won in a manner of speaking. It is instead the continuing struggle of filmmakers to "give life, reality, its historical importance, which exists in every instant"; this war was also aesthetic, a struggle against inflexible aims and methods that reflected cinema's theatrical and entertainment industry origins.[27] If on a smaller, less internationally acclaimed scale than their Italian counterparts, native filmmakers were also interested in transforming a cinema in which, as they saw it, the committed artist, and the photographable real outside the enclosed studio complex, had played roles that had hitherto been too limited.

FIGURE 10 The town of Oxford, Mississippi, here imaged in a series of opening establishing shots, serves as the setting for the Faulkner story dramatized in *Intruder in the
Dust* (frame enlargement).

    The desire to get to the bottom of things, to discover and promote the truth,
energizes this important form of postwar Hollywood filmmaking, but that same
desire makes itself felt in the era's commercial theater as well, indicating the
wider cultural reach of the phenomenon within these related performance arts.
Responding to modernist preoccupations with individuality, the inner life, and
an expanding field of representational possibilities, as well as a cultural climate
drastically altered by years of global war, postwar Broadway witnessed a developing fascination with innovative forms of realism in both acting and staging. With
its focus on the communication of inner, never-expressed truth in dramatization,
the Method approach to performance served an emerging theatrical tradition that
engaged deeply and meaningfully with the private life, which became a principal
subject for playwrights in the period. This can be seen especially perhaps in the
early plays of Tennessee Williams and Arthur Miller, especially *A Streetcar Named
Desire* (1947) and *Death of a Salesman* (1949), both of which won the Pulitzer Prize.
In both its forms, Miller's *All My Sons* (1947; film version Irving Reis, 1948) connected directly to progressive traditions through a focus on conscienceless war
profiteering. Both Miller and Williams rejected the well-made play formula that
had long dominated the commercial theater, which they found inauthentic with
its predictable suspense, surprise, and reversals, while preferring the stark, truth-
telling approach of Henrik Ibsen's dramatic modernism.

Sensing at the end of the 1940s that a newly energized age of American empire was dawning, Miller intended telling a truth that he thought his fellow citizens needed to fully absorb. *All My Sons* was a riposte to the easy chauvinism of postwar victory culture. *Salesman*, as Miller later confessed with all the scorn of a Mark Rudd or Todd Gitlin, would set the "corpse of a believer . . . before the new captains and so smugly confident kings" of a renascent capitalism.[28] With all the zeal of Zavattini and journalist/filmmaking Louis de Rochemont, Miller forcefully proclaimed that in the immediate aftermath of the war the American economic system was hurtling toward "burgeoning calamity," while the perils of an increasingly imperialist foreign policy were "not even hinted at in the theatre and fiction of the age"; in part, the problem was that "the movies were dancing the country into a happy time," a challenge to which postwar filmmakers interested in locative realism could not help responding.[29] Issuing a timely warning, the political theater that was *Salesman* filled a desperate void, or at least that was how the playwright saw it. Miller was inclined in his later years to universalize his protagonist, Willy Loman, understanding him as motivated by a desire "to excel, to win out over anonymity and meaninglessness . . . to count."[30] But for Miller, Willy's tragedy was also historically specific, deeply connected to the drive in postindustrial American capitalism toward individual-crushing, impersonal economic relations. As Zavattini puts it, speaking for many a postwar realist, "The true function of the arts has always been that of expressing the needs of the times; it is toward this function that we should redirect them."[31] Miller and company (including the era's most popular television playwrights, Paddy Chayefsky and Rod Serling) wholeheartedly agreed.

The most honored and successful form of early television, live drama, was dominated by a realist approach, and the film industry took notice. In 1955, Academy members selected Delbert Mann's *Marty* as the year's Best Picture. Based on an acclaimed Chayefsky teleplay, also directed by Mann and originally broadcast in 1953 on *The Philco-Goodyear Television Playhouse, Marty* was a resolutely unglamorous film whose making would surely have been unlikely during the first three decades of the classic studio period. No production of this kind, to be sure, had ever received consideration for this industry accolade, which customarily, at least at the time, went to A-pictures that were star-driven and entertainment-oriented in a traditional sense. Amazingly, this low-budget ($340,000) release also won the Palme d'Or at Cannes, as well as a number of other awards, exemplifying how widely shared was the taste for realist filmmaking among those in the industry.[32] And the film quickly achieved a substantial popularity, even as Hollywood in general was experiencing a significant downturn. *Marty* turned a handsome profit for its producers (Hecht-Hill-Lancaster), with a domestic box office of about $3 million.[33] Mann was an experienced Broadway director, but this was his first film, and the successful transference of this teleplay to the screen depended absolutely on his ability to reach beyond the TV studio soundstage and bring the production literally to the streets where it is ostensibly set, imparting an unmistakable sense

FIGURE 11 Some of the street scenes in *Marty* such as this one were filmed guerilla-style in the Bronx (frame enlargement).

of reality to Chayefsky's touching if unsentimental story. The plot's simplicity reflects the everyday concerns of working-class Bronx ethnic culture. Chayefsky's plain intention, reflecting the realist aesthetic prominent throughout the postwar world, was to dramatize "the most ordinary love story in the world . . . the way it literally would have happened to the kind of people I know."[34] The film's exteriors were all shot at various well-known street locations in the New York borough, including the Grand Concourse, Arthur Avenue, and Gun Hill Road, and these proved to be perfect settings for a drama that resolutely avoids any whiff of glitziness, fantasy, or conventional adventure.[35]

A thirty-something, "heavy-set" Bronx butcher, Marty Pilletti (Ernest Borgnine), finds living with his mother increasingly miserable. His Saturday begins with a failed, humiliating attempt to make a date with a woman he recently met (Marty keeps proposing different days that they might go out until he realizes that she is just not interested). That evening, he meets Clara (Betsy Blair), who is likewise socially awkward and unattractive (Marty observes that they are both "dogs"). The long night of the "date" they then enjoy reveals their deep needs for companionship as well as some transcendence of the repetitive banality of their limited social scene, even as it uncovers their manifold insecurities and fears. The poignant awkwardness of their hesitantly developing connection, not suited to a declamatory style of acting, makes every exchange a minefield; inner explosions, often not surfacing in the words the characters exchange, register instead in the finely detailed acting Mann encourages with carefully lit close-ups and two-shots. But in addition to deploying the camera to render an undramatic personal encounter, the story demanded a careful documenting of a social/geographical context whose economic limitations deeply affect what possibilities for self-actualization the characters might dispose of. Such an encounter with place was, of course, impossible to offer for the teleplay, staged of necessity on the barest of live broadcast sets. A comparison of the two versions quickly reveals that the film's exploration of location proves indispensable to Chayefsky's intention to make his story a slice of ordinary life. Unlike the stage-bound teleplay, the film records the actions of the socially typical characters in an environment whose complexities, if not all made the subject of dialogue, emerge clearly with extended cinematic *ekphrasis*, with pictures that are literally worth thousands of words. The film's street scenes are filmed in a carefully calculated, unprepared fashion that looks backward to neorealist works such as *Bicycle Thieves* and forward to New Wave productions like François Truffaut's *The 400 Blows* (1959).

Despite these international affinities, *Marty* is thoroughly American. Though this story of loneliness seeking a remedy often strikes a note of universality, it also reflects deeply the particularities of Italian American life, offering a penetrating and varied portrait of a Bronx populated by an older generation whose English is shaky and accented, but whose children are thoroughly Americanized, struggling with the anxiety-provoking courtship rituals of a young adult world filled with strangers, with whom introductions must be managed and forms of familiarity painfully negotiated.[36] Marty, his family, and friends actualize the lived-in-ness of the community, which emerges as a series of cramped, interconnected spaces (apartment buildings, small businesses, restaurants, and a tangle of highways) over which the action spills, often in a somewhat restless or rambling fashion.

In a manner that de Sica and Zavattini might have admired, the inhabitants of the Bronx are captured by the camera as either unhappy with or uncertain about their "proper" place in this culture, as they are glimpsed in motion as they look for something to do on a Saturday night, or trapped in the palpable discomfort of tiny kitchens, crowded clubs, and hectic markets. Mann and Chayefsky refuse to lend this community any geographical center or obvious social hierarchy, not even the sense of shared values and traditional practices that an evocation of its inevitable adherence to Catholicism might provide. The camera instead defines the Bronx as a nexus of intersecting highways and bustling commercial thoroughfares that seem to lead to no certain destinations. Tellingly, no glimpse is afforded of glamorous Manhattan, whose famous skyline would be easily visible across the nearby East River, and this gap indexes the irrelevance of the nation's cultural and financial capital to a neighborhood less than ten miles from Times Square.

Reflecting the staging practices of postwar Broadway's most talented art designers, like Jo Mielziner, Mann's small-scale interiors, where privacy comes at a premium if at all, poignantly evoke the existential concerns of an aging generation of widows who are bitter and ashamed to be living with their young adult children. Frustrated at their failure to leave behind the family home, these children are shown to be either eager, like Marty, to marry and establish lives of their own, or desperate, like his friend Tommy (Jerry Paris), to find somewhere else where his mother (Augusta Ciolli) might live, putting an end to her frequent arguments with his wife, Virginia (Karen Steele), who resents her mother-in-law's constant interference. While the film optimistically suggests that Marty might have found a woman willing to share his life, in the manner of postwar realism more generally, fundamental economic and familiar questions are poignantly addressed but remain unanswered, precluding any deep sense of a happy ending. As indicated by the character's dress and their home furnishings, the obviously limited resources of these hard-working middle-class people betray no hint of the unprecedented prosperity buoying the hopes of many others for comfort and security in middle 1950s America. Perhaps the most sympathetic character in the film, Marty's mother (Esther Minciotti), finds herself hopelessly immobilized by her good intentions and straitened circumstances. She seems genuinely pleased that her deeply cherished son might marry, even as she worries about what will happen to her when Marty leaves to start his own family, with his income now needed to support, at least in part, two separate households.

The Catered Affair (Richard Brooks, 1956), based on Chayefsky's sequel to *Marty*, also first performed as a teleplay, proved to be less successful than its predecessor with both critics and filmgoers, though it is in many ways even more realistic, demonstrating in shot after shot how the cramped quarters of a small city apartment shape the relations, often tense and argumentative, of the family that lives there. Here, too, economic privation is a central theme, with the plot focusing, in the Zavattini manner, on the most mundane of events: the plans that a working-class couple (Bette Davis and Ernest Borgnine) make to provide their only daughter (Debbie Reynolds) with a wedding and reception that will consume most of their limited savings, which have taken more than a decade to accumulate. The father, who drives a cab for a large company, wants to buy his own "medallioned" vehicle with the funds, but the mother feels pressure to compete with her daughter's in-laws, who are middle class and affluent enough to promise the newlyweds a rent-free apartment for a year. Plans for the reception, however, soon spill out of financial control, and the painful decision is made for the couple to get married at city hall, forgoing both the church ceremony and the "catered affair" at a ritzy hotel (where the guests would eat caviar, the father quips, even though they'd be happy with corned beef).

The parents' seemingly endless argument about arrangements that eventually go nowhere ironically brings them closer together, as in the manner of postwar Broadway drama: the breaking of the wall of silence that had separated them for years allows them to examine the life they have spent together, in which they find much good, while giving voice to long-repressed resentments. The film ends with an unspectacular but deeply significant gesture of renewal. With his wife's blessing, the husband gets his own cab and some modicum of freedom from a grueling work routine. Exteriors were all filmed at various locations in the Bronx, providing, as in *Marty*, an intriguing portrait of a community where everyone is struggling to make and live a comfortable life. In an acting turn that says much about the aesthetics of commercial production at the time, Bette Davis appears in "aging" make-up, a fat suit, and shapeless dresses that befit a domestic slattern as she cleans house and does the marketing (in a sequence shot at a locally famous venue, the Bronx Terminal Market), portraying the small joys and substantial discontents of everyday living.

If only in part, Hollywood had obviously moved in a very different direction.

3

Of Backdrops and Place

The Searchers and Sunset Blvd.

Cinematizing and Documenting

Sunset Blvd. (Billy Wilder, 1950) and *The Searchers* (John Ford, 1956), two of the best-known and most acclaimed of Hollywood's postwar productions, are heavily invested in quite different forms of cinematic realism in which actual locations are central. Both films exemplify in different ways the movement out of studio soundstages and their inherent theatricality that became such an important general trend in American filmmaking of the period. As part of the growing trend toward spectacular pictorialism that became one of the industry's chief ways of differentiating its product in the period from that pesky rival, television, Ford's film depends on the prominent display of Monument Valley, Utah, a thoroughly *sui generis* and largely uninhabited desert landscape. The unique identity of Monument Valley is reconfigured in this film, as in other Ford entrants in the genre, to suit the peculiar ontology of the western, as the real is turned into backdrop and drained of particularity even while becoming a landscape of peculiarly powerful cinematic appeal. Such an abstracting textualization might seem unusual since the western is surely the most American of Hollywood genres, with its stories all period pieces located in a certain national time and region. The genre is defined, if that is the right word, by its trans-Mississippi geography as well as by its evoked historical period, the roughly half-century between the end of the Civil War in 1865 and the closing of the frontier, which can be variously dated by either the official decree to that effect issued by the Census Bureau in 1890 or, perhaps, the admission to the union in 1912 of Arizona, the last remaining territory in the contiguous North American areas of the country.

And yet in *The Searchers*, as in westerns more generally, geography and history offer reference points that are vague at best. Here Monument Valley stands in for a West Texas with quite different natural features, but this ostentatiously inauthentic gesture does not compromise the film's peculiar connection to the geographic imaginary. Similarly, the narrative's location in time (in the late 1860s) is only occasionally relevant to the story Ford has to tell, which is historically abstract, so to speak, though based ultimately on actual events from decades earlier that have already passed through a fictionalizing process (in the source novel by Alan LeMay of the same name).[1] It is an interesting comment on the western genre, in both its literary and cinematic forms, that westernizing novelization has relieved the story materials of the considerable significance they possess for the narrative of Manifest Destiny and its key concepts, permanent settlement and the rule of law. In the fashion typical of legendary storytelling, *The Searchers* aims to provide a poignant affect: a nostalgic longing for a golden past of the collective imagination, but a corresponding lack of interest in history of the more academic kind, confirming Ernest Renan's famous view of the essential incompatibility of history in the academic sense with the social construct of "the nation."[2] Historians are obsessed with important dates, key figures, and developments of the *longue durée*, and they manifest an enthusiasm-dampening propensity to debunk the very mythology that sustains broader interest in those halcyon days gone by, when an essential aspect of the national imaginary was the self-deceptive notion of "wide-open spaces."

Films like *The Searchers* demonstrate clearly that the American public has less interest in the "real" West than in the idealizing mythology of the region created by journalists, writers, showmen, and film producers. Ford's film, as a result, could have been set anywhere that would readily signify westernness, itself a hard-to-define but nonetheless potent social and geographic category. The brief indication in an opening title that the story to be told took place in Texas during the immediate post–Civil War era could easily have been written out of the narrative, being a stipulation with virtually no truth value once the story was mostly emptied of its historical particulars. Significantly, though Ford was concerned to infuse the western with "realism," the filmmakers gave no consideration to shooting in some recognizably Texas location; authenticity as such, then, was not a factor in production planning. Monument Valley was chosen for other reasons, most importantly Ford's interest in pictorialism, as well as, after several projects successfully shot there, his undimmed enthusiasm for this wild and virtually uninhabited place as a temporary production site where he could practice his art and, in a gesture not inappropriate for the western genre, get away from it all.

Realism with a Human Face

Though *Sunset Blvd.* would eventually be understood as part of the postwar series identified by French critics as film noir, Wilder was not free in the least to select any one of the nation's many cityscapes to serve as the conventional "dark city" of such narratives, one of earliest and most influential of which, *Double Indemnity* (1944), he had himself directed. The script's focus on a fatal romance might be quintessentially noir, but *Sunset Blvd.* is all about a particular place, a well-known street in the "real" Hollywood, whose absence on the screen would surely have been noted had Wilder and producer Charles Brackett chosen either to shoot on soundstages and back lots or if proffered some other American city as a plausible substitute. The film presents itself, in fact, as an exposé of the type quite familiar to the national public, who, at this point in Hollywood history, had become addicted to sensational accounts of the offscreen lives of the national cinema's larger-than-life figures. The narrator's account is to be an "inside" story that purports to tell the truth about a homicide committed by one of the community's most famous citizens, former star actress Norma Desmond (Gloria Swanson), with her victim the might-have-been screenwriter Joe Gillis. The opening sequence of the film locates Gillis's corpse floating in the mansion's pool, with the not-to-be-credited power to narrate the tale of his own demise from this final resting place in the house's most visible sign of wealthy self-indulgence. In the original script, Gillis "speaks" from the morgue where his remains have been transported, but it seems altogether more fitting that his corpse begin its impossible narration from that part of the property that, for most Americans at the time, would have marked it out as quintessentially Californian, a place for sun worship and recreational exertion. This scandal of ill-sorted passionate attachment and subsequent violence constitutes, then as now, the hottest kind of subject matter for fanzines and gossip columns alike, and Gillis hardly shows himself to be especially prescient in predicting the kind of overheated treatment it should surely receive, so different from the cool and self-indicting cynicism of his matter-of-fact narration of the events that led to sudden violence and his demise. Even the filmmakers' bizarre trope, the corpse that tells its own tragic tale, seems to be an appropriate narrational extravagance in the lurid tradition of "true crime" accounts, including the James M. Cain novel that had furnished Wilder and collaborator Raymond Chandler with the material for the aforementioned *Double Indemnity* (of which more in chapter 5). In *Sunset Blvd.*, the narrator's corpse is hardly cold before the shocking events begin their rapid transformation into hot copy, a process the narrator of course cannot forestall, only rival. Reporters and newsreel cameramen arrive on the screen in the same speeding caravan of dark sedans as do the police, suggesting the seamless fit of criminal and journalistic investigations. Both groups seek an exposition of precisely the sort Gillis will provide: a backstory that explains why the screenwriter was at the Desmond mansion and why Norma was moved to put three bullets in him as he walked out her front door with his suitcase. As soon becomes clear, he is the only one who knows it all and can deliver the truth in flashback dramatizations and obtrusive voiceover analysis.

As a post-mortem character of sorts, played by William Holden, Joe contrasts immediately with the person who sets about reporting the initial facts of what will undoubtedly prove to be a sensational story. One of the nation's most recognizable show biz columnists, Hedda Hopper, appears as herself, and is shown phoning in her lead paragraph. Her predictable emphasis is that Desmond's reclusiveness must lie behind the crime of which she is the assumed

FIGURE 12 Gossip columnist Hedda Hopper, playing herself, is caught by Billy Wilder's camera phoning in the story of the Norma Desmond scandal in *Sunset Blvd.* (frame enlargement).

perpetrator. Here, performing herself, the journalist and hammy former actress does the kind of thing she would do were there actually a story. We know, of course, that there is no one at the other end of telephone line receiving her scoop; the fictionalized real is unmasked as dramatic fakery by the presence of the "actual" gossip columnist, one of Hollywood's most important figures, a maker and break of reputations, a source of gratis buzz who often shaped, for ill or good, the box office fates of new releases. Appearing as herself, acting as herself, she strains, if she does not rupture, the story's pretentions to be a story. The operative aesthetic here is a social realism dependent only in part on typology (William Holden as a tough but attractive masculine presence). The film also depends on the pressing into performative service of "real people" in roles similar or identical to those they customarily occupy in the world outside the story. The realism in *Sunset Blvd.*, in other words, goes beyond this standard form of "truth-seemingness," which, however authentic, is still fabulation of a sort. Wilder's engagement with the particulars of place is a more complicated affair, with the film's narrative constituting not simply the inside story of a May-December love affair gone horribly wrong.

    Sunset Blvd. also offers an exposé of the discontents of a not yet buried past that lies just barely beneath the surface of an industry relentlessly devoted to a present of glamour, youth, and acclaim. Desmond is a somebody become a nobody. With the manner of the show business royal she once was, she rules over a some place become a no place, her needs catered to by an ex-husband reduced to a servant, Max von Mayerling (Erich von Stroheim), once a well-respected filmmaker in his own right but now yet another present irrelevance. Experiencing a deep professional and personal crisis and in need of any place that might provide refuge, Joe literally stumbles onto the house, whose frozen-in-time presence awes him even before he has any idea who its strangely matched residential couple might be. Unable to resist accepting the financial support Norma can provide, he soon finds himself trapped by her insatiable need to be loved, with the objective correlative of that possession being his taking up residence in her mansion and wearing the clothes she selects and purchases for him. In the end, he will not be owned, no matter how desperate his circumstances, and the result is his perhaps too obvious retreat from a dependence he hates himself for reluctantly accepting. Norma's meddling prevents him from reclaiming his dignity as well as a personal life and career that seems, against the odds, to have taken a promising turn, as an apparently on-the-verge-of-success partnership with a young scriptwriter, Betty (Nancy Olson), has led to romance. Humiliated by Betty's discovery that he is in effect a kept man, Joe breaks off the relationship. It is after he determines to return to his home in the Midwest, which Norma experiences as a blow to her ego, that she answers with three shots from her revolver.

In summoning his audience, Gillis gestures toward a represented space beyond conventional forms of reporting or textualizing. He imagines a place of pure truth, unshaped by a hyped rhetoric designed to arouse and entertain, and so an accurate reenactment of his recent history. He intends, in fact, more or less what the filmmakers themselves intend. *Sunset Blvd.* thus tells the inside story of his inside story, with the real, in its several forms, appearing as itself, and preferred, if not exclusively, to the strictly fictional elements of the film in which mimesis renders as other people and things that *are*, assigning them stipulated identities. The principal performers "other" themselves by playing a role, but several from the filmmaking community appear, we should say authentically, "as themselves." Suitably decorated soundstages sometimes invite the viewer's limited investment of belief in the manner of the era's typical studio film, but a considerable number of Los Angeles locations, their authenticity suitably flaunted, make it clear that the story was filmed in the city where it is set. But this real place is not simply recast as part of a self-enclosed fiction, becoming a conventional "setting." Hollywood, its people as well as its institutions and built spaces, is only in part fictionalized by being assigned a series of invented names and qualities, whose supposed truth viewers are encouraged to endorse conditionally.

Wilder and Brackett, it must be pointed out, did not invent this semi-fictional approach to portraying America's filmmaking community, with Busby Berkeley's *Hollywood Hotel* (1938) and Robert Florey's *Hollywood Boulevard* (1936) the most interesting predecessors to *Sunset Blvd.* Berkeley's film is little more than a showcase for Benny Goodman and his orchestra, as well as a number of lavishly staged musical numbers including the iconic "Hooray for Hollywood." With exteriors shot at the actual Hollywood Hotel, where Louella Parsons hosted a weekly radio program, the film does incorporate real places (including brief shots of landmarks such as the Brown Derby restaurant) even while featuring personalities, most notably Parsons, as "themselves," but its plot is otherwise thoroughly conventional and as fanciful as in Berkeley's other Warner Bros. musicals. It is less an exploration of the industry than, as its signature tune suggests, a celebration of the kind of engaging fantasy it excelled at producing.

Florey had established himself as a talented documentarian (working on newsreels) and as an experimental filmmaker of some note when he was assigned to the project that would become *Hollywood Boulevard*. The film, as he originally imagined it, would have featured a series of episodes, each filmed at a prominent Los Angeles location, that would be loosely connected to a fictional narrative. *Hollywood Boulevard* would also include a considerable number of cameo appearances by figures from the industry, most of whom would be appearing as themselves. Paramount, however, was less enthusiastic, and the project was shifted substantially toward fictionality and away from its planned deep engagement with place. Wilder and Brackett would be able to accomplish what Florey was prevented from doing in more than a superficial way: using all that was Hollywood to tell something of the story of the industry.

Realism in *Sunset Blvd.* depends more on a self-reflexivity that, among other effects, lays bare the partiality of performance art, in which actors remain "themselves" while also playing characters. Wilder and Brackett achieve something quite similar with setting. The untransformed (if co-opted) real is juxtaposed with its only partly fabulized other, as, for example, in a sequence when Norma Desmond (*played* by Gloria Swanson) dialogues with Cecil B. DeMille, who is both *playing* and *being* himself. In this same sequence, the Paramount soundstage where they meet is both a set in the film and, as depicted by the camera, a working soundstage at the "actual" studio. Wilder's film observes DeMille taking part in the film's dramatic structure, but also as he was in fact at the very moment of the production of Wilder's film, that is, directing his own current project on one of the studio's soundstages. A deep and quite palpable ontological difference separates Desmond from the DeMille who appears in these sequences. Located only in part at the same level of the fictional, they are "characters" but not in the same sense, and their extended, complex encounter reveals as only partial the disjunction between the imagined world in which they play assigned roles and the real Hollywood that is being referenced and represented. The border between the fictional and the real, in other words, is revealed as thoroughly permeable. The filmmakers make it clear that filmic images can function in the conventional fashion as fictional, and yet, as André Bazin affirms, cinematic representation differs essentially from its literary counterpart because as viewers "we are forced to accept as real the object photographed." Brackett and Wilder make sure that

FIGURE 13 The complexities of a Paramount soundstage, fully dressed and staffed, figure as an important aspect of setting in *Sunset Blvd.* (frame enlargement).

we see that the real is indeed real, but this is of course no simple matter since the context for such representation is thoroughly fictional, not in any way a "true story."

The principals (Swanson, costar Holden, and secondary players like von Stroheim, Jack Webb, and Nancy Olson) inhabit roles in the traditional sense, playing characters who are fictional but true to type, as suits a representational regime aiming at a kind of social realism. But Swanson's Norma and von Stroheim's Max are also *á clef*, that is, evoking real but unnamed originals; in an interesting twist for this kind of fictionalizing, these unnamed others are, in part, none other than "their real selves." Norma Desmond resembles in different ways silent-era actresses Mary Pickford, Clara Bow, and Mae Murray, all of whom in their post-career lives experienced something like her personal difficulties and professional disappointments; the script confected by Wilder and Brackett also evokes the drug addiction of Mabel Normand, one of Charlie Chaplin's costars, and her subsequent involvement (though she was never indicted) in the shooting death of lover William Desmond Taylor. The intense interdependency between Desmond and von Mayerling, the star's former director (and ex-husband), recalls both Josef von Sternberg's Svengali-like promotion of Marlene Dietrich (whose career at Paramount declined when the studio fired him) and the similar deep professional/personal connection between director Mauritz Stiller and Greta Garbo (Louis B. Mayer took over Stiller's "role" with Garbo after MGM dismissed him).

The characters played by Swanson and von Stroheim thus reference Hollywood types, with their personal/professional relationship in some sense an industry cliché: the exotic star actress managed by her über-continental artist, both with huge egos and larger-than-life professional images that pose continuing difficulties for studio executives and threaten to end their Hollywood careers. But the biographical real is also evoked by this "fictional" relationship: Swanson and von Stroheim worked together on a number of films, including the ill-starred production *Queen Kelly* (1929). Von Stroheim's dismissal from the project was instrumental in ending his directorial career in Hollywood. It is, of course, as a failed director that von Stroheim appears in the film, playing a version of himself, subordinate to the very star (Swanson) who survived the wreck of that production with career intact. This particular resonance between text and context deepens the film's portrayal of the discontents of celebrity, the darker side of fame and fortune, about which there is more to say below.

Swanson's early career successes were in DeMille films; thus the close professional relationship that Wilder's fiction focuses on here is also in some sense true as well as fabulized, existing, that is, only in the fiction. To put this another way, Swanson's performance history is in some sense shifted to the character she is now playing, as the scene between the two characters on a Paramount soundstage more closely aligns Desmond's personal history with that of the actress playing her. DeMille, as himself, is a character in Wilder's fiction, in which he plays a key role as an important figure at the film's version of Paramount Studios. But, also as himself, he remains the director who coached Swanson in her breakthrough roles in *Don't Change Your Husband* (1919) and *Why Change Your Wife?* (1920), both produced at Paramount. DeMille was as responsible as anyone for Swanson becoming one of the silent era's most successful stars, and in Wilder's film the still-working if now aged director's anguished eagerness to escort the star whose career he had advanced off his set eerily contrasts with the professional relationship the two enjoyed for many years in real life, during which, it should be noted, no such episode occurred.

So cinematic art imitates cinematic life—at least mostly. Or, perhaps better, in this extraordinary place obsessed with glamorous images and entertaining narratives, art *is* life, with the line between being and performing shown as thoroughly permeable, an industry truism here quite subtly expressed. Consider that *Sunset Blvd.*, though it does not portray one, *is* after all a Hollywood success story, featuring the much-lauded return to industry prominence of Swanson, who resurrects her career, if for only one shining moment, by incarnating a fictionalized version of herself delivered to a quite different but equally plausible fate. She is, as the filmmakers thought, perfect for the role. The film details how Norma prepares for her expected professional return with careful dieting, endless beauty regimens, and constant exercise, and if these sequences have a palpable authenticity it is because the character is depicted as following the same routines as the famously health-obsessed actress who plays her. Swanson's only slowly fading glamour and vibrant glow testify to the success achieved by such discipline. Norma's efforts to preserve her beauty and appeal prove pathetically inconsequential; DeMille's disregard for how good she looks precipitates instead a descent into desperate melancholy and, eventually, a dissociation from reality. In contrast, Swanson's self-obsession allowed her, by starring in this film, to write a chapter in her life story that surely seems to be right out of some script entitled *A Star Is Re-Born*. Wilder's film is the proof of the actress's accomplishment in portraying what she might have become but did not, ironically, at least in part because of her moving portrayal of the doomed Desmond, her tragic doppelgänger.

For those in the know, the referential richness of this sequence is enhanced by the fact that what DeMille is shooting is a scene from the biblical costume drama eventually released as *Samson and Delilah* (1949). This future event belongs not to the diegesis Wilder has created, but to the subsequent real history of DeMille, the others involved in the production (some of whom also "appear" in Wilder's film), and Hollywood itself (nominated for five Academy Awards, the film was cited for best costumes and art direction). *Samson and Delilah* appears here in miniature *as itself*, with actor Henry Wilcoxon caught by Wilder's camera as both in character (playing Ahtur) and performing that character as Henry Wilcoxon. In this film-within-a-film, it is only the first of these "performances" that is recorded (or, more correctly, appears to be recorded) by DeMille's cinematographer. The camera operator is played, if that is the right word, by Archie Dalzell, one of Paramount's most experienced and talented professionals, but not, as it happens, one of the crew for *Samson and Delilah*. So Wilder's camera records him doing, or pretending to do, what Dalzell did for years on Paramount soundstages even if he is not really an authentic part of the shoot that Norma's unexpected arrival disrupts.

Wilder's multilayered diegesis identifies itself as in some ways contiguous with but distinct from the Hollywood which is its subject, a complex cultural place it performs, references, and is enfolded by. *Sunset Blvd.* does not designate everything that is seen within the frame as being *for* the story, dependent in other words on the stipulation of identity and significance involved in fictionalization, on some form or other of "putting in the scene." The distinction made here has been approached in a somewhat different manner by Leo Braudy in his study of "what we see" in films. For Braudy, film history is defined by two types of productions, closed and open, that challenge viewers to see what is framed by the camera for them in radically different ways. The closed film presents its world as "the only thing that exists," constituting the frame as the absolute limit of what is there, as containing "every object, every character, every gesture, every action." In the closed film, "everything is totally sufficient . . . everything fits in." In the open film, the frame is constructed as unable to include all that matters, as what it does depict directs the viewer's attention outward as well as inward. The open frame "allows other things into it," including realia that are, and sometimes are not, textualized. The world of an open film is thus "a momentary frame around an ongoing reality. The objects and the characters in the film existed before the camera focused on them and they will exist after the film is over. They achieve their significance or interest within the story of the film, but, unlike the objects and the people in a closed film, the story of the open film does not exhaust the meaning of what it contains." In the closed film, Braudy writes, the frame "defines the world inside as a picture frame does," but in the open film, the frame is "more like a window, opening a privileged view on a world of which other views are possible."[3]

Wilder exemplifies something of this latter approach by dramatizing how an uncalculated, impulsive gesture initiates a line of action that eventually goes nowhere after revealing its particular truth. In response to what she believes is a summons from DeMille, Desmond has herself driven to the Paramount lot. Though she is not booked for an appointment, the gate man, recognizing the famous actress, lets her through, and she proceeds to the soundstage where DeMille is shooting. She has convinced herself that the several calls she has had from the studio are about some new project, perhaps the script she has herself written about John the Baptist and Salome, the holy man's teenage tormenter, a role that though now in her fifties she intends playing. But the desperate woman has deceived herself. Paramount's prop manager made the calls; he was simply eager to rent her car for a current production, ironically a period project for which this still-operative automotive antique would be perfect, its age and unfashionability seen as advantages rather than drawbacks. Realizing at last that Desmond is the victim of an unintentionally cruel misunderstanding, DeMille is reluctant to dismiss his old friend too abruptly; he asks her to take a seat near him while he finishes shooting the scene. Norma is denied a place before the camera, but invited—as we all are—to take a seat and watch. There she is spied by one of the "juicers" on the lighting bridge. The man immediately shines his spotlight on the former star, effectively framing her and immediately attracting a crowd of admirers, who rush to her side. They disperse after a chagrined DeMille, fearful about causing her any more pain, orders the spot switched off in a gesture that is both kind and dismissive. Desmond becomes once again only a spectator, watching from behind the camera and no longer glamorously lit in anticipation of becoming its object as the others go about their business.

In this scene, Wilder and company literally shine a light on themselves and the profession they practice in a gesture that strikingly enacts the spectacularization at the heart of the medium's representational agenda, its selection from what the real has to offer of what is to be textualized and made available for viewing. But this self-reflexive moment, steeped in irony and pathos, also underlines the openness of the framing process. The context makes it clear that only one view of the world among many is selected and briefly privileged, with expressive intentionality the operative force. Reflecting the will of the man who wields it, the camera-spotlight here finds an object of interest in the world dynamically unfolding before it. Such open framing, however, is only momentary. The light will soon be turned in another direction, toward the closed world of the film set where DeMille is in charge, where "all the characters and all the objects . . . are controlled by outside forces, ultimately by the director himself."[4]

Authenticity, Particular and General

Avoiding the temptation to focus on the enigmatic and tragic Desmond, the filmmakers make the industry their main character, and their concern with a scrupulous and multi-faceted realism meant that Hollywood itself would have to furnish the film's exterior and, in some cases, interior locations. This portrait of an industry devoted to producing and selling that complex experience called "entertainment" is achieved through the detailed textualization of key built and cultural spaces. Realism in this instance depends on those spaces being recognized as authentically themselves, corresponding in some fashion to filmgoers' knowledge or assumptions about what had been since the early 1920s the nation's most chronicled and imaged community, with its "personalities" enjoying a celebrity only occasionally extended to others photogenic and charismatic enough to catch the public eye, for example, the pilot Charles Lindbergh, the author Ernest Hemingway, and, more rarely, politicians like Huey Long and Franklin Roosevelt. *Sunset Blvd.* is structured around its incorporation of various forms of realia, with its portrait of a place as much if not more dependent on the real people it deploys. The film emphasizes how thoroughly this unique place is lived in by the industry, which is of course a cultural commonplace. So completely has American filmmaking taken possession of Hollywood's identity and name that it has subsequently seemed desirable for two other national industries to flatter themselves with portmanteau neologisms that refer back to it (Bollywood in Mumbai, Nollywood in Nigeria).

Wilder's portrayal of the community is deep and carefully nuanced, displaying the considerable determination of director and his producer, to purvey a realism that not only represents but includes those things characteristic of real life. This aesthetic is thoroughly documentary in the classic sense as defined by Paul Rotha: "Bringing to life familiar things and people, so that their place in the scheme of things which we call society may be honestly assessed"; Rotha's politically progressive understanding of "familiar," of course, might have to be abandoned since this film devotes itself to anatomizing an extraordinary, in fact unique place that had become entirely familiar.[5] In addition to the principal players, a number of others from the industry, broadly conceived, appear as themselves, including gossip columnist Sidney Skolsky (who figures in an early scene at Schwab's Drugstore, his habitual hangout). Hedda Hopper's rival, and Hollywood's other famous "reporter," Louella Parsons, was invited to appear in the film but declined, perhaps fearing being upstaged by Hopper, who had enjoyed a screen career before turning to journalism.

Others less recognizable are also named as themselves, actor Creighton Hale as well as songwriters Ray Evans and Jay Livingston, while a number of visibly aging studio hands from the early days of Hollywood appear in cameos that only those in the know would be certain to recognize, including Gertrude Astor, Ruth Clifford (a former silent screen leading lady), E. Mason Hopper, Franklyn Farnum, and Eva Novak. Hollywood notables also "appear" in the film as names even though their fleshly avatars do not. In the pitch made to Paramount producer Sheldrake (Fred Clark) for a script he has written on spec, Gillis says that Darryl Zanuck at Fox is interested in it, but that he cannot imagine Tyrone Power (that studio's most important leading man) in the role. Gillis suggests that Paramount's Alan Ladd might be perfect for the male lead. Because they produced *Sunset Blvd.*, executives at Paramount were not unhappy that the film advertised the studio in several ways, including the reference to Ladd, then one of their hottest properties. Not surprisingly, however, Zanuck and Fox refused permission for their names to be used. Wilder and Brackett paid no attention. No legal issues would be raised: realism was all, and so professional courtesy meant little in these circumstances, especially to the constitutionally irreverent Wilder. Interestingly, two traditional characters are the focus of the scene in which the making of a pitch is grounded thoroughly in the contemporary reality of the industry by the mention of actual studio officials and performers. Gillis and Sheldrake are types, fictional creations. They can exist in the same world with Zanuck, Power, and Ladd only through the script's gesturing toward a world that lies (not too far) outside its entertaining fabulations.

Real place for both Ford and Wilder is an important constituent of narrative meaning, reflecting their similar intentions to move beyond the limitations of the soundstage, to which, however, they would each return in later projects. Ford had turned Monument Valley into a kind of soundstage by the time he started production on *The Searchers*, which could have been shot elsewhere in order to communicate, realistically and authentically, the sense of westernness required by the narrative. To be sure, a sense of place is profound and foundational for the story that Ford sets there, but, though to some degree particularized by the story, Monument Valley remains—in fact must remain—general, abstract, which is to say generic. Narratives can be understood as generic only insofar as they connect to a recognizable multiplicity of similar films; a genre develops through serial, imitative repetition, and Monument Valley became generic, as well as a recognizable image of authorship, through its deployment as the real West in one Ford western after another. The location's particularity reflects the tension in any genre between conventional elements (such as themes, images, character types) and their unique inflections in different films. The actual location where Ford's westerns were shot, then, is always already unnamed, never identified as it "is," extratextually speaking. Thus the images of Monument Valley are the representations of a place that is always imaged in some sense as what it is not in the narratives for which it provides a setting. The valley is backdrop, not a particular location that filmmaking, in the sense promoted by Zavattini, can get to the bottom of, discovering and conveying meaning in the very act of transforming it into images. It is authentic only in a quite minimal and thoroughly problematic sense.

In *Sunset Blvd.*, the particularity of location is all. Wilder's film profoundly reflects in its images, narrative, and themes the same institutions that are responsible for its making, and whose history and meaning he is committed to portraying. *Sunset Blvd.* portrays lived space defined by its central role in the national culture industry. Wilder's film provides a thorough anatomy of the discontents of an industry bent on the profitable exploitation of both fantasy and reality, including human talents and physical appeal. The complex and endlessly fascinating thereness of Hollywood is the cultural and geographical fact that made *Sunset Blvd.* possible. Lacking much in the way of cultural significance before Ford's cameras starting rolling, Monument Valley quickly became the nation's most famous movie-made location—its meaning fixed by cinematic representation. John Ford considered it "the most complete, beautiful, and peaceful place on earth," and he was directly responsible for transforming it into the most recognizable of authorial signatures.[6]

A Rugged Landscape to Ride Through

A man on horseback, photographed against a distant bleakness, is "the most natural subject for a movie camera," or so said John Ford. Enthusiasts of Hollywood westerns, especially those directed by Ford, would likely agree that this is indeed a potent combination of actor, action, and setting.[7] And Monument Valley, Utah, located on the Colorado Plateau, was in Ford's view an ideal place to make films in which a man on horseback would be the dominant image. For one thing, the valley offered flat and unobstructed spaces over which riders might travel at speed for some distance (outlaws galloping away from a posse, Indians chasing down a wagon train, cavalry troops on patrol trotting in formation). Such action staged in Monument Valley could be captured from a variety of perspectives, but most spectacularly in sweeping panoramic shots, with the camera placed on a promontory, the most famous of which is now named John Ford Point as a memorial to the director's aesthetic preference. Such framings emphasize the smallness of human figures measured against the massive reddish brown sandstone mesas and buttes that are the area's most obtrusively distinctive feature; as the director surely intended, their scale means that performers, often picked out in extreme distance, are in effect absorbed into the location even as they put it in motion. *The Searchers*, as its title proclaims, tells the journey of a purposive journey, as Ethan Edwards (John Wayne) and his nephew Martin Pawley (Jeffrey Hunter) pursue and finally confront the Comanches who have slaughtered the rest of their settler family, taking off into captivity and sexual subjugation a sole survivor, Martin's sister Debbie (Natalie Wood). Ethan wants justice and so does Martin; both are committed to settling accounts with the raiders. But Martin wants to rescue Debbie, while Ethan soon makes it clear that he intends to kill her, thereby

FIGURE 14 The massive buttes of Monument Valley reduce to relative insignificance the human figures in *The Searchers* (frame enlargement).

erasing what he sees as the family shame arising from her absorption into a polluting culture. This stark drama of cultural collision in a vast wilderness is appropriately set within the large-scale landscape that the valley provides.

Monument Valley, Ford was not hesitant to note, also provided the maker of western films with other advantages, in particular a diversity of geographical locales, all of which are used in *The Searchers*, whose narrative involves an extended pursuit across what is purportedly a huge expanse of territory. The valley, so he proclaimed, is the West in miniature: "It has rivers, mountains, plains, desert, *everything the land can offer.*"[8] Monument Valley thus possessed as well a conveniently impressive malleability, which, as historian Glenn Frankel observes, enabled Ford to "pivot the camera and be rewarded with a series of *differentiated* and breathtaking vistas," as a series of unique rock formations made themselves available from single set-ups, inviting spectacular panoramic shots.[9] "Vista" is clearly *le mot juste*, describing as it does the usefulness of a site that can be photographed in considerable depth, even on a scale that dwarfs the individual figure, suggesting the limited purchase on or relevance of human action to this landscape, as the beholding eye is drawn toward a beautiful and arresting background. Monument Valley is certainly not a location where the foreground in its empty, stage-like barrenness can be configured as a center of interest; the eye moves naturally up from the empty sand across which the characters move to the impossible beauty of the rock formations that contain and frame their exertions.

It seems likely that Ford at first sight understood the location (whose five square miles seems even larger) as a particularly magnificent exemplification of the proverbial "wide-open spaces" central to the concept of the West within the American imaginary. Its ontological emptiness on one level seems consonant with its geography. Monument Valley, after all, is a desert, but that emptiness also reflects the region's geological history as the site of an immense inland sea, which once divided the continent into two halves, Laramidia to the west and Appalachia to the east. The improbably shaped buttes are reminders that the sea has receded, leaving standing some formations—the so-called balanced rocks—that would otherwise be impossibly gravity-defying. Its buttes proclaim that Monument Valley is somewhere that something else once was.

For the most part, the cinematography in *The Searchers* does not privilege objects or scenery of any kind in the foreground. In many medium shots, human figures crowd the frame, enabling little of "place" to be observed. Mise-en-scène, in the sense of significant objects to-be-seen within the frame, in either exteriors or interiors, has here only minimal importance; Ford's westerns do not depend on the genius of art or set designers, but more on what nature has unintentionally provided. Frank Hotaling, an experienced Hollywood professional, did the art design for, among other Ford projects, *The Searchers* and *The Quiet Man* (1952), and the striking use of color schemes and culturally resonant objects in the latter production underlines its absence in the former. It seems no accident that *The Searchers'* two most famous set-ups bookend the narrative with rhyming but contrasting vistas of massive rock formations in the distance framed by cabin doorways: the first of these is the initial shot of a POV sequence in which a female figure looks out toward a distant rider, who turns out to be her brother-in-law Ethan, long absent from the family, and she is caught in silhouette, obscuring but not blocking our view; the second, and more famous, offers an in-depth composition with Edwards posed carefully in the immediate foreground against the rocks in the far distance, looking back toward those in the cabin, including what is left of his family, who are wishing him farewell. Though the camera in both shots is inside the house, it finds nothing of interest there, treating human shelter as little more than a window onto an outside where all that matters takes place. Civilization, flimsy and vulnerable, seems mere frame, registering as something like shadow.

FIGURE 15 The impressive landscape of Monument Valley is first glimpsed in *The Searchers* from the doorway of a settler farmhouse (frame enlargement).

After his initial location shoot there, Ford was drawn to Monument Valley for one western production after another. In this way, the site was so inextricably identified with Ford's western films it became their dominant *assumed* location (though in different fictional guises) even when some sequences were shot elsewhere, with the diegetic geography being in effect a montage of noncontiguous spaces. In the case of *The Searchers*, an Alberta, Canada, location was used to stage a wintry sequence, while the film's dramatic conclusion was shot in what is arguably the most used "natural" exterior of the Hollywood western, Bronson Canyon in L.A.'s Griffith Park, whose first notable use was for the Tom Mix–Zane Grey adaptation *Riders of the Purple Sage* (1925). No doubt, however, that the master location of *The Searchers*, so to speak, is an unnamed Monument Valley, a place that is at one and the same time particular and general, needing the localizing stipulation that one narrative after another would provide (for example, Tombstone, Arizona, in *My Darling Clementine* [1946], the Texas frontier in *The Searchers* and *Rio Grande* [1950], and Oklahoma and Wyoming in *Cheyenne Autumn* [1964]). Perhaps because Ford was singlehandedly responsible for the revival of the A-feature western as a key element of studio production, those westerns, and the place they so reverently represent and celebrate, became the most readily identifiable exemplars of the genre itself. An image "quote" of the valley is all that is needed to reference the thematic and cultural values of that most resolutely national of studio film types.

A brief selection: on their self-appointed journey to discover the country from which they feel so estranged in *Easy Rider* (1969), Captain America (Peter Fonda) and Billy (Dennis Hopper) ride through the valley, moving east from its social emptiness toward different forms of a national life in deep crisis; the eponymous protagonist (Tom Hanks) of *Forrest Gump* (1994), driven by grief and narcissistic self-absorption to run across the country in what seems an attempt to escape himself and history, winds up in Monument Valley, where he comes to the end of his obsessive journeying (at a location now known as Forrest Gump Point), with a change of heart every bit as mysterious and sudden as that of Ethan Edwards himself, who, having captured (rescued?) his niece, does not kill her; and, finally, time travelers Marty McFly (Michael J. Fox) and Doc Brown (Christopher Lloyd) in *Back to the Future III* (1990), stuck in Hollywood's version of the Old West, whose stereotypes they are forced to adopt even as they are eventually reduced, trying to return to their own filmic time, to hauling their broken-down DeLorean across the valley with a buckboard, as genres and historical periods clash in a sequence filled with knowing postmodern humor.

These allusions, it must be pointed out, are all in essence cinematic. They are Baudrillardian invocations not of place *in se* and *per se*, but of the images of that place in Ford's westerns and the meaning it has come to possess as a result of those representational gestures. The valley may of course be deployed in films, as it is in Stanley Kubrick's *2001: A Space Odyssey* (1968), as a generic, dust-covered, rock-strewn landscape devoid of referential possibilities, including its "earthly" identity, but only if the distinctive buttes are banished from the frame. Otherwise, it is arguably the most particularized of American locations whose meaning has been radically altered or fixed by Hollywood, a short list, admittedly, and perhaps topped by the Hollywood sign itself, once a real estate advertisement whose semiotic co-optation by the film industry is one of our national culture's most self-revealing sagas. Something similar happened to Monument Valley when Ford worked his representational magic there. Ever since that initial production, images of the site that feature its most identifiable geological landmarks are always already reuses of the cinematic past, nostalgia-evoking reminders of the important place that the western film, evoking its own forms of wistfulness for an imagined past of epic grandeur, once occupied in the national imaginary.

But it was not always so. In fact, perhaps the most significant advantage that Monument Valley had to offer Ford initially was a certain blankness. Despite a striking and unforgettable magnificence, so suitable to the pronounced interest that nineteenth-century culture took in the geographical sublime, the valley was so remote that it had hosted only a few outside visitors by the time Ford scouted it in 1938 when he was planning the first notable film to be shot there, eventually entitled *Stagecoach* (1939). He likely did not know that a very forgettable Zane Grey adaptation, *The Vanishing American*, directed by George B. Seitz, had been shot there in 1925. Despite its incredible beauty, the area had previously remained nearly completely outside the orbit of American history. Located in a part of the Southwest that had become a state only in 1896, Monument Valley remained more or less inaccessible to visitors until the expansion of the nation's roads after World War II, especially the building of the interstate highway system in the 1950s. It is the national cinema that has transformed it into one of the country's most recognizable natural locations. But except for the Navajos who lived on a reservation nearby, what they call the Valley of the Rocks was unknown to most Americans when it made its first brief appearance in *Stagecoach*.

The contrast with the nation's most famous natural location, Niagara Falls, could hardly be more striking. As historian Elizabeth McKinsey reports, "The basic image of Niagara had become common knowledge by 1776." The site was so well known, in fact, that those writing about it felt no need to offer even a brief description.[10] The idea of the natural sublime, an emotional state characterized by both transcendence and irresistibility, had taken root in American culture earlier in the century, following the publication of Edmund Burke's widely read treatise on the subject.[11] Niagara Falls, according to McKinsey, corresponded at almost all points to Burke's catalog of those qualities in nature that give rise to this complex emotional state. Niagara is "a vast, powerful, magnificent waterfall, its outlines obscured by mist, difficult to get to, a seemingly infinite succession of waters creating an incessant roar, surrounded by the deep solitude of the wilderness, inspiring terror in the observer."[12] Monument Valley likewise conforms to several of Burke's sublime-inducing categories. It also is "difficult to get to" and "surrounded by the deep solitude of the wilderness"; it too gives the viewer impressions of "vastness," "magnificence," and "infinity," even though the valley lacks anything like the continuing drama of thousands of gallons of water tumbling over a precipice, making a deep, rumbling noise that can be heard for miles and generates towering clouds of mist.[13] As Frankel observes, Ford deploys extreme long shots of the valley landscapes "like some modern directors use special effects—to create drama and stun the audience," affectual intentions that are consonant with providing the experience of sublimity, which his representations of Monument Valley have inspired in many a filmgoer.[14]

Niagara Falls provides a useful point of reference in yet another way because it belongs to a familiar geographical category, the waterfall, one that is generically associated with the experience of the sublime. Monument Valley's rock formations, in contrast, are thoroughly *sui generis*, immediately identifiable in their particularities of shape and color. More important, perhaps, with the ancient seabed constituting a stage of considerable expanse, the valley, even in its undramatic stillness, provides an ideal place for the staging of action on a grand scale, permitting filmmakers to exploit to the fullest one of their medium's most essential qualities: its fostering of the illusion of motion by the representation of moving human figures, a seamless matching of cinematic form to content. If it has also become, like Niagara, what Jonathan M. Smith calls a "symbolic landscape," a place that for a culture "condenses and clarifies a meaning that is elsewhere found in a diffuse and ambiguous form," then that meaning inheres more in representational rather than geographical tradition. Monument Valley, perhaps, seems in one sense the exemplary American landscape which, in the words of Agnew and Smith, is nothing less than an "image of exemption from the trials of history . . . a clean geographical slate on which the ideals of America could be inscribed." And yet this blankness proves to be a mirage. In *The Searchers*, and similarly in other Ford westerns, the hero who dominates this place carries with him a heavy baggage of history and cultural values.[15] Niagara is a place of swift and ceaseless natural motion to gaze upon with awe. Monument Valley, in contrast, is actualized by human action, a place to be *in*, not *near*; it can hardly then be exempt from the foundational human dialectic between creation in God's image and the innate depravity that is the unfortunate legacy of Original Sin.

The tradition of American sublime landscape painting in which Niagara is a frequent subject often makes use of human figures observed from a distance in order to measure scale and provide context. These figures, as McKinsey points out, are often contemplative, their faces turned toward the falls in order to provide a metatextual point of reference, a place to look from that is simultaneously outside the landscape and inside its depiction. These "transfixed viewers" serve "to emphasize Niagara's impact as spectacle." We look with those who look so we can see what they see; what is a site thus becomes a sight, a location defined as an object of contemplation. In the rhetorical turn known as a *mise-en-abîme*, representation in the Niagara landscapes conflates image and image-making, confirming the social constructedness of what is being put there for us to see. With its several scenes of viewing and "communing" with the falls, Henry Hathaway's *Niagara* (1953), an extraordinary shot-on-location production discussed in chapter 5, captures observer characters doing much the same, turning the film's viewers into tourists twice-removed.

Ford's use of human figures in his Monument Valley westerns is quite different, avoiding their deployment as intratexual agents of reverential gazing. As scholars have pointed out, Ford's compositions often reflect the watercolors of Charles M. Russell, whose images of Native Americans, cowboys, and assorted western folk capture their subjects on elevated ground that functions like a pedestal framing them against distant mountains. The filmmaker differs from the painter, however, in the prominence he gives the Monument Valley buttes, which often dominate the upper half of the frame even when the human figures are posed on some promontory.[16] Russell's human figures are most often seen from a medium distance, often in substantial detail, and he is unconcerned with constructing the mountains barely visible on the horizon as objects of contemplation. The painter's interest is in depicting the West in human terms; for him the distant high places are backdrop or frame and little more, indications of a westernness that is more significantly depicted in the distinctive dress and manner of the region's exotic types, who are glimpsed more often in action rather than in some static pose. Russell's figures are easily transformed into statues; significantly, he worked as much in cast bronze as with watercolors. With their emphasis on the essential relationship between foreground and background, Ford's long shots defy such a reduction of representational reach.

The rocks of the valley, to be sure, are backdrop for Ford as well because the focus of his films remains the human dramas staged in their foreground. But the buttes, in their impressively solitary verticality, also seem symbolically central to the cultural mythology his westerns both evoke and modify. This landscape resonates with the human characters, both American and Comanche, who find themselves more or less at home in the Valley of the Rocks. *The Searchers* focuses on a self-sufficient and isolated outsider (in essence, the proverbial "man of the west"), and so is his Indian double, Scar (Henry Brandon), a warrior of impressive strength and resolution who has his own reasons for exacting revenge by murdering the Edwards family. Ethan is an outsized hero whose devotion to family just barely outweighs the homicidal impulses of a grief-stricken revenger, eager to right unnumbered wrongs even though he has reason enough to doubt the efficacy of devoted effort to a cause. He seems as hard as the stones he easily maneuvers among. From the beginning, he is dominated by an anger that can be no more assuaged than the inhospitality of a place he comfortably inhabits might be softened by civilizing efforts, which he, of course, has no intention of making.

This barren landscape, where little grows beyond tumbleweed, is a reverse image of the virgin paradise inhabited by an American Adam that dominates the national mythology. North America was first understood by its European settlers as a land of verdant plenty where the human story might be given another chance, perhaps avoiding a second Fall. Ethan Edwards, however, is an Ishmael, not an Adam, a wanderer upon the earth rather than its ordained master.[17] "The American Myth," as R.W.B. Lewis writes, "saw life and history as just beginning": "It described the world as starting up again under fresh initiative, in a divinely granted second chance for the human race. . . . It introduced a new kind of hero, the heroic embodiment of a new set of ideal human attributes . . . the hero of the new adventure: an individual emancipated from history, happily bereft of ancestry, untouched and undefiled by the usual inheritances of family and race. . . . His moral position was prior to experience."[18] In *The Searchers*, it seems a mockery of common sense that hot sand and red dust might successfully be farmed, though this is the avowed intention of its inhabitants, whose supposed crops and livestock are more or less invisible. Ethan finds his way back to a wasteland where the self must discover forms of being that are more likely to be destructive than life-sustaining. Returning from a war that his army lost and abjuring the surrender designed to restore peace, Edwards is hardly "emancipated from history," but rather trapped by its grim irresolutions. Yet this is hardly the scene where these collisions of collective intentions have played out. He is the rogue outlier of a national family riven by self-inflicted wounds, forced by circumstances toward a reunion that, faithful to the perdurability of his oath to the Confederacy, he cannot accept and perhaps, so the narrative hints, has actively resisted. And he is hardly "untouched" by "the usual inheritances of family and race," whose complexities the disturbing narrative brings to the surface but does not resolve. The family he returns to is his and not his. Its center is a woman he loves but will never possess, and whose horrific violation and murder will permit him to turn a flooding anger against her killer and, so it seems for much of the chase, against his enemy's other victim, the daughter she bore his brother, now a captive. This child could have been his but is not. His beloved lives on in her, and yet the child is now alienated from him by fiercer, unforgivable, and irreversible acts of estrangement, a kidnapping and rape that he sees as blood-polluting, regretting that they have not yet been followed by some slim but redeeming mercy of death.

Life has left Ethan with the taste of ashes in his mouth, and his feelings of dispossession in its several senses are appropriately imaged by the postlapsarian bleakness that is Monument Valley, a place that seems ideal for pursuit as well as, because it registers the nearly complete lack of civilization, a bloody settlement of accounts that is both personal and ethnocentric. Most important, of course, is a restoration of white-eye superiority, which startlingly reverses the social and cultural values of that most famous of American pursuit and rescue narratives, James Fenimore Cooper's *The Last of the Mohicans* (1826). Yet even in that fiction one of the heroines prefers suicide to a degrading death to be delivered by the phallic knife of her revenge-obsessed Indian captor. Edwards, in any case, is no Natty Bumppo, though, like his literary predecessor, he "knows" the Indians better than do the other whites. He speaks their language, understands their customs, and has made his own their wisdom about how to live in this unforgiving wilderness. But he is not one of "them," and the name that the natives have assigned him ("Big Shoulders") confers no honor, instead a reference to his physical presence.

An ideal setting for an anti-Rousseauvian narrative in which no savages are noble, Monument Valley hardly evokes the "virgin land" of the American dream whose natural bounty can at last be turned to human use, nor does this frontier invite civilizing gestures meant to tame its only apparent wildness. The valley is the West conceived in quite another fashion altogether: preternaturally natural on a gigantic scale, unshaped by history yet a stage ideal for the exercise of an iron will, and terrifyingly savage in its relentless exposure of those buried truths and repressed horrors that constitute an irresistible call to violent action. Dwarfing the importance of all other duties and desires, what must be searched out is to be found somewhere in a seemingly trackless wilderness, a coherent mapping of which Ford's camera absolutely refuses, giving the journey something of the undirected directedness of a medieval *avanture*. Much like the dark forest in twelfth-century romance, in fact, the Ford-invented Monument Valley is the landscape where morality plays can be staged in geographical and cultural abstractness. Despite their period-correct weapons and clothing, his westerns hover on the outside of the era they often only vaguely reference. These films connect indirectly at best to the dynamic history of the West, roiled by the restless forward motion of events and the serial solidification of real places into socially defined and individually named locations that are claimed for a central government. It is impossible to imagine how Monument Valley, at least as depicted in *The Searchers*, might ever fulfill such a geographical destiny.

Ford's westerns only rarely celebrate the progressive nation-building at the heart of the American story. It is telling that the director's most historically engaged and demythologizing western, a film that thematizes the painful birth of settled culture, *The Man Who Shot Liberty Valance* (1962), was shot not in Monument Valley, but on Paramount soundstages and back lots, with some exteriors staged at California locations not far from Los Angeles. The decision to bypass Ford's favorite real location may have been made by the studio and dictated by finances (with two A-list stars the budget may well have been stretched), but, as Tag Gallagher suggests, it seems as well to be a response to the story, which is "theatrical" and privileges "statehood as opposed to territory, civilization as opposed to wilderness."[19] In any case, the film's realism is a kind of reverse effect achieved by the refusal to engage the hyperreality of a thoroughly mythologized Monument Valley. Ford instead conjures up a generically ungeneric

West in which the traditional hero (played of course by John Wayne) dies a pathetic drunk, forgotten by everyone except the crusading politician (James Stewart), whose distinguished career he furthers with a deception that ironically costs the true western hero what he loves most, sinking him into a self-destructive melancholy from which he never emerges. In this film, the legend of the western hero—his eminence established by homicide—is shown to be a pathetic, destructive, if socially useful lie. *The Man Who Shot Liberty Valance*'s black-and-white cinematography begs interpretation as a refusal of the naturalness of that spectacular valley. In his other westerns, Ford captures this scenicness with Technicolor and VistaVision, in extravagant stylizing gestures that had, in large part through his practice and influence, become *de rigueur* for the A-westerns by the middle of the 1950s. The exceptions would, of course, be films devoted to deconstructing the genre. Consider, for example, Arthur Penn's *The Left-Handed Gun* (1958), based—of all things—on a Gore Vidal teleplay. Photographed in muted black and white, this stagey drama portrays the existential crisis of gunslinger Billy the Kid, artfully incarnated as a kind of nineteenth-century James Dean by the Method-trained Paul Newman.

For the most part, Ford's West is as real and unreal, as in time and out of time, as King Arthur's Britain. His westerns, of course, cannot avoid entirely the grand narrative of trans-Mississippi settlement in the post–Civil War era, but they most often do no more than gesture at momentous events whose more than mumbled discussion would, so it seems, violate some taboo. Their narratives sometimes center on alternative or fictionalized versions of key events of legend or history (the Gunfight at the OK Corral and Wyatt Earp's civilizing efforts in *My Darling Clementine* [1946], but, even more tellingly, the sideways treatment of George Armstrong Custer and the Battle of the Little Big Horn in *Fort Apache* [1948]). Similarly, a historical event, albeit less sweeping, and thoroughly fictionalized in LeMay's novel, can with difficulty still be glimpsed in *The Searchers*, though its most significant figure—the *mestizo* Comanche chief Quanah Parker, child of a captive woman later rescued—had already been written out of this narrative of abduction and redemption by the time it came to Ford. Interestingly, Parker's story suggests the inevitable interdependence of native and European peoples, their constitution, despite war and hatred, of precisely that kind of mixed society that Ethan Edwards views with such horror and from which he "rescues" Debbie (who has somehow, though it strains credulity, been exempted from bearing her captor's children).[20] The narrative invented by LeMay, and further refined by Ford, reinvokes the "lost boundary" separating white settlers from the natives they have largely displaced, as Debbie is rescued before the conception and birth of a "breed" like Quanah Parker can take place.

From the point of view of its own mythologizing history, the tale in *The Searchers* is thus appropriately staged in a distinctive landscape suspended between somewhere and nowhere. Such indirection characterizes as well the film's engagement with perhaps the darkest, most morally reprehensible element of the national character: a visceral, murderous disgust at what might be best described as race shame. Though English offers no word to describe this most virulent form of racialism, it is a persistent theme of both American social engineering (with its long-enduring prohibitions of "miscegeny," finally declared unconstitutional in 1967) and also fictionalizing (as in *Mohicans*). Only occasionally, however, does it surface in some fully articulated form, most notably, perhaps, in D. W. Griffith's *The Birth of a Nation* (1915), where the reestablishment of impermeable racial boundaries, politically and socially, is shown as foundational of sectional reunion. In *The Searchers*, Ethan will provide Debbie with the death that by all rights she should have dealt herself rather than submit to continuing violation, in the process abandoning her identity to embrace being a Comanche. Only *in extremis* does the narrative unexpectedly and without explanation sidestep this truly horrifying possibility, having earlier forecasted its inevitability and never hinting that Ethan could be other than unmoved in his resolve to salvage something of family and ethnic honor in the only way it seems possible.

Through the films he set there, subsequently released to global audiences, Ford turned Monument Valley from a location into a place defined by generic and personal meanings. The corresponding eastern stereotype is that frighteningly untraversable denseness that begins as soon as the rocky shore ends, a sunless, impenetrable forest where lurk hordes of hostile savages eager to annihilate intruders, as they do so spectacularly in that most visually arresting of "easterns," Michael Mann's version of *The Last of the Mohicans* (1992). This film was shot in the Blue Ridge mountains of North Carolina, which offers, if not old growth stands of trees, substantial secondary woodland that readily stands in for the story's location in what is now upstate New York. The eastern forest is thickly overgrown and requires clearing in order to be civilizable through a series of pioneering gestures that always intimate at the dispersal or cleansing of the native population as well. As geographers John A. Agnew and Jonathan M. Smith suggest, in the early years of the national history "an image prevailed of North America as a pristine wilderness, available for European 'development.'"[21] In the early writings of European settlers, like John Winthrop, William Bradford, and Jonathan Edwards, North America is conjured up as a crowded landscape, teeming with wildlife, dense forest, and inconvenient primal residents. Clearing that land will install there a quite different form of living. In his famous co-optation of a biblical prediction of preeminence (Matthew 5:14), Winthrop imagines America, shaped by divine will, as a "city on a hill." The dominant quality of Monument Valley, in contrast, is its barrenness—clearly referenced by the possibility it presents of extreme long shots in which, despite distance, viewers can still pick out small groups of human figures dwarfed by an immensity of nothingness, a place where any purchase of European-style culture, dependent on agriculture and animal husbandry, is difficult to imagine. To be sure, hills proliferate there, but the building of a city on any of them hardly seems in the offing.

Though unrecognizable as a previously existing place (or perhaps because it was unrecognizable as such), the Monument Valley landscapes that were introduced to national and global filmgoers in *Stagecoach* immediately established themselves as archetypally "western" in a general sense, so thoroughly did they conform to the long-developed cultural stereotypes of the region's wide-open spaces. With its otherworldly wildness, its unsettled desert emptiness stretching for miles toward the horizon, its irregular rock formations sculpted to an unintentional beauty, Monument Valley signifies the West as the other of the national cultural imagination, not a nature to be made clean and then rebuilt free from the impediment of a past, but an unconstructed, unwelcoming landscape where the rough individualism of the western hero could be inscribed, if not as the basis for permanent habitation. In this sense, *The Searchers* is archetypal: a peripatetic narrative centering on a determined unsettledness that is the main character's *idée fixe*, his psychology writ large in the shadow of a suicidal civil war. In a gesture toward the relentless movement of manifest destiny, Ethan's arrival is always the prelude to a departure toward some yet unglimpsed beyond that the spacious blankness of the valley evokes, the somewhere else that is not here.

Ford may not have been exaggerating when he confessed that "the real star of my Westerns has always been the land," meaning, of course, Monument Valley, not the canyons and desert of suburban Los Angeles. The latter locales were where the exteriors essential to the western genre, then enjoying a period of substantial aesthetic decline in the still-evolving sound cinema of the 1930s, were mostly shot until Ford determined to provide *Stagecoach* with key sequences filmed in a more impressive and authentic setting.[22] During the silent 1920s, the genre had made fine use of actual locations in productions such as Ford's own *Iron Horse* (1925), sequences of which were shot at several Nevada locations, including Dodge Flat near Wadsworth. The conversion to talking pictures meant that dialogue was best recorded on soundstages, to which western filmmaking largely decamped for some years, dominated for a time by B-series, which often featured singing cowboys like Gene Autry, Tex Ritter, and Roy Rogers. Because *Stagecoach* restored the notion of significant, appropriately rugged landscape to the genre, the industry, as well as influential critics, took good notice. Reviewing the film in the *New York Times*, Frank S. Nugent, fascinated by Ford's brilliantly executed panoramic vistas and effective refounding of the cinematic genre, enthused:

In one superbly expansive gesture . . . John Ford has swept aside ten years of artifice and talkie compromise and has made a motion picture that sings a song of camera. It moves, and how beautifully it moves, across the plains of Arizona, skirting the sky-reaching mesas of Monument Valley, beneath the piled-up cloud banks which every photographer dreams about, and through all the old-fashioned, but never really outdated, periods of prairie travel in the scalp-raising seventies, when Geronimo's Apaches were on the warpath.[23]

There is some dispute about how Ford "discovered" Monument Valley, but the most convincing explanation is that local resident Harry Goulding (he ran a trading post near the reservation) heard that a location scout working for Ford was looking at potential filming sites around Flagstaff, Arizona. As he confesses, Ford was impressed not only by its natural beauty, but by its inaccessibility (it was many miles from anything that could be called civilization). Filming there was like an extended camping trip, allowing him to "get away from people who would like to tell me how to make pictures."[24] In 1938, Ford, busily preparing the project that would become *Stagecoach* for producer Walter Wanger, was contacted by Goulding, who showed the director still photographs he had taken and argued that the place would be ideal for the western he would soon shoot. He also informed Ford that there were many underemployed Navajos living there who would be happy to work cheaply as extras. Like the valley itself, these local people found themselves represented either stereotypically (as the generic "Indians" whose antipathy to stagecoaches, settlers, or wagon trains needed no explanation) or particularized according to the demands of the narrative. In *The Searchers*, they are cast as Comanches, but, like all indications of historical, cultural, or locative particularity in the narrative, this is only a half-hearted gesture toward the real. Ford was quickly sold on the valley when, chartering a plane the next day, he made a quick tour of the area, establishing in his own mind that it could also serve as a production center. The rest is film history and, perhaps to some degree, legend, as for one production after another "his crews built towns, forts, ranch houses, and Indian villages," creating and re-creating that minimal built space the area lacked but Ford's films required.[25]

Frankel cannot avoid using a theatrical analogy to illuminate the director's attitude toward the place where his films were set: "Like Shakespeare and the Globe Theatre, Ford used one mythic setting for his stage . . . he made the valley his personal film set." The director did indeed impose a form of flexible meaning on a natural space. This unique location is established through the power of serial representation to be generic, rendering it adaptable to a potentially unlimited number of staging and backdrop uses, even as it is emptied of its ability to signify itself except insofar as it signifies a someplace else that is always fictional. If John Wayne always plays John Wayne through, but along with, his impersonation of some required character, Monument Valley does much the same, except that Wayne had a life outside the acts of representation to which he submitted his body. The repeat performances of the valley, as it were, refer viewers more to previous films than they do to the thereness of the world captured by the camera, a place whose precise identity and actual history are never evoked in the act of their cinematization. This wondrously beautiful place was transformed by Ford into one of the nation's most recognizable and admired landscapes, with its name and location forever unknown to most filmgoers.

The opening of *Back to the Future III* is set, *mirabile dictu*, in a drive-in theater improbably located in Monument Valley; the film's time travelers speed toward the screen in order to launch themselves back into the past, with the famous buttes as backdrop. The film thus humorously invokes the site's paradoxical ontology. Its "reality" is always an effect of its serial fictionalization and defining function as an adjunct to Hollywood filmmaking. Monument Valley is where the screen is located through which the characters have access to a "history" that eventually returns them to Monument Valley because it is simply a fictional effect. Through the perdurability of classic Hollywood representations, Monument Valley can be summoned as the most potent of generic markers, making it possible for filmmakers to engage with national history through the invocation of once-valued representations, a national history of a less than academic kind with which the Zemeckis film, with its several homages to Hollywood, has a good deal of not unpoignant fun.

The Realist Moment of Charles Brackett and Billy Wilder

Sunset Blvd. was the last as well as one of the most notable and profitable of the fourteen collaborations between Wilder and Charles Brackett, working as screenwriter/producer. The Brackett/Wilder films are routinely counted among the best pictures that Hollywood produced during the 1940s and 1950s: *The Major and the Minor* (1941), *Five Graves to Cairo* (1943), *Double Indemnity, The Lost Weekend* (1945), and *The Emperor Waltz* (1948), just to identify the most notable. With two notable exceptions, *Foreign Affair* (1948) and *Sunset Blvd.*, none of these can be considered a realist production, though some featured sequences that were filmed on location, lending them a certain extra-soundstage authenticity. *Double Indemnity* was filmed at or in a number of Los Angeles locations, including an office building on North Kingsley, a family home on Quebec Drive, and the Burbank Southern Pacific Railroad Station. These real spaces, however, serve as useful, convenient stages rather than as locations whose preexisting meaning is explored in any more than a minimal sense. To be sure, because they are real and not simulacra, the Los Angeles locations lend *Double Indemnity* a certain aura of authenticity that melds interestingly with its restrained deployment of noirish antirealist stylings that would often be imitated in similar productions, especially darkly lit soundstage set-ups in which low-key lighting creates interesting chiaroscuro effects.[26]

Still, the film's locations are in effect backdrops for a drama that puts into play not the particularities of some urban space, but rather characteristic elements of contemporary American culture in general. These were the promotion of life and accident insurance through high pressure door-to-door sales to those uncertain about the future, as well as the rootless isolation from extended family and community then characteristic of urban life, especially in the country's fast-growing metropolitan areas with its neighborhoods of newly arrived strangers. *Double Indemnity*'s plot begins when an unmarried man on the make seizes guiltlessly on the opportunity for erotic indulgence seemingly offered by a chance encounter with a bored housewife. Their connection appears at first to respond simply to the frustrations of a gone-stale monogamy, but eventually reveals much darker forms of narcissism and sociopathy that in comparison make their adultery seem mere misbehavior.

These discontents of contemporary living go to the heart of the social contract, and, it hardly needs emphasizing, are not location-specific. *Double Indemnity* is not a film about Los Angeles in particular except insofar as Los Angeles is appropriately called upon to represent the most up-to-date forms of archly-transient American urban life. The film's pessimistic take on human nature, as French critics immediately registered, resonated with other national cultures as well, and it is not surprising that in the postwar period film noir was well on its way to becoming an international phenomenon, with the anomic modern condition writ large providing stock characters, themes, and settings.[27] Until the end of the war, Wilder was in no way committed to a realism that might explore in any depth the unlimited semiotic possibilities of a particular location. The interest he would eventually show in this kind of filmmaking, moreover, was not long-lived, lasting for only two consecutive projects, both in partnership with Brackett, who would go on, working with Henry Hathaway, to write and produce one of the most notable of postwar realist films, *Niagara*. Before and after, most of Wilder's films were closed rather than open. And this was true for Brackett's career after *Niagara* as well.

Closed films, as Braudy suggests, emerge from creating a place rather than finding one, taking shape from organizing the materials of the world "into a totally formed vision" rather than making an attempt "to discover the orders independent of the watcher."[28] Closed films are theatrical in their centripetal energies, featuring interesting performance "business" (e.g., Jack Lemmon straining spaghetti through a tennis racket in Wilder's *The Apartment* [1960]), and less reliant on telling images than on the kind of snappy dialogue for which the writing/directing team had become famous. Brackett and Wilder, as Braudy observes about closed filmmakers, are generally interested in "the truth of subjectivity," whose focus is "the obsessions of the individual." *Sunset Blvd.* could have been this kind of film and would have resembled other celluloid treatments of the artist frustrated by institutional change, advancing age, creative blockage, or personal demons (e.g., Federico Fellini's *8½* [1963] or Luchino Visconti's *Death in Venice* [1971]). Instead, it is open in the sense of considering "the truth outside the self," refusing Forsterian round characters in favor of flat ones that represented general rather than personal truths.[29] Brackett's later projects as screenwriter and/or producer, working with a number of directors (George Cukor, Mitchell Leisen, and Henry Levin chief among them), were all studio-bound, filmed almost entirely on soundstages. This essentially theatrical approach was very much the house style at Paramount, where for a number of very good corporate reasons the kind of realism sponsored by Zanuck at Fox, or by Harry Cohn at Columbia, was not at all in favor.[30] The two Wilder/Brackett location films are interesting and important exceptions to their studio's well-established preference for glamorous drama and entertainment productions (especially musicals) featuring its extensive stable of A-list leading players.

The temporary shift in the filmmaking approach of the team seems to correspond directly to an unexpected turn that Wilder's career took at the end of the European war. Born in Austria, Wilder had worked as a screenwriter in Berlin for some years before the Nazis came to power; he quickly left, first for Paris, and then to Hollywood, where, beginning in 1933, he resumed his career and soon became one of American cinema's most talented director/screenwriters. In the summer of 1945, the American Military Government (AMG) in Germany needed the services of an experienced professional to help manage the restart in the western occupied zones of film production as well as exhibition. Wilder was a canny businessman, charming and good with people, and, more important, he was something of an "old boy," well acquainted with many of the filmmakers still working in the industry he had left only a decade before. He could speak to them in their own language, in every sense of the word, and so was the natural choice for the position of film czar. Seeing this as an opportunity to serve his country and advance his own career, Wilder quickly agreed to being posted to Germany even though no one was sure exactly what he or indeed the AMG should do about either production, halted since the surrender in May, or exhibition, then largely stalled because of a lack of films to project. Months earlier, Allied military authorities had failed to fill Italian screens with ideologically correct American films as hostilities wound down there, which was seen as an opportunity lost to shape what soon proved to be a politically chaotic situation. The AMG hoped to do better with Germany, where the stakes were considerably higher, as the possibility of yet another onset of German revanchism dominated European politics and U.S. concerns about regional instability in the early postwar era.

At first, Wilder was put to work on a series of documentary films, collectively entitled *Todesmühlen* or "Death Mills," compiled from the considerable footage that Allied combat photographers had shot of the concentration camps the armies had liberated in the closing weeks of the war. Germans were forced to sit through regular screenings of these documentaries in order to receive the weekly ration cards upon which, in a society where food was scarce, life depended. Though he participated willingly, Wilder thought the project more or less pointless, and he was probably correct. Wilder asked: "Will Germans come week after week in the cinema in order to play the guilty pupil?"[31] Few if any involved in directing the occupation thought the answer might be "yes," especially if they had witnessed a compulsory screening attended by largely disengaged or sleeping spectators. But the project was popular with the occupation authorities, who had been adamant since the discovery of the camps that Germans be faced with their collective crimes. Many in the country had protested ignorance about the hitherto unexampled mass murder perpetrated during the war, and the films gave the lie to such thinking.[32] In retrospect, the program, though certainly justified on moral grounds, seems largely punitive. Did the reconstruction of the country depend on discrediting the Third Reich by exposing its criminally homicidal nature, making sure that all Germans should come to acknowledge what had been done in their name (or in many cases by them, since Hitler's "willing executioners," in Daniel Goldhagen's compelling phrase, were legion)?

It seems not. In absolute control and possession of the country, the victors would scarcely allow National Socialism to regather its forces, while the huge social and existential challenges that defeat entailed (including the absorption of huge numbers of their ethnic brethren from Eastern Europe) disposed most Germans to develop a useful amnesia about the recent past. Military impotence, destruction, and want made the people quite receptive to the unfamiliar social institutions, government institutions, and foreign policy (especially dramatically redrawn borders) that the Allies were requiring them to accept. Americanization in the western zones proceeded without either widespread protest or political recidivism, a miracle perhaps as remarkable as the more acclaimed *Wirtschaftswunder* (economic miracle) that restored Germany to a place of economic preeminence within a decade or so after the war ended.

With their vivid, accessible dramatization, and concrete representation of social issues, feature films, more subtly rhetorical than the documentaries produced by Wilder and others, could be a useful tool in the furtherance of Germany's prescribed cultural transformation. Hollywood entertainment, designed to please rather than instruct, would hardly fill the bill any better than guilt-inducing documentaries about atrocities. The kind of release that did well in U.S. distribution, as Wilder observed, would not "particularly help us in our program of re-educating the German people."[33] Hollywood, he thought instead, should commission a "very special love story, cleverly designed to help us sell a few ideological points," a project for which he volunteered his services and was able eventually to get his employer, Paramount Pictures, to support. What might keep the German public glued to the screen, so Wilder came to think, were feature films that addressed the issues then facing them and concluded with a positive ideological message, precisely the kind of mildly propagandistic production that Hollywood, in cooperation with the Office of War Information, had been moved to make during the war, two of the best of which were the Brackett/Wilder collaboration *Five Graves to Cairo* and fellow exile Fritz Lang's *Hangmen Also Die!* (both 1943). In the so-called Wilder Memorandum that the director sent to his military superiors in the Information Control Division (ICD), he observed that while the semi-documentary British film *Target for Tonight* (1941) was well received by American audiences, "it took a Hollywood film—an 'entertainment film' based on a fictitious story—to really tell us what was going on." The film was MGM's *Mrs. Miniver* (William Wyler, 1942), and, Wilder reports, as soon as President Roosevelt saw a preliminary version, he "urged Metro to put the film on the market as quickly as possible."[34] Moving operations to Berlin, Wilder discovered that the city, largely obliterated by Allied bombing and Russian artillery, had become something of an eerie moonscape, offering the filmmaker the opportunity to capture the incredible human capacity for self-destruction in striking images. He decided then that he would devote the rest of his time in the country to a feature project that would be cleverly designed. As he wrote his military chief Davidson Taylor, such a film "would provide us with a superior piece of propaganda; they would stand in long lines to buy and once they bought it, it would stick. Unfortunately, no such film exists today. It must be made. I want to make it."[35] Wilder got permission from the AMG, then engaged Brackett and eventually two others, to work with him on a screenplay; the filmmakers returned to Paramount for studio work after shooting a number of exteriors in Berlin. To add authenticity to the soundstage work, he brought with him street signs, posters, even a doorbell, all of which became part of the mise-en-scène designed by Hans Dreier and Walter H. Tyler. Wilder's plan from the beginning was to explore the relationship, at turns exploitative and tender, between a GI stationed in Berlin and an attractive widow. Boy does not get girl but returns home to his world, while she has seen enough that is positive in him, and thus in Americans generally, to decide that life is worth living. Wilder framed this ending sardonically: when the gas gets turned back on, she decides to roast the few measly potatoes she has been rationed rather than stick her head in the oven, her previous plan. At an early stage, the film was, however, transformed into more of a comedy of manners. It was eventually released in the United States, and quite successfully, as *A Foreign Affair* (1948).

Affair interestingly touches on, if it does not explore in depth, many of the problems that in the war's immediate aftermath challenged both the occupied and also their erstwhile masters. As the double entendre of its title suggests, *Affair*'s agenda is both diplomatic and erotic, as the plot revolves around a triangle in which an American officer, John Pringle (John Lund), has to choose between Erika von Schlütow (Marlene Dietrich), the German woman whose favors he has enjoyed for some time to their mutual profit, and the aptly named Phoebe Frost (Jean Arthur), a congresswoman come to police the moral ruination visited upon American servicemen, an unexpectedly attractive woman whose *froideur* (explained by her coming from Iowa) Pringle eventually melts. With its frank acknowledgment of the occupation's regrettable sexual politics, the film offers an unflattering portrait of Americans failing to inhabit the moral high ground that, as Phoebe demonstrates, is a central feature of their still-puritanical national culture.

Wilder, it is fair to say, engages with an aspect of the occupation of which the folks back home would remain willfully ignorant, breaking official silence about an issue that hardly shed a flattering light on the U.S. mission to Germany. The film is certainly a "very special love story," with Pringle tiring of the opportunistic if charming Erika, realizing that, after his initially pretend affections have transformed Phoebe into a submissive, giggly female, he has fallen in love with a good old-fashioned American girl. But this is a film that centers on sexual exploitation, which would become one of the writer/director's main themes. Just as in *The Apartment* (1960), where the married executives of a giant corporation seem to spend most of their time and energy pursuing the company's female employees, the occupation troops in *Affair*, from the officers down to private soldiers, exploit the city's women who, dependent on the meager rations that their captors provide, are capable of only limited forms of protest or refusal; in the aftermath of defeat, women alone were forced into what amounted to casual forms of prostitution, and Wilder does not shrink from depicting the economic basis of these relationships, just another form of slightly illegal barter like the black market. In depicting their plight, Wilder also anatomizes the pervasive, hypocritical puritanism of American culture, hardly promoting a positive view of the occupation authorities and the values that the Germans were being not so gently forced to embrace.

Not surprisingly, the film did not pass ideological muster with the ICD. It was only approved for exhibition in Germany by Wilder's successor as film officer, Erich Pommer, another German Hollywood émigré brought back to help in the reconstruction of his homeland. Pommer was more positive than Wilder about the prospect of a renewed domestic production helping in the continuing ideological struggle. He must have thought that Germans would benefit from the film's biting humor (not concealing completely a quite penetrating appraisal of the defects of the American character). In any case, the film was not screened for those it was intended to make laugh but also instruct. Audiences still living in the crumbling ruins of their cities, and worrying every day whether they would have enough to eat, might well have appreciated *Affair*'s almost despairing depiction of everyday life under the watchful eyes of the conqueror, who is intent on identifying and dealing appropriately with unregenerate ex-Nazis. Reduced to working in a nightclub and "entertaining" an American officer, Erika, who once consorted with leading Hitler's inner circle, lives out the contradictions of the era, as she finds herself pursued by one of her ex-lovers (a Gestapo agent in hiding) and also investigated for her dubious wartime connections by the very officer who has made her his schatzie. But it is hard to see how the film fulfills in any way Wilder's avowed intention to "sell a few ideological points," unless he aimed to debunk the occupiers' self-satisfied sense of moral superiority. But then anyone living in the occupied western zones would hardly have been surprised to learn that American officers were using their considerable economic power to establish "friendly" relations with the many single local women who were then often on the verge of starvation.

Germans did not have the chance to see *A Foreign Affair* until 1977, when it ran on state-sponsored television, long after the political issues of the postwar era had been made irrelevant by the so-called economic miracle that witnessed the transformation of an erstwhile totalitarian socialist nation into a lively democracy, with fully "Americanized" consumerist values. Despite the continuing relevance of its critique of the American occupation, *Affair* must have then seemed quite an antique, with its evocation of a time of deprivation and misery that those who lived through it were largely eager to forget. In 1948, official Washington was shocked by what one congressman said was the film's "false picture of a decent and honorable army of occupation," and even the urbane Bosley Crowther, giving it a positive review, opined that "under less clever presentation this sort of traffic with big stuff in the current events department might be offensive to reason and taste."[36]

Brackett and Wilder anatomize the strange new world that had emerged during occupation in which two quite different cultures found themselves intriguingly symbiotic. *A Foreign Affair* offers a penetrating, often disturbing glimpse into the social and cultural contexts of the occupation, even engaging with persistently difficult issues such as de-Nazification and the punishment, if any at all, that should be meted out to the friends of the recently decapitated regime. Yet *A Foreign Affair* played its own role in postwar politics, as one of a number of U.S. productions, including *The Big Lift*, that explained the contemporary German crisis to American filmgoers, with the unofficial aim of rendering acceptable U.S. aid to and military support for a defeated foe. Economic and political problems in the western zone were considerably ameliorated in 1948, as noted in the introduction, by the establishment of the Federal Republic of Germany and a new currency, the Deutschmark (backed by the United States), but, ironically, these same events ended the partnership between Germany's western and eastern occupiers. The Soviet blockade of Berlin almost immediately followed, turning the Federal Republic into a frontline state in the struggle against communism. With the establishment of a substantial long-term American military presence in West Germany after the successful Berlin Airlift, German–American relations (including the exploitation of German women) continued to be a theme for realist productions, two of the most provocative of which, Gottfried Reinhardt's *Town Without Pity* and Wilder's *One, Two, Three*, were not released until 1961 (both films were shot largely in Germany).

With bitter satire that pulled very few punches, *A Foreign Affair* succeeded in bringing home to American filmgoers the economic desperation of a once-modern society now reduced to bartering. Food shortages posed a genuine threat of starvation to the conquered population; locals were allowed at best 1,500 calories a day, even as American soldiers found that their own generous food rations, which included abundant supplies of cigarettes nearly impossible otherwise to obtain, provided them with enormous trading power. As the film unflinchingly demonstrates, the nation's soldiers became enthusiastic partners in a sordid black market economy, exchanging food and tobacco for sexual favors and other goods. GIs were able to enjoy a power over women that would come to an end when they were finally posted stateside, a move that many were eager to postpone indefinitely. Crowther got it right when he wrote that Brackett and Wilder "have turned out a dandy entertainment which has some shrewd and realistic things to say. . . . Congress may not like this picture . . . and even the Department of the Army may find it a shade embarrassing."[37]

In the event, the making of *Affair* seems to have prompted Wilder and Brackett to make another film that demythologized a real location with no little satire. They had been interested for some time in doing a black comedy about an aging silent film actress who becomes involved with a young man, eventually murdering him in a jealous fit. The comic elements in the script, however, were gradually downplayed, much more so than they were in *Affair*, which also ends with violent death. The film's title signals a focus on location, with one of Hollywood's most famous thoroughfares an easily understood metonymy for the film community itself. In large part, of course, Wilder and Brackett serve up an intriguing mixture of shrewd social comment and crime melodrama, fueled by plotting that is not terribly different from what had proved a successful formula in *Double Indemnity*. Both films focus on ill-sorted romantic relationships, motored by exploitative self-interest, that end violently and disastrously, with a justice-restoring retribution required by the Production Code dramatically delivered in memorable closing sequences. At some point in the development of the project after Wilder returned from Germany and work was completed on *Affair*, the decision was made to shift the film decisively away from its noir plotting toward an exploration of a famous community through a thoroughgoing commitment to the incorporation of the real in numerous ways. Much more work was then expected from the location scouts at Paramount, who were quickly put to work by Brackett and Wilder, as Ed Sikov reports:

> Paramount's location scouts were busily finding excellent examples of the way Hollywood's citizens variously lived. The Alto-Nido apartments at 1851 North Ivar at the top of the hill at Franklin would work well for the drab barracks of an unemployed screenwriter. For Norma Desmond's mansion, they had to look farther afield than the 10,000 block of Sunset Boulevard, on which the fictitious house is situated in the script. They found it, about six miles away, at the northwest corner of Wilshire and Irving Boulevards. . . . More ghostly than derelicts, the building itself fit the filmmakers' description superbly, as did the vaguely seedy-looking yard and garage.[38]

With its extensive on-location shooting, *Sunset Blvd.* surveys the cultural and physical environment of the capital of world filmmaking, including the forms of work that take place on soundstages. The ostensible main characters, much as their counterparts do in *The Remains of the Day*, animate the complex connections between institutional and domestic spaces. Their struggles for success or continued relevance reveal the discontents of this world, with its too easy passage, often traversed, between the personal and the professional: the unintentional cruelty of technological change, the self-destructive energies of writer's block, and the sadomasochistic dependence of the director, unknown to the filmgoers who enjoy his work, on his charismatic star, who, under his often tyrannical instruction, can light up the silver screen or, failing to do so, soon consign him to irrelevance, with his fall from knownness even more complete than her own. The main characters exemplify the different if interdependent activities of filmmaking (acting, screenwriting, and directing), whose interactions, personal and professional, bring to the surface the discontents of an industry that, dependent on the attractive photographing of the human body, fosters a narcissism always already undermined by age, changing fashion, or creative exhaustion.

The psychologically useful distinction in modern culture between private and working selves founders on this constant public display. Performance tends to conflate with being, enacting a well-known truth about the so-called "film community," whose ostentatious *moyen de vivre* was quickly turned by the industry into an audience-enhancing source of interest, a world of wealth, romance, and modern values as carefully constructed for an eager reading public as the films in which these larger-than-life celebrities appeared. This sad truth plays out in the film's memorable closing scene in which aging star Desmond, her already tenuous grip on reality weakened by the trauma of the shooting, is arrested at her home by the police and a crowd of reporters, who, she imagines, have arrived to shoot the close-ups for a long-desired comeback. This moment of delusional misunderstanding cruelly mocks the now unwanted actress's unquenched desire to be transformed into appealing representations. Flashbulbs popping, the assembled paparazzi snap her picture, eager for yet another sleazy industry scandal whose hook will be Norma's haggard image. In the manner of much Hollywood "news," Desmond's sensational crime opens up to public scrutiny her domestic space, whose faded magnificence remains a constant reminder of former success and eminence, even as she becomes once again the main character in a story that the public can be easily persuaded to take an interest in. Hollywood is here epitomized as a preeminent site for the confection of intriguing stories—journalistic and cinematic, personal as well as fictional—that center around the essentially exploitative photographic capturing of images, and the catering to the desires of the public, some more regrettable than others, for the various pleasures they might provide.

The filmmakers' experience with *Affair* afforded them invaluable experience with both the technical challenges posed by extensive location shooting and the aesthetically rich ways in which location could be made an attractive, intriguing feature of the film. The location footage was integrated with the film's dramatic and thoroughly fictional story, offering screenwriter and director many opportunities to comment, often with a biting sarcasm that was politically provocative, on the social conditions then prevailing in a prostrate Germany under total allied domination. The bulk of *Affair*, however, was shot on soundstages or exteriors erected on the Paramount lot in Hollywood; reflecting the film's production history, Berlin figures in the film more often as backdrop than as a location properly speaking. Interestingly, the film's "tour" of a wrecked Berlin's notable "attractions," from the burnt-out Reichstag to the rubble-strewn Brandenburg Gate, was shot at Paramount, through the time-honored technique of back projection. The obtrusive theatricality of many sequences relieves the narrative of the seriousness of its very dark subject matter, enabling it to emphasize the comedy of sexual manners at its center, where an unsophisticated American puritanism becomes the chief target of biting satire that is hardly softened by a Marcusean discarding of sexual repression. The result is a thoroughly implausible redemption of the main character, a U.S. Army officer who finds himself falling in love with a visiting congresswoman who sheds her glasses, mannish clothes, sensible shoes, and inhibitions, enabling him to abandon his German "girlfriend" for the more sanctioned love and pleasure she can provide him with. The moralizing conventionality of the finale, of course, is more or less Brackett and Wilder's knowing wink at the Production Code.

As in *The Remains of the Day*, the locative center of *Sunset Blvd.* is a semiotically rich residence. Norma Desmond's house is revealed to be a relic from, and a repository of, human and material remains belonging to a bygone era, which, in a sense, the building chosen by Paramount's location in fact is. The property at 3810 Wilshire Boulevard was the former residence of local bigwig William Jenkins, built in the 1920s for the then-amazing cost of $250,000. Jenkins's outsize investment in self-promotion, showing in the late 1940s signs of age, provides a perfect setting for Norma's story of meteoric rise to and sudden fall from industry preeminence and attendant wealth. The property fits perfectly Gillis's famous description of it: "It was a great big white elephant of a place. The kind crazy movie people built in the crazy twenties. A neglected house gets an unhappy look. This one had it in spades. It was like that old woman in *Great Expectations*—that Miss Havisham in her rotting wedding dress and her torn veil, taking it out on the world because she'd been given the go-by." The "real" needed only a few further touches so that it would suit its current owner, who is no Miss Havisham, but a still attractive woman in her fifties who has the money and ego to remain stylish. Norma remains interested in men, and her desire for Joe (whose body she carefully appraises several times) is genuine. In costuming the very fit and healthy Swanson, Edith Head decided to combine "Jazz Age materials with so-called New Look styling . . . an hourglass form and tightly cinched waist that created a kind of rigid femininity . . . employ[ing] current fashion trends but adding the odd element here and there."[39] Paramount built a pool on the property (though it was only barely functional) and upgraded the house's interior with stained-glass windows and an organ, which von Mayerling plays to great effect in one scene. These additions give Desmond's residence a certain panache, enhanced by other furnishings that are definitely not of the Miss Havisham variety.

Desmond's misfortune is that she lives on—as a rich businesswoman with an honored Hollywood past—in a present that holds a place for her, even if it is not the one she truly desires. She is not like her former film industry colleagues, the group she derisively calls "the waxworks," who seem to possess a life only when Desmond allows them one, and her house and car are still operative, if in need of updating and some further maintenance, which Desmond is happy to provide. She opens up her pool so that Joe can use it and accompanies him to one of Beverly Hills' toniest men's shops, outfitting him with contemporary clothes that suit her own only slightly eccentric stylishness. Not a purpose-built simulacrum, the film's principal playspace is shown by Wilder's camera to be slowly decaying, if still redolent of outsized, out-of-fashion opulence, like the monstrously elegant and period correct 1929 Isotta Fraschini Tipo 8A in which her chauffeur, and former husband, drives her to the studio for the embarrassing meeting with Cecil B. DeMille.

This portrait of the film community as it then was in the postwar period is completed by the number of other recognizable locations around the city that are self-consciously evoked, including, in a metafictional gesture whose complexities were discussed earlier, Paramount Studios, as the film's producing company in effect appears as itself. All the real locations in the film are connected in some way with the motion picture industry that had transformed suburban Hollywood into a world entertainment center: the Bel-Air Country Club, Paramount Studios, Schwab's Drugstore, the corner of Hollywood and Vine, Bullocks Wilshire (the men's clothier), and Perino's Restaurant chief among them.[40] As film historian Sam Staggs suggests, "For purposes of the film, pieces of Hollywood and the rest of Los Angeles were assembled as if from a kit." Even the film's purported location of Desmond's mansion on Sunset Boulevard (its house number, 10086, was never actually assigned to a building) was authentically faked, as Staggs points out: "The fateful driveway that Gillis careers into when a tire blows was part of the Janss home at 10060 Sunset Boulevard," and through the locative magic of montage it becomes the mansion's ostensible entrance.[41]

The "waxworks" provide an impressive *tableau vivant*, more decorative than performative, and hence are best considered part of the film's extended description of Desmond's residence. Three once-famous Hollywood personalities are captured, with absolute authenticity, as their now-forgotten selves, reduced to the mundane activity of playing cards in order to pass the time: "stars" Buster Keaton, H. B. Warner, and Anna Q. Nilsson, all of whom had long slipped from notice when the film was made but remained "names" of some recognition. Desmond appropriately completes the quartet, in one sense a character socializing with actual industry personalities, but, of course, on a deeper level a human presence exactly like them, Swanson's own career having gone into decline about the same time as their own. Like the house and their hostess, the "waxworks" are forms of the living dead, yet more wreckage from an institutional past that has not suffered complete obliteration, a fact that can surprise a now-indifferent audience. A time traveler to a distant era, Gillis registers our collective but only momentary sympathy for a celebrity that ends before life itself, with Desmond and her guests inhabiting something like an antechamber to eternity, where they mark time, having lost what made their lives most worth living.[42] Reduced to silence (in a potent historical irony, they are not asked to "talk" in this film), the waxworks seem the simulacra of the selves they once were, exhibits in the museum of the once-was. But this is a fate that Norma, still relatively young, vibrant, and attractive, has not quite yet embraced. At film's end, she will be saved from this demeaning recognition by madness.

The much-reduced presence of the once famous and rich bears silent witness to the truth of Norma Desmond's own bitter feelings about the celebrity she once enjoyed, explaining her deep fears of further abandonment and her self-preserving delusion that her career is not over, only stalled. The film's "romantic" pairing matches a then-rising star, William Holden, with one of the most famous actresses of the 1920s, Gloria Swanson, who had not been seen in a film for almost ten years and would make only three more in the remaining twenty-five years of her professional career. In a profoundly metafictional moment, Desmond screens for her young *inamorato* a clip from one of her own purported films, actually a sequence from Swanson's most notorious project, *Queen Kelly*. The filmmakers' choice here undoubtedly reflected the actress's own wishes (she held the rights to the European release, which could not be shown in the United States, and so this sequence would not have been possible without Swanson's cooperation). A romantic costume epic, the production was marred by troubles and disputes of all kinds, especially complaints from Swanson that she had been deceived about the script, which ended with her character taking up residence in what was self-evidently a brothel. The upshot was the dismissal of its director, none other than the very Erich von Stroheim who in his role as Desmond's butler is seen running the projector in this scene. Reconstructed by Swanson and producer Joseph Kennedy, *Queen Kelly* was released in Europe but not in the United States because of a clause in von Stroheim's contract. Yet another production among the several that he failed to oversee on time and within budget, the film was the last major directorial project for von Stroheim, who continued to work, in both Europe and the United States, as an actor but whose considerable artistic talents as a filmmaker were lost to the industry. The *Queen Kelly* screening is one of many invocations of the true or the historical in the film that enhance its authenticity, at least when recognized by cognoscenti, as they surely were meant to be. Screening the film from which he was fired by the actress/producer unhappy with his vision for it, von Stroheim in his current fictional avatar as Desmond's servant seems condemned to performing a strange and particularly cruel form of penance. That he appears in the film as an ex-director, and in a fictional role, distinguishes him absolutely, and perhaps cruelly, from his erstwhile contemporary DeMille, who appears only as himself and thus as the practicing and still quite eminent director he then was.

Their real careers alluded to in the narrative, Swanson and von Stroheim, along with "the waxworks," exemplify the spectacular forms of success and failure that, so Brackett and Wilder suggest, characterize the workings of an industry that must respond to ever-unpredictable public taste while placing a premium on youthful beauty and energy. Once meant to display the prestige of its owner, Desmond's house is now inhabited by those whom Hollywood long ago discarded, in the form of characters and "real selves." They are persistent relics from an otherwise forgotten era that can be otherwise registered only in the continuing, if seemingly pointless, existence of the mansion's owner, her body and face no longer as loved by the camera as they once were. Desmond's physical and mental disconnection from the present registers the partial irrelevance of a star-driven Hollywood cinema flourishing in the late 1920s, with its push toward artistic eminence radically reoriented by the talkies and the substantial aesthetic changes that came in its technological wake. "I am big. It's the pictures that got small," Desmond complains in a remark whose truth is only slightly diminished by her pathetic narcissism. The confining of film production to often-cramped soundstages was necessitated by the limited technical abilities of primitive microphones and the general technology of primitive sound recording and editing. The discontinuous history of the industry is imaged by the house in decline, which is still big, like its owner, who still lives there, but now a destination reached only by mistake. It is classy but also creepy, overgrown with vines and vegetation, not unlike how Hollywood has imagined Dracula's castle. Suspended in time, estranged from an ever-advancing present, the anachronistic but still functioning edifice comes into the narrative only when Joe pulls up the driveway with a flat tire as he attempts to elude the finance company men intent on repossessing his car. The technical change that has sidelined her, ruining her career, is only partly contradicted by the presence of a still-working DeMille on a studio soundstage that likewise has survived industrial upheaval. As DeMille makes clear with a painfully patronizing friendliness that only thinly disguises his desire to be rid of her, the parade has passed her by.

But *Sunset Blvd.* is also a film that explores the meanings that adhere to place, with its focus on a microcosm (the house suspended in a past turned unchanging present) and its connection to a larger industrial and urban community, a place of work, recreation, and ordinary living, such as the well-known apartment building where Gillis has his digs at the Alto Nido. With apartments fashioned in what was then known as the New York style (open floor plan, including full bathrooms, galley kitchens, and snazzy Art Deco stylings), the Alto Nido opened its doors in 1930, advertising itself as "Hollywood's Premiere Apartment Hotel," a part of the continuing construction boom fueled by film industry dollars. In the 1950s, the building's owners continued to take pride in the considerable number of younger filmmaking professionals who made their homes there, their cramped if not inelegant quarters, so many must have hoped, simply way-stations to their own stand-alone mansions on Sunset or further up in the Hollywood hills.[43] Like "Desmond's house," the Alto Nido, located in a thriving city neighborhood, is a relic from Hollywood's Golden Age, completed just as the conversion to sound radically changed the industry's aesthetics and the Depression sliced box office profits to the bone. Even so, the Alto Nido expresses the continuing relevance of what once was and still is. It is like the Paramount studio lot, whose old-fashioned sign is the very image of the industry's persistent relevance and essentially unchanging function within American culture. The business plan upon which Hollywood was founded as a production center remains successful (if in some decline) with long-term employees still at their studio posts, where Wilder's camera finds them. Soundstages continue in operation, and producers show themselves eager for quality screenplays to serve as the vehicles for stars such as Tyrone Power and Alan Ladd, who are singled out as representative of a new generation of performers.

Of course, a different way of regarding Hollywood history is suggested by Desmond's out-of-time and ghostly residence on one of the community's most famous and traveled thoroughfares, hidden from the contemporary Angelenos rushing by. A past whose darkness cannot be kept from casting a shadow on the present is a persistent theme in film noir. Both Norma and Joe find themselves at professional and personal dead-ends, thrown by a chance meeting into a working and then romantic relationship based on interlocking needs and pathologies that can lead nowhere. No future is possible for them either separately or together. Gillis proves unable to successfully revise her script for *Salome*, but she is in any case far too old to play the part. As so often in the film, however, the fictional seems a strange echo of a real life that is much less grim. Viewers versed in Hollywood history would perhaps have remembered how Gloria Swanson managed to land her most famous role when pictures were indeed "big." Even though she owns the script, circumstances deny Norma the opportunity to play the *femme fatale* most vilified in Christian history. Swanson, by way of contrast, won her own struggle to play the eponymous temptress capable of moving a man of God to lose his religion in the notorious *Sadie Thompson* (Raoul Walsh, 1928). Based on the controversial stage play *Rain* (adapted by W. Somerset Maugham from his short story), the property had been declared off-limits for Hollywood production by Will Hays, president of the Motion Picture Producers and Distributors of America. Through a complex series of negotiations, however, some more than a little shady, Swanson first convinced Hays to take the material off the blacklist and then obtained the filming rights from Maugham, even signing the eminent author to pen a sequel, which was, however, never made. Getting the film produced her way cost Swanson dearly, however, as her perfectionism led in large part to its going over budget, and the star had to sell one of her properties in order to get it completed. But *Sadie Thompson* proved a huge box office and critical success, and Swanson's performance was especially praised. The actress turned producer knew evidently what she was doing when she developed the project and the role of a lifetime it would offer her.

To her portrayal of the pathetic if conniving Desmond, Swanson brings more than a little of her own considerable force of personality and determination, which shows in her obsessive supervision of Gillis's rewrite efforts, and, after the meeting with DeMille, her unflagging efforts to get in shape for a project and the inevitable close-ups that she mistakenly thinks are in her professional future. Unlike the other former stars in the film, Swanson was still working in show business when Wilder and Brackett asked her to take on the role of Norma Desmond (she had a radio show on New York's WPIX). Swanson never fully inhabits the tragic role that the script assigns her; she can only portray Desmond's disconnection from reality, not live it. The filmmakers surely intended this to be the case (Mae West was their first choice for the part), eager as they were to blur the boundary between the fictional and the real but certainly not intending to dismiss the appeal, glamour, and charisma of the medium in which they too had been so successful, and which this slickly professional film reverently embodies as well as evokes.

4

An American Neorealism?

Of Cinematic Modernisms, Foreign and Domestic

It certainly seems true enough, as Mark Shiel suggests, that "few moments in the history of cinema have been as hotly debated and by succeeding generations as the moment of Italian neorealism": this series of innovatively realist films began to be produced in years following the end of World War II (1945) and was essentially played out by the middle of the 1950s, even though neorealism in various ways continued to mark Italian filmmaking for at least the next decade, arguably even longer.[1] Significant within their own national context because they were intended as interventions in the ongoing debate about what direction a post-Fascist Italy should take, neorealist films, as far as world cinema culture is concerned, were most important because of the startling success they achieved in their overseas release, especially in France and the United States. It is their American reception that will concern us in this chapter.

Recent discussions of neorealism continue to offer competing versions of the movement's corpus, as well as the precise nature of its connections to what came before and followed after that national cinema.[2] Most film historians, however, would agree with Shiel that the advent of this archly realist form "marked a significant stage in the transformation of cinema," as the classical forms of filmmaking that had emerged in Hollywood and other national industries eventually made way, at least in part, for the modernist art cinema, which was characterized by a radically different aesthetic or, perhaps better, a complex array of different aesthetics.[3] As it turned out, the welcome embrace generally accorded literary and artistic modernism in the postwar commercial cinema included a focus on concerns about verisimilitude, roughly speaking, the sense in which representation should accurately reflect both the "world" and our experience of it.

Verisimilitude, of course, deeply shapes the principal subject of modernism: subjectivity, the inner life, the personal as opposed to the supposedly "objective" realms of experience, access to the truth of which, of course, is problematized by the various epistemological difficulties recognized since Descartes. However marked by purely aesthetic innovations and the interrogation of what constitutes the real, key modernist literary texts (James Joyce's *Ulysses*, D. H. Lawrence's *Lady Chatterley's Lover*, Vladimir Nabokov's *Lolita*, perhaps most notably) likewise manifest the urge (or desire) that art tell a truth that had never before been fully or adequately told.[4] One way of looking at neorealism is to see it as extending to the cinema literary modernism's impulse toward taboo-breaking truth telling, while putting to one side the question of how exactly we can come to "know" what social reality might be. The result was, as Julia Hallam and Margaret Marshment put it, the advent of a key theoretical moment (hardly the last in cinema history) "when realism was the subject of intense critical attention and reflection to illustrate the different codes and conventions that are 'claimed' as 'realist.'"[5]

Neorealism, in Shiel's subtle formulation, was characterized by a "disposition to ontological truth," that is, manifesting a desire to represent the world and its people as they are (even if that desire is not fully realizable). These films evidenced a special commitment to a rhetoric of revelation. Neorealist filmmakers intended to show viewers what they otherwise might not come to see or, if seeing, would neither understand nor feel sympathy for.[6] Commercial filmmaking, in contrast, had long provided for the most part plausible fantasy that appealed to consensus values and dramatized what viewers wanted to believe was true, if only because, aware they were enjoying fiction, they consented to investing a limited belief in the "reality" projected in light and shadow on the screen. To achieve this effect, plausible fantasy need entertain no particular "disposition to ontological truth," nor does it often do so. The early work of the neorealists, especially Luchino Visconti, Vittorio de Sica, and Roberto Rossellini, provided a strong contrast to the Hollywood releases that constituted the bulk of the films screened in the postwar era by Italian exhibitors. Rossellini's war trilogy—*Rome, Open City, Paisà* (both 1946), and *Germany Year Zero* (1948)—offered authentic visions of a European culture nearly destroyed by war, with an approach to collective disaster (of which the twentieth century provided what we might cynically call rich materials) that had never been taken up before by the commercial cinema. These films struck viewers as essentially distinct from the ordinary commercial product because they had been quite obviously shot in the very locations where the dramas depicted had taken place. But neorealist productions also seemed "true" by contrast with what Hollywood normally turned out, films whose orientation was toward the various easy pleasures associated with the desire to entertain. With a mixture of wonder and admiration, Bosley Crowther said that *Paisà* is "the antithesis of the classic 'story film'" because it threw out "glints of meaning which are strangely unfamiliar on the screen."[7]

Crowther's fellow Americans might have found unfamiliar a film that was committed to limning what he thought was a "terrifying picture of the disillusion, the irony, the horribleness of strife." Americans were accustomed to the more comforting chauvinism of the Hollywood war movie, even whose less glory-shedding productions, several of which are discussed in the introduction, affirm a national unity of purpose that is always marked by a certain amount of self-righteousness. No doubt, the industry's war films share the socially upbeat affect of American commercial film production in general; it is difficult to imagine how they otherwise would have found a viewership, especially in the national exhibition marketplace. Rossellini's commitment to a startling form of verism had little in common with the late Victorian poetics that dominated the Hollywood model, which was based on notions about the rhetoric of the cinema that were, intriguingly enough, largely consonant with the protocol of moral uplift "imposed" on the industry by the Production Code in 1930, to be later enforced after 1934 by the Production Code Administration (PCA).[8] Hollywood had never been in the business of producing pictures that were (except in a pleasurable and temporary way) "terrifying," even, perhaps especially, when such films addressed the horrible orgy of self-destruction from which world culture was only beginning to reemerge, with the final result—it bears remembering—very much in doubt, especially in Europe, where at war's end there was no obvious path to social, economic, and political recovery.[9] Postwar Italy was riven by political violence (for a time a communist-led revolution seemed likely), sectional disaffection that challenged the authority of the central government and the property rights of traditional landholders, widespread corruption, and the constant threat of starvation in the poorer areas of the southern Mezzogiorno.

The U.S. film industry was by and large satisfied with essentially mindless escapism, even as a strain of democratic modernism was making its presence felt in the wake of the conversion to sound (which attracted writers and intellectuals of some note to Hollywood) and the consequent increased politicization of society epitomized by the Rooseveltian New Deal. Challenges were developing to the Victorian aesthetic that had largely prevailed in filmmaking until the late 1920s. American culture in the first half of the twentieth century, pushed by a series of landmark legal decisions about First Amendment rights, was in the process of accepting the principle that art might, perhaps should tell the truth, however disagreeable or threatening, and that, so occupied, could claim exemption from censorship and, more importantly, prosecution for obscenity. If prewar Hollywood manifested only an occasional "disposition to ontological truth," vexed questions raised by literary modernism's preoccupation with violating convention were being asked and answered in the courts. What emerged by the time of the landmark case *Miller v. California* (1973) is that representations previous generations would have found unproblematically obscene (and thus lacking First Amendment protection) might now be found to have "redeeming social value" if their legitimizing vocation was an "art" whose truth-telling aims were not seriously questioned by the court.[10] The spiritual turn of phrase, perhaps exemplifying American religiosity, appropriately revealed how Rossellini's filmmaking, with its redefinition of what might be profitable subjects and style for the commercial cinema, thus suited the evolving legal reconfiguration in the United States of art's special exemption from those Victorian protocols enshrined in the Production Code. The Code enjoined filmmakers to "recreate and rebuild human beings exhausted with the realities of life," to escape from the real, in other words, not embrace its "exhausting," much less its "terrifying," nature. The cinema, in this older and soon residual view, must stand above the real, "lifting men to higher levels," making an "appeal to the soul through the senses," excluding whatever inconvenient truths might trouble such stirring visions of human possibility.[11]

This aesthetic proclaims in somewhat lofty terms what the American film industry had for the most part actually been doing for years, providing paying customers with visions of human action that were both escapist and socially affirming, depicting the extraordinary in aid of eventually reestablishing and endorsing the essential rightness of consensus values. In the early 1930s the industry, attempting to staunch a decline at the box office, had exploited sex and violence in order to entice reluctant filmgoers. Once this initiative met firm opposition from the Catholic Church's Legion of Decency, however, producers accepted without much complaint a Production Code that outlined in detail what "decent" motion pictures could be and as well as an office, the PCA, to oversee the implementation of those principles.[12] We might say that so-called pre-Code sound films are intriguingly realist in that they inaugurate the screen representation of organized crime, with its violent methods of doing business, and social issues such as adultery and divorce, whose discussion and, especially, sympathetic dramatization had once been quite taboo. Releases such as *Public Enemy* (1931) and *The Divorcee* (1930) were more realistic in thematic terms than the studio films that preceded them, even if overall they offered plausible fantasy little different from the standard Hollywood product. In any case, as soon as the PCA assumed its oversight function under the watchful eye of its head censor, Joseph Breen, the industry accepted substantial restrictions on content, eager to continue its profitable role as provider of uncontroversial cinematic entertainment.[13] It hardly seemed desirable, or practical, to many in the industry that their films display a disposition to ontological truth. Glamor, eroticism, and suspenseful narrative were proven lures to keep customers coming back to the theater week after week.

For Cesare Zavattini, conventional cinema, dependent on constructiveness and facile appeals to unproductive pleasure, results from epistemological failure. If our "first, and most superficial reaction to daily existence is boredom," the reason is that we cannot "succeed in surmounting and overcoming our moral and intellectual sloth." We must simply learn to look at reality in the proper fashion to realize that an emphasis on preexisting story "imposes death schemes onto living events and situations." The task of the filmmaker then is not to entertain or enlighten with an engaging story, but rather to make the viewer "think about reality precisely as it is." Hollywood, on the contrary, busies itself with the attempt to make viewers satisfy themselves "with a sweetened version of truth produced through transposition," that is, through a rearrangement of the real that preempts the "non-abstract and concrete study of man."[14] In practice, the lofty goals of neorealism were unsurprisingly realized, as David Overbey points out, "more in the theory and criticism of neorealism than . . . in the films themselves."[15] But, as critics agree, neorealism did manifest itself in a radically distinct approach to filmmaking and visual style that, in Shiel's useful summary, was typified "by a preference for location filming, the use of nonprofessional actors, the avoidance of ornamental *mise-en-scène*, a preference for natural light, a freely-moving documentary style of photography, a non-interventionist approach to film directing, and an avoidance of complex editing and other post-production processes likely to focus attention on the contrivance of the film image."[16]

To put this in a slightly different way, what the neorealists aimed to create, in an always self-conscious and rhetorical fashion, was the impression that, in Zavattini's useful formulation, "the contents always engender their own expression, their own technique," even though, of course, "imagination is allowed," if only on the condition that "it exercise itself within reality and not on the periphery." The result would be "a cinema of encounter." Give us "an ordinary situation," Zavattini says, " and from it we will make a spectacle," converting what seems at first unworthy of our attention into a compelling object for the gaze we share with the camera. If, as he points out, commercial cinema has traditionally been centrifugal, dispersing its energies in a movement away from the reality that constitutes its ultimate subject, neorealism would be centripetal. Not remaining "content with illusion," neorealism would embrace instead "a powerful movement toward facts" that would be energized by a "desire for comprehension," altering in effect the workings of visual/dramatic pleasure as the commercial cinema had solicited and channeled them.[17] Yet this was a tradition not very interested in exploiting/exploring the particular event, which is to say that its realism was more literary or fictional than journalistic, only rarely concerned with the re-creation of a specific past and even then not on the scale of a Hollywood "event" films such as *The Big Lift*.[18]

Arguably, one of the signal accomplishments of modernism in both its literary and cinematic forms (including the verist materialism of the neorealist movement) is its colonization of the unlimited terrain of life itself, its claiming of lived experience in all its forms as the objectness proper to representation, dramatization, and performance. Crowther's shocked enthusiasm for *Paisà*, and all the films that at the end of the 1940s became recognized as neorealist, surely indexes the liminality of his cultural moment, with his previous attachment to quality entertainment from Hollywood challenged, yet still intact. Confronted by a radically different film aesthetic, he now persuades himself to view Hollywood productions as "classical," emphasizing the contingency of that description with questioning quotation marks. Attracted toward a form of cinema that had not yet become a central part of his viewing experience, Crowther yet proves able to embrace both its strangeness and groundbreaking accomplishment, as his criteria of evaluation rapidly shift in ways for which, strangely enough, he finds himself already prepared. His reviews of the period regularly express his willingness to see film, at least in part, as an art with an affinity for the real, and so he is receptive to *Paisà*.[19] And yet, still thinking from within the Hollywood paradigm, he confesses to being surprised by Rossellini's discomfiting, unglamorized vision of an Italy in ruins, riven by continuing war and internecine conflict. It is a world whose truth can never be captured or summarized, only suggested by disconnected vignettes and subsumed within the vaguest generalities of a title ("countryman") that hints (perhaps ironically, given the civil war that erupted upon Italy's surrender to the Allies in 1943 and continued after the general end of European hostilities) at a still elusive sense of national unity.

Rossellini's images reflected the complex realities of his postwar world and were staged in it for the most part, but, with some major exceptions, they were not found in some newsreel and then creatively redeployed as part of an onto-logically complex montage melding the typically verisimilar to images that were authentic in a different sense, reflecting in part a world that existed before the shaping intentions of the filmmaker. In an essay that interestingly incorporates the insights and blindness of the neorealist position, Zavattini proclaims, as he reflects on the essential difference between this style of filmmaking and the entertainment cinema more generally: "The most important characteristic of neo-realism, i.e., its essential innovation, is, for me, the discovery that this need to use a story was just an unconscious means of masking human defeat in the face of reality."[20] Nonetheless, his films, like Rossellini's, remain firmly rooted

FIGURE 16 Like the de Rochemont semi-documentaries, Roberto Rossellini's *Paisà* includes documentary or newsreel footage to provide authenticity (frame enlargement).

in narrative, which, with its twists and turns, sympathetic characters, thematic concerns, and dramatic resolutions, provides the structure upon which the evocation/exploration of real place and the various meanings it holds in the contemporary moment might unfold. He could imagine a time when this tradition of filmmaking would dispose of "no scenario written before, and no dialogue to adapt," but in fact that moment never arrived.[21]

It is not the politics of the film that engages Crowther deeply. Instead his reaction is thoroughly Hollywood, almost all affect, not analysis, the result of the juxtaposition of a different regime of representation, including, especially, what should be shown, with that to which he is more accustomed. A few years after the release of *Paisà* and the other key films of the late 1940s, Zavattini was able to proclaim that "the cinema should take as its subject the daily existence and condition of the Italian people," moving the viewer toward the analysis of the intriguing spectacle of a world just rediscovered by the camera.[22] But Crowther hardly finds himself seized by this "desire for comprehension": he is instead shocked by the pleasure he experiences at what the film represents and how it represents, at Rossellini's skillful expansion and deepening of the boundaries of what the camera may record and offer the receptive viewer. *Paisà*, Crowther enthuses, "cannot fail to rattle the windowpanes of your eyes." Many a viewer will leave the theater with "emotions limp." The cumulative effect of the film's understated episodes, played for anticlimax, have an "oddly disturbing effect." Viewers accustomed to Hollywood's reassuring melodramatics, however, might leave the theater with a "sad sense of emptiness," resulting from the film's skillful exploitation of an anti-triumphal form of catharsis. Crowther, in short, finds no distanciation in the film's appeal. Zavattini would perhaps be disappointed, for he argues that the neorealist cinema should not concern itself with the Aristotelian goal of "bringing the audience to tears and indignation by means of transference." This new kind of film should instead "bring the audience to reflect . . . to think about reality precisely as it is," a goal similar to that of Brecht's epic theater in its privileging of ideas (and their truth) over emotions.[23]

Later entrants into the developing series (shaped carefully by American exhibitors who were watching a growing market niche) would similarly impress Crowther. He was just as moved by de Sica's *Bicycle Thieves*, in the viewing of which he found himself captured by a "feeling of genuine compassion which swells and overflows in this film, offering a purge of emotion for those who possess humility."[24] For him, Giuseppe de Santis's *Bitter Rice* (1950) was notable not for its engagement with worker politics, but because in this film "passion toils and tumbles . . . like the wrestlers in a gas-house free-for-all, and torments of carnal hunger are boldly and rawly exposed."[25] This seems a more appropriate response to a film intended for grindhouse rather than art house exhibition. Of course, the idea of "exposure" is not entirely inconsistent with the way in which *Bitter Rice* exhibits its "bombshell" female lead, Silvana Mangano, who seems to spend most of her working life in a skin-tight and soaking wet blouse. What's more worth noting here, however, is the emphasis once again on affect rather than politics. A realism so conceived would suit Hollywood's disposition toward Aristotelianism, the way in which by the early postwar era American films had been organized around arousing and then satisfying exactly the kind of emotions Crowther felt himself experiencing when encountering these otherwise strikingly different narratives from Italy. His reactions point toward the successful formal approach that was then being taken by many of the American filmmakers similarly concerned with representing the "real." A different regime of representation, one often described by industry insiders like Fox's Darryl F. Zanuck as "factual," was for commercial reasons to be balanced by "drama," meaning characters and action with which viewers would easily find themselves emotionally engaged, could in fact "root for."

Neorealist films, even if somewhat misunderstood as "personal" stories by American viewers like Crowther to whom their political messages might be difficult to decipher, offered a powerful alternative to the mainstream domestic product, a significant rival for admission dollars. It is a bit surprising, then, as Robert Sklar has pointed out, that we must "credit the U.S. film industry with early and powerful recognition of post–World War II Italian cinema."[26] In 1947, Hollywood awarded de Sica's *Shoeshine* (1946) its first-ever special Oscar for a non-English-language film, recognizing the film's "high quality" and surprising emergence from a recovering industry in "a country scarred by war." Sklar might have mentioned that it was the exhibition of Rossellini's *Rome, Open City* at New York City's World Theatre that inaugurated what Tino Balio calls "the foreign film renaissance on American Screens." Rossellini's film played to overflow audiences for twenty-one months after its opening on 25 February 1946, shattering records previously held by *The Birth of a Nation* and *Gone with the Wind*, and it went on to gross $5 million in U.S. release, substantially more than any foreign film had ever previously earned and substantially more than the vast majority of domestic productions, for which a gross of only half that amount would have been counted as an outstanding success.[27]

Crowther's receptivity to this radically different kind of film was obviously shared by many educated urbanites, particularly in a cosmopolitan New York City culture that has never been widely endorsed by the country as a whole. Such filmmaking did not generally meet with the same enthusiasm and acclaim in Middle America, but obviously a not inconsiderable vein of national taste had been revealed, and it was soon to be explored by the distributors and exhibitors who during the next two decades created and then helped make flourish what would become known as the international art cinema.[28] In the first postwar decade, neorealist films were "always a minority" of Italian production and were never particularly profitable or commercially successful in their own country.[29] However, matters were quite different across the Atlantic. In 1952, *Time* magazine called attention to "Rome's New Empire," which was, so the argument went, now firmly ensconced in an appreciative North America, for Italy had become "second only to Hollywood as the major supplier of films to the US."[30]

The undoubted popularity of Italian Neorealism with the American intelligentsia, however, has been misunderstood, at least as far as the history of postwar Hollywood is concerned. As Sklar goes on to report, the widely credited notion that neorealism influenced American filmmaking of the period is "among the mysteries of historiographic fashion." In his view, the supposed impact of neorealism on "the aesthetic practices of U.S. filmmakers in the immediate postwar years" must be considered little more than a "breezy generalization and common cliché" that still awaits the discovery, increasingly unlikely at this late date, of "significant nodes of specific affinities and practical interactions."[31] One brief example from the work of one of the most reliable and careful of film historians must here suffice as an illustration of this mistaken view. In discussing Alfred Hitchcock's decision to make *The Wrong Man*, Patrick Gilligan suggests that for various reasons, chiefly his admiration for Roberto Rossellini, "[Hitchcock] wanted to sink his teeth into a neorealist project."[32] But Hitchcock's film is a re-creation of a "true story," never an approach favored by the neorealists though quite common in American realist filmmaking of the period, with two of that particular cycle's most notable releases, *Boomerang* (1947) and *Call Northside 777* (1948), cited by Hitchcock himself as his film's immediate context (these Fox releases are discussed in the next chapter). Like *The Wrong Man*, they are re-creations of true stories that had attained a certain national notoriety through newspaper coverage and feature stories in magazines such as *Reader's Digest* and *Life*.[33] Far from calling attention to neorealism, Hitchcock thus reminds François Truffaut in their famous interview that the American postwar cinema manifests its own burgeoning realist traditions, forms of filmmaking that contrast strongly with the conventional Hollywood product even though they are produced, distributed, and exhibited in much the same way as the more strictly entertainment cinema of the era. Tellingly, his French admirer asks for no clarification about why Hitchcock would be interested in a project similar to these films produced by Louis de Rochemont and directed by two of postwar America's most acclaimed practitioners, Elia Kazan and Henry Hathaway. Despite his own deep enthusiasm for neorealism, Truffaut never suggests that Hitchcock showed any interest in the Italian production cycle per se with this film or others.

Undeniably, the patrons of the era's art cinemas (the only sector of American film exhibition that increased in both scope and profitability after the war) were enthusiastic admirers of a neorealism whose initial wave of American box office successes peaked during the early 1950s. And neorealism continued to exert a powerful influence on "post-neorealist" Italian production, producing a further number of films that did very well in the American market, including at least two, Federico Fellini's *La Dolce Vita* (1961) and *8½* (1965), that rank among the most profitable foreign releases from 1945 to 1973. But the American filmmaking establishment did not take up the challenge to imitate or appropriate the neorealist style. As historians such as Luca Barattoni have shown, the "post-neorealist" Italian cinema, however, left its mark on evolving Hollywood practice in the 1960s and, especially, the 1970s.[34] The influence of the international modernist art cinema in general is easy to read out from the films of the so-called Hollywood Renaissance filmmakers of the 1970s such as Robert Altman, Martin Scorsese, Francis Coppola, Jerry Schatzberg, and Hal Ashby. American filmmakers of an earlier era, however, did not take up how neorealism offered a "way of thinking" about a war that had hardly marked or reshaped North American society. As Shiel points out, however, they were deeply influenced by the Italian art cinema's subsequent turn at the end of the 1950s toward a focus on "the material, psychic, and social character of peacetime society, especially in relation to urban modernity," whose discontents for the personal life were endlessly anatomized in films from both national traditions in the 1970s.[35]

Once the fiction of neorealist influence has been abandoned, however, how else to understand the sudden advent and flourishing of an American realist cinema during precisely the same era when neorealist films were playing a central role in reestablishing the profitability of foreign films on American screens? Sklar and Saverio Giovacchini argue that we should understand neorealism from the very beginning as "global" rather than as a national movement subsequently gone international. The various realisms of the international postwar cinema would then be a multilayered "bricolage" resulting from complex processes of imitation and independent development. Could developments in the United States be traced to an "international conversation about realist cinema that began in the 1950s . . . [and] was absorbed with varying results into national cinemas, thereby becoming a global style?"[36]

From the case histories we have examined thus far, this seems plausible enough as a general approach. We should indeed credit a series of divergent and only occasionally overlapping developments (including in other performance art forms, especially postwar Broadway and early television theater) for the emergence of a more realist cinema in postwar Hollywood, including films with a marked locative agenda. *The Big Lift* was part of a series at Fox that took advantage of a renewed interest in World War II and its political aftermath. *Sunset Blvd.* emerged from an international conversation of sorts; its deep engagement with lived and natural place connects not so much to institutional developments as such, but to the filmmakers' previous experience with *A Foreign Affair*, which was a production meant to engage, in an entertaining fashion, with the realities of postwar Germany, reflecting a collective state of mind while confecting entertainment from the foibles of occupiers and occupied alike. Because of its origin in Wilder's plans for a remaking of the postwar German production, this film is best explained in terms of authorship. In any case, for a variety of industrial, economic, and political reasons, the trend that Wilder imagined never materialized. Though it connects to the established tradition of films about Hollywood filmmaking, *Sunset Blvd.* is in essence a sequel, an attempt on the part of Wilder and Brackett to repeat what had proven with *A Foreign Affair* to be a critically acclaimed and popular formula (the film was among the top twenty earners of the year). Partnering with Henry Hathaway, Brackett would promote in *Niagara* yet a third iteration, this time with a focus on a natural landscape rather than on Los Angeles that was then arguably America's most semiotically rich city. *Niagara* was yet another box office hit, grossing about $6 million worldwide on a production budget of less than $2 million.[37] The institutional and aesthetic developments that produced this quite unusual and intriguing release of the first postwar decade are traced in the next chapter.

No "international conversation" about the desirability of real location shooting led John Ford to abandon studio sets, back lots, and nearby Branson Canyon for the "true West" of Monument Valley. Ford was interested in a pictorialism dependent on the appropriately spectacular real, but one "blank" enough to be easily accommodated to the needs of a well-established genre for infinite repetition. He sought out Monument Valley for a series of western projects, including *The Searchers*, in what was a move back to the future, not a response to the particular conditions of the postwar era, which, in any case, his decision to film there antedated by some six years. *The Searchers*, of course, is realist only in a quite limited sense, as I argue in the previous chapter. For his own artistic and career-boosting reasons, Ford worked to restore to the western the sense of place it had lost with the coming of sound and the rise of B-series, often stagey productions that featured singing cowboys like Gene Autry. These were not developments that he was completely against, of course, as witness his promotion of John Wayne as his own continuing star and the musical numbers that regularly appear in his westerns, including the specially composed theme song for *The Searchers*, sung (uncredited) by the Sons of the Pioneers, the most famous of all western musical groups. But the performance of western culture in the film is completely subordinated to staging within a landscape, conceived, as W.J.T. Mitchell argues, "as an instrument of cultural power, perhaps even an agent of power that is (or frequently represents itself as) independent of human intentions."[38]

In the postwar era, Ford's pictorialism suited the industry's general strategy to offer cinematic experiences qualitatively different from the unreliable black-and-white images and tinny audio available from television, then the medium's most dangerous competitor. In a time of declining attendance, Hollywood's attempt to win back its audience by offering filmgoers impressive eye candy made the fifteen years or so after the end of the war an age of outsized visuality, fueled by the increasing popularity of the various widescreen processes recently invented or perfected, with the revival of 1920s biblical epic one of several related generic developments suiting this rapidly evolving exhibition technologies. Norma Desmond's desire to make a film about Salome and John the Baptist demonstrates her correct reading of current production trends rather than her disconnection from filmmaking realities, and DeMille's *Samson and Delilah* proved to be the industry's top box office draw in 1950, earning about $11 million in its initial release and prompting soon afterward a second and similarly profitable one.[39] Fifties cinema, not surprisingly, found itself dominated by a series of successful entrants into the production cycle DeMille had refounded, in all of which pictorialism, whether ersatz or based on real locations, is a principal attraction. DeMille even found himself remaking a film he had made nearly thirty years before, *The Ten Commandments* (1923). The 1956 version features extensive location shooting in Egypt's Nile Valley and the Sinai Peninsula, though many of the most arresting sequences were staged and shot on the largest film set ever built, surpassing the gigantism of D. W. Griffith's *Intolerance* (1916), whose impressive centerpiece was a studio lot re-creation of the city of Babylon, a set so big it proved too expensive to disassemble until it eventually fell into ruin.

If Hollywood applauded the small-scale realism of Delbert Mann's *Marty* in 1955, the next year the industry saved most of its praise for the largest-scale travelogue film ever made, Mike Todd's *Around the World in 80 Days*. Shot in 70 mm, *Around the World*'s striking Technicolor images seemed larger than life when projected onto huge screens. Exhibition was restricted at first to theaters that could accommodate this new technology; six-track stereophonic sound (by Westex) provided an appropriately dense and all-encompassing aural accompaniment. Like most Hollywood productions, *Around the World* centered on star performance, with Britain's David Niven and Mexico's Cantinflas as an international duo of adventurers who lead the fast-paced narrative, set in the late nineteenth century. The story traces their successful attempt to circumnavigate the globe in only eighty days by taking advantage of modern means of transportation, in particular the railways. In terms of substance and theme, *Around the World* offered little more than an ordinary adventure narrative. It was all flash and fluff—entertainment with a knowing wink that reflected Todd's P. T. Barnum sensibilities. The greater part of a huge budget for the period ($6 million) was spent on location shooting (112 separate filming sites in thirteen countries) as well as on elaborate sets that were constructed for some sequences. Todd reportedly turned more than a 600 percent profit in domestic exhibition, not counting overseas box office, which was considerable.[40]

Monument Valley, photographed in black and white, had impressed knowledgeable critics like Frank S. Nugent when first introduced to cinemagoers in 1939's *Stagecoach*, but it was infinitely more impressive in Technicolor and in the aptly named VistaVision, whose expanded screen the valley was quite capable of filling. Ford's restoration of real place to the western was taken up in earnest by David O. Selznick in his 1946 epic production *Duel in the Sun*, intended as a kind of sequel to his *Gone with the Wind* (1939). The adaptation of Margaret Mitchell's novel had been filmed largely on soundstages and back lots, as well as at various Los Angeles area locations, but the filmmakers, especially last-in-line director Victor Fleming and Selznick himself, were not much interested in communicating any sense of real southernness; Tara was a façade constructed by art director Lyle Wheeler. *Duel in the Sun*, in contrast, was shot on a variety of southwestern locations, especially in Arizona, though none, including Squaw's Head Rock, where the climactic "death in the sun" shootout is staged, possessed the impressive

FIGURE 17 *To Catch a Thief* offers one tableau after another of glamorous views of the French Riviera, then just coming into its own as a tourist destination (frame enlargement).

natural beauty of Monument Valley. A similar form of pictorialism dominates even in westerns of the era in which the "real location" is more or less a mirage, such as John Sturges's *Bad Day at Black Rock* (1955), filmed at Lone Pine, California, whose "town" was in effect an elaborate purpose-built set. Much the same may be said about William Wyler's *The Big Country* (1958), appropriately photographed in Technirama and Technicolor, but not making use of locations more exotic than California's own Red Canyon State Park.

Only slightly more authentic as an exploration of a real place is Alfred Hitchcock's travelogue thriller *To Catch a Thief* (1955), shot principally on location in Cannes, Monaco, and—most spectacularly—the mountainous Grande Corniche highway connecting these seaside locations. The film's narrative is little more than an excuse for the sexy pairing of glamorous stars, and Hitchcock spends minimal energy in making plausible Cary Grant's superficial incarnation of a former *résistant*; Grace Kelly has an easier time portraying a spoiled rich girl. But however much the film accurately and spectacularly evokes a French Riviera then being extensively promoted as a tourist destination, *To Catch a Thief* offers only customary Hollywood romantic fantasy; it is in no meaningful way an exploration of place. Pictorialism does not necessarily serve a realist agenda, a proposition proved by *To Catch a Thief* and many other so-called location films of the period. William Wyler's very successful *Roman Holiday* (1953), for example, was shot largely in the title city whose principal architectural landmarks, such as the Spanish Steps and the Piazza Venezia, the filmmakers make every effort to show. But, much like *To Catch a Thief*, the film's focus is a glamorous romance that could have been staged almost anywhere. The "eternal city" functions simply as visually attractive backdrop. Lacking power because it is represented in a largely decontextualized fashion, Rome is not an urban landscape in the sense promoted by Mitchell, since its long history, concretized in world-renowned architecture and public art, is reduced through a kind of photo-tourism to little more than charming decoration.

In contrast to the pictorialist trend, many postwar productions that utilize real locations are similar to *Sunset Blvd.* in displaying a "disposition toward ontological truth." These films share affinities with (if not direct connections to) the neorealist instant classics then enjoying a substantial popularity in U.S. art theaters. Neorealist and American realist films of the period equally feature serious cultural and social themes; on-location shooting and the use of place as "itself"; historical re-creations and actuality footage (both more common in American productions); a deglamorized approach to mise-en-scène; stylistically unobtrusive cinematography; naturalist acting styles; and non-actors, at least in minor roles. Consider, simply by way of examples, the following films, distinguished from the standard Hollywood product by this general sort of cinematic realism, though not necessarily sharing all the elements mentioned above: *None Shall Escape* (1944), *Boomerang* (1947), *13 Rue Madeleine* (1947), *T-Men* (1947), *Call Northside 777* (1948), *The Search* (1948), *The Naked City* (1948), *Berlin Express* (1948), *Canon City* (1948), *He Walked by Night* (1948), *Border Incident* (1949), *Intruder in the Dust* (1949), *Thieves Highway* (1949), *Lost Boundaries* (1949), *The Woman on Pier 13* (1949), *Christ in Concrete* (*Give Us This Day*) (1949), *The Lawless* (1950), *The Big Lift* (1950), *The Men* (1950), *Night and the City* (1950), *Whistle at Eaton Falls* (1951), *Decision Before Dawn* (1951), *Walk East on Beacon* (1952), *The Sniper* (1952), *The Juggler* (1953), *Little Boy Lost* (1953), *The Wild One* (1953), *Salt of the Earth* (1954), *On the Waterfront* (1954), *Down Three Dark Streets* (1954), *The Phenix City Story* (1955), *Marty* (1955), *The Catered Affair* (1956), *The Wrong Man* (1956), *The Garment Jungle* (1957), *Middle of the Night* (1958), *Vertigo* (1958), *Wild River* (1960), *Man on a String* (1960), *The Intruder* (1962), *A Child Is Waiting* (1963), *An Affair of the Skin* (1963), *Black Like Me* (1964), *Nothing but a Man* (1964), *The Train* (1964), and *The Pawnbroker* (1965), among numerous others, perhaps a hundred or more altogether.

The filmmakers involved constitute an honor roll of the generation that for the most part came of age during the war and after: Elia Kazan, Stanley Kramer, Henry Hathaway, John Cassavetes, Louis de Rochemont, Edward Dmytryk, Sidney Lumet, Robert Wise, Mark Hellinger, Fred Zinnemann, Alfred E. Werker, Roger Corman, Anthony Mann, Clarence Brown, Herbert Biberman, John Frankenheimer, László Benedek, and Alfred Hitchcock chief among them. This postwar tradition (which may be too grand a term) hardly constituted a self-conscious movement, never generating, in the Italian fashion, a self-appointed post-facto spokesman like Zavattini to codify and theorize. But it lasted longer, assuming a number of divergent forms, and produced more films than its Italian counterpart. Of course, any dispersal of energy from production into self-promotion or memorialization would, in any case, hardly have been possible within the American film culture of the age, which was substantially anti-intellectual, even though some of the filmmakers involved, such as Dmytryk and Zinnemann, would surely in other industrial contexts have been less reticent to discuss their political and aesthetic views outside the occasional interview or production history. As in the case of neorealism, this American tradition of locative realism never dominated production during the two decades of the postwar experience, nor, once again like the neorealists, did these filmmakers devote themselves exclusively to the making of realist films in which place plays a central role. American postwar locative realism cannot be reduced to any master narrative, and is best considered as only paralleled at points by neorealism in terms of aesthetics, themes, and production strategies. It is certainly too extensive and diverse an aspect of the era's production to be covered in a single volume.

The most important cycle of locative realist films within the American industry was unlike anything that occurred in Italian filmmaking of the period. The evolution of what might best be described as pictorial journalism (which numbers *The Big Lift* among its most important releases) exerted substantial influence on Hollywood developments, lending them a distinct national character. It is this tradition that will be the focus in the remainder of this study.

Pictorial Journalism and *The March of Time*

The postwar theorizing about the various possibilities of a realist cinema in the works of Bazin, Kracauer, and Zavattini, among other notable thinkers, was symptomatic of certain intellectual and political preoccupations. But in the United States, the most important trend toward the expressive, engaged use of real locations emerged from outside the industry, and not from the academy. It was a commercial, not an aesthetic development per se, part of an emerging trend toward the featurizing of documentary materials of one kind or another in a format known as the weekly newsreel. Newsreels, generally no more than twenty minutes in length, consisted of actuality footage of real people, places, and events, brief stories, so to speak, some of which were truly serious and newsworthy, others (and these constituted the bulk of most weekly "issues") possessing only what the business came to call "human interest."

Pioneered by the French producer Pathé, which for decades dominated the field, the newsreel had by the 1920s become a standard feature of the "program" offered at the nation's movie theaters, with a number of U.S. producers competing for screen space. In the competition for subscribers, Fox, Paramount, Hearst, and Universal all supported newsreel units. One of Paramount's units is clearly, and ironically, visible in the final sequence of *Sunset Blvd.*, with the clear implication that Norma Desmond will, after all, once again appear on the silver screen, just not in the main feature; she has a future of sorts with the studio since she continues to serve, if unwittingly, Paramount's need for appealing forms of story. Of particular significance for subsequent film history was the *March of Time* series, developed not by a Hollywood company, but by what was then as now one of the most important publishers of news commentary and summary, Time, Inc. As historian Raymond Fielding reports,

> At its height, in the United States alone, the American newsreel was seen weekly by at least 40 million people, and throughout the world by more than 200 million. For many people, especially the illiterate, it was a principal source of news until the coming of television. . . . By the middle of the 1920s, American producers dominated the international newsreel business, employing a world-wide network of news-gathering facilities . . . in their competitive struggle to make motions picture records of newsworthy events in times for exhibition deadlines.[41]

Despite the ostensibly journalistic intentions of newsreel producers, however, the form, as Fielding reports, was "compromised from the beginning by fakery, re-creation, manipulation, and staging."[42] In other words, much of the discussion in chapters 1 and 2 about the notions of "authentic" and "true" in regard to the deployment of settings is relevant, _mutatis mutandis_, to the aesthetic traditions of newsreel production. In the program developed by American exhibitors, newsreels came to occupy a strictly subordinate place as one short feature among several, but, as Fielding points out, they brought a distinctly different kind of cinematic experience to most American viewers: "It was the _March of Time_ alone which successfully introduced and established the documentary format for film audiences in the United States. And all of this occurred before the films of Pare Lorentz, Joris Ivens, Willard Van Dyke, and Herbert Kline."[43]

Certainly, these current event short features hardly qualify as journalism in the traditional sense. They are far from unmanipulated, objective recordings of "things that happened." Instead, they are closer to fictional or at least fictionalized representations in which the authentic or true shares space with the strictly fabulized or faked. But practices of re-creation and staging do not prevent a newsreel story from being realistic or from communicating the truth of an event even while "simulating" its representation. A re-created event might be rendered more or less faithful to its unfilmed original by remaining true in some sense to the event depicted, even if this meant deceiving viewers by using look-alike actors to speak the words of well-known figures for whom actual footage was not available. It seems important, in other words, to differentiate in terms of truth value or authenticity what appears on the screen from the events in the real world to which reference is made. Re-creations or stagings, to be sure, are not realia as such, but they can be (and often were in the newsreel tradition) more or less reliably authentic representations of the news, with a truly journalistic standard of the truth being upheld, if only on the level of the signified rather than the signifier. A look-alike actor may read onscreen the important speech made by a political figure, but the text of the speech might be precisely what in fact had been said. The news is accurately conveyed even if viewers have been persuaded to consider true what is, superficially speaking, a simulacrum.

This practice was more justifiable, perhaps, when the image was designed to stand in for or index general rather than particular truths. Crumpled "corpses," smeared with fake blood, could truthfully, if not authentically, depict the deadly effects of bombing raids during the Spanish Civil War or the Japanese assault on China; these images, however staged, referred to historical facts that were beyond dispute, lending concreteness and vividness to events that were far distant and for which actual footage was unavailable. They encouraged viewer empathy and interest. Similarly, voiceover "readings" aurally superimposed on not easily identifiable images made it possible to fix and particularize what they could be understood as meaning. The image of a thatched-roof farmhouse set ablaze meant something particular when the voiceover narration lamented the easy triumph of German *Blitzkrieg* in the Battle of Poland. Such manipulation, if that is the right term, is of course a standard feature of most documentary and photojournalistic traditions, and it seems unexceptional when the commentary is no lie, but a truth that can be usefully exemplified or illustrated by what is depicted even if the image is quite other from what the narrator suggests it is. De Rochemont was fond of arguing that reenactments were "frequently sharper and more 'detailed' than the real thing," an Aristotelian view about the unique value of fiction's suppositionality that demonstrates how his attitude toward the "truth" was more that of the social realist than the journalist.[44]

If journalism holds up as its inviolable standard an accurate rendering of particular truths, *including* the images deployed to express them, then newsreels should not be considered journalism. When the newsreel makers engaged writers to render dialogue that could reasonably be assigned to figures (or perhaps we should say characters) whose views and predilections were well known from other sources, surely then the line from news reporting to fictionalization had been crossed. Even in such cases, however, the resulting representations, while neither strictly true nor authentic, could still be, and often were, meaningfully realistic. In the newsreel, the line between journalism properly speaking and fictionalizing often blurred, and no opprobrium perhaps should attach to those who filled in with supposition and invention in order to make the news both more interesting and, if in somewhat paradoxical ways, more authentic. The news *depicted* (and this is a key term) in newsreels thus differs substantially from the reporting that filled the pages of newspapers devoted to objective reporting.

In the course of the 1920s, another form of journalism emerged with the advent and flourishing of a new type of newsy weekly magazine, *Time*, which offered, as Fielding describes it, "an appraisal of current events—a summary of the week's news which interpreted it in the light of past events, social and political trends, and prognostications of future change."[45] Much like TV news in the twenty-first century, the articles published in *Time* depended on accounts, facts, and figures gleaned from more traditional sources, in this case mostly the *New York Times*. The magazine quickly attained a substantial popularity with middle-class readers who did not mind being gently guided in their thinking about domestic and international issues as long as these were discussed from a contemporary perspective that was not easily identifiable as either Republican or Democratic. *Reader's Digest*, which started publication in 1922, appealed more blatantly to the same readership, who were eager to be informed and yet too busy (or reluctant) to read full versions of political/cultural commentary and middle-brow fiction (*Reader's Digest Condensed Books* series met with similar success when it appeared in 1950). In early 1931, Roy Edward Larsen, general manager of *Time*, decided to expand the corporation's operations into radio. His idea was to produce a bi-weekly radio program, *The March of Time* (*MOT*), which would feature stories of current news, sometimes utilizing "real" audio but mostly requiring the services of a considerable staff of writers, actors, and production personnel. The show was a considerable success (in 1945 it would end its fourteen-year run), and Larsen was persuaded early on that the news magazine should have a newsreel counterpart, with each filmic issue focused on important current events or trends and featuring the kind of mildly directive commentary that *Time* had pioneered with both its flagship magazine and radio program. Newsreels quickly came to constitute an important part of the composite program that emerged as standard during the 1930s after the conversion to sound and the concomitant discontinuation of live performance.

In 1934, Larsen persuaded one of the short subject/newsreel producers at Fox to head up the new operation. Louis de Rochemont turned out to be an inspired choice, and the new series proved immensely successful, especially in its later years when, under his direction, it offered thoughtful and detailed commentary on Europe's gathering storm.[46] A year before hostilities commenced, the release of "Inside Nazi Germany—1938," directed by Jack Glenn and widely believed to be based on actual footage smuggled out of Europe, aroused considerable furor from isolationists and interventionists alike at a time when the industry was still reluctant to confront the growing Nazi threat. This issue of *MOT* depicted in part a Germany recovered from the worst effects of the Great Depression, a country exuding nationalist fervor where enthusiastic crowds thronged to be harangued by a Hitler then enjoying his greatest popularity. Intended as a warning to complacent Americans, these sequences were read as pro-German by many of the regime's more virulent transatlantic critics, even though they were balanced by the filmmakers' condemnation of the country's increasing militarism and its promulgation of anti-Jewish legislation. Noted film critic Otis Ferguson, for example, writing in *The New Republic*, understood that de Rochemont was issuing a measured warning about the growing threat to the other democracies and to its own citizens posed by the Nazi regime. The film was, in his view, "an editorial with pictures, an editorial for democracy and against suppression, militant nationalism, and shoving people around."[47]

"Inside Nazi Germany—1938" was, in aesthetic terms, very much a mixed form, incorporating some real footage that de Rochemont's operatives had obtained, but it mostly consisted of re-creations of typical events, making use of actors—in the loosest sense of that term—following scripts fashioned by the writers for the series. One of the most interesting sequences features what appears to be a middle-aged *hausfrau* and her pipe-smoking husband listening intently to a radio broadcast whose subtitled text reads: "Hundreds killed in riots of communist strikers in Detroit." German radio, for years at this point under the artful direction of Dr. Josef Goebbels, Reich minister of propaganda, did in fact produce carefully calculated misinformation designed to convince the national public that the United States was more riven by ideological, racial, and class conflict than was the case, but this snippet of film does not record a telling moment of its domestic reception. Jack Glenn staged the sequence in Manhattan, using nonprofessional German Americans in a gesture toward type that would have met with the approval of Sergei Eisenstein. The film also featured a number of what we might call authentic stagings. Glenn persuaded Bund leader Fritz Kuhn to appear as himself in order to read from a script in several scenes written for him that featured the pro-Nazi and anti-Jewish opinions he heartily endorsed; these enactments were staged in Glenn's New York offices. The precise truth value of this material is debatable since the words he speaks are not exactly his own, and he is being prompted to speak them as what only can be called a performance. It would be difficult, however, to deny this speech a considerable amount of authenticity since Kuhn agreed with what the text contained even as he was eager to take advantage of the free publicity for himself and his movement that this *MOT* appearance provided.

If neither real nor documentary in any narrow sense, *MOT* depended on an effective, and artfully seamless, mixture of reality effects, achieved by splicing together actuality footage (sometimes of events, sometimes just of locations) with re-creations or stagings of various kinds, the whole stitched together by craftily written scripts. To be sure, there is an ontological difference between faux tableaux (two nonprofessionals pretending to be rapt listeners of Goebbels's programming) and sequences in which some public figure like Kuhn appears as himself, even if the event is staged. In terms of rhetoric, of course, such differences may well be unimportant. Once viewers were convinced that what they were seeing on the screen was "real," their limited investment of belief carried them beyond the occasional absurdity. Why and how did some newsreel camera photograph an elderly couple listening to a propaganda broadcast? This was not a question that even sophisticated viewers like Otis Ferguson found themselves inclined to ask. As the filmmakers well knew, whatever the precise nature of its constituent parts, the whole would seem real enough, would in fact *be* real enough since it was convincingly supported with relevant facts and corresponded to views that were already generally held about the current state of German society.

Even with their various techniques of "enhanced" journalism, the *MOT* documentaries were substantially true, and in being true, more or less, the form remained faithful to the *Time* policy of engaged advocacy. De Rochemont never tolerated either off-putting stridency or boldfaced partisanship. Though some on both sides of the interventionist debate might fault what he produced, viewers in general considered these featurized newsreels films of fact, not fiction. It is simply that the cinematic facts were often not sufficient to the journalistic aim of telling a comprehensive and affecting story. The production history of "Inside Nazi Germany—1938" is instructive in this regard. Though the actuality footage obtained at great expense and risk depicted some of what was happening in Germany, there was, as Fielding reports, "nothing that was politically controversial or revealing." The film smuggled out of Germany was "a disappointment" to de Rochemont, who was forced to do what scriptwriters, film directors, and producers do in order to build the story of political repression, concentration camps, and accelerating re-armament that he wanted to tell.

The major, if not the only, strand of postwar Hollywood locative realism can be traced to the hybrid formula de Rochemont developed while working during the 1930s on *MOT*. As the international situation worsened, Roy Larsen persuaded de Rochemont to begin feature production using the same formula. The result was *The Ramparts We Watch*, released in 1940; as far as Hollywood history is concerned, the film is most important because it was the progenitor of a new form for Hollywood: the semi-documentary. The semi-documentary, as *Ramparts* exemplifies, depends on the creative incorporation of disparate elements whose different claims to truth or authenticity must be mutually accommodated: newsreel footage depicting actual people, places, and events, its meaning fixed by an authoritative narrator in the fashion first pioneered by *MOT* and staged sequences, meant to evoke typical social situations that were filmed in actual locations and with nonprofessionals as performers. An earlier project, which he never brought to completion, had been to use considerable footage shot by expeditionary newsmen Roy Phelps and Armand Denis in the Belgian Congo; the film was to have been an extended cinematic essay on the future of colonialism, at the time fast becoming a provocative issue in which many Americans took a deep interest. Time, Inc. passed on the project, which was picked up and completed by Denis-Roosevelt Productions, eventually released in French as *Magie Africaine* in 1938. But his bosses at Time did greenlight de Rochemont to work on a similar extended essay film that addressed the worsening international crisis from an American point of view. A conventional theatrical promotion and release would be arranged for the late spring of 1940.

The Ramparts We Watch was to be part essay, part propaganda screed, and part fictional dramatization. This combination of elements was quite new in a feature film, though anticipated by some 1930s releases (especially Warner Bros. films such as *I Am a Fugitive from a Chain Gang* [Mervyn LeRoy, 1932] that seemed inspired by what was then in the news). Unlike the *MOT* features more generally,

Ramparts looks to the past in order to understand the conditions and developments that led to a renewed outbreak of European hostilities on 1 September 1939. De Rochemont had at first intended to present an argument against U.S. involvement on either side by refreshing viewer's memories about what he thought were the devious forces that had drawn this country into conflict with Germany in 1917, and, more generally, an eventually frustrated and abortive involvement in European affairs as the postwar settlement spun out of American control by the end of the 1920s. As initially conceived, *Ramparts* would be advocating for a wary and careful non-intervention in the ongoing continental hostilities; the film would neither discount nor exaggerate the dangers Hitler's expansionist policies posed to American interests. This would have distinguished the directedness of *Ramparts* from the more stridently isolationist and pacifist line eventually taken by the America First Committee and its chief spokesman, Charles A. Lindbergh. This organization would boast of nearly a million members before the Japanese attack of Pearl Harbor on 7 December 1941, and Hitler's subsequent declaration of war against the United States four days later led to its immediate disbanding.[48]

As *Ramparts* demonstrates, American postwar realism emerges in large part from documentary/journalistic traditions in which exhortatory, obtrusive narrators play a central role; many of its experiments with form involve the reach, configuration, and function of the non-diegetic narrative voice, which does not issue from the image, but rather controls or contains it. In this developing American tradition, the extradiegetic narrator proves a much nuanced formal feature, one that does not similarly figure in Italian neorealist films of the period. Neorealism develops from feature film traditions that are marked by political engagement, for the cinema during the fascist era, roughly 1939–1943, could hardly escape functioning in this way. Committed to showing rather than telling, however, the Italian films offer no equivalent for the relentless presentness of the narrator's voice in *Ramparts*. De Rochemont's film could hardly have emerged in the form it finally assumed, and to the enthusiastic reception it immediately was accorded, had it not been for the energies released by increasingly disturbing international circumstances to which *MOT* had been devoting substantial attention for the past several years. Resonating with the national public, this advocacy anticipates the commitment to social portraiture felt so strongly by de Sica and the other neorealists later in the decade. Consider how, in the broadside issued for the premiere of *Ramparts*, de Rochemont and his collaborators characterized their approach to dramatizing the collective mentality of small-town USA as the international situation worsened in 1917:

> Characters in the film are the ordinary people most Americans have for next-door neighbors. . . . In a time of crisis, these people discovered within themselves unsuspected energy, generosity, and courage. Most important was their discovery that as Americans working together with a common will, they could do a job magnificently. To make clear how the destiny of

ordinary people is interwoven with kings and generals, "The Ramparts We Watch" is richly documented with historic newsreels, selected from the priceless and heretofore unreleased collections of the U.S. Signal Corps, the Imperial War Museum in London, and the Archives Cinématographiques in Paris.[49]

This reconstruction of the past was hardly "historical" in the usual sense; as its production proceeded, the film struggled to keep up with a rapidly changing European situation. De Rochemont and his collaborators soon found themselves among the increasing number of their fellow citizens, including and especially President Roosevelt himself, whose support of rearmed and watchful neutrality was weakening. A drastic change in the fortunes of the battlefield suddenly put the United States in more vulnerable long- and short-term positions. In spectacularly rapid fashion, the Wehrmacht had won the Battle of France, receiving the French surrender just the week before the Republic convention, on 22 June. The remnants of the British Expeditionary Force had been rescued by the Royal Navy at Dunkirk, but the army had been forced to abandon most of its equipment. A severely weakened British Empire was at one stroke the only obstacle standing in the path of a German domination of Europe since the Low Countries and much of Scandinavia had by this point fallen into Hitler's hands. Once again American trade with the United Kingdom was threatened, even more severely than it had been during the First World War because the Kriegsmarine, disposing of an impressive fleet of submarines, now occupied French ports. The effect of these events on American politics was immediate. At the Republican convention that same month, the "determination to see Hitler stopped emerged from nowhere," as historian Charles Peters recounts, "to inspire thousands of volunteers whose enthusiasm overwhelmed the political bosses and allowed [Wendell Willkie] to seize the nomination."[50] *Ramparts* was already in production when, against all odds on 28 June, the committed internationalist Willkie became the Republican presidential candidate, providing the final proof that the isolationist moment was passing and prompting both parties to form a united front in opposition to German aggression. The political message of *Ramparts* would be transformed accordingly.

De Rochemont was not the only Hollywood producer moved deeply by the fall of France and the increasing prominence of Willkie as a spokesman for military preparedness to produce a pro-British film. Darryl F. Zanuck, his former boss at Fox, had determined about the same time to go ahead with a project, eventually titled *A Yank in the R.A.F.*, directed by Henry King and released in 1941. As historian Peter Lev outlines, Zanuck, among other Hollywood notables, had in 1940 been summoned to appear before a Senate committee, chaired by D. Worth Clark (D-Idaho), investigating the supposed war-mongering of the film industry on behalf of the British. As it happens, Willkie had been hired by the Motion Pictures Producers and Distributors of America as the legal representative of the studio executives giving testimony, and he was, according to all reports, easily able to demonstrate the insubstantiality of the paranoid theorizing about the interventionist position promoted by senators whose antisemitism was only thinly disguised (international Jewry was goading America into war, or so they affirmed). Films did not then dispose of First Amendment protection (not found to be speech in the U.S. Supreme Court's 1915 *Mutual* decision), so Zanuck was surely brave to assert that filmmakers like him should be able to deal with "the same vital developments which today fill our newspapers, magazines, books, the radio and the stage."[51] Utilizing gun camera footage made available to Fox by the RAF, *Yank* does exactly that, offering American filmgoers something like a running account of the Battle of Britain (including an impressive reconstruction of the Dunkirk evacuation) in addition to a sparkling romance between a photogenic couple, Tyrone Power and Betty Grable (who was able to persuade Zanuck to include one of her signature song-and-dance numbers). The combination of glamorous stars, a romantic subplot (Zanuck himself penned the script), and engagement, decidedly if attractively partisan (handsome young man becomes dashing fighter pilot), with current issues made the film one of the studio's most profitable releases that year. If put in the service of fairly conventional entertainment (the predictable course of the romance dominated screen time), the film's politics were unmistakable, as Zanuck's exemplary "Yank" found himself persuaded by Britain's predicament to take part in the air war that followed quickly upon the Dunkirk evacuation.

Ramparts underwent a quite similar radical remaking in early summer. The film eventually opened in the capital on 30 August. Most interestingly, perhaps, de Rochemont cut substantial portions of the story body of the original version in order to make room for the more than sixteen minutes of captured footage chronicling the German victory over Poland in September 1939 and some staged "German" sequences that improbably announced Hitler's plan to attack the United States once victory in Europe was secured. This new material put a quite different twist on the film's exploration of the national mood in the years preceding the U.S. declaration of war in 1917, which, if in a more shortened form, was still the focus. Now President Wilson's decision to opt for war was presented as the only reasonable option, a measured reaction to German plans to invade (by persuading Mexico to attack in the American Southwest in order to reclaim territory lost in the Mexican Cession). The drastic change in the film's rhetoric and political stance required extensive reshooting, which was accomplished after the team trouped back to location, doubling the original budget of $200,000 or so.[52] Here, indeed, was a film that continued throughout its production to grab from the headlines.[53]

In its final form, *Ramparts* argues the United States should join forces with the British by supplying them with the materials of war in order to thwart the German domination of the continent, and for many of the same reasons that had been relevant two decades earlier. The film's avowed inspiration was Major George

Fielding Eliot's book *The Ramparts We Watch*, in which the famed military analyst, journalist, and radio commentator argued strenuously that the nation should be building up its military in anticipation of coming conflicts with both Japan and Germany that likely could not be avoided.[54] This plea for preparedness was widely read when the book was first published in 1938, even though it did little at that time to change widespread support for isolationism and against any geopolitical moves that might be seen as war-mongering, including the substantial expansion and modernization of American land and air forces that Eliot recommended. Most of the book consists of detailed analyses of the American status of forces, and those of its likely opponents, material that obviously could not be adapted for the screen. But de Rochemont did borrow from Eliot the major's reasoned sense of the dangers America was facing.

What made *Ramparts* important for the subsequent development of engaged, realist filmmaking in the United States, however, is that, in addition to promoting Eliot's views, the film offers a fictional tale of ordinary Americans living in a typical small town (location filming was done in New London, Connecticut), whose lives are caught up in and radically changed by the events, both national and international, that finally led to Wilson's declaration of war. In the manner of a traditional documentary, the film offers sequences of archival footage detailing the outbreak of the European conflict in 1914 and the murderous stalemate that soon developed, along with the launching of submarine warfare against Entente shipping by the Germans and the British naval blockade of German ports, events that deeply affected the United States, which as a nonbelligerent was determined to maintain economic relations with both sides. The meaning of this often rare actuality material, much of which had been unearthed by de Rochemont's researchers, is fixed by authoritative voiceover narration.

But this documentary approach, with its emphasis on notable personalities and public events, was of little use in and of itself in dramatizing the gradual change in public opinion that prepared the way for Wilson's decision to ask Congress to declare war. So de Rochemont hit on the idea of including dramatic enactments in which the views of typical American characters might find expression, even if the fiction in which they were caught up is never developed in the structured manner prescribed by Hollywood screenwriting practice. These vignettes feature a gallery of continuing characters, all played by nonprofessionals. Joe Kovacs, an immigrant from Hungary, receives a draft notice and, feeling an obligation to the country of his birth, returns to fight in the Austro-Hungarian army. His daughter Anna, now needed to help support the family, drops out of school. Neighbors begin to suspect that the Bessingers, who are of German extraction, are sympathetic toward the Central Powers; in an emotional scene, the wife and teenage daughter are prevented from participating in a bandage-making drive meant to resupply the Allies. Walter, son of one of the town's leading citizens, decides to join the Lafayette Escadrille and departs for France. Discussions about the political and moral issues raised by the war erupt throughout the town, especially after the sinking of the *Lusitania* in 1915. Joe is killed fighting in Russia, while the Bessingers' son is refused entry into the U.S. armed forces because his parents are technically enemy aliens. These, and many other short scenes, exemplify the movement in American public opinion toward the declaration of war against Germany, a decision, so the film suggests, that in the end was forced on America by the German declaration of unrestricted submarine warfare in early January 1917 and, several months later, the revelation through the so-called Zimmerman telegram that the Kaiser's government had been seeking a military alliance with Mexico and Japan to invade the American Southwest.

As the filmmakers responded to a rapidly changing situation, *Ramparts* became more of an essay film—and more heterogeneous in the kinds of materials it incorporated. The reedited final version, changed enough to require a second copyrighting, controversially incorporates key sequences from a German propaganda film called *Feuertaufe* (Baptism of Fire), a print of which was captured by the British Royal Navy and then, so it seems, made its way to de Rochemont through his contacts in the Canadian government, which was obviously eager that material that might prove very useful in an anti-Nazi production should be made available to the producer.[55] *Feuertaufe* itself exemplifies the ways in which the war was then transforming international feature film production more generally. Directed for UFA (the most important German producer and distributor of fiction films) by Hans Bertram, who also collaborated on the script, *Feuertaufe* was an elaborate production, with its series of combat scenes of the war in Poland skillfully intercut with authentic footage of Nazi figures, military parades, and various ceremonies, the whole set to an original score of military music. De Rochemont must have admired the skill shown by the filmmakers, who were doing much the same thing he had done for *MOT*, though without resorting, it seems, to substantial fakery of any kind.

In the event, UFA accused Time, Inc. of pirating a commercial release to which they held the copyright and distribution rights. De Rochemont responded, somewhat weakly, that the print he had used constituted the spoils of war and had been obtained not directly from the British, who had captured it, but from the Canadian government, who authorized its being handed over to him for journalistic purposes, which, he argued, were strictly legal. The case might have made for interesting legal arguments about the rights of nonbelligerents, as the Americans were in the summer of 1940, but the issue became moot in December 1941. RKO, which distributed *Ramparts*, was in any case warned by the German government that there would be reprisals, but this threat of course was preempted by the rapidly worsening relationship between the two countries, especially once the Lend Lease Act providing substantial military aid to Britain was signed into law by President Roosevelt in early January 1941. Needless to say, American filmmakers did not customarily find themselves in such international political controversies, but de Rochemont was trying to make a very different kind of commercially released feature.

If *Feuertaufe* is strictly a documentary film, offering significant parallels with de Rochemont's work for *MOT*, Bertram's next contribution to the German war effort, *Kampfgeschwader Lützow* (Battle Squadron Lützow, 1941), which treats the experiences of a "typical" bomber crew during the Polish campaign, offers the same kind of fictionalized realism deployed with such good effect by de Rochemont in *Ramparts*. The melding of documentary stylings with low-key fictional narrative was hardly confined to German and American filmmaking. Consider, for example, British director Harry Watt's *Target for Tonight* (1941), which, like Bertram's very similar chronicle, focuses on a bombing mission. The suspenseful, even harrowing, narrative that sees the crew barely make it back to base after a successful run against an industrial target was carefully scripted, but acted by serving Royal Air Force personnel and filmed in part during an actual nighttime attack. It too is a mixture of actuality and fictional footage, with the sequences filmed during the mission straddling the border between the two forms. The Crown Film Unit was in charge of production, acting for the Ministry of War Information, but commercial distribution was handled by Warner Bros. in both the United Kingdom and the United States. The film was given a special Academy Award and enjoyed a quite successful run at the box office, much as *Ramparts* had done the year before.

Like de Rochemont, Watt had begun his career as a documentarian, working with the justly famed John Grierson and the Empire Marketing Board documentary group on productions such as *Night Mail* (1936) and *North Sea* (1938). Ealing Studios director Charles Crichton, who after the war would achieve a considerable reputation as the director of such films as *The Lavender Hill Mob* (1951), got his start in the business with a similar production, *For Those in Peril on the Sea* (1944). The film details the work of the Air Sea Rescue Unit, recently set up by the RAF, which was eager to promote its effectiveness in rescuing Allied pilots forced to ditch in the English Channel. Sailors and airmen were used in place of professional actors in most roles, and on location shooting around the port of Newhaven in Sussex they lent authenticity to the film's low-key, unglamorized drama. *For Those in Peril* is only one of a number of similarly conceived fictional/documentary films produced by Ealing in order to aid the imperial war effort and remind Britons of their patrimony; consider Crichton's *Painted Boats* (1945), a nostalgia-fueled docu-drama about life on England's inland canals, making use of many of the techniques (including omnipresent narration) used by both de Rochemont and Scottish documentarian John Grierson. The semi-documentary, it is clear, is hardly just a product of the particular conditions of the American industry and the role of journalists like de Rochemont in bringing a new kind of realism to feature filmmaking that remains fictional, but only in part. A certain internationalism is also clearly in play here as these realist forms emerge to fulfill similar propaganda purposes in different national industries. Lines of direct influence are difficult to establish, but the British films mentioned above were all exhibited in the United States and, as mentioned earlier, did not fail to be noticed by American filmmakers, especially Darryl F. Zanuck.

Feuertaufe, to be sure, offers a stern and impressive chronicling of the might of the German war machine, but de Rochemont draws out the more frightening aspects of the Wehrmacht by appending further material meant to establish how the *Blitzkrieg* is an expression of the national will for seemingly unlimited conquest. The style of this footage suggests an origin in yet another Nazi documentary, one substantially more aggressive than that of the only mildly triumphalist *Feuertaufe*, whose narrator strains at times to sound almost conciliatory, explaining the invasion as a preemptive defensive attack against a Polish army that was poised to invade Germany. De Rochemont and company staged these additional sequences, hyping their aggressiveness in order to raise the political temperature of the actuality footage lifted from Bertram's film. These ostensibly German sequences leave no doubt about Hitler's long-term plans for the domination of the continent and the eventual carrying of the fight to North America. A series of images depicts the countries already occupied by the Wehrmacht. The names in this clip are in their customary English forms, leaving little doubt about the actual source of the material. But this is simply one of the absurdities that viewers, carried along by the argument, were not expected to find troubling. An onscreen narrator, apparently delivering his German-language harangue into a radio microphone (an English translation appears in subtitles) issues a stern defiance to the American people, who (once again absurdly) are imagined as the audience for this production. He proclaims that "when we are ready to take the stride into overseas space, we have the means of awakening our friends in America . . . there will be no Wilson rising up to stir up America against us," a none-too-subtle reference to those Americans sympathetic toward Hitler who might prevent America from coming to Britain's assistance, and an interesting hook to the film's earlier sequences in which the former president and his views play a prominent role.

The threat, of course, was not entirely empty. The German-American Bund had on Washington's Birthday 1939 staged a march in New York City that attracted some 20,000 participants and ended with a rally at Madison Square Garden where Fritz Kuhn railed against the man he called "Franklin D. Rosenfeld" and his "Jew deal." Hitler had his admirers in the United States, a number of whom were in high places. De Rochemont answers the charge that America could not produce another Woodrow Wilson by cutting in complementary sequences of footage of both FDR and Willkie talking tough about the nations threatening the world order and proclaiming their joint opposition to isolationism. No matter who wins the election that would follow in November, de Rochemont seems to saying, America will stand strong on the side of Britain. These images of bipartisan solidarity are meant to respond positively to the onscreen narrator's charge that America's so-called "inferior" soldiers could do nothing to stop their fearless, well-trained German counterparts, who were certain, so affirms the narrator, that hostilities with an undisciplined and mongrel populace would quickly end in Aryan triumph.

De Rochemont's inclusion of these genuine and fabricated German materials was not approved universally as *Ramparts* moved through its exhibition runs. Such partisanship was disliked by many who remained determined that the nation maintain its neutrality in the conflict and not be seen as advocating for intervention on the British side; others thought that de Rochemont had turned into a warmonger who was needlessly alarming the public about unlikely threats to their collective safety and well-being. The Pennsylvania Board of Censors, for example, required that the sixteen minutes of this footage be cut from the film if it were to be approved for exhibition in that state, concerned that screening of this material would have a "terrifying effect on the masses," which was, of course, precisely the filmmaker's intention. De Rochemont had offered a free screening of the film for two National Guard units in Reading, Pennsylvania, but this plan was abandoned after the board's decision. A compromise seems eventually to have been reached, as the controversy subsequently dropped out of the news.[56] To those who accused him of terrifying the public and inflaming anti-German opinion, de Rochemont responded that "the thing you are doing is promoting appeasement—surrendering to fear—the most dangerous thing facing America today," making a stronger case for intervention than even Roosevelt had yet dared to advance at this time.[57] Such political engagement, it goes without saying, was highly unusual for a commercial filmmaker to put at the center of a feature film; for a number of very good reasons, the industry generally chose to adopt a low profile with political questions, especially international ones, since advocacy might have adverse consequences for the foreign exhibition of the Hollywood product, a crucial source of revenue.

Ramparts, however, offers a compelling brief. With historical precedent firmly in mind, the narrator argues that America should certainly be on its guard: "A new and greater German war machine is on the march," intones the narrator, with the threat much more dangerous than the ham-fisted attempt of the kaiser's ministers to conclude an alliance with Mexico. This time, however, there was no official document to outline German intentions, only the triumphalism of *Feuertaufe* and the fabricated footage suggesting, if quite improbably, that on German radio a news reader had been so bold as to issue a clear defiance to an America not yet completely convinced of the necessity of engaging the Nazi threat. This hubristic insult to American opinion might have seemed especially unlikely to a careful observer since the Battle of Britain had just begun, with its outcome therefore still very much in doubt. *Feuertaufe* attempts to do much the opposite, proclaiming that even though Germany was forced to go to war against an aggressive Poland, what Hitler wanted was to limit the war and make peace as soon as possible.

Having uncovered and detailed the supposed German threat, *Ramparts* cuts back to New Year's Eve, 1918, dramatizing the town's celebration of the recent victory. The leading citizens of this unnamed community say, with an optimism soon to be sullied, of course, that they are looking forward to a bright future for their country and the world. The Great War is now over, but it has a lesson to teach, or so proclaims the district congressman in his function as toastmaster. He reminds his fellow guests that future generations of the country will be given the duty to "hold the ramparts of our democracy and freedom until kingdom come." A key passage in this speech is a quotation from Wilson's Declaration of War (which, printed in the newspapers, had been shown earlier as enthusiastically received by the townspeople). Wilson's words are meant, of course, to resonate just as meaningfully with the 1940 cinema audience of his fellow countrymen. In an anticipation of his more famous "Fourteen Points" address (delivered on 8 January 1918), Wilson proclaims that we will fight "for democracy, for the right of those who submit to authority to have a voice in their own Governments, for the rights and liberties of small nations, for a universal dominion of right by such a concert of free peoples as shall bring peace and safety to all nations and make the world itself at last free."

Its ideological message stirringly communicated, *Ramparts* concludes with a carefully edited montage of shots of what might best be called national "places of memory": a huge American flag tossed by the wind; the Lexington Minute Man statue; a country church, suitably Protestant in appearance; a vista of the Rocky Mountains; another vista of a mountain stream; and a closing seascape in which the camera eventually locates "Plymouth Rock" and its "1620" carved legend. A solemn choral rendition of the national anthem furnishes the musical accompaniment. This comforting conclusion contrasts strikingly with the film's opening image, a warning siren that fills the screen and lets out a huge wail, bruiting a threat for which, the film has tried to suggest, Americans have a ready and appropriate response.

Bosley Crowther saw *Ramparts* in September 1940 at New York City's Radio City Music Hall, one of the nation's most famous first-run theaters; its booking there testified to the confidence of the producers (Time, Inc. and RKO) and distributors that this was a film audiences would be eager to see. Crowther opines that *Ramparts* was no "entertainment film in the ordinary sense of that word." Instead, it "deals in historical facts as they fall into a grim, dramatic pattern."[58] Though warning viewers that "there has never been a motion picture just like this one," Crowther finds himself so startled by this thoroughgoing reworking of feature film conventions that his review offers only a vague idea of its complex structure, especially the carefully articulated mixture of "real" and fictional footage. The critic, however, was deeply appreciative of the film's rhetoric, acknowledging that "a more provocative or challenging motion picture has not been placed before the public in years—or maybe, on second thought, never [*sic*]."

Journalistic in its intent to offer current news and the most relevant understandings of the rapidly moving international crisis, the film de Rochemont produced could not help but lack some of the sources of pleasure to which Hollywood had long accustomed cinemagoers, even as it issued quite different and, as acceptable box office results showed, successful appeals. Though he concluded that it was a "stirring document," Crowther also thought that *Ramparts* "lacks suspense, that it drags in spots."[59] No fair-minded reviewer would disagree. Like all propaganda films, moreover, *Ramparts* deals in half-truths, in precisely the manner to which Americans would soon become accustomed when, after Pearl Harbor and the German declaration of war, Roosevelt's Office of War Information enlisted Hollywood in the production and dissemination of similarly slanted information in the struggle to maintain national morale. But Crowther only briefly touches on the criticisms at the end of his review, perhaps recognizing that a desire for "suspense" was inappropriate in talking about a straightforwardly historical account of fairly recent events. The facts could always be made more dramatic, displacing (in the Aristotelian fashion usually well exploited by Hollywood) the actual in favor of something more pleasurably plausible, as truth was reshaped the better to arouse and satisfy emotion. And, in fact, a more thoroughly fictionalized version of regrettable international developments, and the threat they posed to America, had been released by Warner Bros. just the year before, creating something of a stir since this film marked the first time that Hollywood had directly confronted the Nazi threat.

Based on the experiences of former FBI agent Leon Turrou (whose publishing of these case files cost him his job with the Bureau), *Confessions of a Nazi Spy* (Anatole Litvak, 1939) focuses on the successful pursuit of a German espionage ring by agent Edward Renard (Edward G. Robinson). With a script written by playwright John Wexley, who, fluent in the language, more or less specialized during the period in German subjects (his most famous script was prepared from a story penned by Bertolt Brecht for Fritz Lang's *Hangmen Also Die* [1943]), the narrative is energized by the kinds of twists and turns, surprises, reversals, and moments of anxious suspense that viewers had come to expect from Hollywood, with the broadly political issues raised by Turrou's story, including the presence in America of large numbers of Nazi sympathizers in the American Midwest, transformed into crowd-pleasing melodrama. The first sequence features an onscreen narrator, seated in dark shadow at a microphone, and (with substantial physical resemblance aiding the effect) actor John Deering sounding and acting just like Walter Winchell, the era's most famous radio commentator and syndicated newspaper columnist—and a well-known interventionist and anti-Nazi. Winchell was an appropriate figure to evoke, if only indirectly, at the beginning of the narrative, which is thus construed in a sense as one of his stories, making Hollywood fiction seem more than a little bit like a journalistic account. Making obvious but vague reference to the Günther Rumrich spy case, whose well-publicized trials had concluded in 1938, the narrator proclaims that "the story brought out at those trials is stranger than fiction," a well-worn if extravagant trope for journalistic storytelling.[60]

But, in contrast to *Ramparts*, this is strictly faux journalism, a series of gestures that, like the would-be Winchell figure shrouded in darkness, vaguely reference an "ontological truth" that hardly shines through, despite the talents of screenwriter Wexley and director Anatole Litvak, both chosen in part because of their familiarity with the German culture so central to the film's portrayal of an immigrant population still attached to the Fatherland. The reason is simple; the "true story" did not obviously redound to the glory of American counterespionage. Unprepared to deal with this kind of national security issue, the FBI bungled the case, allowing the ringleader, Dr. Ignatz Greibl, to flee the country after he passed a polygraph. Catching the steamship *Bremen* out of New York, he returned to Europe in style, there to resume his career as a gynecologist. The film completely rewrites this unsatisfactory conclusion to the affair, as the viewer's righteous anger is satisfied by a conclusion in which a lightly fictionalized Greibl, here portrayed as both the head of the American Nazi Party and a German agent (Paul Lukas), meets with failure and then finds himself turned over to his own people for "liquidation." An FBI misadventure, the responsibility for which went as high as J. Edgar Hoover himself, was transformed into an investigatory and national triumph. If controversial because it attracted the fire of confirmed isolationists, *Confessions* was very successful at the box office even though eighteen foreign countries, including most of Hollywood's biggest customers in South America, banned its exhibition. But when the chief of production at Warners, Hal B. Wallis, was asked by Crowther if *Confessions* might be the start of a trend in "anti-Nazi, pro-democracy pictures," the movie executive gently reminded the reporter that "there is only one type of picture in which we—we at Warners, anyhow—endeavor to specialize, and that is the picture which is interesting and entertaining."[61]

Recognizing that *Confessions* and its anti-Nazi successor at Metro, *The Mortal Storm* (1940), were the kind of pictures "we should have seen about five years ago," Crowther found himself lamenting Hollywood's earlier reluctance to confront the Nazi threat. *Mortal Storm*, he concludes, "throws no new light upon matters of which most informed people have long since been painfully aware . . . is really no more than an inflammatory re-statement of long-known facts." For Crowther, the sad fact is that "Hollywood stood idly by while the mortal storm arose."[62] Implicit in Crowther's critique of the industry, however, is his view that Hollywood should have played a significant role in the evolving national understanding of international events, providing information and dramatically stirring representations of what was going on in Europe, therefore educating its public. And yet he knew quite well that American commercial filmmaking always set its sights on the financial bottom line; as a business, Hollywood was hardly then in a position to do otherwise. Speaking of the heart-wrenching family drama in *Mortal Storm* that could have been screened after the publication of its source novel by Phyllis Bottome in 1938, Crowther's rhetorical question is quite disingenuous: "If it was to be told at all, why wasn't it told then?"[63] Films about the growing Nazi threat could certainly have been made earlier and in a manner that was both "interesting and entertaining," as Wallis might say. Crowther, however, knows the reason why this did not happen: that "so long as European markets were open to any business . . . the American film industry would go no deeper into the most vital and pressing subject."[64]

Significantly, no such charge of stale irrelevance emerges in the critic's judgment of *Ramparts*: "No one can say that it does not recapture a memorable and poignant phase of our national life, that it fails to remind us effectively of our vital heritage," pointing out the "sickening parallel between events in those days and current happenings," and doing so with enough realia footage that it could hardly be dismissed as make-believe, despite the slanting of the truth effected by de Rochemont's German re-creations, which were probably accepted as authentic by most viewers, including Crowther. At the time of the film's release, the *Feuertaufe* sequences depicted events that were only one year old at most, and what they depicted was certainly news to many filmgoers, who might never before have seen photographic evidence of the speedy destruction accomplished by combined-arms lightning war.

De Rochemont was by no means loath to work with the established industry as he began, with *Ramparts*, to enter feature production. Eager to make money like any movie entrepreneur, he wanted his films handled in the customary fashion by commercial distributors and exhibited at the nation's cinemas. Very soon he would enter, much as other independent producers had done and would do, into a multi-picture deal with a major studio, Twentieth Century–Fox, creating a unique partnership with the Reader's Digest Corporation in order to establish a firm base for the series of projected films, each of which would draw on current events. Unlike most other industry players, however, de Rochemont remained committed to an engaged form of essentially journalistic filmmaking, one that like the shorts he had produced for the *MOT* series would provide viewers with information and, as appropriate, promote political or social viewpoints that the very serious-minded de Rochemont favored. As we will see, despite his hopes to transform the industry in part, this essentially journalistic model for feature filmmaking simply could not satisfy for long the public's already well-established taste for an entertainment cinema in which glamour and fantasy played key roles.

Planning for *Ramparts* began with de Rochemont's intent to portray what he considered to be the "less tangible, less comprehensible, but much more vulnerable rampart of our national defense, the mass mind of the American public," as he would confess to Crowther when critic reporter visited the production as shooting progressed.[65] The worsening international situation meant that what we might call the national morale needed strengthening; providing information in the attractive format pioneered in the *MOT* series would not suffice. This was a subject to which a strictly documentary approach, with its carefully calculated interplay between real footage and explanatory commentary, could hardly do sufficient justice. Dramatization through individual if typical characters would be more effective in depicting the change in public attitudes during the chain of events that eventually led to an American declaration of war, including, especially, the conflicts thereby unearthed and explored in a society hitherto united (at least in the view of de Rochemont).

And so the "mass mind of the American public," as he told Crowther, must be both exemplified and anatomized, and this, de Rochemont concluded, could be done only through the dramatic if, strictly speaking, fictional means of conjuring up a typical American small city, whose people could illustrate and exemplify the various issues faced as European war was brought increasingly closer to home. Based in New York rather than Hollywood, de Rochemont searched for a small city not far from the metropolitan area whose "look" had not changed substantially since 1919, deciding eventually on New London, Connecticut, whose downtown and suburban neighborhoods were much the same as they had been in 1913. Interestingly, the filmmakers commissioned a nationwide survey to pick a typical American small city, and the results were reportedly used in the final selection process, which was, of course, also influenced by considerations of convenience and expense. America in a sense was recruited to pick the location that would exemplify its society. If it did not appear as itself in the film, New London was filmed as itself, as Crowther reports: "Twice the main street in New London was decorated with bunting and crowded with costumed extras for a Peace and a Preparedness Day parade. Houses, buildings, and a theatre in the town served as perfect backgrounds, with slight alterations (such as neon signs removed for significant action)."[66] The town, however, was not used simply as a series of backdrops for the fictional sequences or, perhaps better, vignettes since most lasted no more than a minute or two. In order to shoot interiors, de Rochemont set up a temporary studio in New London that also served as his production headquarters.

FIGURE 18 *The Ramparts We Watch* deploys an actual Connecticut community as a typical American small town (frame enlargement).

More interesting, perhaps, given what Rossellini and company were to do a few years later, he involved the townspeople themselves heavily in the project, in part to keep costs down (de Rochemont was the stereotypically penny-pinching New Englander), but also to make sure that the drama would be as authentic as the settings in which it would be staged. There are no professionals in the cast, and the film even omits the usual credit sequences in which roles are identified by their performers. As *Times* reporter Thomas Pryor observes, "A studious effort was made to obtain realism in casting as well as in production."[67] A reported 1,400 local residents were used in the production, with 73 having speaking roles. The part of the elderly German professor torn between residual loyalty to his homeland and a desire to remain faithful to his adopted country is played by a local medical doctor (Alfredo Wyss), while, as Pryor relates, the "roles of a Hungarian housewife and a clergyman are interpreted by real-life counterparts."[68]

While the "actors" were held to a prepared script more or less, de Rochemont provided only limited coaching, emphasizing in this way the naturalness of their performances or, perhaps better, enactments, one again anticipating how neorealist directors would attempt to shape performance as well. These enactments do not conform to the protocols of naturalistic acting in the professional sense, with its emphasis on "getting into character" and the achievement of a smooth delivery that effaces the marks of preparation. This smoothness, somewhat contradictorily, also serves as an earnest of that preparation and ability (for people, as we all know, do not customarily speak without hesitations, uncertainties, and false starts). Fluency is thus a conventional marker of naturalness, but an index of acting ability as well. In *Ramparts*, the townspeople generally speak their lines without any noticeable "interpretation," manifesting a naturalness of a different kind—a sort of antiprofessionalism—that emerges from their correct but somewhat disengaged enunciation of the prepared script, in a manner akin to the "dramatic monotone" that producer Jack Webb, much influenced by the several de Rochemont projects he worked on, adopted for his famous TV series *Dragnet*. Webb's performers were encouraged to read their lines, and for the first time, from a teleprompter as cameras rolled.[69] De Rochemont's crew, though experienced and well trained, were instructed to use, as Pryor reports, "no panning, trucking, or trick shots through the strings of a harp."[70] The film is dominated by a very plain visual style (almost all group medium shots) with little of the formal blocking or framing in the traditional Hollywood manner, enabling easy matches between the documentary and story sequences in which a deemphasis on glamorization dominates (no elaborate costumes, makeup, flattering lighting, or flashy set decoration in the few interior sequences).

The most important element of neorealism, as least for Zavattini, was that its filmmakers demonstrated an "unlimited confidence in things, events, and in men." The reason was simple: "they have been attracted by truth, by the reality which touches us and which we want to know and understand directly and thoroughly." In Italy, Zavattini proclaims with more than a little pride, "there can never be a lack of truth" because "every hour of the day, every place, every person, can be portrayed if they are shown in a manner which reveals and emphasizes the collective elements which continually shape them."[71] Despite Hollywood's postwar domination of the world's cinema screens (especially in Italy, where American films were more popular than the native product), Zavattini suggests that "the Americans are undergoing a crisis; they have no idea what subjects to use," meaning that they have to "use a story" in order to make a film, but this is nothing but "an unconscious means of masking human defeat in the face of reality."[72] We neorealist filmmakers, Zavattini affirms, "work to extricate ourselves from abstractions." This commitment to the contingent and the particular describes equally well de Rochemont's approach to the making of *Ramparts*. To be sure, the film did not result from an "encounter" with the real that, sympathetically analyzed, yielded up its otherwise hidden significance. De Rochemont chose a particular place because it exemplified a more general truth the film was intended to communicate, unfolding in a series of authentically dramatized encounters that effectively illustrate and personalize larger historical trends (such as the growing distrust of German Americans). Working diligently to escape from abstractions through the authentic fabulizing of particulars, de Rochemont found himself committed to a real world whose truth his camera could communicate. In *Ramparts*, there is no story that is a "death scheme" that the filmmaker imposes on a reality emptied of its meaning so that it might serve as the appropriate backdrop for a preconceived drama.

The real is present throughout *Ramparts* in a series of forms melded to shape a convincing kind of truth: in its documentary footage, much of which has been retrieved precisely to serve the filmmaker's purpose, including the serendipity of the recovery of *Feuertaufe*, the film's "incontrovertible" witness to Nazi intentions; in its nonprofessional players, whose rootedness in the community that the film reimagines is entirely authentic; and, most of all, in the place itself, in the location that, as Bosley Crowther argues, is important to the filmmakers not because its "adjuncts" could be used as sets, but rather "the town itself" could be evoked in order to express a generality that was otherwise uncommunicable, for it could only be grasped in the specific textures of the (largely) unreconstructed.[73] If de Rochemont starts with an abstraction (the intention to represent the changing mood of a nation), he finds in his encounter with New London what Zavattini terms "a non-abstract and concrete study of men." In this encounter, as in neorealism, it is place (space both built and natural, including the people who inhabit it) that matters more than anything else. Location shooting is the *sine qua non* that defines the particular qualities of neorealism films (several of which, like *Rome, Open City* and *Germany Year Zero*, draw their titles from the particular spaces in which they are set and where they were in large part filmed). This use of real place is every bit as constitutive of American postwar realist filmmaking as much of its essence. Here, too, is a filmmaking tradition eager to promote the discovery of meaning within a palpable materiality infused with culture, rejecting completely what Zavattini understands as the "superimposition" at the heart of the Hollywood commercial enterprise at large, its subordination of the real to imagination or, perhaps less grandly, to a process of reshaping designed to provide predictably profitable forms of visual and dramatic pleasure.

As an essay film, *Ramparts* would perhaps have been more effective had it offered a more detailed presentation of America's current historical situation as opposed to its concern with dramatizing the collective *mentalité* of a small town of some two decades earlier. At least this was the opinion of George Fielding Eliot, whose endorsement of the film that was in some ways based on his book was not wholehearted:

> When first this picture was planned, it was going to tell more. It was going to tell also the details of our national defense problem of today, as the book does. But as work went on, it became more and more apparent that there was not room in one picture for anything save the message that the story has for them. To add to it, to attempt to explain it, to seek to draw a moral from it, would be an insult to the intelligence and to the patriotism of American audiences. No American who sees it will ever forget it.[74]

The message, as Eliot recognized somewhat to his regret, was in its story, however undramatic and sketchy it might have been, rather than in any dry marshaling of relevant facts. De Rochemont had invented a form that would work with audiences, even if it required some modification to make it more commercial. If de Rochemont's project was, as one of his collaborators, Edgar Anstey, enthused, "the reconstruction of modern history for the screen," then *Ramparts* was a success, even if less in a form that would be commercially viable, and more as a novelty adroitly addressing international politics and domestic policy at an unusual time when these matters were at least of some interest to average filmgoers. Anstey predicted that the film would "have more influence on the development of cinema than any other film of recent years," and that is true enough, if a bit of an exaggeration.[75]

After *Ramparts*

Although the executives at Time were pleased by the film's generally positive notices and the mild controversies it aroused, much as edgy entrants in the *MOT* series had been doing for some years, *Ramparts* was not a hugely profitable project for the company. Thoroughly *sui generis* in its elaborate bricolage of materials from archival sources, as well as in its journalistic openness to continual updating, *Ramparts* did not provide the American film industry with an obviously useful model for reinvention. In order to operate on a very limited budget, de Rochemont had forsworn the use not only of name performers but of professional actors in general. Even if performers had been signed up for the project, they would have found no extended narrative in which to develop even the sort of minimal flat characters that were the staple of industry dramaturgy. The filmmakers disposed of no screenplay as such, though the credits list two writers (Robert L. Richards and Cedric R. Worth) who penned the brief dialogue for its several vignettes. Story construction, if that is the proper term, was minimal at best. As the film's editor Lothar Wolff remarked, "There was really no script when production started. . . . The scenes were usually written the night before."[76] De Rochemont expected the film to be barely profitable if at all, and he was proved correct.

Hollywood's business model was constructed around the glamor provided by attractive performers and impressive production values. The appealing world thus conjured up was then put into intriguing motion by suspenseful, easily readable narrative that was designed to keep viewers glued to their seats and returning regularly to their local theaters for more of the same. De Rochemont had designed *MOT* around a different set of attractions. These editorializing newsreels featured visuals that were compelling because they were current and at least seemed to be, "real," offering news that could be *seen* (which was then still something of a novelty), while viewers were engaged by the dynamic presentation of political, social, and cultural issues in which they were invited, sometimes exhorted to take an interest. With its social realist evocation of small-town American life, its reverential memorialization of key public events (such as Wilson's declaration of war), and its effective blending of rare historical film clips with recent actuality footage, *Ramparts* conforms closely to this well-established pictorial journalism formula. It resembles the customary Hollywood product only in length and in offering something like a fictionalized story world. Moreover, unlike the entertainment turned out by the country's studios, the film was unapologetically political, as critics were quick to note. *Ramparts*, Crowther opined, "emerges as a straight propaganda picture, solemnly bidding the people of this land to gird themselves for defense, bugling America to the alert."[77]

If the professionalism of studio contract players made for performances that, in their apparent casual effortlessness, demanded to be understood as natural, then de Rochemont's amateurs inhabited their characters with an unsmoothness that, so Crowther understood, made for a very different effect, "imparting the illusion of photographed actuality," and so turning a performative deficiency into a representational virtue. But for obvious reasons, the industry could hardly base continuing production on the use of amateur actors. In addition, lacking suspense and poorly paced, *Ramparts* did not make for compelling viewing; spur of the moment story construction had no wider application because it was inclined to be undramatic. Yet the film had its special qualities. Its mission was "to remind us of our vital national heritage," which it accomplishes with an emotional power that Eisenstein might have admired. And, with its "stirring re-creation of an era," *Ramparts* purveys a strong sense of authenticity, creating for viewers the illusion that they were being accorded a privileged view of "the real," which Hollywood storytelling customarily ignored in its profitable purveyance of appealing fantasy.[78]

Ramparts's realistic reconstruction of the not-too-distant past was surely a representational achievement that was worth further exploration by the industry, but even here de Rochemont's approach might not have seemed particularly commercial to most of his contemporaries. The widespread appeal of the film's unembarrassed chauvinism also indicated that the filmmakers had contacted a key element of current viewer taste that might make for box office success, at least as long as the experience of total war encouraged a gung-ho enthusiasm for national institutions and values. However, Hollywood's formula for historical films, so to speak, was for the most part "costumers" that involved an elaborate marshaling of resources to summon up some romanticizable past; even when such films were overtly patriotic (e.g., *Yankee Doodle Dandy* [Michael Curtiz, 1942]), they were not intended to move filmgoers to some particular action. Costumers, moreover, were certainly not customarily graced with the intellectual labor required to explore an era's "structure of feeling," to use the term popularized by critic Raymond Williams. But portraying the lived experience of those inhabiting a particular time and place was the principal focus for de Rochemont, who, as Anstey pointed out, had been interested for years in the "reconstruction of modern history for the screen."[79] Costumers usually did not contain much history of this kind.

As Bosley Crowther recognized, the film could only have assumed the form it did at this certain moment of uncertainty, when international danger was becoming increasingly present but the public might still have opted for a delay in preparing to meet this challenge; in an era of total war, delay could well have made eventual victory unachievable. Its army chased from the continent, Britain might fall either to air assault and then cross-Channel invasion, or to a starvation of vital resources following the destruction of its merchant marine. If that happened, any American invasion force intending to take back Western Europe would have lacked the large, "unsinkable" staging area of the British Isles. German continental hegemony would then likely have been irreversible. With the form and content of *Ramparts* determined for the most part by the peculiar exigencies and opportunities provided by a crisis point in the enlarging global war, it hardly seemed likely that the American industry would be turning out any other films with such an effective mix of historical reconstruction and partisan exhortation.

As the fighting in Europe drew toward the unconditional surrender of enemy forces, de Rochemont was able to interest Fox's Zanuck in the project he initially termed *Now It Can Be Told*, a title and concept that were at first thoroughly journalistic, with the film's promise to reveal the details of a hitherto secret FBI case that involved the bureau's central role in foiling a dangerous threat to national security. Compared to the question of continuing American neutrality anatomized in *Ramparts*, this was a much more straightforwardly documentary subject, with the filmmakers having no political ax to grind beyond the promotion of J. Edgar Hoover's operation and no pressing issue to work over with filmgoers, who were simply called upon to applaud the heroic and indefatigable police work that continues to keep them safe. This material, in fact, was on its face better

FIGURE 19 *The House on 92nd Street* features a sequence depicting FBI director J. Edgar Hoover in full executive mode (frame enlargement).

suited to *MOT* treatment since it need not involve a fictional story at all; de Rochemont had access to surveillance materials, and he could have used interviews with the FBI personnel to whom Hoover gave him direct access in order to fill in the details of the case, with narrative continuity supplied by voiceover, just as he had recently done with *We are the Marines* and *The Fighting Lady*. But *The House on 92nd Street* quickly assumed a more fictional direction once Zanuck saw its commercial potential, which, so he thought, existed in its realist effects and patriotic message. Zanuck showed de Rochemont how to transform a documentary into a fictional film that would be built up around a compelling narrative. As it turned out, such films could be reoriented in part as star vehicles (e.g., Paramount's *Appointment with Danger* [Lewis Allen, 1951], which focuses on Alan Ladd's considerable appeal), but they need not be, providing a low-budget formula particularly suited to Poverty Row producers with no access to A-list performers, and it is in this area of postwar Hollywood production where the semi-documentary most obviously flourished.

The revised script for *House* was penned by a team of writers, including Barré Lyndon, who had the year before produced a suspenseful and exciting version of the Mary Belloc Lowndes novel for John Brahm's *The Lodger*. A strong generic connection to conventional Hollywood production was established by emphasizing the case's crime story elements, with the foiling of the gang's plans providing effective action scenes. The investigation to uncover the ringleader's unknown identity gave the plot a usable enigma, revealing a considerable surprise since the man in question turns out to be a woman who adopts drag as a disguise. In documentary fashion, the offscreen narrator reveals almost at the outset that German espionage never gained a foothold in the United States, so it was up to the narrative to generate the requisite what-happens-next interest. His character having been based only in part on the details of the actual case, a double agent was carefully deployed to meld the two often separate parts of the narrative. Naturally, this FBI plant finds himself in constant danger from his erstwhile colleagues, even as the rounding up of the ring is never in any doubt. Hoover, of course, would never have approved a script that suggested for a minute the bureau was caught off-guard or genuinely challenged by this threat to national security, so only this form of dramatization, often tied to some supposed "true event," with a focus on a sympathetic main character, could be used to generate a narrative whose conclusion would be uncertain. Here was a formula that could be, and soon was, adopted by the industry, as discussed further in the next two chapters.

5

Noir on Location

A Troika of Realist Filmmakers

"Marilyn Monroe and *Niagara*, a raging torrent of emotion that even nature can't control," reads the poster banner, which features a full-size image of the smiling actress, in a skin-tight evening dress reclining across, and visibly dominating, a miniaturized Horseshoe Falls, the rushing water spilling across her ample hips. This Fox production stages its violent drama of marital discord, psychopathology, and self-destructiveness not in some version of the darkly shadowed, rain-swept, and inhospitable urban spaces that had for almost a decade become conventional for crime melodramas of this kind. Almost perversely, perhaps, the film's story unfolds in what had earlier in the century emerged as the best-known of North American honeymooner destinations, the most hallowed place for the celebration of a fundamental social rite: the cementing of the physical bond between husband and wife.

The advertising campaign, however, offers an account of the film that is far from accurate. Despite her startling sex appeal, Monroe's character cannot master the erotic power that the river and its magnificent falls come to represent, and even her innocent and unglamorous brunette other, the "good" woman who plots neither adultery nor spousal murder, barely escapes the dangers posed by this impressive landscape, which are both geographical and metaphorical. As the prominent presence of a sexy femme fatale suggests, Hathaway's film is in many ways thoroughly conventional, treating, if with a somewhat different twist, the destructive illicit triangle first introduced to American filmgoers in Billy Wilder's earlier *Double Indemnity* (1944). During the next decade or so, *Double Indemnity* inspired a cycle of films centering on fatal romance, including *The Strange Love of Martha Ivers* (1946), *Sorry, Wrong Number* (1948), and *Out of the Past* (1947). Along with a steady stream of similar productions, these films were identified by French critics, beginning in 1946, as "dark cinema" or *film noir*, and the cinephiles in Paris noted their kinship with a much-celebrated French series from the 1930s, the poetic realism productions of Marcel Carné, Jean Renoir, Pierre Chenal, and others.[1] Often displaying a modernist interest in the portrayal of troubled subjectivity, the film noir explores an interior reality not previously much depicted in Hollywood films, constructing thereby its own peculiar form of real location, one dependent on what are in some sense antirealist visual stylings and mise-en-scène to reference what cannot be photographed as itself, which is, paradoxically, a realist aim. There's more to say on this in chapter 6.

What is remarkable about *Niagara* is not its competent, if predictable, recycling of a plot and themes that by 1953 had become almost hackneyed. Writing in the *New York Times*, A. W. complained that the filmmakers were dramatizing a story that was "scarcely a tribute to their imaginations," and it is difficult to dispute that judgment.[2] But *Niagara* is much more than a run-of-the-mill crime melodrama, as those in the industry then would have called it. To be sure, the film achieved a certain notoriety for its inventively carnal representation of a young actress named Marilyn Monroe, whose previous roles had only suggested the extraordinary sex appeal she was now carefully coached to display. But the film lays claim on other grounds to a significant place within Hollywood history. Following the formula invented by Louis de Rochemont with *Ramparts*, producer/screenwriter Charles Brackett, Fox studio head Darryl F. Zanuck, and director Henry Hathaway had for the previous five or six years been in the forefront of the accelerating trend in the industry toward location shooting, and it is their collaboration that led to the conception and then successful production of this most unusual film, which interestingly reconfigures noir visual conventions. Brackett's developing interest in a cinematic realism based on the deep exploration of the meaning of place was discussed in chapter 3; it would not be inaccurate to consider *Niagara* a sequel of sorts to both *Sunset Blvd.* and *A Foreign Affair.* While not abandoning a conventional focus on compelling narrative, within the noir series *Niagara* significantly shifts the center of viewer interest toward the exploration of a natural place that had been complexly reconfigured for social purposes. At the time of the film's production, Niagara Falls as a tourist destination was still in a process of transformation, assuming in a rapidly evolving postwar America a hitherto unrealized position of cultural prominence. Thinking of Hollywood films more as entertainment than as either art or social commentary, the *Times* reviewer was not disposed to acknowledge this extended, and at times complex, engagement with place as an aesthetic accomplishment. Reviewers closely connected to the industry were more sensitive to the film's innovatively extensive exploration of a real location. *Variety* appropriately enthused:

> The unusual use of Technicolor in a suspense film and the interesting background of North America's honeymoon haven combine to assure it a good reception in all situations. Plot line has been carefully moved to maintain interest and the natural scenic background is used as part of the story, rather than as an adjunct, to heighten credibility of impact . . . [with the filmmakers] skillfully injecting some sightseeing scenes to maintain

realism while deriving fine scenic interest from the famed locale. . . . The natural phenomena have been magnificently photographed on location by Joe MacDonald. Trip around the cascade via boat, the Horseshoe Scenic Tunnels, and caves around the falls have all been made integral parts of the script.[3]

Henry Hathaway and City Portraiture

Several years before, Henry Hathaway had made a city portrait film that features the re-creation of a true story and, with its extensive evocation of a city, seems a study of sorts for his later work on *Niagara*. *Call Northside 777* (1947), produced by de Rochemont for Fox, explores the seedier sections of Chicago as well as the several institutions of "official" Illinois. The film opens with a brief history of the city that is narrated against impressive panoramic shots of the Loop and downtown newspaper office facades. A number of subsequent, illustrative sequences are staged in the diverse locations where the events re-created in the narrative actually occurred. These include the prison in Stateville with its extraordinary panopticon watchtower, as well as various government buildings in the state capital of Springfield, photographed documentary-style. The realism in *Call Northside 777* depends on a consistent fidelity to its extraordinary story of justice deferred, with the script as scrupulously journalistic as the reporting of newspaperman

FIGURE 20 *Call Northside 777* was shot in a number of real locations in Illinois, including the state penitentiary, which featured a distinctive panopticon central guard tower (frame enlargement).

James McGuire (P. J. McNeal in the film, played by James Stewart), whose crusading efforts result in the freeing of the wrongly convicted Frank Majczek (Wiecek in the film, played by Richard Conte), who was wrongly convicted of a policeman's murder:

> *Time* reported on the case in August 1945 when Majczek was released. After *Reader's Digest* published a story entitled "Tillie Scrubbed On" in December 1946, Twentieth Century–Fox sent producer Otto Lang and writer Leonard Hoffman to Chicago in January 1947 to interview participants and writers connected with the story. In February 1947, Fox purchased from McGuire the rights to an unpublished story and other material concerning Majczek. McGuire subsequently was hired as a technical advisor on the film.[4]

In writing the synopsis of the film to be submitted to the PCA, Fox publicist Harry Brand enthuses, and accurately enough:

> "Call Northside 777" is a true story, lifted right out of the headlines of Chicago newspapers. . . . The millions and millions all over the nation who daily real the details of the real-life story, re-enacted in "Call Northside 777," as it appeared in the newspapers will eagerly await this 20th Century-Fox picture. . . . Henry Hathaway filmed "Call Northside 777" in Chicago and at the Illinois State Prison in Stateville, near Joliet, using actual backgrounds wherever possible and following the story as faithfully as could be done. . . . All the events and characters depicted in it are *not* fictional, and any similarity with actual persons, either living or dead, is intentional.[5]

Here was a feature film that quite self-consciously extended the journalistic life of a story that had captivated millions of readers after the initial run of articles in the *Chicago Tribune* with the subsequent appearance of a *Reader's Digest* version.

De Rochemont had formed a partnership with the magazine (RD-DR Productions) to turn out a series of semi-documentaries either based on (or themselves inspiring) articles in one of the nation's most widely read and admired magazines. Most would be crime-centered in one way or another, but two addressed what de Rochemont identified as pressing cultural issues. The most successful and significant of these was *Lost Boundaries* (Alfred E. Werker, 1949), a ground-breaking treatment of racial prejudice, and the only one of de Rochemont's films to have received due notice from critics.[6] The film centers on the plight of a light-skinned "Negro" couple who, after the father, a doctor, experiences difficult in establishing a practice within the African American community because he is not dark-complected enough, decide to pass for white, which they do for some years, taking up residence in a small New Hampshire town where there are no people of color. De Rochemont's idea to make a film about labor/management relations, with a script prepared by a Harvard Business School professor, was less inspired. Both these films are discussed in the conclusion to this volume.

With its focus on the solving of a criminal case, *Northside* fit more easily into accustomed Hollywood patterns of production, while offering something quite different. Reviewers often praised effusively the film's engagement with the real on a number of levels, hinting that these depictions were more appealing to viewers desiring to see their world represented than the somewhat stale and hackneyed story of a crusading newspaperman whose reporting proves crucial in righting a judicial error. Consider, for example, these comments from the *Hollywood Reporter*:

> Few motion picture formulas have proved so continuously effective as the semi-documentary technique which takes a real-life story and presents it as a straight from the shoulder statement of facts. Drama, then, is enhanced by its accuracy, and emotional strength is drawn from its realism. . . . [It is] difficult to state whether the spectator's interest is held to the greatest degree by the human points involved, or the informative value contained in the actual shots of the Illinois State Penitentiary, the actual operation of an AP wirephoto, or the inner-workings of a large police department.[7]

Call Northside 777 was a sequel designed to capitalize on the interest filmgoers had shown in the portrait of a small Connecticut city (Stamford, standing in for nearby Bridgeport where the events in question took place) in Elia Kazan's *Boomerang* the year before, also produced for de Rochemont at Fox, and based once again on a *Reader's Digest* story. In fact, in an interesting modification of usual industry practice, the studio did not send a synopsis or "treatment" to the PCA office for preliminary evaluation, but rather a copy of the relevant article from the magazine.[8] *Boomerang* was also an investigative thriller based on an actual crime, the murder of a local priest that occurred in 1924 and had subsequently been written up as "The Perfect Case," a reference to the fact that no one was ever brought to justice, which was a source of continuing embarrassment for the authorities in Bridgeport. This is probably why the producers were refused permission for the film to be shot there.[9] A suspect was brought to trial, but he was subsequently acquitted by the efforts of the prosecuting attorney, who became convinced of his innocence as the trial proceeded and undermined his own presentation. It was de Rochemont who brought this unusual material to Zanuck's attention. The script then resulted from a complex collaboration between the author of the original article, Fulton Oursler, Kazan, screenwriter Robert Murphy, and producer Darryl F. Zanuck, who was concerned with heightening the drama of a story that did not reach a conventional conclusion. As in *Ramparts* and *House*, a narrator (the omnipresent Reed Hadley) proclaims the truthfulness and the authenticity of its reenactments, even as he advises that what happened there could have happened in any American small town. As in *Call Northside 777*, the public and private

FIGURE 21 *Boomerang* opens with an impressive panorama shot of its location, here Stamford, Connecticut, standing in for nearby Bridgeport, where the true story the film dramatizes actually occurred (frame enlargement).

institutions of the state collaborate in the provision of justice, exonerating the falsely accused and thereby confirming the impression of civil order created by opening urban panoramas that emphasize the solidity and continuity of city center built space, a standard feature of de Rochemont's semi-documentaries firmly established by *The House on 92nd Street*.

The industry took notice that *Boomerang* was exceptionally invested in authenticity, but, as the *Hollywood Reporter* noted, also represented a "something of a novelty inasmuch as not a foot of the feature was filmed in Hollywood, or in any studio, but all of it on location."[10] De Rochemont's previous film for Fox, *13 Rue Madeleine* (1946), had been largely filmed on the studio lot in Los Angeles, with some location work in French Canada (substituting for the story's "real" locations in both the UK and France). The publicity chief at Fox, Harry Brand, writing copy for its release, made much of the film's authenticity, but, unlike *Boomerang* and *Call Northside 777*, this espionage thriller was by no means a re-creation of an actual series of events in the *MOT* tradition, though it did feature, much like *House*, some fascinatingly detailed filming of actual OSS procedures:

> "13 Rue Madeleine" is a newsdrama of the Office of Strategic Services, for which 20th Century Fox writers have taken facts and fashioned them into a screenplay that is as authentic as this week's newsreel and as exciting

as the most fanciful adventure fiction. The source material was gathered in the vaults of the Bureau of Archives, where the official records of the nation are kept, and used to make a thrilling story of the courageous men and women who worked behind the lines of a shrewd and wary enemy.[11]

De Rochemont had tried to convince Zanuck that authentic locations would have made for a better result, one that would have had more impact on the audience. But the producer rejected his argument, reporting that director Henry Hathaway

> is completely satisfied with the Quebec and Boston locations that he has personally selected. While I appreciate your experience with factual films you must also realize that we have made many location expeditions and we know something of the hazards involved. It is difficult for me to understand your continued refusal to accept our decision on the European trip and I was particularly surprised to learn that you have not personally seen the Quebec locations. . . . I think it is ridiculous to have a producer doing the job of purchasing locations when there are many more important issues at stake. . . . If you decide to accept our production decisions and remain on the picture you should come to the coast at once.[12]

De Rochemont responded immediately in a telegram of his own: "I am more convinced than ever that the realism we are seeking to achieve in London and French sequences can best be obtained by going to Europe," but Zanuck held the purse strings and had his way.[13] *13 Rue Madeleine* turned out to be more of a conventional actioner and less of a breakthrough chronicle of a relatively unexplored aspect of the European war than de Rochemont had intended. The script by two industry professionals, John Monks Jr. and Sy Bartlett, managed to include almost every spy story cliché. Bosley Crowther complained about the production's "drift into full-blown melodrama after a neat 'documentary' approach. . . . The plotting is vague and confused after the boss spy—the hero [James Cagney]—gets going in a peculiarly Anglicized France." De Rochemont, Crowther concluded, "let this one get away."[14]

Boomerang was a different matter since the location involved was within U.S. borders; filming in a Europe still suffering in 1946 from the disastrous aftereffects of the war would have posed a significant challenge, and Zanuck was probably correct in urging the use of plausible substitutes, with Quebec sites offering something of a French/English atmosphere even if sophisticated viewers like Crowther were not fooled. But de Rochemont was zealous in pursuing a locative realism for his productions; he had little patience for the opinions of industry executives, including those like Zanuck who were sympathetic to his approach for very sound reasons. Since breaking into feature film production with *Ramparts* in 1940, de Rochemont had dreamed of establishing the East Coast as a production center to rival Hollywood, with a much different kind of product in mind: films of fact and information that dealt with the most pressing issues of the day (an issue explored further in the conclusion). With such a vision, it made sense for him to form a partnership with the American magazine best known for offering the reading public accessible features that emphasized human and cultural interest rather than either straight news or political comment. RD-DR offices were located in midtown Manhattan's theater district, but this was as close as de Rochemont got to establishing a production center that might rival what the West Coast had to offer. The New Englander gained prominence within the industry only after partnering with Zanuck, who for a few years saw the "film of fact" as a usefully profitable cycle for the studio to exploit, with relatively low-budget productions sold on current interest and realism rather than star power and spectacle.

With its focus on a Chicago that had never before been the focus of an extended filmic portrait, *Call Northside 777* was undoubtedly the most influential of the de Rochemont/Zanuck partnerships in the immediate postwar period. It would quickly be followed by an interesting cycle of more or less realist productions that likewise offered city portraits and followed the same formula, especially the emphasis on location shooting and representational authenticity of different kinds. These included three semi-documentaries: of Los Angeles in *He Walked by Night* (Alfred E. Werker, 1948), produced for Eagle-Lion; of Phenix City, Alabama, in *The Phenix City Story* (Phil Karlson, 1955), produced for Allied Artists; and of New York City in *The Naked City* (Jules Dassin, 1948), produced by Mark Hellinger for Universal. More traditional fictional crime thrillers, such as *Kansas City Confidential* (Phil Karlson, 1952), made for Associated Players and Producers, offered an ersatz version of this locative realism (the film was shot entirely at Samuel Goldwyn studios in Los Angeles, though some publicity falsely claims that some sequences were staged in Tijuana and Guatemala). *Chicago Deadline* (Lewis Allen, 1949) similarly attempted to capitalize directly on *Northside*'s success, but it only gestures at the realism of its model with some brief exteriors shot on location in Chicago. This portrait of yet another newspaper reporter, Ed Adams (Alan Ladd), is thoroughly conventional and lacks documentary stylings. Implausibly, Adams finds himself sidetracked from his official duties into investigating the mysterious death of a young woman, a quest that leads him into fistfights and wisecracking flirtations with glamorous women in bars. The coroner thinks she died of natural causes, but Ed knows better and sets out to solve the case, in the process becoming yet another version of that hard-boiled stereotype, the private detective. Much later, *Chicago Confidential* (Sidney Salkow, 1957) would offer a closer imitation of Hathaway's film, but its story is also right out of the crime melodrama formulary. A district attorney is fooled into successfully prosecuting an innocent man, then sets out to prove him innocent, in the process discovering, with the aid of the innocent man's glamorous girlfriend (Beverly Garland, who plays similar parts in most of these films), that union mobsters were behind the frame-up. Based loosely on fiction penned by an experienced newsman (Jack Lait, former editor of the *New York Daily Mirror*), *Chicago Confidential* also makes effective use of some location shooting, but its engagement with the real and true is minimal at best. Much the same might be said of *New York Confidential* (Russell Rouse, 1955), filmed entirely in Hollywood's Samuel Goldwyn Studios and "located" only by some nondescript stock footage. An "exposé" of the New York rackets, the film is Mafia-lite, centering on themes of gang rivalry and betrayal that had been explored more successfully in the gangster cycle of the early 1930s.

And yet *New York Confidential* was reasonably successful and quickly spawned a sequel of sorts, *New Orleans Uncensored* (William Castle, 1955), which includes some sequences shot, documentary-style, on location in the French Quarter, with a de Rochemont–style prologue dominated by a narrator who offers an interesting sketch of the southern port over a montage of newsreel images, including de rigueur shots of cotton bales. This B-production is less a true story than yet another pot-boiling crime melodrama that lacks the behind-the-scenes accounts of institutional procedures that are featured, to the delight of critics and filmgoers alike, in the de Rochemont films, and their close imitators such as *He Walked by Night*, produced by Brian Foy with the technical assistance of the Los Angeles Police Department. If lacking access to the "inner workings" of law enforcement agencies, such films were limited in the amount of properly documentary sequences they could offer. The realism of this cycle of city confidential films, in which producer Edward Small and director Phil Karlson played prominent roles, is atmospheric at best, with only fleeting attempts to explore the meanings of these quite distinct urban spaces. Because it modifies considerably the journalistic model pioneered by de Rochemont and company, the only entrant meriting further discussion is *The Phenix City Story*, which, based on a series of actual events, was written effectively by Crane Wilbur. In addition to his script work for *He Walked by Night*, Wilbur would later direct three prominent entrants in the prison noir cycle, *Outside the Wall* (1950) and, as previously noted, *Canon City* and *Inside the Walls of Folsom Prison*. The interesting experiments of Wilbur with pictorial journalism are discussed further in chapter 6.

Hathaway's interest in cinematic realism of an authentic kind ran in some ways even more deeply than Wilbur's. He was a lifetime Hollywood professional with decades of experience in the industry, having been introduced to filmmaking as a child, appearing in several Allan Dwan films, but military service in World War I interrupted his acting career. Back from overseas, he reentered the film business behind the camera, working as an assistant director during the last decade of the silent era, often under prominent professionals like Fred Niblo, Victor Fleming, and Josef von Sternberg. Like most directors during the classical studio era, Hathaway labored on disparate projects, not all of his own choosing, but he was arguably most successful in inaugurating with de Rochemont the Fox cycle of noir semi-documentaries. *The House on 92nd Street, 13 Rue Madeleine*, and *Call Northside 777* all focus on stories avowed to be true, even though fictionalized to different degrees and dependent on reenactments. The films divide their attention between the activities of a criminal or enemy underworld (the realm of dramatic fiction featuring professional actors) and those public institutions, including the fourth estate, charged with its surveillance and control, where in large part real people appearing as themselves are shown performing their accustomed duties. Official America is thus depicted always heroically and in authentic actuality footage as well as in true-to-life restagings, mostly, if not always, shot in the actual or suitably real locations. De Rochemont, Zanuck, and J. Edgar Hoover were in enthusiastic agreement about this approach, and Hathaway was an ardent acolyte.

Early in his career, Hathaway had fancied himself something of a documentarian, traveling in India and collecting material for a film on pilgrimage, so it was perhaps appropriate that, as a Fox studio hand mired in ordinary costumers and genre pictures, he lobbied successfully to direct when he read a script that de Rochemont was developing and that eventually became *House*. As he reports in an AFI-sponsored oral history, Zanuck told him one day, "We got Louis de Rochemont here . . . and we don't know whether this type of documentary picture will be interesting to the public." Hathaway immediately volunteered his services: "It was a whole new sort of technology. I was mad about 'The March of Time' . . . and I loved the idea of getting away from the studio, and the FBI interested me as well."[15] Hired to direct, once production began Hathaway found himself filming several sequences guerilla style on the streets of New York, collaring passers-by who wandered into the frame and getting them to sign the required releases. The FBI even provided the filmmakers with a special surveillance van from which they could film street scenes without attracting the attention of startled pedestrians. Accustomed to more conventional methods of obtaining footage (even his horse epic *Lives of the Bengal Lancers* [1935] had been shot in the hills around Los Angeles), Hathaway found the project exhilarating.

House was in part intended to glorify the investigative power of a government institution dominated by its larger-than-life founder and director, J. Edgar Hoover, who appears in an opening sequence to bestow a visual imprimatur on what, so a written prologue avers, is a careful re-creation of an actual event:

> This story is adapted from cases in the espionage files of the Federal Bureau of Investigation. Produced with the F.B.I.'s complete cooperation, it could not be made public until the first atomic bomb was dropped on Japan. The scenes in this picture were photographed in the localities of the incidents depicted—Washington, New York, and their vicinities; wherever possible, in the actual place the original incident occurred. With the exception of the leading players, all F.B.I. personnel in the picture are members of the Federal Bureau of Investigation.

Variety came closer to the truth, promoting to potential exhibitors the film's "exploitation possibilities offered by [its] hook-up with the current atomic bomb publicity. Picture should be one of the sensational grossers of the year. . . . These references were probably added after the pic had been filmed, but studio execs insist they knew during the filming at least in a general way that it was the atomic bomb that was the object of the spy campaign."[16] Hoover had not been pleased by a previously Bureau-sanctioned production, the James Cagney gangster film "*G" Men* (William Keighley, 1935), but he was not especially interested in historical accuracy. Like *Confessions of a Nazi Spy, House* did draw on bureau files dealing with the FBI's discovery and penetration early in the war of a New York–based German spy ring, the so-called Duquesne Case. At the time, the roundup of a considerable number of enemy agents had been a public relations triumph for Hoover and company, not secret in the least, with "perp walks" featured in newsreel segments. Fox executives were speaking with forked tongues about the film; German intelligence was not trying to discover the details of U.S. atomic bomb research, which was just in its beginning stages when the last of Hitler's erstwhile agents were delivered to justice. Hoover was evidently pleased with the positive publicity that the filmmakers provided to the Bureau. In a telegram to de Rochemont, he enthused: "We are all most happy over the developments in connection with your picture of the FBI and I personally appreciate the interest that you and Mr. Zanuck are taking in it."[17]

On other levels, there was a good deal of truth conveyed by the film. *House* was indeed mostly shot in the locations where the events in question had taken place, and in the sequences that detail bureau operations current FBI personnel were in fact used, not Hollywood professionals. Hoover also dispatched "technical advisors" to Hathaway and de Rochemont, eager that the film should reflect well on the Bureau's effectiveness in thwarting a significant national threat. As producer, de Rochemont had earlier shopped the project to MGM, where it received a sympathetic reading from staffer Phillipe de Lacey, who perceptively identified what made it attractive. MGM passed, but de Rochemont must have been cheered to learn that an industry insider recognized the commercial value of the particular forms of realism at its core (in story, incorporation of newsreel materials, and on-location reenactments):

It is only in the manner of presentation that a story and screenplay such as this will rise above the ordinary and run of the mill crime motion pictures. The audience must be made to believe at every instant that what they are seeing on the screen is true; they must be almost deluded for the time they are in the theatre into thinking that a camera just happened to be there, to record this amazing story of espionage. This is the core of the technique that should be used, and there is only one man in Hollywood today who understands, and can create this illusion. For this reason, I personally strongly advise that the director of this picture be Louis de Rochemont. . . . The use of actual backgrounds and locations should be encouraged and utilized as much as is practical technically. Only in scenes with much dialogue do I think it necessary to build sets. Those sets that are built should be exact duplicates to the minutest detail of some true location. . . . The camera work on this picture is probably the most important element in creating a sense of reality. It should at no time have the Hollywood over-polished, back-lighted, effect-ridden camera work.[18]

What Lacey did not mention was the crucial innovation that *House* represented, as the semi-documentary form was melded to the spy thriller, one of the several strains of crime narrative then developing into what would later become known as film noir, all of which would in time be grist to the semi-documentary mill. He did, of course, appreciate the appeal of the kind of realism it would offer filmgoers, realizing that, at least in large measure, it would depend on the sophisticated manufacture of "illusion."

The irony of this celebration of FBI competence in preventing the supposed theft of atomic secrets is that the wall of security surrounding the Manhattan Project, with work also being done in both Canada and Great Britain, had indeed been breached, but by Soviet rather than by German agents. De Rochemont would not be involved, but Fox would not long afterward commission another semi-documentary to deal with this disturbing betrayal, *The Iron Curtain* (William Wellman, 1948). While acknowledging the success of Soviet espionage, this film features a domestic morale-building reversal in dramatizing how a Russian embassy official posted to Ottawa, Igor Gouzenko (Dana Andrews), becomes enthralled by Western prosperity and freedom and disenchanted by the lies he has been told by his own people. He turns traitor to help foil the continuing espionage efforts of his erstwhile countrymen as some who were involved in the theft of atomic secrets are identified, tried, and imprisoned. Many sequences were shot in the Ottawa area where the events in question took place, and, in the manner of many Fox semi-documentaries produced under Zanuck's oversight, the script was based on a nonfiction source, in this case Gouzenko's several sensational magazine articles detailing his experiences. (Gouzenko would compile these in a book, *The Iron Curtain: Inside Stalin's Spy Ring*, that was timed for publication in conjunction with the film's initial release.)[19]

Partly fictionalizing actual events to produce a cinematically appealing story may well be morally problematic; the promotion of misinformation masquerading as the truth is exactly what journalists are expected not to do, and it was certainly not the practice of *MOT*. *The Iron Curtain* stays closer than *House* to actual events; those involved in this later project determined that the main facts of the case, their dramatic value carefully heightened, constituted a hook current enough to appeal to audiences. *Variety* enthused: "William A. Wellman's direction carries out documentary technique, pointing up factual material and dramatic values by never permitting a scene to be overplayed. Stress on underplaying and the absence of obvious meller tricks goes a long way in adding to realistic air with which the film is imbued."[20] By the time that *Iron Curtain* was being produced, Zanuck and company had learned their lesson about implausibilities, one both notable and far from unnoticed being the climactic sequence of *13 Rue Madeleine*, where James Cagney's OSS agent is killed in his Gestapo prison cell before undergoing torture that might have forced him to divulge vital information. An American bombing run called in especially for the purpose does the job, wiping out the reptilian double agent (Richard Conte) in the process along with his Neanderthalish minions. In a moment of *in extremis* hilarity that seems in retrospect a study for his over-the-top death scene in *White Heat* (1949), Cagney roars with laughter as the bombs explode and the building tumbles in ruins around him. At the end of this semi-documentary, there was plenty of "overplaying," and the "realist air" present in the impressive early sequences of the film had vanished altogether, flaws that Wellman would carefully avoid. An overabundance of what Zanuck characteristically termed hokum was found also in the closing sequence of *House*. A raid on the residence that furnishes the film with its title climaxes in the revelation that the ringleader the FBI had been seeking is actually a woman who goes about "his" business in male drag, a plot twist that Hathaway confesses was Zanuck's gimmicky idea.[21] In neither *Madeleine* nor *House*, however, did these excesses hurt box office, but they were generally avoided in the later Fox entrants in the cycle, whose entertainment elements were more restrained and documentary values heightened.

Compared to *Madeleine, House* is a plainer production, more de Rochemont and less Zanuck. Less invested than *Curtain* in either affecting melodrama (provided by A-list players like Andrews and costar Gene Tierney) or the accurate re-creation of events, *House* features an extensive repertoire of documentary materials, including newsreel clips and footage recording the surreptitious FBI surveillance of the German spies. There are no headlining stars (supporting performers Lloyd Nolan and Signe Hasso are the only "names" in the cast), and Hathaway takes a generally deglamorized approach (no romance, but plenty of gritty locations). Zanuck told distributors that they were to sell the mysterious house featured in the new title he had crafted for the film. Hathaway reports what took place at a pre-release marketing meeting: "He turns around to the guys and he says: 'This is an extraordinary movie, boys . . . this is one of the pictures we're going to sell on a gimmick. Every bit of advertising will be on the mystery of 'What is the house on 92nd Street?'"[22] Thomas Pryor proclaimed in his *New York Times* review that "Louis de Rochemont, the producer, and his director, Henry Hathaway, have achieved a most successful blending of the documentary and conventional techniques, thus proving that realism can be entertaining, too."[23] Studio head Spyros Skouras was more than pleased by the reaction of the preview audience, as he reported in a telegram to Zanuck:

> Just this minute returned from packed projection room screening house ninety second street. Audience was actually jumping in their seats and emerged breathless from dynamically dramatic impact of the picture. Action of this picture is like machinegun jampacked with suspense and

dramatic realism that is practically hypnotic. LOUIS DE ROCHEMONT AND
HENRY HATHAWAY have made what probably will be looked upon as the
top picture of its kind and William Eythe Lloyd Nolan and all other members of the cast acted with such sincerity and naturalness as seldom before
seen. It's a whopper!![24]

Critics were as enthusiastic as Skouras, and they appreciated the reconfiguration
of the *MOT* formula to suit Hollywood's dramatic requirements. In a canny assessment of the film's supposed facticity, *Variety* observed: "Twentieth-Fox, employ-
ing somewhat the technique of The March of Time, has parlayed the latter with
facilities and files of the FBI in arriving at The House on 92nd Street. It doesn't
matter much whether it's east or west 92nd—the result is an absorbing documentation that's frequently heavily-steeped melodrama."[25]

Darryl F. Zanuck

Zanuck took credit for the film's critical and commercial success, the latter coming in at $2.5 million in domestic rentals. This made what had been a very low
budget ($400,000) production extraordinarily profitable, in fact the studio's best
earner that year, and as a result it established a production cycle that the studio,
unable to rely on star vehicles for the bulk of its projects, would continue to
promote.[26] In his early career, while supervisor of production for Warner Bros.,
Zanuck had showed a strong interest in what film historian Peter Lev calls projects
that were "convincingly grounded in contemporary reality," a series that became
a kind of studio specialty. The most famous of these was *I Am a Fugitive from a
Chain Gang* (1932), based on a true story that had been a journalistic sensation and
offering a biting exposé of the Georgia penal system.[27] At Fox, Zanuck was at least
in large part responsible for what Lev terms that studio's "broad tendency toward
social realism" in the decade and a half or so after the war, including the cycle of
noirish semi-documentaries as well as a series of problem films such as *Gentleman's Agreement* (1947) and *No Way Out* (1950). Though a strongly pro-business
Republican, Zanuck, as Lev points out, "at times . . . showed a populist streak
and a strongly developed sense of injustice, and in the late 1940s his populism
seemed to dovetail with the needs of the audience." He would sponsor a kind of
"vaguely leftist filmmaking," including, as we will see, the work of more committed left-leaning directors such as Kazan and Jules Dassin, but only, Lev cautions,
"as long as the public was receptive."[28] Screenwriter Philip Dunne remembers a
Zanuck who was no ideologue, but very concerned with fairness in the treatment
of political subjects:

> I think he always knew that the pregnant issues were going to be liberal
> issues, unpopular, to some extent. He was interested in a good story with
> good news value. Now, you see, at the very time that he was fighting the

[Screenwriters] Guild, we made *How Green Was My Valley*. Which, after all, was a very powerful statement in behalf of labor organizations. We talked about it very frankly. He'd grin at me and say, "You've got your propaganda there." "You want to throw it out?" I said. "No, no," he said, "Leave it alone, but express both sides."[29]

Also a Republican by inclination and temperament, de Rochemont held political views before the war and after that were "vaguely leftist," as Fielding, his most careful chronicler, observes:

> Louis himself could not by the wildest stretch of the imagination have been considered part of any left-wing persuasion. And yet, the films that he created were more consistently liberal, progressive, and militantly anti-fascist at a time when it took courage to attack "prematurely" the totalitarian adventures then under way in Germany, Italy, Spain, and Japan. His films were critical, though somewhat less vigorous in their treatment of Soviet communism. . . . His films consistently championed the racially oppressed and doggedly exposed theater audiences to the emerging horrors of anti-Jewish persecution and genocide.[30]

Sympatico politically even if holding very different views about what commercial filmmaking should be, the two enjoyed an interesting partnership during the first years of the postwar era.

Hathaway was arguably the most successful of the filmmakers at Fox who were called upon by Zanuck to make "factual" films, many of which dealt with World War II and the Cold War that soon followed. Other directors, however, were pressed into service and achieved some notable success with this genre, including that most famous of Hollywood's *literati*, Joseph L. Mankiewicz, whose two thrillers for Fox made extensive use of authentic locations: *Escape* (1948), which, as A. W. was pleased to note in his *New York Times* review, was "filmed in England against the background of moors and the lush, rural countryside," the location in question being the wilderness areas and village near Dartmoor prison; and *Five Fingers* (1952), with a number of sequences set in various locations in Istanbul and Ankara, of which more below.[31] Like Mankiewicz, whose reputation today rests more on his success with stagey films such as *All About Eve* (1950) and *Sleuth* (1972), Anatole Litvak arguably did his best work in intimate dramas like *All This and Heaven Too* (1940) and *Sorry, Wrong Number* (1948). But he also became part of the realist movement at the studio, directing in 1948 one of the era's most famous social problem films, *The Snake Pit* (1948), a dramatization of life in a mental hospital, many of whose sequences were filmed on location at the Camarillo State Mental Hospital in California. *The Snake Pit* made good use of extensive, painstaking research into the treatment of the mentally ill.

Litvak also directed *Decision Before Dawn* (1951), a sequel of sorts at Fox to *The Big Lift*, and one of the most important of the American films that were filmed in and depict a devastated and defeated Germany that would soon become, because of the tangled politics of the immediate postwar era, a staunch ally in the Cold War confrontation with the Soviet Union and the Eastern Bloc. The *Reader's Digest* condensed version of George Howe's *Call It Treason* (1949) had aroused a great deal of interest in the lightly fictionalized experiences of a German POW who agrees to spy on his own country during the last days of World War II, and Zanuck eagerly bought the rights to the book, though the resulting production would not involve de Rochemont. Like *The Big Lift* and several other Zanuck films, *Decision* bore a kind of institutional imprimatur, having been made with official cooperation, as an opening title proclaims: "This motion picture was filmed in its entirety in Europe, where the story actually took place. 20th Century–Fox expresses its appreciation to the United States Army, Navy, and Air Force, as well as to the Armed Forces of France, without whose generous cooperation this film could not have been made." If *Decision* is then arguably official in some important ways, it is also authentic, as a further title proclaims with the sly directedness of a brief commentary in the tradition of the *MOT*: "This story is true—the names of the people have been changed to protect those who survived, but the basic incidents took place only a few years ago in these same ruins, left as tragic reminders of the regime which brought suffering to the world and destruction to its own country." Making use of locations in Wurzburg, Mannheim, and Nuremberg, *Decision* featured haunting images of German cities reduced to shattered buildings and piles of bricks, constituting alone with several other U.S. productions (*The Big Lift, The Search, The Devil Makes Three, Berlin Express*, and *A Foreign Affair*) a cycle of films featuring the same landscape as the most notable production trend of the newly reconstituted German cinema, the *Trümmerfilme* or "rubble films."[32]

Zanuck's proudest achievement as producer (working with a team of directors) was *The Longest Day* (1962), an epic reenactment of the 1944 D-Day invasion of Normandy. Important sequences of the film were staged at the locations where the events took place (including Pointe du Hoc, Sainte-Mère-Église, and Bénouville). The film even featured several original members of the Allied and German forces as cast members (including one of the Rangers who repeated his feat of scaling the sheer cliffs to spike German guns at Pointe du Hoc). Zanuck was never a man to slight his own considerable accomplishments in managing a production that required teams of directors and screenwriters, in addition to a huge cast of Hollywood and foreign stars in cameo performances. But, given the huge efforts made to make the film both truthful and realistic, he may be forgiven perhaps for boasting that his invasion was logistically more difficult than the operation directed by Supreme Allied Commander General Dwight D. Eisenhower, who, in Zanuck's words, at least "had the men and . . . the equipment. I had to find both." As Cornelius Ryan, the author of the nonfiction account on which the film was based, observed, no film will ever again match the impeccable realism of the Zanuck production, which made use of period equipment—including the two light cruisers USS *Springfield* and *Little Rock*—that would never again be available.[33] Steven Spielberg's *Saving Private Ryan* (1998), while offering compelling, even horrifying reenactments of the same campaign, seems realistic, but hardly authentic in comparison. His "Omaha Beach" was scouted out and carefully constructed in County Wexford, Ireland, while other action scenes in the film were shot near Hatfield, Oxfordshire (where the "town" of Ramelle was built as an elaborate set, like David Lean's "Aqaba" in *Lawrence of Arabia*). Even Ma Ryan's farmhouse was actually an exterior constructed in Wiltshire, England, not on the great American prairie where this sequence was ostensibly set. *Saving Private Ryan*'s present-day frame was the only sequence shot in France and at the actual site, the American military cemetery at Pointe du Hoc, one of the nation's most significant places of memory and impossible for many reasons to fake in any way. Even though expediencies and limitations of various kinds forced him to use soundstage "exteriors" for some of the sequences of *The Longest Day*, Zanuck was certainly more invested and interested in providing a sense of authenticity by making creative use of the relevant realia, including actual sites and "participants," both human and material.

As he admitted in an interoffice memo, Zanuck became intrigued by the possibilities of fact-based filmmaking when he first met in 1944 with de Rochemont and decided to distribute the two armed forces documentaries designed for wartime morale-building that he had made. Eager to make the move into more mainstream fiction filmmaking, de Rochemont brought Zanuck the initial treatment for the film that would eventually become *House*. As initially conceived, this "true" story (much of the script was fictional or fictionalized) would have been undramatic, or so Zanuck thought. He saw little in the way of commercial possibilities for a film without "a vital personal story and characters whom we understand and appreciate." Documentary and fictional elements should be melded, Zanuck advised, with the resulting mix more similar to the standard Hollywood product than de Rochemont had initially imagined. Every scene, however realistic it might be, must also have "movement and drama," requiring the casting of qualified, talented performers in featured roles calculated to encourage viewer identification. Only when de Rochemont agreed to combine his "factual technique" with what Zanuck defined as "factual dramatization" was the project greenlighted.[34] This "blending of fact and drama" made for what the studio head insisted was a "vital" formula, and it was one that Fox, occasionally imitated by others in Hollywood, would exploit throughout the 1940s and 1950s. As Zanuck wrote to de Rochemont early in their collaboration on *House*:

> One thing I do know is that there is no money or reward in factual pictures
> of this type unless they are produced with every box office ingredient and
> trick you can find. . . . The FBI is old hat as far as exploitation is concerned. . . .
> I am in favor of using actual locales wherever we possibly can, and in going

for realism, but when it comes to box office there is no use in kidding ourselves. The factual pictures have consistently failed. *Desert Victory* [Roy Boulting (1943), a straightforward documentary sponsored by the British Office of War Information] was the biggest hit, and it grossed in this country less than $500,000. While *Roger Touhy, Gangster* [Robert Florey (1944), a biopic with some interesting location sequences] was a cheap, lousy picture but had a couple of box office personalities, it will gross domestically no less than $750,000. It is already at $600,000.[35]

In a memo about another World War II drama, also based on a true story, which would eventually be released as *Five Fingers*, Zanuck discussed the uses of authenticity for encouraging spectator belief and engagement. As noted earlier, the Fox director in this case was Joseph L. Mankiewicz, who would supply, working with a script by Michael Wilson, the requisite sophistication. Bosley Crowther recognized that *Five Fingers* was an effective entrant in the then-current cycle of realist dramas because it offered a true story whose important exteriors were shot at the very locations where the events in question took place. But, as he noted, the film's considerable box office success depended as well on its well-written script and Mankiewicz's directorial finesse. In short, the production's careful cultivation of authenticity was important, but not sufficient to its audience appeal:

> To be sure, what IS added to the relish of this spicy adventure that is played in a particularly suave and crafty manner by James Mason in the central spy role is the fact that the story of it is almost a literal account of a fantastic piece of spy work that was accomplished in Ankara, Turkey, in 1944. . . . A good deal more has been added by Mr. Mankiewicz and Michael Wilson, who wrote the script. And it is this good deal more, including a wonderfully smooth and urbane romance between our man and a Polish ex-countess, played by Danielle Darrieux, that rounds out a racy melodrama into a meaty, full-flavored adventure tale. As was demonstrated by his direction of "All About Eve," Mr. Mankiewicz is much more distinguished as a "dialogue" than an "action man," and his pre-eminence at conversational staging is again made evident here.[36]

Zanuck must have been very pleased to see confirmed by one of the nation's most influential critics his thoughts about how to make an audience-pleasing realist drama. As he pontificated in an interoffice memo:

> The great value of any semi-documentary picture . . . lies in the fact that while the story need not be true in every case, it must be presented in such a way that the audience *thinks* the whole story is true. This is . . . something you simply must have. . . . You can dramatize and take certain liberties and licenses as we did . . . provided you start out with a convincing opening.

If you start out with a feeling of authenticity you immediately have the
audience on your side and they tell themselves that while this seems an
incredible story, it must be true.[37]

Location shooting in Turkey furnished the filmmakers with opening and extended
chase sequences that lent *Five Fingers*, much of it filmed on a studio soundstage, a
palpably authentic feel; these included some very unusual boating scenes shot on
the Golden Horn. As Zanuck was well aware, *Five Fingers* remained only generally
true to its source, bending the facts, for example, by having the Mason character
discover that German agents paid him counterfeit money for his photographs of
secret British documents. This ironic reversal was thought to be needed in order
to provide the requisite sense of poetic justice (in 1952 the Production Code was
still very much in force in Hollywood).[38] It was also Zanuck's decision, or at least
so he reports, to make the German spy played by Mason the main character, with
his link to the equally ethically challenged Polish countess played by Danielle
Darrieux providing the dramatic and romantic interplay that Crowther found
"smooth" and "urbane."

Box office returns for the cycle of realist films produced at Fox and, more spo-
radically, by others in Hollywood proved Zanuck correct, at least until audiences
tired of those serious political and social realities for which four years of total war
had given them a taste. In 1946, a big box office year from Hollywood in general,
only the studio's musicals earned more than the relatively low-budget *House*. But
just a few years later, in early 1950, Zanuck already sensed that the public no longer had any enthusiasm for realist productions that were "downbeat in nature, or
deal[t] with sordid backgrounds, unsympathetic characters and over-emphasized
'suffering,'" especially if that suffering was connected to some current social problem, as in Fred Zinnemann's *The Men*, which focused on the problematic recovery and social reintegration of paraplegic veterans. It was, of course, produced
by a powerful rival producer who was also committed to making films drawing
their material from current headlines, particularly themes connected to the war:
Stanley Kramer, releasing through United Artists.[39]

Kramer was as enamored of realist dramas as Zanuck, committed to an artistically and politically engaged form of filmmaking. When he died in 2002 after a
long and illustrious career, he was remembered as "a passionate Wunderkind . . .
eager to shake up the status quo with a string of socially conscious films in the
early 1950's that raised many of the issues . . . that mainstream film companies
were often too timid to explore."[40] Among other Kramer productions whose
narratives reflect current events, consider *The Juggler* (Edward Dmytryk, 1953),
a film that is largely now forgotten but was one of the first features to be shot
on location in the recently constituted state of Israel, providing many American
filmgoers with their first views of a country then very much in the news. Unlike
other Hollywood productions of the period (most notably Otto Preminger's
Exodus [1960]), Kramer's film does not melodramatize the obvious political themes,

opting instead to push continuing conflict with the country's Arab neighbors to the margins. A filmmaker of considerable intellectual sophistication and deeply held liberal beliefs, Kramer refuses to provide a simple-minded public relations promotion for the experiment in the founding of a Jewish homeland. Instead, his film deals with the chaos, personal and national, that attended the end of war, making it possible for Israel to emerge from the partitioning of Palestine (mandated by the just-founded United Nations).

But what of those who fled there, leaving behind the only identity they had ever possessed? *The Juggler* focuses on the emigration to Israel of an assimilated German Jew with the very Aryan stage name of Hans Müller (Kirk Douglas), a vaudeville performer once famous throughout Europe and much honored especially in the land of his birth, where, so he recalls, little children would tell him that he was their idol. Comfortable in his Germanness, Müller could not convince himself that Hitler's ascension to power, and the promulgation of anti-Jewish legislation that quickly followed, should mean disaster for someone as privileged as he felt himself to be. He delayed for too long his departure from the country, which he had the means to accomplish with ease and thus doomed his family to destruction at the hands of a once-benevolent state. Never having abandoned this sense of self, Müller seems thoroughly *stadtlos*, feeling that he belongs nowhere and that nowhere belongs to him. He thus finds himself living out that most dehumanizing of antisemitic stereotypes in a nightmare version of the "Jewish question" as formulated by Zionist polemicist Theodor Herzl. Müller is a man without a country trapped by his feelings of estrangement from the place that has welcomed him "home," having not yet thoroughly abjured the culture that made him a pariah and sought his death, a fate from which only good luck has saved him. Quick-tempered, mistrustful, easily rattled, but possessed of considerable strength, Müller is a danger to himself and others. He strikes out against authority of every kind, including the Israeli policeman who simply asks to see his identity card and is then kicked into unconsciousness. Confused and terrified, Müller runs away from the scene, and only after a pointless flight to nowhere through the countryside does he begin to trust again. Befriended by a young boy and a young woman, Ya'El (Milly Vitale), he allows them to help him adjust to a world that once made sense and is only just beginning to seem a safe and rational place once again. The Michael Blankfort novel that is the film's source hints at the religious source of Müller's acceptance of grace (no criminal charges will be filed for his attack on the policeman); Ya'El, it is revealed, means "the strength of God." Despite this flavoring of religious allegory, the film remains thoroughly grounded in its authentically detailed portrayal of Müller's discontent and the unique location (a land of strangers welcoming other strangers) in which it might be relieved through a process of self-reclamation whose contours are only hinted at, not rushed toward some faux conclusion.

An unusual film that dares to take on a legacy of the war not so easily dramatized, *The Juggler* follows its source in providing Müller with a love interest,

but thoroughly eschews Hollywood glamour and the easy pleasures of suspenseful narrative in favor of anatomizing the foundational spirituality of a reborn
Holy Land. Bosley Crowther observed that "it offers a fast and fascinating journey
through modern Israel, in addition to an intriguing and often touching study
of a man."[41] Despite these virtues, the film did only limited business at the box
office; its reception from American audiences was just as disappointing as that of
Kramer's *The Sniper* (1952, also directed by Dmytryk), one of the better noir semi-
documentaries, which featured extensive on-location shooting in San Francisco
and five years earlier would likely have drawn larger crowds. Like *The Juggler*,
The Sniper dramatized the working out of a psychopathology across an urban environment photographed in detail (here a misogyny that leads a desperately lonely
young man to start shooting women he picks out at random in the city until he is
hunted down by the police).

By the early 1950s, in an era of solid economic prosperity and growing amnesia about global conflict and its aftermath, it became apparent that American
cinema's realist moment had begun to wane, interestingly enough at just about
the same time that neorealism was also running its course, domestically and
internationally. Most historians would date the end of that cycle with the release
of Vittorio de Sica's *Umberto D* (1952), which was screened in the United States
only toward the end of 1955 because its producers felt it would no longer appeal
to U.S. tastes, as Zanuck had predicted. Bosley Crowther is surely correct in suggesting that "the merchants obviously were anxious about the market for such a
film." The reason was not far to seek:

> It is an utterly heartbreaking picture, almost from the word go. The plight
> and destiny of the aging hero, who has only a mongrel dog and the casual
> friendship of a rooming-house slavey to comfort his loneliness, are plainly
> without prospect or hope. The only thing that could save the old gentle-
> man is a happy contrivance of some sort. And this you may be sure that
> Signor De Sica, with his uncompromising integrity, will not invent.[42]

Uncompromising integrity or not, de Sica soon tried to reconcile himself to the
current taste for entertainment pictures, with his next important project being
Stazione Termini (U.S. title: *Indiscretion of an American Wife*, 1953), a tragic romance
starring Jennifer Jones and Montgomery Clift that also seems to have been too
downbeat for American tastes. It too bombed at the U.S. box office, even in a
considerably reedited and Hollywoodized version.

Niagara: A Different Kind of Realism

A new direction for locative realism was needed, and Charles Brackett at Fox hit
on a concept that, while not easily repeatable, was found more appealing by the
era's filmgoers. The project eventually titled simply *Niagara* would certainly not

be "heartbreaking," and it earned $2.35 million in its U.S. release, proving to be one of the studio's most profitable films that year.[43] Reading the marketplace correctly, Hathaway, Brackett, and Zanuck would avoid the twin traps of sordidness and preachiness by devising a melodramatic frame to contain the noir bleakness of the tragic story at its center and by injecting it with healthy doses of suspense. These entertainment qualities, however, do not in the least detract from how the film deeply engages with contemporary American culture, in the manner of worldwide postwar realist films. To be sure, no social problem is at issue, nor does the film comment on or analyze national institutions. It also refuses an engagement with history, broadly speaking, even though a traumatized Korean War veteran is one of the main characters.

Niagara is no semi-documentary either because, unlike *House* and the other entrants in that cycle, it does not use its real locations to restage the events of a story that is in some sense true, but rather to lend its fiction the sense of authenticity that Zanuck considered important to gaining and retaining audience interest. Instead of relying on newsreel footage to provide background and context, its meaning fixed by authoritative voiceover narration, *Niagara* is more oriented toward standard forms of fictional narrative construction, with interlocking character arcs, reversals, and a crosscutting, suspenseful finale in the style pioneered by D. W. Griffith. The film's success depended also on its canny promotion of Marilyn Monroe in what was intended to be at first a supporting role as the villain of the piece. Her part was expanded after Anne Baxter declined the female lead, to be replaced by the lesser-known Jean Peters. In a sense, with its focus now shifted toward a sexy rising star, *Niagara* marked a return to the studio past and, in particular, to the successful formula Zanuck hit on with *A Yank in the R.A.F.* (1941), a film that not only made the pro-intervention political point Zanuck was committed to promoting, but firmly established relative newcomer Betty Grable as a bankable performer. Within two years, she had become the studio's biggest moneymaker, featured in a number of highly profitable musical comedies. *Niagara* did much the same for Marilyn Monroe, who provided *Niagara* with a sexy glamour otherwise entirely absent from most realist productions. Hathaway's work with producer and cowriter Brackett could hardly be more different from the more journalistic filmmaking he had practiced with de Rochemont. In a gesture toward entertainment value and the drama that Zanuck thought necessary to audience engagement, *Call Northside 777* dutifully provides James Stewart with a supportive wife (played by the unknown Helen Walker). This character proves useful as the reporter works through his doubts about the imprisoned man's innocence, but otherwise adds neither sexiness nor glamour to this somber black-and-white chronicle of a journalistic crusade. *Niagara*, in contrast, has sizzle of the kind that only an experienced production head like Zanuck could provide, far beyond what the stolid New England newsman de Rochemont would have been interested in conceiving, much less promoting.

If the semi-documentaries tended to focus on unsensationalized cityscapes and compelling law enforcement problems, *Niagara* offers a quite different form of entertainment for the eye. In fact, it is one of the first Hollywood releases to identify the taste of postwar filmgoers for color travelogue entertainment that turned them into armchair tourists. In a memo to Fox publicist Harry Brand, producer Brackett explained the genesis of the film:

> When a motion picture producer has to settle on his next project, he goes through a long period in labor. . . . He's looking desperately for something that will stir in him and, hopefully, in the audience, a genuine excitement. . . . There was one Old Beauty who had been a top box office attraction in American for almost two hundred years, and a pin-up beauty for the rest of the world. She had hardly been touched upon by motion pictures. . . . I sent a note to Mr. Zanuck asking if it might not be a good idea to make a feature-length picture with Niagara Falls for a star, and got his instant approval, if a story could be found. . . . No merely frivolous story could do justice to that star we had chosen, and yet in the story there must be plenty of fun, plenty of typical Niagara Falls transients. In fact, the place must be seen through the eyes of quite ordinary visitors. Our story must cover every aspect of the place—the rainbows, and the roaring Cup of the Horseshoe Falls, invaded a dozen times a day by the tiny Maid of the Mist; the spidery bridges of the Cave of the Winds; the dark tunnels under Table Rock House; the whirlpools below the Falls; and, eventually, that spot above the falls where the calm river drops into the most savage and terrifying rapids in the world. . . . And over all our story there must be the ringing of the bells from the carillon in the International Bell Tower—that sound which, with the roaring of the waters, is the sound of Niagara. . . . In those rapids there still looms a coal barge which would have been swept over the brink of the falls had the men aboard not been inspired to scuttle it, so that it grounded on the shallow lip. That coal barge gave us our final scene. . . . Hathaway and McDonald and their assistants were thirty days on location, shooting from sunrise till that point in the afternoon when a camera will no longer register the light. They were scarcely dry for an hour, and several times they were in real peril.[44]

Brackett and Zanuck, it turns out, were trendsetters in making spectacular locations a central attraction of a postwar cinema determined to compete with its fast-developing rival television by offering a richer form of visual experience. With beautiful images of exotic places, the travelogue film became one of the most successful film types of the era, best exemplified by *Around the World in 80 Days*, which made intelligent and cost-conscious use of real locations, in accordance with the production trend we have been tracing here, and Mike Todd was not above using various forms of traditional fakery to provide "real atmosphere."

Enhanced by Technicolor and the widescreen process Todd-AO, the film's visual splendor was impressive.

Released the same year, *Second Chance* (Rudolph Maté, 1953) offers some superficial similarities to *Niagara*; this RKO film is likewise a color noir thriller that in true sub-Hitchcockian style features an exciting finale, in this instance a struggle between the protagonist and villain staged "at a great height" from an aerial tram suspended over a steep gorge. This sequence was filmed at Cerro de Atachi in Taxco, Guerrero, Mexico, as *Second Chance*'s filmmakers made inventive and exciting use of a real location, which is not identified in the narrative. Though unimpressed by the insipid and tired plotting that precedes it, Bosley Crowther found that "once they get aboard that tramway—Mr. Mitchum and Miss Darnell, coming down off the mountain and trailed by Mr. Palance—the drama begins to crackle. And once that cable snaps, the picture becomes a welter of cliff-hanging terror and suspense."[45] The "terror" Crowther felt was certainly enhanced by the 3D format in which *Second Chance* was shot and released; the gimmick lives up to its billing only in its conclusion. The tramway sequence, including the exciting rescue, seems, at least according to Crowther, to have been based on a real event, a difficult rescue from a malfunctioning mountain tram in Rio de Janeiro.[46] The finales of both these color noirs are archly Aristotelian, arousing a potent combination of terror and suspense that is then purged. In *Niagara*, the endangered main character is plucked from the river just before the boat in which the villain, who had abducted her, plunges over the falls; the villain and his intended victim are the recipients of similarly differentiated forms of poetic justice in *Second Chance*.

These finales, however, contrast markedly in terms of their cultural reference. In *Niagara*, the spectacular demise of the psychopathic but sympathetic murderer reenacts a perilous, usually fatal descent that has been repeated often enough over the years to become truly archetypal.[47] It is a cultural commonplace that the falls embody the threat of being carried by the irresistible current to a crushing death on the rocks below, a danger that has been tempting daredevils since the nineteenth century (the latest such stunt to engage with this form of experiencing Niagara is tightrope walker Nik Wallenda's June 2014 walk across the falls). *Niagara*'s finale, then, is as real as it is fictional, insofar as it is an exploration of the meaning of location from, as it were, within. Always alert to just this possibility of a stalled boat getting trapped in the current, the famed river patrol motors into action but fails to extricate the woman from her precarious perch on a rock outcropping. A police helicopter arrives on the scene in the nick of time to provide an against-the-odds happy ending. Though the concluding sequence makes use of some back-projected soundstage shots, it mostly offers authentic documentation of both the dangers of the rushing river and the intrepid professionalism of those charged with preventing the loss of innocent life in a constantly threatening landscape, taking advantage of the sunken wreck at the lip of the cascade as the last and most suspenseful of the various settings around the falls that were scouted out by Brackett and company.

In *Niagara*, the falls, as well as the national park that contains them and the cities on either side of the national divide, figure as locations whose sociocultural meanings are constantly the focus of representation. The Taxco tramway in *Second Chance*, by way of contrast, provides no more than a useful setting; its geographical particularities are neither recognized nor invoked beyond a vague sense of Mexicanness that they are coaxed to portray in order to provide local color. The tram could be just about anywhere, its location only slightly more particularized than the Connecticut stream from which the threatened infant is snatched in Griffith's *The Adventures of Dollie*. Even if its action sequences do not lack for authenticity, *Second Chance* lacks facticity. The film does not engage with any particularities of place or invoke a history well known to viewers. In fact, the history of Taxco would be irrelevant to the working out of the film's conflicts; it is better left unidentified and uninvoked. *Second Chance*'s geographical realism, we might say, is merely operational.

In *House*, and many other productions in Fox's realist cycle, facticity is journalistic, a matter of the specific events the film was committed to reenacting or embodying through the use of documentary footage. In *Niagara*, facticity is ekphrastic, to be found in the careful documenting of place, a complete sense of which was to be achieved by the stitching together of different episodes staged in various locations in the town and the national park, exactly as Brackett had imagined from the outset. It seems clear that although over his career Hathaway showed himself to be the more consistently committed realist, *Niagara* was in all essentials a Brackett film whose carefully considered dramatic and entertainment values—surely the heritage of the screenwriter/producer's many years at MGM—were very much in line with Zanuck's concept of an audience-pleasing production.

A Different Kind of Cinematic Geography: The Spaces of Film Noir

As in *Sunset Blvd.*, the story dramatized in *Niagara* becomes a tangled, disturbing examination of a natural location with a complex cultural history. By the early 1950s, Niagara Falls had become something close to an indispensable institution of American life. The film's narrative connects the natural power of this carefully managed tourist destination not only to the custom of honeymooning (which had become its most vaunted reason for existing), but also to the overindulgence it slyly but unmistakably encouraged. What emerges as a central thematic concern in the film are the darker sides of that sanctioned excessiveness: compulsive eroticism and the overwhelming jealousy it can engender, amorous states of mind that become motives for decoupling, in fact for murder and self-destruction. *Niagara* invites the viewer to see the grandeur of its much-admired vistas in a radically different way, transforming the powerfully cascading water from a backdrop to be contemplated into a series of interconnected playspaces that contain and shape all the events of the tragic plot. The narrative moves through the various "attractions" of the resort like a sightseeing expedition, which is fitting since the main characters are in fact tourists (a point insisted on by Zanuck), if in the case of the adulterous couple faux ones.

Much as Brackett and Wilder had done in *Sunset Blvd.*, the filmmakers here thoroughly recontextualize well-known narrative and thematic conventions soon to be retroactively identified as noir, then an emerging story type that hitherto had been staged for the most part in entrapping or threatening urban spaces, photographed in a dark and gloomy style, where shadows prevent full visibility, hinting at a disturbing unknown. This was a Hollywood tradition in which they had each done some exemplary work, from Brackett's collaborations on *Lost Weekend* and *Edge of Doom* (Mark Robson, 1949) to Hathaway's noir projects such as *The Dark Corner* (1946) and *Kiss of Death* (1947). As many commentators have noticed, film noir reflects continental modernisms (not only Expressionism but also Surrealism) and does not customarily offer the kind of engagement with specific, complexly layered natural/built space that *Niagara* does, reflecting the thematic and formal concerns of postwar Hollywood realism and its interest in particular places.

From the outset, however, setting had been important in film noir, as definitive in this emerging series as wide-open empty spaces had become for the western, framed in the distance by mountains. The darkly criminal themes and narrative movements of film noir are essential in the form's evocation of the anomic dark city of the national imagination. Here setting seems a correlative to the breakdown of traditional values at the center of noir narratives, as urban built spaces could easily be framed or lit as inhospitable, impersonal, and unwelcoming (a feature of noir visual style discussed in more detail in chapter 6). In its promotion of existential isolation, of a modern world where all are strangers, the dark city evoked in these films contrasts with the conventional small-town of Hollywood melodrama where all are known by all, where single-family residential and small business spaces are animated by a complex web of enduring relationships, providing no opportunity for solitariness, let alone the alienation that seems to be the spiritual condition of every noir character.

The doomed characters in *Niagara* are no exception: the ill-sorted trio of George (Joseph Cotten) and Rose Loomis (Monroe), and her handsome, younger lover, Patrick (Richard Allan), who tries to murder the now-inconvenient husband but instead winds up being thrown by George into the gorge from the wooden walkway of the Cave of Winds attraction, where, as its website excitedly if in the present instance somewhat ironically proclaims: "Rushing Bridal Veil Falls creates tropical storm-like conditions. Talk about a rush! Nowhere else on Earth gets you closer to the Falls!"[48] George believes wife Rose's promise that a second honeymoon will revitalize their failing relationship, and yet he is shadowed by her young lover, a reminder of the promiscuous past she had promised to leave behind when marrying George. The other belated honeymooners, Ray and Polly Cutler (Ross Showalter and Jean Peters), do not enjoy the marital renewal they sought, but find themselves caught up in the murderous triangle at the plot's center, with Polly, abducted accidentally by Loomis, almost sharing his fate when his stalled boat goes over Horseshoe Falls as he attempts to flee from the police.

This sequence contrasts with George's killing of Rose in an ironically appropriate and claustrophobic interior space, where the woman, desperate to escape a righteous vengeance, finds herself trapped in the resort town's bell tower, source of the romantic melodies requested by visiting honeymooners. As the betrayed husband trails her through the town, the film seemingly abandons its visual concern with real space for an expressionistically conceived dead-end, a series of narrow corridors, locked doors, and empty rooms that seem all swirling shadows and strange angles, where the bright Technicolor of the film's exteriors is drained away, leaving Rose to expire in the most minimal and abstract of soundstage settings, an unpopulated no-exit worthy of the genre's misogyny and fatalism. Despite the stylizing gestures, however, the viewer cannot forget that the bell tower is in fact "real," a famous landmark that exemplifies the commercialization of the famous place in which it is centrally located. *Niagara*'s transformation of film noir's *topos* speaks to the power of the postwar realist moment, in which a very different kind of location becomes the focus of the filmmakers. In this film, the dark city, more often than not a confection of soundstages and back lots, becomes the wildness of an awesome natural phenomenon in a movement toward the exteriorization of alienation, self-destructiveness, and unruly passions.

The Cutlers, who seem in every way to exemplify respectable middle-class values, have driven to Niagara intending to alleviate the perhaps unavoidable staleness of monogamy. This is a problem evidently exacerbated by Ray's overinvestment in work; in fact, his eagerness to get ahead in the company to which he seems completely devoted seems to be his dominating quality, the source of his bonhomie and energy. Polly and Ray are childless, it appears, and this may be a clue to Polly's evident ennui, her eagerness that this trip, and the "time alone" it will give them, be a success. Polly, not Ray, is the one looking forward to making good the honeymoon they had been years before forced to postpone, but now, of course, the honeymoon does not mean what it then, at least conventionally, would have meant for them. She hints to Ray that the visit to the falls should be even more satisfying now that she has her "union card," an invitation whose erotic edge Ray only dimly recognizes and for which he shows little enthusiasm. In an unintentional slight to Polly, who is expecting to enjoy his attention, Ray has brought along a number of books to read, including, almost improbably and quite humorously, one of the thick volumes of Churchill's *The Second World War*, which could hardly seem less an inspiration to romantic abandon.

Ray's lack of interest perhaps explains why Polly shows herself less than confident in her own beauty, especially when measured against the extraordinary sensuality of the woman they befriend at the tourist cabins, who provides a spectacle that entrances even her business-minded husband. As quickly becomes clear, he has been persuaded to make the trip only because it can be combined with a visit to his firm's headquarters, located on the American side. We are reminded that the two cities, located near the border marked by the rushing waters, are not just tourist locations, but working communities. Being in Niagara will give Ray the opportunity to indulge in some politically useful socializing with one of the company executives. As the Cutlers approach the falls, Ray erupts with excitement but does so as the cereal factory that employs him, not one of the continent's most impressive natural sights, comes into view, displacing the falls as an object of veneration and expressing thereby his corresponding indifference to the prospect for sexual indulgence that the vacation spot is meant to afford.

Pert, attractive, but not in the least provocative in either manner or dress, Polly exemplifies the socially sanctified prettiness on pictorial display in the magazines of the era that catered to the middle-class homemaker. She does not turn heads, and she knows it. Taking her snapshot in yet another typical gesture of the postwar American on vacation, Ray attempts to coax Polly into showing off her excellent figure to better advantage, but she seems embarrassed, even bewildered by the request, showing herself to be reticent in ways that interestingly complement her husband's indifference. Rose Loomis, by way of complete contrast, is all cocktail-lounge sexiness, eminently aware of the effect she has on men, using skills she honed as a waitress, which is how she met George and, thinking he would provide amply for her, why she connived to marry him. Rose makes it known to the Cutlers that she has brought George to Niagara in the hopes of restoring him to his former self, but this is soon exposed as a lie. Not only has she lost interest in her husband; she is eager to get rid of him. Rose's role in this plot is to make such a conclusion plausible by provoking her husband into acting out in public, and, when she easily makes him jealous, he obligingly displays his violent temper and self-destructive urges for all to see. Like Polly, Rose expects to find romantic fulfillment in Niagara, just not the officially sanctioned kind, and she has attracted a man willing to murder in order to claim her as his own.

If Polly remains dependent on Ray, whose desire for her she must rekindle, Rose takes her romantic fate into her own hands; Patrick figures as no more than a shadowy figure, waiting in a cheap rooming house for Rose's calls, not the author of the murder plot but its obedient functionary. He is so marginal that his deadly encounter with George does not draw the camera's attention, which takes place (where else?) in the falls themselves, in the tunnels and walkways built for tourists at the Table Rock Center. The Cutlers had visited this site earlier, and Polly had caught a glimpse of Rose and Patrick embracing in a dark corner, which they convert into an illicit lovers' lane. Dressed in the full-length raincoats and boots required of all visitors to the spray-drenched site, Patrick and Rose make a strange-looking pair of lovers. The next day Rose lures George to Table Rock, where Patrick is waiting for him. The attempted murder fittingly takes place just where the lovers' assignation had occurred twenty-four hours earlier.

Viewers are left to imagine how George proved himself able against his younger attacker, throwing his body over the falls and then emerging from the tunnel to claim the dead man's shoes, leaving his own behind. Rose would surely identify the mangled body retrieved on the rocks below as his, for without this lie how could she explain Patrick? And this is what happens. George now can be officially dead, or so he tells Polly when he returns briefly to the cabins, and he would be free at last from the woman who has sought his death if only Polly would keep his secret. She does, telling the police merely that George is still alive when it becomes clear that, unable to get beyond his jealous obsession, he has thrown away his chance to escape and now intends to kill Rose. Though freed officially from his own identity, George simply cannot seize this opportunity to start a new life. In a movement that ironically reverses the plot in which he failed to be ensnared, he lures Rose from the hospital, where she had been admitted after fainting at the unexpected sight of Patrick's body in the morgue. He does this by arranging for the song he knows was "theirs" to be played on the carillon, whose constant intoning of romantic melodies can be heard all through town. At first a lovers' anthem, the song (Lionel Newman and Haven Gillespie's "Kiss") now informs Rose that George is alive and out for revenge. Rose desperately tries to buy a ticket out of town, but Loomis blocks her way, and she flees—inevitably, it seems—toward the carillon tower itself, now empty. She scales the steps to the very top, followed by George, who, without a word, strangles her, then sits by the body and says how much he loved her. This act of fulfillment and failed disengagement is imaged by a succession of brief shots of the carillon bells, a dynamic montage that emphasizes their silence, with the illicit romance they signified, as well as the revenge taken for this betrayal, having both come to an end.

But the considerable energy of Rose's passion and conscienceless betrayal has not exhausted itself; George must pay for the murder he committed as he now attempts to escape from the falls and all it means. And the cycle of betrayal and revenge now also threatens the "normal" couple who are the temporary neighbors of the Loomises. Officially dead, George becomes something of a nonperson, shadowing the Cutlers and hoping to convince Polly that he had to kill his rival in self-defense and then could not stop himself from tracking down and strangling Rose. Unlike Rose, Polly remains committed to the marriage; Ray, after all, is a solid provider, not a psychologically damaged veteran who is no longer able to support his wife. The Cutlers would seem to be immune from self-destructive passion. With Ray's frequent absence on what has become more of a business trip than a honeymoon, however, Polly finds herself with time to develop a friendship with George, who is fully aware of the deepening crisis besetting him and eager to find a sympathetic female ear. She almost becomes collateral damage as a result, her brush with death perhaps an object lesson that ratifies abstention, willed or not, from erotic abandon, even at second hand, as she simply gets too close to the tumultuous passion that dooms their erstwhile friends.

Raymond Borde and Étienne Chaumeton, authors of the first full-length study of noir, conclude that these films "give the public a shared feeling of anguish or insecurity . . . a state of tension created in the spectators by the disappearance of their psychological bearings." Watching a film like *Niagara*, filmgoers "no longer encounter their customary frames of reference . . . a logic to the action, a clear distinction between good and evil." The resulting disorientation is an affectual intent also to be seen in surrealist works that, as Susan Hayward writes, are "concerned with depicting the workings of the unconscious (perceived as irrational, excessive, grotesque, libidinal)."[49] These themes are also central in the film noir, whose texts often trace the borders not only between modes of living, but between modes of experience, particularly the (dis)connection between dreaming (along with other alternative states like amnesia) and ordinary consciousness, in which other forms of psychological discontent emerge such as George's fits of anomic violence and Norma Desmond's disconnect from reality, both of which prompt a finally self-destructive homicide.

Liminality also memorably plays out in noir mise-en-scène. Vivian Sobchack persuasively argues that film noir is most deeply marked by its unique representational response to a culture in transition between the collective, public experience of a world war that required the widest marshaling of all the nation's resources and the desired, collective return to "the family unit and the suburban home as the domestic matrix of democracy."[50] This national experience of in-betweenness finds its most substantial visual reflex in what Sobchack says are the "recurrent and determinate premises" of this Hollywood type, its obsession with the dark city. In film after film, a crowded yet impersonal modernity takes shape as built spaces invite casual, impermanent connection even as they preclude, in their refusal to support traditional moral values, any establishment of family life. Sobchack importantly turns critical attention toward mise-en-scène, the characteristic settings of this film type such as "the cocktail lounge, the nightclub, the bar, the hotel room, the boardinghouse, the diner, the dance hall, the roadside café, the bus and train station, and the wayside motel."[51] These are the publicly accessible (if hardly socially approved) spaces of entertainment, dining, travel, and lodging, whose function is to provide for those literally, and also metaphorically, in transit. They substitute for what cannot be obtained in a world where nothing is "settled," where the secure and self-sufficient family home is unimaginable because it would depend on relationships (economic, sexual, and nurturant) that in noir narratives are not yet finalized and perhaps never will be. Such formal elements of mise-en-scène, Sobchack plausibly suggests, are the geographical reflexes of "existential, epistemological, and axiological uncertainty."

In characteristic noir fashion, *Niagara* conjures up transient spaces in which such uncertainty dominates and strangers encounter strangers, while Rose and George figure as the dark other of that happy-enough twosome, Ray and Polly. As a place shaped for and devoted to tourism, Niagara is no community in the ordinary sense; its characteristic structure is not the single family dwelling, the locus of family life, but the tourist cabin designed for the twinned activities of landscape gazing and sex. To be sure, in the film this transience is connected to domesticity by the trope of renewal, the hoped-for return to desire that the oxymoronic second honeymoon is designed to provide, with Rose planning one way to solve the problem of a marriage turned sour and Polly another. The two forms of romance that the film dramatizes connect as much as they contrast, with both depending on the harnessing of a passion symbolized by the crashing waters of the falls and the rushing river that feeds them. It is thus strangely appropriate that Polly finds herself borne along to the brink of disaster by the same powerful current that proves George's undoing; the action differentiates between the dissimilar kinds of sexual dissatisfaction each suffers from, to be sure, but the river is the same for both. Notably absent is the complex articulation of guilt and innocence that characterizes similar noir narratives, which sometimes delivers morally ambiguous protagonists from death but refuses to exculpate them (Guy Haines in *Strangers on a Train* [Alfred Hitchcock, 1950], for example). The importance of the form that the ending takes in *Niagara* lies rather in how it expresses the meaning of the location where it occurs, effectively enacting the contradictory meanings, social and natural, of Niagara Falls. The cultural work of *Niagara* is dramatizing the connection of natural magnificence with the force of the erotic.

The film refigures as one the two meanings of the falls, with the natural environment no longer, in the manner of euphemism, the means through which what cannot be spoken of directly can be provided with an acceptable excuse. Instead, the falls are shown to be not displacement, but the appropriate image of what it is that American culture has asked them to stage, with the impressive volume of cascading water coming not so much to substitute for but more to embody sexual passion as an irresistible and at least potentially destructive force. The falls, and their surrounding areas, had been established by the early 1950s as the most sought-after place for the honeymooners, who could, in their more reflective moments, contemplate a carefully reengineered "natural" landscape of considerable grandeur, whose water flow and appearance, more generally, had been significantly altered in order to transform a natural feature that was inherently a source of wonder into an even more effective, because more spectacular and less variable, lure for tourism. This ameliorative work reflected the shaping intentions of America's most famous landscape architect, Frederick Law Olmsted, the designer of, among other famous national landmarks, New York's Central Park. The falls were to be yet another site for "recreation," a concept then signifying the kind of spiritual refurbishing that the unnatural bustle of nineteenth-century urban life made necessary, especially desirable, perhaps, for young couples just embarking on the arduous journey of married life. This aim was furthered by the establishment of the state park in the 1880s, a project that succeeded in spite of intense opposition from the state's business community, which was eager to take full industrial use of its hydroelectric capacities. The "Free Niagara" movement in which Olmsted's detailed report and plans for development played a significant role helped preserve the falls in something like their natural state (which was, arguably, enhanced rather than spoiled), even as facilities for tourism (of which more below) allowed visitors to experience the natural wonder from up close or within, and not just as a breathtaking vista.[52]

Ginger Strand, Niagara's most perspicacious cultural historian, recounts that the promotion of the site as a tourist destination responded to how "a market need had been established for sexual fulfillment. Selling sex manuals was one way. Selling honeymoons would quickly become another."[53] And so, Strand continues, exploring the sense of place now came to be firmly attached to what, a century before, had been one of several possible stops on the bridal tours taken by young marrieds of the wealthy classes:

> After World War II, Niagara's honeymoon promoters aimed to leverage the postwar travel boom. . . . The postwar Niagara honeymoon was now promoted as an American tradition. Honeymooning at the falls was every American's birthright. . . . A visit to Niagara was, like much of postwar culture, a reassuring encounter with what the nation had just been fighting for: the American way of life. What did it mean? It went beyond democracy and freedom to embrace a host of lifestyle ideals valorized as simply the way things should be: the wholesome family life of *Leave It to Beaver* and *Father Knows Best*, the small-town community values of Norman Rockwell and *Life* magazine, the modernity and progress represented by the torrent of household consumer goods Americans adopted en masse. . . . The marriage manuals of the era affirmed the natural order: the man was to dominate and the woman was to let him.[54]

The falls licensed that necessary domination, which was a new way of appreciating their natural magnificence. A nineteenth-century guidebook describes Niagara as "the ever-lasting altar, at whose cloud-wrapt base the elements pay homage to Omnipotence," thus imbuing those who gaze upon it with a sense of awe at the immensity of divine power and its transcendent beauty.[55] There was nothing erotic about such neoplatonic transport, which moved powerfully in the opposite direction, from the physical to the divine.

In the 1950s, Niagara Falls was certainly still thought to be awe-inspiring, a reminder of human insignificance measured against metaphysical immensity; the site, after all, continued to be constructed as an object of contemplation that was intended to be "sublime" in the sense of offering the experience of the sublime, which was by definition not available in the course of living in ordinary natural or built spaces. But by the time that Hathaway and company set about the making of *Niagara* the falls had taken on another meaning entirely—no longer "an altar to be gazed upon in reverence." They were instead scenic backdrop, the sightseeing excuse furnished to couples whose more compelling desire was to shut the door on the world in order to place themselves within what Strand calls the natural order of married life. The centrality of this rite, in fact, was so uncontested that the honeymoon untasted could be seen, as it is in *Niagara*, to be a missing piece of proper marriage, one that the long-married could fill only by making the requisite sensual pilgrimage to Niagara, where troubled relationships perhaps might also find remediation.

After a fashion, the two women in Hathaway's film offer a conventional noir contrast between the virtuous, life-sustaining soulmate and the aggressively erotic femme fatale, the woman who is the source of her lovers' death and also her own. But Polly and Rose exemplify as well the contrasting qualities of the falls: which is at one and the same time, a suitably tamed, carefully redesigned, and thoroughly exploitable attraction, self-evidently "there" for human enjoyment, as well as a natural force flowing irresistibly toward destruction from which those who tempt fate by surrendering to it can be rescued only by good fortune, if at all. The film's suspenseful finale reminds us that during the nineteenth century Niagara became the nation's preferred site for daredevil stunts, from high-wire crossings (starting with Blondin Gravelet's successful walk in 1859) to going over the falls in a barrel (Annie Edson Taylor survived unharmed in 1901, the first of many to make the attempt, most of whom were not so lucky).

The falls often fill the screen, thus providing not only a visually rich setting full of "grandeur," but, in a manner long traditional for this place, the opportunity to engage with feelings of "the sublime," a state of mind that, as Philip Shaw suggests, "marks the limits of reason and expression together with a sense of what might lie beyond those limits. . . . [It] is dark, profound, and overwhelming and implicitly masculine."[56] As Shaw reminds us, in the writings of the Romantics,

FIGURE 22 Niagara Falls dwarfs the figure of George Loomis (Joseph Cotten) in the opening sequence of *Niagara* (frame enlargement).

the "lofty mountain peak or the swelling ocean . . . became the scene for darker meditations on the nature of the self and its relations with the external world."[57] The film's opening vista, with its bird's-eye view (from the Canadian side) of the two cascades, quickly abandons travelogue descriptiveness for a dramatization of such meditations. A human figure becomes barely visible in the bottom right of the frame, moving dangerously close to the falling water. A second series of shots locates a man, his clothes drenched, wandering in this solitary and threatening place.

The falls, he says in voiceover, have summoned him to this encounter, and their purpose is to humble him through a demonstration of their immensity and (he continues to anthropomorphize) remind him of his weakness. He can approach the torrent of falling water but cannot enter it, even though soaked to the skin by the spray. But this man refuses to be intimidated; he will challenge the falls by demonstrating his own ability to overcome and become "independent." In his defiance of nature, he is a universal figure, only latterly to "fall" into the narrative that catches him up and provides him with an individual identity. Like many a noir protagonist who finds himself trapped by circumstances and his own incapacities, George cannot escape from erotic bondage. But, in a more universal sense, he also cannot stand up to Nature. The falls have the last word; they do destroy him. In true noir fashion, the proclaimed power of George's inner discourse with such sublimity is demonstrated to be nothing but self-deception, as it would be of course for anyone. First seen from a distance, then experienced as a series of safe, accessible spaces that testify to the natural landscape's taming reconstruction, the river and the falls toward which it rushes become transformed at film's end into a danger from which only those more pure in heart may be rescued, if only barely.

Of course, *Niagara* must be found guilty of what the Hollywood industry is in general guilty, at least according to Zavattini. Like the artistically inferior *Second Chance*, this film too superimposes a death scheme "onto living events and situations" because of the felt need "to use a story" even when, as Brackett reported, a real place was the project's starting point.[58] Hathaway's film, however, deploys a story that permits the complex meanings, social and natural, of Niagara Falls to emerge. Like several of the director's other productions, *Niagara* is named for a place that the film is photographically committed to exploring in an act of extended description that draws the director's camera to parking lots, a souvenir shop, a hospital, even—in a movement of excess that Roland Barthes would term a "reality effect"—the city morgue (actually the Canadian side post office building), which, in its appropriate late Victorian exuberant ugliness, the film memorializes in what can only be a gesture of respect for what is there, which it allows us to see. If a substantial team of carpenters was employed by Hathaway to build the "Rainbow Cabins" in a spot overlooking the falls, that set went up on location and in a style that seamlessly matched the unchallengeable authenticity of the real into which it does not seem to intrude.

6

The Legacies of
The Ramparts We Watch

The Settling of Accounts

Surprisingly, perhaps, Louis de Rochemont's reconstruction of an era's structure of feeling in *The Ramparts We Watch* seems to have inspired one of the more interesting, if largely forgotten, films of the war, André de Toth's *None Shall Escape* (1944), the first Hollywood production to dramatize events from what has since become known as the Holocaust. To be sure, de Toth's film, produced and distributed by Columbia, does not feature the pictorial journalism of its model except for the brief inclusion of some newsreel footage. More than fifteen years later, de Toth was to work with de Rochemont on the Cold War thriller *Man on a String* (1960), jointly produced by Columbia and RD-DR Productions, and based closely on the tell-all autobiography of former Soviet agent Boris Morros, which had very much been in the news. Coming at the very end of the cycle of semi-documentaries, this later film more closely follows the example of *Ramparts* in retelling a "true story" and relying for its setting on then-rare actual footage that the filmmakers managed to shoot in the notoriously camera-shy Soviet Union. De Toth would perhaps have preferred to have done much the same with *None Shall Escape.* But with the film set in interwar Germany and Eastern Europe, real location shooting was obviously out of the question as long as the war continued, and de Toth could not for this reason use authentic, nonprofessional performers.

None Shall Escape does not recount a true story in the pattern later established by *Boomerang* and *Call Northside 777*, which center on the re-creation of a particular event; instead, in the manner of *Ramparts,* using fictional characters meant to represent types, the film tells the story of a period through the experiences of an unsympathetic protagonist that reflect widely shared trends. De Toth and his screenwriters (Lester Cole, Alfred Neumann, and Joseph Than) were eager to provide an explanation of the rise of National Socialism and its genocidal energies while lending their voices to the debate about postwar crime trials, though this aspect of the project seems not to have been emphasized in the original script (entitled *Lebensraum*, a reference to the Hitlerian policy of advocating conquest of the Slavic East in order to provide "living room" for an expanding Germany). Much like *Ramparts, None Shall Escape* offers an understanding of the present through a careful analysis of the past, looking back to the aftermath of German defeat in the Great War in order to dramatize the growing appeal of National Socialism's political vision and the moral degeneration to which it gave rise, spelling death for many millions and destruction for much of the continent. This was precisely the kind of re-creative realism that de Rochemont had invented some four years earlier. The cultural importance of the production did not go unnoticed by those in the industry, who were informed by the *Hollywood Reporter*, arguably the industry's most important house organ:

> It is fitting that the Motion Picture Industry, which has grown so much in world importance during the past four years of war and which has become recognized by all nations as the foremost force in spreading the world of truth and freedom throughout the universe, should make the first loud cry for retribution and swift vengeance against the enemies of these ideas when the day of reckoning arrives. And it is also fitting that, through the medium of the screen, the simple peoples of the earth, the little fellow who has suffered most, shall be given the opportunity to voice that cry. . . . Hollywood was fortunate indeed that André de Toth was forced to flee the men he tells us about here, for his treatment of the subject, his handling of the actors, and his unbelievable ability to create new departures from routine procedures are evidence of his artistry as a director.[1]

In looking at the origins of fascism from the viewpoint of those attracted to its message, the film hardly addressed an academic question of historical causation, but rather a pressing political problem, one requiring some preliminary discussion. The rapid spread throughout Europe of various forms of ultra-nationalistic authoritarianism during the 1920s and 1930s had been viewed by many in the democratic West with enduring alarm, prompting, especially after the war began, a number of scholarly analyses. Among them was Siegfried Kracauer's *From Caligari to Hitler: A Psychological History of the German Film,* published in 1947, but with an early chapter, released as a pamphlet by the Museum of Modern Art in 1942, that was devoted to an analysis of German propaganda film. Kracauer's reading of selected Weimar era films prompted much debate then and ever since because it depends on the notion that ideas and values that can be gleaned from popular films "reflect" underlying social predispositions, providing the critic with a handy way to read the national culture for which such productions are intended and in which they find widespread approval. For our purposes, however, it does not matter whether Kracauer's analysis of German culture based on supposedly popular films is correct. What is important is his argument that National Socialism was a movement that found widespread support from the German people themselves, that Hitler and his inner circle were not a criminal gang who had somehow hijacked the government of a civilized society, but instead were representative of widely shared predispositions, fears, and values. Kracauer was not alone in understanding the emergence and flourishing of National Socialism in this way (not much different, of course, from how the Nazi leadership itself would have presented its success, as an expression of the national will, with the party, as in Soviet Russia, understood as "taking a leading role").

The most influential of the several antifascist studies published in the United States during this period was undoubtedly Erich Fromm's *Escape from Freedom* (1941), which became one of the most widely read and respected nonfiction books of the war years. Fromm was a public intellectual associated, like Kracauer, with the Frankfurt Institute for Social Research, most of whose principal members relocated to the United States after leaving Nazi Germany. Like Kracauer, Fromm argued that National Socialism answered the Germans' collective need for a new order that would restore national pride and purpose after disastrous defeat in the Great War and the subsequent imposition of the harsh terms of the Versailles Treaty (1919). Promising a delivery from threats both internal and external, the collectivism of National Socialism embraced a freedom *from* freedom itself, to be achieved by an authoritarian politics that made possible the abrogation of individual responsibility and the exercise of free will. In an interwar era of great political, social, and economic uncertainty, this "escape from freedom" energized a collective reaction against the weak democratic institutions of the Weimar Republic, setting into motion political events that led to the establishment of a Nazi state in 1933. Modern German society, as Fromm saw it, had been built on both moral individualism of Lutheranism and the self-justifying energies released by Calvin's doctrine of predestination, a reading of that national culture antici- pated by Max Weber's celebrated *The Protestant Ethic and the Spirit of Capitalism* (1904–1905). The advent of National Socialism involved a wholesale retreat from this commitment to radical forms of individualism and entrepreneurship, as the freedom from an authoritative church provided by Reformation theology proved burdensome in the wake of collapse on the battlefield and on the home front in the fall of 1918.

The key to understanding the rise to power of Hitler and the Nazi Party was thus the unstable social conditions unleashed by an exhausting war that ended in a socialist revolution that toppled the Kaiser. In the imposed peace that fol- lowed, the country's territory was shrunk, and the extensive redrawing of national boundaries put many ethnic Germans behind unfamiliar borders or in countries now hostile to their presence. Widespread economic insecurity, worsened by the global financial crisis beginning in 1929, made many feel helpless, in the grip of forces they barely understood, and increased the appeal of a leader who spoke eloquently of a brighter future that would exchange defeat for victory. Fromm advanced a nuanced view of how a nation might go collectively wrong, even as he refused, unlike influential others, to indict German society as inherently

lacking in moral compass, as constitutionally unable to support the Enlightenment political values espoused by Western culture more generally. Fromm thus
argued against the simplistic view that Hitler and his leading supporters were
gangsters who had somehow seized control of a modern society, a view that, as
Michaela Hoenicke Moore writes, badly misrepresented a much more complex
and problematic series of trends: "American commentators and officials used metaphors of 'disease' and 'gangsterism' to characterize the Third Reich from the very
outset. They served the purpose of superficially reconciling or concealing conflicting assessments of the relationship between Nazism and German society at large."[2]

Metaphors like "disease" and "gangsterism" possess little explanatory power,
but this approach made for exciting cinema because it enabled history to be
personalized. Using look-alikes and "reconstructions" in the stylistic, if not the
intellectual, tradition of the *March of Time,* John Farrow's *The Hitler Gang* (1944, for
Paramount) is a pseudo-documentary that traces key events in Hitler's life and his
subsequent rise to power in what, unfortunately, has become the pattern for later
Hollywood treatments of National Socialism. These films blame the supposed
madman for leading a helpless nation to launch an aggressive war that eventually
led to mass murder on a horrific scale. Reviewing *The Hitler Gang* in the *New York
Times,* P.P.K. provided an accurate summary of its take on Nazi Germany: "The
cold facts are, certainly, that here is a man who, propelled by assorted psychoses,
set out on a campaign of conquest and annihilation with cynical disregard for
accepted honor or decency."[3] Blaming the leadership of the National Socialist
movement in effect exculpates the German people, who become the dictator's
first victims, even as they are relieved of responsibility for actions undertaken to
support the regime.

An alternative theory, morally problematic in a different way, was to suggest
that Hitler exemplified an enduring national pathology that called out for some
kind of collective punishment and then reeducation on a massive scale before a
defeated Germany could rejoin the community of civilized nations. Such a "structural" explanation tended to ignore individual responsibility for particular acts.
During the war, Columbia University's Richard Brickner explored this issue in
Is Germany Incurable?; he concluded that the country did persistently suffer from
"a paranoid trend" that had become firmly ingrained in the collective character.[4]
Fromm acknowledged, with scholars like Brickner, that the Germans were predis-
posed toward an unthinking respect for strong leaders, but he emphasized how
historical circumstances had turned many good people in that country toward a
darkly amoral view of civilization, making it eventually possible for them to commit atrocities they would have in other circumstances found completely abhor-
rent.[5] Germany, in short, remained "curable" despite recent events, and much of
the blame for its aggressive and murderous policies must ultimately be ascribed
to a confluence of social, political, and economic developments. But, as far as
Fromm was concerned, such historical circumstances did not excuse individuals
from responsibility for the actions they had taken; with its emphasis on the sense

of free will that psychological balance affords, his neo-Freudianism demanded that those who had violated accepted standards of civilized behavior pay the appropriate price for their transgressions, which, however, still required explanations more sophisticated than reflexive invocations of some vaguely metaphysical form of "evil."[6]

Though the cultural critic is not acknowledged as a source, Fromm's views about the rise of National Socialism would find interesting cinematic expression in de Toth's film, which addressed, directly or indirectly, a number of pressing issues. Was the German nation to be held collectively guilty for Nazi aggression and genocide? If so, how would they be punished and, more important, how would they be led to abandon values that many, perhaps most, had enthusiastically embraced and vigorously defended? How did individual malefactors come to embrace political ideas and practices that seemed so inconsonant with Western European values? It was with this current hook in mind that a script was developed at Columbia Pictures, by Alfred Neumann, Joseph Than, and, especially, the talented Lester Cole (later one of the witch-hunted Hollywood Ten), who were charged with imagining how the trials might unfold, as well as what history they would reveal. Their script captures much of the confusion in an Eastern Europe transformed by the complexities of the settlement after the Great War, reflecting decisions made in Versailles and the treaty's resolution (sadly only temporary) of conflicting nationalisms. At a time when the German characters in Hollywood films were cartoonish stereotypes, the protagonist in *None Shall Escape* is an essentially good man undone by circumstances, a well-educated and decorated veteran of the kaiser's army who returns in 1919 to his home in what had been East Prussia. The village of his birth, and where he had become a leading citizen as a young adult, is now part of the newly emergent Polish state established by the several improbably successful military campaigns conducted by the legions of Jósef Pilsudski (bitter conflicts that the film passes over in silence).

The appropriately named Wilhelm Grimm (Alexander Knox) demonstrates immediately that he has been embittered by the defeat of the Central Powers and by what the war has cost him (one of his legs, requiring him to walk somewhat uncertainly on a wooden substitute). As part of the German-speaking educated class previously dominant in the town, Grimm is greeted somewhat coldly, but respectfully, by the erstwhile Polish neighbors, who wonder why he has dared to come back (his return can be understood as a response to Pilsudski's announced intention to make Poland a functioning multi-ethnic society; this extension of good faith persuaded many ethnic Germans to return to or remain in the new nation). Hoping, in much the same spirit, that past communal rivalries might be forgotten, the town's religious leaders, Father Warecki (Henry Travers) and Rabbi Levin (Richard Hale), seem genuinely pleased to see him. They suggest, in fact, that Grimm reassume his position at schoolmaster, a reestablishment of the accepted order to which no one in the town would strongly object—of this they are certain. Though the obvious linguistic, legal, and cultural difficulties of their

FIGURE 23 The end of the Great War reunites the ethnically diverse inhabitants, including the German schoolmaster (Alexander Knox), frame left, whose return has not been expected after Paderewski's declaration of a Polish republic in *None Shall Escape* (frame enlargement).

invitation are left unaddressed by the film, de Toth's meaning is clear enough. Borders shifted as a result of the war, transforming the status of millions caught up in this painful process, but postwar Eastern Europe had the chance to become a peaceful society if only tolerance, fortified by a certain amount of historical amnesia, had prevailed.

The plot certainly holds out this possibility, reflecting Pilsudski's firm belief that Poland should be a multi-ethnic polity. When war broke out, Grimm had been engaged to a Polish woman, Marja (Marsha Hunt), and his fiancée has waited for him. Reunited by good fortune with Grimm, she gives voice to her readiness to marry the man she fell in love with years before. Thus the film's opening sequences suggest that all can be as it was, or was intended to be, with the new political arrangements not compromising the traditional intercommunality of village life. A man who might consider himself fortunate to have survived the just-concluded conflict, as well as those who could hardly help but celebrate a political change that the war has unexpectedly brought, are shown poised to reassume their accustomed roles, with the victors (generously, one might say) offering to make social room for their fellow citizen who, true to his own bonds of blood loyalty, fought and sacrificed for a different outcome.

But the Wilhelm Grimm who left to serve the kaiser is not the crippled veteran who has returned from the war. Four years of European fratricide have unleashed in him both blood lust and intolerance. The schoolmaster has become virulently ethnocentric, believing now in the inferiority of Poles in general and of Marja in particular, who, he thinks, will be Germanized by their marriage and only in this way become a suitable mate for him. As he tells the horrified woman, Grimm still dreams of a Greater Germany occupied with colonizing the Slav lands to its east, including the territory that has now become Poland. With bitter disappointment, he recalls that German arms had proven victorious on the Eastern Front in 1917, forcing the Russians to conclude a peace treaty that ceded much of what had been Western Russia to the German Empire, which is of course now defunct; the kaiser, having abdicated, lives in Dutch exile and a democratic government has been installed humiliatingly in the provincial town of Weimar. For Grimm, the war is not a horror best forgotten, but a lost personal opportunity still deeply regretted. He was promised a leading role in the postwar exploitation of Germany's new territories, but defeat on the Western Front has ended all these hopes. At least as he sees it, his future is now limited by his disability and by the new political arrangements that have prevented Germans from political control of the east. It is hardly surprising that Marja quickly finds her former lover domineering and his views of Polish racial inferiority unacceptable, as she tells Father Warecki, who suggests she go to Warsaw for a while to reconsider her promise to marry.

In her absence, Wilhelm, consumed by feelings of rejection and anger, seduces and then rapes a young girl, a former student who looked up to him. She commits suicide out of shame, and it becomes known that he was the man involved. Put on trial, Wilhelm, however, is found innocent when solid evidence against him cannot be produced, but all his fellow citizens, including Marja, are convinced of his guilt and there is no question of his remaining among them. Asking the priest and rabbi for a loan, he then heads for Germany to restart his life among his "own people." Grimm's criminal behavior, so we are given to understand, is uncharacteristic of someone who had long been a law-abiding and socially responsible member of the community, but whose moral sensibility has been warped by his experience of Germany's defeat, with his fiancée's uncertainty about their future life together pushing him over the edge and his moral restraint weakened by notions of German ethnic superiority that the war has only served to strengthen.

Arriving in a Germany where these feelings of dissatisfaction and indignation are shared by many, Wilhelm soon becomes one of National Socialism's earliest and most fervent adherents, advocating for the overthrow of the "imposed" democracy now governing the country. He participates in Hitler's failed Beer Hall Putsch (November 1923). In the 1930s, he rises steadily in the party ranks, eventually accepting, after German victory over Poland in 1939, the position of *gauleiter* for the very district where he had grown up and where Marja (now widowed) still lives. Once again, Grimm returns to the place of his birth, but this time wearing the uniform of a conquering army and wielding almost absolute power over those who once were his fellow citizens. When orders are issued for the rounding up of

the town's Jews, Wilhelm eagerly complies, ordering his troops to kill the deport-
ees assembled at the railway station when, obeying Rabbi Levin's command to
stand firm, they refuse to board the trains scheduled to deliver them to a death
camp. This is but the last in a series of increasingly horrific and murderous acts
that Grimm commits with an apparently clear conscience, as for the sake of the
party and the glory of a "Greater Germany" he betrays all who have shown him
kindness and concern: his brother and family, his former neighbors, and the two
men of religion who enable him to escape from Poland after his trial and make
a fresh start across the German border. Though horrific and thoroughly meriting
condemnation, Grimm's actions are dramatized as emerging directly from the
unintended consequences of the Great War, while, interestingly enough, neither
the Versailles Treaty nor political treason (the famous "stab in the back" of the
1918 socialist revolution) is advanced as an explanation for the aggressiveness
of National Socialism. Instead, the problem of Germany is seen as a virulent
ethnocentrism (a condition that in a milder form is shown to manifest itself in
Grimm's Polish neighbors as well). Believing in the exceptionalism of their supposed Aryan heritage, the Germans identify cultural others as inferior and hence
either exploitable or disposable, even as they are inspired to dreams of colonizing
conquest and race-purifying genocide.

   But, so the film suggests, these sociopathic dispositions are only brought to
the surface by the thoroughgoing dislocations occasioned by the war, which created a new world in which the losers could not easily regain their place despite
the best of intentions. The irremediable effect of the war on Grimm is neatly
imaged by his loss of a limb and his persistent, narcissistically motored obsession
that everyone dismisses him as a cripple. Had war not come, he would have married Marja and persisted in his career as the village schoolmaster. His pride in
being German in culture and language would have found unpleasant but rather
harmless expression in the uppity stiffness of his dealings with the Poles whose
children he had undertaken to educate for their own good (he is remembered by
more than one of them as an inspired instructor).

   In a manner reminiscent of Welles's *Citizen Kane* (1941), Grimm's story
emerges in a series of flashbacks as he stands trial before an Allied Commission,
accused of crimes against humanity and confronted, as if on the Day of Judgment,
by all those whom he has harmed; he is found guilty and sentenced to death,
anticipating more or less what would happen to Nazi leaders in late 1945 after
Germany's defeat. When de Toth was making this film, however, the convening
of war crimes trials was by no means a settled matter, and his film was seen as
an argument that such legal proceedings should conclude the conflict, as testimony establishes the unfortunate circumstances leading to German society's
escape from freedom into the amoral, transindividual expression of a perversely
conceived national will. Doubtless a victim of history, Grimm (and by implication
other powerful Nazis) still found himself called upon to choose at key moments
in his life (as when his brother asks him to flee the country or when the village

priest and rabbi implore him not to murder his Jewish neighbors). It is for such
choices that he is found guilty and condemned to death. De Toth's film advocates
for an informed and just accounting of Nazi crimes, with the trials permitting
surviving victims to tell their stories to the world. *None Shall Escape* can be seen
as a kind of cinematic advocacy for such a public and collective accounting even
as it avoids simplistic moralizing and the obscurantist over-personalizing of historical developments, particularly the assessment that the advent and flourishing
of National Socialism was the direct result of a single madman's energies and
calculation.

As Allied victory in Europe became increasingly certain in 1944, one of the
most vexing of political questions was what punishment should be visited on the
German people and, especially, on individually culpable Germans; in the court of
world opinion, they could hardly be found other than guilty of having caused the
two most disastrous wars in human history. As early as October 1943, the Soviet
Union, the United Kingdom, and the United States promulgated a "Declaration
on German Atrocities in Occupied Europe" as part of the Moscow Declaration
meant to guide a postwar settlement. This section of the agreement pledged
the Allies to deal judicially with Germans who had committed atrocities (later
called "crimes against humanity"). The presumptive victors agreed to pursue the
guilty parties "to the uttermost ends of the earth . . . in order that justice may be
done. . . . The above declaration is without prejudice to the case of the major war
criminals whose offences have no particular geographical location and who will
be punished by a joint decision of the Government of the Allies."[7]

Even so, summary execution on a considerable scale was also advanced
at various meetings as an appropriate punishment of the German leadership,
such as Tehran (1943), where Soviet leader Joseph Stalin, in apparent seriousness, advocated shooting out of hand as many as 100,000 Wehrmacht staff
officers once surrender had been finalized. Roosevelt, it appears, did not object
strenuously to this plan for mass executions, perhaps because harsh treatment of
defeated Germany was supported by powerful figures within his administration.
The evolving official if highly secret U.S. position at the time on the management
of postwar Germany might well have been the plan put into final memorandum
form in early 1944 by Secretary of the Treasury Henry Morgenthau Jr. The Morgenthau plan would have solved the problem of continuing European warfare
by deindustrializing and "pastoralizing" Germany, separating the country from
much of its mineral resources and industrial base. If in a less draconian fashion
than Stalin had suggested, those involved at higher levels of the Wehrmacht
and Third Reich government would be submitted to harsh, summary judgment,
and many would in fact have been slated for execution.[8] The British, especially
Churchill, displayed little enthusiasm for what Morgenthau had in mind for the
Germans, but the Soviets would have been pleased to see Germany reduced to
military and economic impotence.

In the event, Roosevelt was put in an embarrassing position when the details of this proposal were leaked to columnist Drew Pearson, who broke the story just a few days after the plan had been finalized at the Second Quebec Conference. A firestorm erupted, and the Germans quickly made propaganda hay out of the revelations, quite probably strengthening their already firm national resolve to fight to the bitter end. Roosevelt quickly denied that any such plan existed, but in September 1946, more than a year after the president's death, Secretary of State James F. Byrnes in a speech in Stuttgart in the American Zone still felt it necessary to issue an elaborate if indirect denial that anything like the Morgenthau plan had ever been official U.S. policy.[9] In any case, in September 1945 the Allies had agreed in the London Charter to hold the trials in the American Zone, with only the principal military, judicial, and government officials of the Third Reich called before the bar.[10] And yet the notion of collective responsibility, and so in some sense punishment, was not entirely abandoned. Plans for de-Nazification went ahead, as we have seen in chapter 3, with director Billy Wilder, among others in the film industry, put in charge of making the documentaries about concentration camps collectively known as *Todesmühlen* (death mills). All German civilians were required to watch these documentaries in order to get the ration cards indispensable for continued survival.

The first and most newsworthy session of trials began that November in the Bavarian city of Nuremberg (an important center of Nazi Party activity) and ended the following October with the execution or imprisonment of most of the accused. The complex, perhaps ultimately intractable issues raised by the Allied definition of "crimes" of actions that were perfectly legal within the system of National Socialism were subsequently explored in Stanley Kramer's *Judgment at Nuremberg* (1961), a screen adaptation of a successful teleplay that interestingly bookends *None Shall Escape*. With location shooting in Germany making possible a convincing re-creation of the immediate postwar era, *Judgment at Nuremberg* offered a complex meditation on U.S. relations with its once deadly enemy, now an indispensable ally in the Cold War with the Eastern Bloc. The film dramatizes the events of the subsequent series of trials, in which German judges were the accused. The American judges who sit in their judgment refuse in the end to let their erstwhile colleagues off with lighter sentences because of the worsening international situation.

Among the defendants, mostly party hacks, the central figure is a noted jurist, based on the most sympathetic of the defendants, Franz Schlegelberger, called Ernst Janning in the film (Burt Lancaster). Janning, who had compromised with the Nazi reorganization of the justice system despite his deep intellectual and moral misgivings, is portrayed as a flawed but "good" German who accepts with equanimity the prospect of extended incarceration after admitting his guilt in a dramatic courtroom speech that in effect supports the American case that judges should be subject to a higher law. The recipient of many industry

FIGURE 24 The American judge (Spencer Tracy) encounters the surviving massive monuments of Nazi-era Nuremberg in *Judgment at Nuremberg* (frame enlargement).

accolades, Kramer's film was timely, released the same year as yet another Berlin crisis erupted: the walling off of East Berlin to prevent the continuing exodus of the country's best and brightest to the west, a move that the Kennedy administration (along with many West Berliners) thought might be the prelude to a total Russian takeover of the divided city. It is instructive that by the time *Judgment at Nuremberg* hit the theaters, Schlegelberger had been out of prison for more than a decade and was receiving a substantial pension from the Federal Republic.

With extensive location shooting and accurate fictionalization of events in the still-visible urban wreckage of post-Hitler Germany, *Judgment at Nuremberg* demonstrates the power of postwar Hollywood realist filmmaking at its moment of highest seriousness, completing the engaged advocacy for the commission of crimes against humanity first brought to the national screen by André de Toth. Spencer Tracy plays the senior American justice, Dan Haywood, a judge from backwoods Maine who, as he knows, was far down the list of those asked by Washington to participate; his more famous and prominent colleagues saw little value to this assignment, as the Allies, having already tried the Nazi leadership, were now faced with the question of what to do with those charged with working within and for a government that, in retrospect, has been judged to be essentially criminal. Committed to making the proper moral judgment of his colleagues on the bench, Haywood wanders the city, much of it still rubble-strewn wasteland, as he attempts to understand what had gone wrong with one of Europe's most civilized cultures.

One of the film's most poignant framings captures him in long shot, a small and seemingly frail figure wandering in front of the *Reichsparteitagsgelände*, the oversize stadium where the annual outdoor party congresses were held. In his apparent insignificance, the individual figure is threatened by the very weight and scale of the mass movement represented by this structure, and yet it is individualism, in the person of the elderly, frail, but firm-minded judge, that has conquered, reducing the empty theater where mass rallies were once held to something like a tombstone. The American judge now wields the power even though he is dwarfed by the empty shell of a culture that only recently had dominated most of the continent. Haywood holds out for a just condemnation of his German counterparts, not just the party hacks but the internationally famous and scholarly Janning. This decision is eventually compromised by the West's growing dependence on a morally and politically restored Federal Republic of Germany, the new nation that, in response to the political and economic needs of the American, British, and French occupiers, comes into being just as the trial concludes. It is a tribute to the power of Kramer's film that when *Judgment at Nuremburg* was screened in West Berlin it was met with derision and anger, as the producer/director reports: "The film went on, and when it was over there was a deafening silence. . . . It was the most frightening evening in my life. The film was totally rejected."[11] Few Germans were ready even in 1961 to examine their National Socialist past, though the Eichmann trial, then in its preliminary stages and scheduled to begin later that year, soon brought the Holocaust to the center of Western retrospection about World War II. In the United States as well Kramer was condemned by many for making a film with such an overt message, which is hardly either simplistic or triumphalist. What he and screenwriter Abby Mann had to say about the morality of political judgments, and the compromises that had to be made for the sake of expediency, seemed to go over the heads of many reviewers.

As he shamefacedly confesses, Janning accommodated the Nazi ideology he despised for the sake of domestic peace and because he loved his country. He is the moral opposite of the diehard party ideologue Wilhelm Grimm in *None Shall Escape,* who is essentially unfazed by those who confront him with his crimes. But then postwar America needed to think that "good" Germans among the Third Reich's leadership were repentant for committing what they knew were horrific crimes. And this moral lapse, so the trial in *Judgment* suggests, is not so terribly different from the expedient reluctance of the U.S. government to curtail further examination or discussion of German guilt once Soviet hostility over the founding of the Federal Republic turned Washington and Bonn into de facto allies. That relationship was solidified by the improbable logistical success of the Berlin Airlift in defeating the Russian blockade of West Berlin (1948–49), an event that, as the film reports, was still in its first and shocking stages as the judges deliberated their verdict (discussed in full detail in the introduction). Insofar as he is able, Haywood resists increasing pressure from the U.S. military and political establishments to take it easy on the accused, but the film makes it clear that in the final analysis political necessity trumps even the highest-minded of moralisms, undercutting what Mann and Kramer present as arrogant U.S. claims of ethical exceptionalism.

None Shall Escape's groundbreaking appropriation of de Rochemont's interest in the re-creation of a historical period likewise went largely unappreciated by filmgoers in the last stages of the war, even though the screenwriters were nominated for the Academy Award for Best Original Story. The film has subsequently been mostly lost to view, meriting, for example, few references in the now considerable literature devoted to screen treatments of the Holocaust.[12] Bosley Crowther inaccurately observes that this was just "another picture which says nothing about the Nazis that hasn't already been said," ignoring the film's strikingly original and resolutely even-handed portrayal of the German postwar *mentalité,* trapped between competing feelings of persecution and superiority. It is also quite unfair to de Toth's treatment of German society (with Grimm's brother and his family, for example, advanced as "good" characters unimpressed by and impervious to the Nazi messages) to characterize the film as "obvious in its piling on of odium . . . with a grim, relentless will."[13]

A microcosm for German culture, the educated Grimm is wounded grievously fighting for a lost cause. His sociopathic tendencies are energized by deep feelings of injustice and persecution, and his desire to make something of himself not surprisingly finds fulfillment in a political movement dedicated to the subordination of supposedly inferior others. Grimm, as de Toth presents him, is very much a product of a thoroughgoing continental disaster, but he is also a man with the capacity to choose, based on his clear vision of the difference between right and wrong. It would be too simple to call him evil or a "gangster." The trials of the Nazi leaders, de Toth suggests, should inform the world of how they came to do what they did even as they are held responsible for their crimes and punished accordingly. Much like Kramer's *Judgment, None Shall Escape* speaks a complicated and, at least for many, an unwelcome truth about the power of historical circumstances to shape human action, even while demonstrating that there can be no excuses for a depraved indifference to elementary human values.

Noir Semi-Documentaries: *Southside 1–1000* and *The Phenix City Story*

De Toth's film is structured by a double rhetoric that makes it atypical of Hollywood filmmaking: it aims both to inform by presenting filmgoers with an entertaining and suspenseful narrative but also to argue for an international tribunal to adjudicate the misdeeds of National Socialist Germany. In its rhetorical designs on the viewer, it is much like the noir semi-documentaries that constitute the other significant legacy of *Ramparts.* Because they have been understood in part as an aspect of the much-discussed and more inclusive noir cycle, many of these films are already well known and merit little further comment here. However, two of the most interesting noir semi-documentaries have hitherto received very little attention from historians and critics. They will be the focus here since they illustrate the formal and rhetorical complexities of the form, including its connection to film noir and its deeply contrasting, yet also complementary, forms of cinematic realism.

Boris Ingster's *Southside 1–1000* (1950) begins with what amounts to an extended civics lesson on the importance for a modern society of a national currency and the institutions needed to support it, only then shifting gears toward a more conventional concern: narrating the admirable exploits of Treasury Department agents in apprehending a gang of counterfeiters, whose activities, if successful, would have disrupted the country's economy. Though it constitutes most of the film's running time and provides its title, this rather conventional story, in which law enforcement inevitably triumphs, is positioned as subordinate to the opening essay; it asks to be understood as one illustration among many of the workings of an important American institution charged with providing the material basis of national financial life and protecting the dollar from uncertainty and devaluation. Unmistakable are *Southside*'s affinities with both *MOT* and with the succession of de Rochemont factual fictions produced in the postwar era at Fox. Similarities are also evident with the cycle of films produced mostly at Hollywood's Poverty Row studios, including Phil Karlson's *The Phenix City Story* (1955), whose unusual concern with journalistic truth in the de Rochemont manner differentiates it from most other semi-documentaries. Karlson's film focuses on what was an ongoing story of consuming national interest, the rooting out of widespread criminal activity in America's most notorious wide-open town; the film is not just a re-creation of real events in the de Rochemont manner, but a multileveled probe in the best tradition of muckraking reportage, a representation of contemporary events that is every much as sensationally journalistic as it is cinematic. Both films belong to a cycle of productions whose complex interconnections also bear further discussion.

In *Southside,* the investigation of the counterfeiting ring, or so the film avers, is drawn from the files of the U.S. Secret Service, whose important function in national law enforcement had been praised three years earlier in Anthony Mann's *T-Men* (1947), a film that is more crime fiction than documentary, less a measured portrait of an important institution and more a platform for the effective staging of violent action that pushes the limits then permitted by the Production Code. And yet, in addition to a focus on a federal agency, *T-Men*'s flat, unglamorized style and ostentatious deployment of real locations (sequences were shot in Boston, Detroit, New York, Washington, D.C., and, of course, Los Angeles) closely connect it to the production trend then gaining in popularity in the wake of *The House on 92nd Street*'s substantial, and quite surprising, box office and critical success. *T-Men* was the first in a series of low-budget noirs produced by Eagle-Lion, a small company developed by British mogul J. Arthur Rank to turn out B-pictures to accompany his feature films in their American release; Mann would be for several years one of the company's most successful directors, especially talented at conveying a compelling sense of "place," which is also a feature of his widely celebrated westerns such as *The Far Country* (1954). Bosley Crowther's *New York Times* review is full of praise for Mann's engagement with cinematic realism in *Border Incident* (1949), his follow-up to *T-Men*:

> Latest of Government agents to be cast in heroic mold by the ever-resourceful producers of "realistic" adventure films are the men of the Immigration Service, who are made to look mighty good in MGM's "Border Incident," which came to the Globe on Saturday. But far more impressive than the heroes in this melodramatic report is the beautiful scenery in the area along the border between California and Mexico. Photographed almost entirely in the flat and fertile farmlands to the north and in the sand hills to the south of the border, this routine adventure film has the virtue of honest recognition of dramatic locale, at least.[14]

An urban drama located in a gritty version of the contemporary city, *T-Men* also proudly proclaims its special access to the realia therein depicted: "The United States currency and the credentials of the Treasury Department shown in this film were photographed by special permission of the Secretary of the Treasury. Further reproduction of said currency or credentials in whole or part is strictly prohibited." Just as Hoover provides an introduction to *House* that attests to its veracity, so Elmer Lincoln Irey, the retired chief coordinator of the Treasury Department's police units, does much the same for *T-Men*. Marketing emphasized Irey's point that this was the first film to be based on actual Treasury Department law enforcement files (once again a clear reference to de Rochemont's vaunted access to FBI facilities and materials), while the film's poster proclaimed that it was "tough, tense, terrific, true," marked, in other words, by a realism in its portrayal of shocking violence (not something that de Rochemont or Zanuck were particularly interested in), as well as in its re-creation of actual events. A further guarantee of authenticity, suitably ballyhooed in press releases, was that associate producer Turner B. Shelton had once worked for Treasury and presumably could be depended on as a technical advisor to get the details right.

Though *T-Men* undoubtedly affords more viewing pleasure, *Southside* embodies more completely and faithfully the representational and stylistic changes that, put into motion by de Rochemont and Zanuck in the 1940s, had resulted in the growing popularity of crime-themed semi-documentary filmmaking that was at this point being taken up in earnest more broadly in Hollywood, including by those working at its margins. Released by Allied Artists, *Southside* was produced by King Brothers Productions, another small company that worked with other Poverty Row outfits producing mostly low-budget films, including the critically acclaimed noir romance *Gun Crazy* (Joseph H. Lewis, 1950) and the show biz melodrama *Carnival Story* (Kurt Neumann, 1954). Realism was one of the industry trends picked up by King Brothers. All three of the films mentioned above make extended and quite artful use of actual locations and, in the case of *Gun Crazy*, documentary stylizations (including an extended bank robbery sequence filmed guerilla-style in Montrose, California, with unaware ordinary citizens wandering in and out of the frame).

Contextually speaking, it is hardly surprising that the semi-documentary noir, as opposed to other noirish crime story forms, found one of its most significant subjects in the attempts of foreign enemies to subvert American society and those forms of criminal enterprise that threatened to destroy the national way of life from within. The noir semi-documentary generally presents an America under continual assault from within and without but protected by large-scale and efficiently organized institutions whose essential quality is their unflagging devotion to discovering, cataloguing, and interpreting facts. Once the Cold War began to dominate the discussion of international affairs, it proved easy enough to adapt the semi-documentary form to the portrayal of a new threat. Not German spies or greedy forgers this time but communist agents became the enemies eager to steal American defense secrets or destabilize the nation with some deadly threat.

Consider, for example, yet other neglected but interesting entrant into the series, *Big Jim McLain*, directed by Edward Ludwig and released by Warners in 1953. After a brief prologue in which the voice of a ghostly and deeply worried Daniel Webster appears in order to inquire if all is well in his country, the film proper opens with a House Committee on Un-American Activities hearing in which an obviously guilty communist (the viewer knows this because he is a shifty-eyed man with a foreign accent) pleads Fifth Amendment protection when asked if he is a communist. Apparently hampered by the freedoms afforded citizens in the Bill of Rights, the committee must turn to less formal (that is, strong-arm) methods of getting at the truth. It is a matter of national security that all members of the Communist Party be made known to government agencies. Two hulking investigators, Jim McLain and Mal Baxter (played by John Wayne and James Arness, respectively), are dispatched to Hawaii, where they are to identity local members of the party in order to foil the subversive activities in which it is suspected that some or all are involved.

In line with film noir sexual politics, McLain hooks up almost immediately with a local communist, Nancy Vallon (Nancy Olson), who also by film's end becomes disillusioned with the party's tactics. Aided by Vallon, McLain makes his way through a political version of the dangerous noir underworld (including a brassy but harmless landlady memorably played by Veda Ann Borg). The various lowlifes McLain runs into are largely now disillusioned ex-communists who, formerly taken in by appeals to unionism and egalitarianism, have now realized that the party's real aim is the destruction of the American way of life. The seriousness of their plotting emerges when, having kidnapped Mal, the communists accidentally kill him with an overdose of truth serum. With the help of the political converts, McLain is finally able to make sure that Mal's murderers (including the group's cold-blooded leader, Sturak, played superbly by Alan Napier) are brought successfully to justice. But the others, not implicated in any specific act of law breaking, only find themselves testifying before a special session of the committee. They too "plead the Fifth" and must be released from custody. McLain's righteous indignation at (what the film wants the viewer to believe is) a cynical exploitation of American freedoms is assuaged somewhat by his witnessing, at film's end, an army unit parading through the reconstructed docks of Pearl Harbor. This sequence completes the patriotic tour of the base that had begun earlier with a heart-rending visit to the *Arizona* memorial, a visible reminder of defeat turned into victory. With this image of a resurgent America fading from the screen, the narrator resurfaces in order to answer Webster's question about the state of the republic, proclaiming enthusiastically that all is well, a happy state of affairs for which, according to the film, the nation's intrepid law enforcement officers are largely to be credited. They are preserving the freedoms for which Americans paid a heavy price in the global conflict concluded only a few years before.

A New Cycle Emerges

In the wake of the box office success of *The House on 92nd Street,* Twentieth Century–Fox quickly commissioned a sequel of sorts, sending screenwriters to work with FBI files to which J. Edgar Hoover had afforded the studio access. The film that eventually resulted, directed by William Keighley, was *The Street with No Name* (1948). Lloyd Nolan reprises his role as Inspector Briggs, but ordinary crooks, not enemy agents, are this time his target; the FBI schemes to plant one of their own, Gene Cordell (Mark Stevens), in a gang specializing in elaborate heists run by Alec Stiles (Richard Widmark). Though this plot is obviously modeled on that of *House,* which was also structured around the FBI's penetration of the gang of malefactors, organized crime was not the original focus of the project but juvenile delinquency. The script had been developed, as Colonel Jason Joy at Fox informed Joseph Breen, in close cooperation with the FBI, which was eager to launch another effort at self-promotion by bringing to the attention of the nation's filmgoers what Hoover and company considered to be a serious crime wave, particularly characterized by juvenile delinquency. Here was a project, Joy told Breen in no uncertain terms, that not only dealt with a troubling contemporary social problem, but had been the brain-child of the man who was undoubtedly the government's most powerful unelected executive: "When this is assigned to members of your staff, I wish you would let them know that this is the story which J. Edgar Hoover personally asked Mr. Zanuck to produce. It has been developed in Mr. Hoover's office, and he believes that it will be of great assistance to him and other law-enforcement organizations in the control of delinquency, both juvenile and adult."[15] Joy and Zanuck were well aware that the treatment they were sending for the consideration of the PCA sketched out a story that violated a number of hitherto sacrosanct Code provisions, as Breen was quick to remind the studio only two days later, pointing out that there was no way he could approve sequences dramatizing the detailed preparation for a robbery, the subsequent killing of an FBI agent, and the kidnapping of a minor child.[16] A meeting between studio and PCA agents revealed Fox's intransigence about the matter. After all, this would be, Zanuck hoped, another low-budget but immensely profitable release, and it fit neatly into the series of social problem projects that he was planning for what he correctly read as an enthusiasm on the part of filmgoers for serious cinema. The memo for the files written after the meeting confirms that Fox was not willing to modify the script whose confection Hoover had supervised: "Colonel Joy insisted that an exception should be made for this picture. He was advised to obtain such an exception a direct appeal would to be taken to Mr. Johnson [sic]. . . . While our letter of June 6 is not detailed, there seemed to be no necessity for going into details since the violations of the Code were so obvious re details of crime, killing of FBI man, kidnapping, etc."

Formerly active in the Chamber of Commerce, Eric Johnston had become president of the Motion Picture Association of America in 1946 and, as such, he was officially Breen's boss and the last court of appeal for Code decisions. Fox wanted exceptions made to Code provisions because of the particular nature of the story, which was, Zanuck insisted, not cynical exploitation of hitherto prohibited topics, but a production that would serve the public interest in important ways and continue the cooperation between Washington and Hollywood established during the war. Johnston quickly answered Zanuck's request with a firm "no": "Am terrible [sic] disappointed I cannot cooperate with you on proposed picture 'The Street with No Name.' Code specifically forbids showing of kidnapped child. I cannot change Code only Board can. . . . Breen's office informs me they have turned down 16 requests thus far this year for pictures dealing with kidnapping of children."[17] Not willing to give up, Zanuck answered with a long telegram message in which he defended his interest in making this kind of film:

I do not need to tell you that I have consistently endeavored to develop pictures which are of value not only as entertainment but also as social documents, and I join with the FBI in considering this to be one of the important contributions to fighting the crime wave which has grown out of all the various reasons which have made juvenile delinquency possible. Incidentally these reasons are emphasized in the picture. Were there a way of circumventing or substituting some other crime than kidnapping and yet retain the message we wish to convey we would most certainly recommend to the FBI that this be done and not ask you.[18]

But it was not to be. Eager to rush some kind of sequel to *House* into development, Zanuck commissioned Samuel C. Engel and Harry Kleiner to do a thorough rewrite of the script they had researched with FBI assistants, removing every one of its controversial elements and substituting the safe topic of "gangsterism" for the projected focus on youth crime. PCA approval, with a few quibbles about language, followed very quickly.[19] Somewhere in the course of this process Louis de Rochemont dropped out of the project, and Engel was assigned the producer's role.

In a few years, de Rochemont would return to the FBI as a production partner. With the filmmaker's encouragement, Hoover wrote (or had written) an article entitled "The Crime of the Century: The Case of the A-Bomb Spies" for *Reader's Digest*, published in the May 1952 issue; the piece dealt at some length with the (in)famous Ethel and Julius Rosenberg spy case. Produced by RD-DR and released through Columbia, *Walk East on Beacon* (1952) offered a substantially fictionalized account of the various agents who passed atomic research secrets to the Russians, ignoring the controversial particularities of the Rosenberg situation and exaggerating the counterespionage efficacy of FBI attempts at preserving national security. Not even a shadow of a tangled web of connections between the Rosenbergs, her brother David Greenglass, and Klaus Fuchs was to be found in the film, whose narrative was a tissue of spy fiction clichés. Alfred E. Werker directed, with much of the photography done on location in Boston and with the usual access provided to FBI file footage. De Rochemont's camera was permitted, as before, to photograph Bureau facilities and record the details of operational procedures.

Hoover waxed enthusiastic about the film's entertainment values, but he also praised its usefulness as propaganda since, in his view, it offered a timely intervention in what he understood as a clash of civilizations:

> "Walk East on Beacon" is not only very fine entertainment but constitutes an excellent medium to convey to every American some measure of the common danger which we face today. This film turns the spotlight on treachery and reveals inhuman blackmail which uses lives as pawns. The brazen methods of infiltration and the brutal disregard for human decency which mark the path of those who adhere to the doctrine of Communism are set forth in a revealing manner. . . . "Walk East on Beacon" . . . will I hope help Americans understand the evil force which is attempting to bring about the destruction of our free form of government.[20]

A most ardent admirer of the film was Senator Richard Nixon, then one of the Republicans in Congress most eager to hype fears about the so-called "Red Menace." Hollywood productions are not often the topic of speech-making in Congress, but Nixon, apparently convinced that the film was more truth than fiction, read the following statement into the *Congressional Record*:

> "Walk East on Beacon" shows one small but exciting portion of the continuous battle which is being constantly waged for the life of this Republic. The underground enemy is revealed in startlingly ordinary guise and in varying walks of life. . . . "Walk East on Beacon" shows the dark side of the picture. It also discloses a reassuring bright side in the revelation of FBI counterespionage activity. . . ." Walk East on Beacon" is an education and a warning. I urge every American to see it.[21]

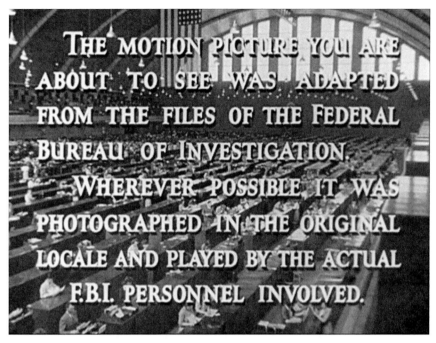

FIGURE 25 Like most of the semi-documentaries, *The Street with No Name* begins with a title card affirming that the story about to be told is true, but this is not exactly the case (frame enlargement).

Deprived of its ability to treat a problem affecting every American city and town, hence the general reference of the title, *The Street with No Name* proclaims its source in an actual case to which the filmmakers were afforded access, but in its considerably reconfigured form the script was no more a re-creation of some "true story" than what the filmmakers offered in *Walk East*. The film's opening title, if not an outright lie, certainly bends the truth almost beyond recognition: "The motion picture you are about to see was adapted from the files of the Federal Bureau of Investigation. Wherever possible, it was photographed in the original locale and played by the actual F.B.I. personnel involved." As would not be the case with both *Boomerang* and *Call Northside 777*, there was in fact no "original locale" to serve as an authentic setting for what was largely rather conventional fiction. A number of sequences for *Street* were shot in official Washington at the FBI training facilities in Quantico, Virginia, and these provided the realism for which *House* had whetted filmgoers' appetites; the rest of the film was photographed at various locations throughout the Los Angeles area (including the FBI branch office and the Royal and Gilbert Hotels). If more confection than truth, the film received an official endorsement of its message that the producers were not reticent to emphasize.

Hoover appears onscreen in order to plead for public awareness of the crime wave then supposedly sweeping the country: "The street on which crime flourishes is the street extending across America. It is the street with no name. Organized gangsterism is once again returning. If permitted to go unchecked three out of every four Americans will eventually become its victims. Wherever law and order break down there you will find public indifference. An alert and vigilant America will make for a secure America." The last line of Hoover's screed sounds like it was grabbed right out of *Ramparts*. A cynic might be moved to observe that Hoover was using Zanuck and Fox in order to argue the continuing importance of the FBI to the preservation of national security now that the war was over; if juvenile delinquency could not be dramatized because of Code prohibitions against the depiction of child kidnapping, then the specter of Prohibition-era gangsterism might usefully be raised. Of course, the Cold War and the threat of communist subversion soon provided the FBI and its director with an even more important mission, which was very quickly documented by *Walk East on Beacon*, following up on Hoover's *Reader's Digest* piece, the two "productions" reflecting the continuing cooperation between de Rochemont and DeWitt Wallace, the magazine's editor. The two films that Hoover sponsored and that in important ways sponsored him were good performers. Columbia did very well with *Walk East*, racking up a reported $1.35 million in rentals, which made it one of the studio's best earners in a year of declining profits. *Street* was not as successful for Fox as the other semi-documentaries exhibited in 1948, finishing at fiftieth place in the yearly rankings of Hollywood releases, but it was still a profitable project for the studio, encouraging the production of other semi-documentaries like *Southside* at the Poverty Row or independent studios that likewise made good use of the undercover agent focus in order to create drama and suspense.

Southside connects closely to this production cycle in several ways; it too is concerned with the exploits of yet another federal institution with broad investigatory and enforcement powers. Here again national security and prosperity are said to be at risk. Here, too, public apathy and ignorance must be overcome so that well-hidden but deadly criminal conspiracies might be brought to judicial light. In *Southside*, the forgers are identified through patient work in the Hoover style, and then an intrepid agent (Don de Fore), posing as a criminal, infiltrates the gang, the members of which are eventually rounded up after an elaborate and suspenseful pursuit that ends up on location at the Los Angeles "Angels Flight" cable service. The faux banknotes are safely kept from circulation, as an important arm of the federal government proves its indispensable value to safeguarding peace and prosperity. Directed by the Weimar émigré whose is credited with inaugurating the noir phenomenon with *Stranger on the Third Floor* (1940), *Southside* exemplifies the shift within the noir series toward the documentarianism and political engagement that characterizes postwar Hollywood realism in general, with Boris Ingster embracing more enthusiastically and creatively than Mann, Keighley, or Ludwig the pictorial journalism pioneered by de Rochemont.

The influence of *Ramparts* and its documentary progeny is obvious from the outset. In its length and ideological ardor, *Southside*'s introductory essay is strongly reminiscent of the wartime films of fact and persuasion meant to inform military and civilian audiences about the workings of American society and the threats or problems facing it. Most prominent among these were the documentaries in Frank Capra's *Why We Fight* series (1942–1945), the seven films by prominent Hollywood directors in uniform that were produced for the U.S. Office of War Information in order to better inform military and civilian filmgoers alike about the nature of the two conflicts in which the country had become embroiled, even more importantly identifying what was at stake in these deadly struggles. A successful follow-up to the series, Capra's *The Negro Soldier* (1944), focuses like *Southside* on a single political issue (the service of black men and women in a still-segregated armed forces), also offering a meditation on the history and established virtues of national institutions while demonstrating how the core values of American society are sometimes threatened from within.

Though he never promotes de Rochemont as a formative influence, the series that Capra produced for the government, especially the final entry, *War Comes to America* (1945), shows an obvious and quite substantial debt not only to his two wartime documentaries, *We Are the Marines* and *The Fighting Lady*, but also to *Ramparts,* especially in the incorporation of "enemy" footage to demonstrate the designs of aggressive foes for global conquest. *War Comes to America* traces how after Pearl Harbor American public opinion moved from a near-universal isolationism and desire for continued nonbelligerency to a determined acceptance of the necessity for the total mobilization of national resources so that European fascism and Japanese militarism might be defeated. Capra thus chronicles exactly the shift in the national mood that de Rochemont promoted in *Ramparts*; he too goes back to the events leading up to America's participation in World War I in order to make the case about Germany's long-standing plans for European and perhaps even global conquest. Capra even deploys restagings whenever appropriate "genuine" documentary footage was not available, continuing the practice that had proved so effective with the *MOT* and the period's newsreels more generally.

Largely because of its essay prologue, done in a style quite distinct from the fictional story that follows, as we shall see in detail below, *Southside* shares more in common with the de Rochemont/Zanuck collaborations and the *Why We Fight* series than with Ingster's previous noir project. *Stranger on the Third Floor* (1940) does not divide into two modally distinct sections but is uniformly fictional in the usual studio fashion. Moreover, instead of the pronounced jingoism of *Southside*, which reflects the victory culture that came into existence after 1945, *Stranger* is marked by the social pessimism that is characteristically associated with transplanted Weimar filmmakers like Ingster, whose work in Hollywood was central to the emergence of the film noir. Compare not only Billy Wilder's *Double Indemnity, A Foreign Affair,* and *Sunset Blvd.,* but also Fritz Lang's *Fury* (1936), which, like *Stranger,* focuses on the inadequacies of the American justice system.

The shortcomings are shown to be structural rather than accidental and hence impossible to resolve in a narrative that treats only an individual judicial error. All these noir films have much to say about various forms of human weakness and pathology, perspectives on human behavior that are notably absent in *Southside,* whose criminals are motivated by the same desire for profit as those working in the legitimate economy.

In a Hollywood devoted to the production, distribution, and exhibition of compelling narrative that often lacks much in the way of engagement with social or political issues, *Stranger* promotes an American form of cinematic modernism in which the uncertainties and ethical dilemmas of the inner life are shown to be connected to larger political and social problems, including, most importantly, the question of whether state institutions can deliver on their promise of the just, efficient, and secure management of communal life. Like the other noir semi-documentaries, *Southside* answers "yes" to this question, but *Stranger,* like most noir melodramas, responds with a resounding "no." In *Stranger,* the convention-ally required provision of justice offered by way of a conclusion is found to rest on the fortuitous accidental death of the real murderer, whose identification is not made by a police force thoroughly baffled by the case and resistant to outside help. Amateur sleuthing on the part of those affected is primarily responsible for the release from custody or from continuing suspicion of those who are shown to be innocent of wrongdoing, if only more or less.

Reflecting Zanuck's insistence that de Rochemont's pictorial journalism be made dramatically effective and otherwise attractive to filmgoers, the semi-documentaries similarly oscillate in their representational regimes between pro-viding information and offering conventional dramatizations. Caught between journalistic and fictionalizing approaches, the semi-documentary is ambivalent or contradictory, but only occasionally, in its presentation of politics, social relations, and moral issues, largely because, in order to retain viewer interest, sympathy can be uncomfortably generated by the attractive malefactors who in part lead the narrative. In *Stranger,* by way of contrast, a split between measured obedience to the law and the unreflective acting out of violent impulses is located within the human self itself—constitutes in fact its essential quality as the film moves the Hollywood cinema's presentation of character observed from the outside toward the recognition of the existence of a rich (and problematic) inner life that offers no "camera-reality" to be recorded and must instead be evoked figuratively.

And yet here too in those noir melodramas of an expressionist bent is the contrast between the individual and a society whose chief function seems to be the passing of judgment, a theme that will often reappear in the postwar semi-documentary, especially those that reflect the melding of journalistic techniques to various forms of crime narrative. *Stranger* offers a form of modernism whose realist impulses are directed toward the representation, however antimimetic, of what previously had been considered off-limits to the kind of drama the cinema was thought capable of staging. Even though its visuals are not dependent in the least on the incorporation of photographable realia, *Stranger*, like many noir films, does pursue a pronounced realist agenda. The anatomizing and dramatization of the inner life in the noir series challenge the comfortable conformism of most Hollywood films, as what is called into question is the seemingly indispensable notion of an undivided moral character, on which the distribution of poetically just fates is managed in the conventionally "happy" endings that Hollywood narrative customarily trades in. *Stranger*'s world is fallen, like our own, a troubled landscape of buried emotions and barely suppressed guilt where good luck counts for more than virtue, which in its unalloyed form is conspicuously absent. *Stranger* tells a kind of truth that Hollywood films had not been accustomed to proclaiming, a contestation of official social values that French critics were quick to recognize as one of the signal features of this "dark cinema." Its particular brand of realism is worth exploring at further length because it contrasts so sharply with the journalistic objectivism of *Southside* and the noir semi-documentary more generally.

Stranger traces the most customary passage of noir experience: a self-reflexive turn toward a morally vexed interiority away from the exterior dramatics hitherto characteristic of the standard Hollywood product of the era, in which the narrative is advanced by dialogue and action. *Stranger* begins in a brightly lit and bustling American metropolis, where two young people, eager to get married, are enjoying what seems to be a lucky break. Here is a film that is substantially more realistic than the ordinary studio release of the era, but in a fashion quite different from the location-oriented approach of a decade later. Mike Ward (John McGuire) is a young reporter who seems to have happened on a murder scene in his neighborhood; his role as a star witness will, he hopes, translate into a regular byline and an attendant promotion, with a salary raise that will allow him to marry at long last his girlfriend, Jane (Margaret Tallichet). At the trial, which Jane attends in order to witness her fiancé's big moment, Mike testifies that he came across Joe Briggs (Elisha Cook Jr.) standing over the body of a café owner, whose throat has been cut. Quickly found guilty, Briggs screams his innocence as guards haul him away, shaking Jane badly as she begins to realize that she and Mike are profiting from another's terrible misfortune. Instead of uniting the couple, the trial divides them; Mike, obsessed with the marble statue that dominates the courtroom, of blind Justice balancing her scales, now swathed in shadows, departs for home deeply troubled after talking to a colleague in a pressroom that suddenly grows dark and crisscrossed by entrapping bars of light.

In an extended voiceover, Mike mulls over his part in proving Briggs guilty and soon disabuses himself of the notion that he would not be likely to commit the same kind of impulsive violent act. He finds his neighborhood and rooming house abruptly darkened and filled with swirling shadows, seemingly reflecting his own distress, and on the front stoop he runs into a stranger with cringing manner and bulging eyes whose secret sharer he will soon become. About to open his door, he spots the stranger leaving the apartment of the man who lives across the hall, Mr. Meng (Charles Halton), with whom Mike has had several run-ins. Thinking that Meng might have been murdered, Mike flashes back to these confrontations and to his own expressed desire to kill him. Falling asleep, he dreams he had murdered Meng, and in an interrogation and subsequent trial staged in a style that *New York Times* reviewer Bosley Crowther opined was derived "from a couple of heavy French and Russian films," finds himself convicted and condemned in the theater of his own mind.[22] Waking, Mike discovers that Meng is indeed dead, his throat slashed in the same fashion as that of the café owner. Because he discovered both bodies, Mike falls under suspicion. He is released by the police only after Jane chases down the stranger, who turns out to be a mental hospital escapee; the man confesses to both killings. The film closes with the young couple reunited and once again planning their wedding.

Stranger's descent into interiority depends on what are essentially antirealist techniques: first, a chiaroscuro relighting of the studio set/exteriors; and then a retreat into a dream world that is evoked in distinctly Brechtian terms. And yet, in comparison to the standard industry product, *Stranger* is intensely realist in a larger sense because of its focus on the unconventional in both collective and personal terms: the failure of the justice system to assign guilt accurately; the impossible distinction, in any case, between guilt and innocence in the human heart; the seldom-bridged gulf between public and private selves. In *Niagara*, by way of contrast, the passions of those seeking to master or channel their sexual desires are projected onto locations that reflect their intensity, appeal, and destructive power; these locations, to be sure, express the passions and feelings of the characters, but they do so in a way that avoids a psychologizing movement toward inner states, the contours of which emerge mainly through dialogue and, in one startling sequence, voiceover. At film's beginning, as noted previously, George approaches the falls and addresses them with his own unspoken resentment about their quite apparent superior power and "being," as he dreads his own creeping sense of insignificance, an essential element in the experience of the sublime landscape that is Niagara. But this moment of focused introspection passes quickly, as the film moves toward a more conventionally dramatic mode of displaying fears, thoughts, and, especially important here, obsessions, psychological states that, once projected, find their objective correlative in the ambiguous nature of the falls, which welcome sexual overindulgence even as they reveal the destructive power of unbridled Nature for those who go too far. Locative realism, just to make the obvious point, is all about exteriorization.

The narrativizing of the inner life in *Stranger* displaces for a time the film's zero-degree surface realism (what theorist Matthew Potolsky calls "a set of conventions so familiar" that no one recognizes that it is "trafficking in conventions rather than describing objective reality").[23] Instead, Ingster and his collaborators install the expressive theatricalism so characteristic of Weimar filmmaking, in which richly symbolic forms of staging, acting, and even sound recording defy, but do not reject completely, forensic forms of representation. Events continue to unfold, but now in a subjunctive mood as the mindscreen throws up for contemplation the possibility of a horrific future. The dream's setting internalizes exterior experience even as it puts into play characters fully charged with complex feelings that are only barely accessible to the conscious mind of the protagonist/ dreamer. The "real" trial scene of the film's opening is restaged in the theater of Mike's unconscious, where, in effect, the agonized man finds himself guilty, obviating the need for a justice system whose judgments prove incorrect (as do his own, for despite these premonitions he is never brought to trial, and justly so since he is in fact innocent of any crime). A world more revealing of difficult truths emerges from within the opacity of surface everydayness where the conventional presentation of self predominates and deeply buried thoughts and emotions unsurprisingly cannot reveal themselves.

In tracing this passage from exterior to interior and back to exterior, the narrative in *Stranger* moves progressively through three distinct stylistic regimes. The brightly lit and thoroughly objective approach of the beginning and closing segments contrasts with the noir stylization (mostly a switch to low-key and more or less naturalistic chiaroscuro set-ups) of the film's interiors and exteriors that follows Mike's perception of the brutality of the justice system and the role he has accidentally come to play in it. If noir film, as is commonly thought, exposes the hidden underside of American life, the darkness here is self-evidently contingent. It reflects the protagonist's shifting mental state and is a matter of how he perceives the world, becoming the objective correlative of his unanticipated encounter with moral and existential questions that are profound, difficult, and, so the film's ending shows, insoluble—except through a transfer of guilt that only technically exculpates Mike. Accordingly, this stylistic transition is marked by the sudden access the viewer is given to Mike's subjectivity. Dialogue is abandoned almost completely and the drama the film now treats is not expressed by exterior action; it becomes instead a mental journey toward accepting responsibility for the conviction of Briggs.

This train of thought leads to Mike's premonitions about Meng's death (something he had himself wished for and was willing in some sense to accomplish). He disavows but then accepts his own capacity for violence. These memories include a violent grappling with Meng when the man had cast a lascivious eye on Jane, as well as Mike's angrily expressed protestation to a friend that he would indeed enjoy killing him, a reaction that is wildly disproportionate to the offense Meng has given. Such burdensome thoughts propel Mike into a troubled sleep, where he dreams of crime and punishment, recapitulating the scene and characters of Briggs's trial with himself now as the innocent accused. The trial ends with his conviction after a false deliverance, for the judge takes no notice that a still-living Meng is in the courtroom as he sentences Mike to death. An exaggeratedly gestural and anti-naturalistic declamatory acting style in these sequences is complemented by dialogue rendered eerily threatening through use of an echo chamber. Interiorized as the locus of a set of values and procedures that shape human self-understanding, the courtroom becomes an abstract play space as ceiling and walls are replaced by crisscrossed patterns of light and dark. Mise-en-scène is rendered even more abstract by symmetrical blocking (a neat circle of interrogators haranguing a desperate Mike, the jury members with heads uniformly bowed down suddenly rising together as if on signal to proclaim his guilt) as well as furniture that "expresses" the power of the law (for example, as Mike speaks to Jane, a guard sits between them on an unnaturally high stool in a direct quotation of a similar set-up in *The Cabinet of Dr. Caligari* [1920]).

If the opening and closing segments of *Stranger* depict a world that seems "normal" and "realistic" within the context of Hollywood filmmaking, it is true that these representations are chiefly melodramatic in the sense described by Margaret Hallam and Elizabeth Marshment: they further the film's interest in "situation and plot" and the presentation of "a fixed complement of stock characters or emblematic types."[24] Mike and Jane constitute the irreplaceable center of melodramatic plotting—the romantic couple—while the stranger is the villain who blocks their happiness by putting Mike in jeopardy and then, in the scene where she confronts him, attempting to kill her. His death restores the moral order as he is forced to confess the truth of his crimes. While the studio-built interiors and exteriors in these segments are realistic in the sense that the city, its people, and its customs evoke contemporary American culture, they do not offer what Hallam and Marshment suggest is the signal quality of realism: a "concern with observation and depiction of character psychology, situations, and events."[25] Interestingly, then, it is in the sections of the film that are either lightly or heavily stylized, and thus antirealistic in one sense, that the film manifests more investment in the real through an examination of themes that are both social (particularly the inevitable inadequacies of the system of justice, which, having no access to subjective truth, can only guess at motive) and ethical (that Mike's success depends on Briggs's misfortune; that he shares in a generalized sense of guilt for having wished the murder of Meng, of which in retrospect he appears more than capable and desirous). In a movement that interestingly parallels the preoccupation in literary modernism with a multileveled subjectivity, the melodramatic flatness of Mike's character as the romantic lead achieves a Forsterian roundness only when the action shifts from a world of objective relations to the unwilled self-dramatization that follows a reflexive yet profound *crise de conscience*. It is in these sequences that the film becomes more art than entertainment, leaving melodrama behind for a heavily Europeanized emphasis on the inner life.

In *Stranger,* as in other American films noirs incorporating expressionist themes and styles, the work of representing the real in any unconventional sense is accomplished by a retreat from public experience to the individual conscience and hence, often if not always, consciousness, where the intimations of self-analysis assume a fully dramatized form that contrasts markedly with the actual trial that had occurred earlier. But this noir vision of the darker side of human nature finds its limits within the generally more socially optimistic narrative tradition of classic studio filmmaking, with which it is generally forced to compromise. In a move that will be reprised often in the developing tradition of film noir, Mike awakes to live out only in a provisional sense what his dream has revealed. He is not surprised to find that Meng has indeed been killed and that, by the same kind of circumstantial evidence that had condemned Briggs, the police quickly identify him as the murderer. The film's melodramatic framing structure soon identifies the guilty party as "the stranger," installing a poetic justice that rewards virtue and punishes villainy in order to produce a conventional happy ending.

Southside, in contrast, abjures any exploration of subjective truth for the particular, thoroughly exterior facticity of Ramparts, whose directive yet nonpartisan politics successfully imitates the peculiar engagement of MOT and Time magazine editorializing. This is critical in its identification of problems but unabashedly chauvinist in its promotion of national virtues, which are never seriously challenged by wrongdoers. Like de Rochemont's films in general, Southside pursues a journalistic agenda, not just to celebrate institutional power, but also to explain why such power is needed to maintain the social and economic relationships of ordinary life, which we unreflectingly tend to take for granted even though they depend on collective arrangements that, it is easily shown, need careful management. Ingster's later entry into the noir series demystifies the workings of the marketplace rather than those of the individual soul. In the world's largest capitalist democracy, Southside affirms that a Smithian invisible hand is permitted to exert impersonal power, except when the mutual pursuit of self-interest proves inadequate to guarantee the continuing equity of contracts. The reliability of the medium of exchange is crucial to economic and social well-being, and, as Southside makes clear, only the government is equal to the task of maintaining it. The reason is simple. Currency's value is a matter of collective agreement, but this unreflective trust is easily undermined by counterfeiting, by the pollution of the economic public sphere with the false coin of criminal intent, a problem beyond the ability of any individual to properly identify and correct.

In its concern with financial stability, the film reflects its historical moment; it was produced just a few years after the international establishment of the Bretton Woods system in 1944, in which the global economy became dependent on a "solid dollar" backed by fixed-value gold reserves. The dollar, in short, not only underwrote the rapidly escalating prosperity of postwar America, but the financial stability of the capitalist world order. The education of the national citizenry, perhaps uninformed and certainly apathetic about such matters, is self-avowedly one of the film's aims, connecting it to the similar rhetoric in both Ramparts and the Capra documentaries, especially Americans at War. There is nothing similar in T-Men, whose framing prologue is more concerned with establishing the truth-value of the story whose re-creation soon follows. In Street, Hoover's overly general jeremiad against increasing gangsterism in the postwar era seems strangely out of date, more appropriate to the lawlessness of the late Prohibition and "public enemies" like John Dillinger and Al Capone, whose disturbances of the national order provided the director with unassailable reasons why the FBI should be expanded. *T-Men*'s government agents are just another species of detective, while the precise nature and functioning of the institution they support only perfunctorily come into focus. Lewis Allen's *Appointment with Danger* (1951), yet another entrant into this cycle, dramatizes a similar "true case" in which the focus falls on the United States Postal Inspection Service, whose agents track down the murder of one of their own and, in the process, foil an attempt by a criminal mastermind to steal $1 million that the Post Office is committed to safely transporting, with its inspectors said to be "the nation's oldest police force." In the manner of *Southside*, if more perfunctorily, *Appointment* begins with a prologue in which, over a montage of shots of different offices, a narrator explains the workings and history of American mail delivery, whose speed and reliability are said to be vital to the smooth functioning of the national economy. But the narrative itself is simply a sub-Hitchcockian study of suspense and terror, as the only witness to the crime—a frightened if resourceful nun—must be protected from the crooks intent on silencing her for good. In *Walk East on Beacon*, little attention is paid to how Russian-backed espionage about nuclear secrets threatens the security of the West (NATO, founded in 1949, had established ties of mutual defense among the principal noncommunist states, with an American nuclear umbrella providing a counter to the Red Army, the continent's most formidable military machine); the film is more cops and criminals than political or ideological treatise, fittingly beginning and ending with investigations and pursuit.

And yet *Southside* shares with all these other films, including the wartime documentaries, a certain *mentalité*. The peaceful everydayness of American life, with its peculiarly informal rhythms and ignorant self-containment, is shown to be threatened by unexpected forces that are eager to exploit unpreparedness and inattention. Those forces can be defeated only by concerted effort channeled through the institutions (the military, the presidency, the Treasury Department) that American society has created to provide for its safety and well-being. Unflagging surveillance is vitally required if democracy and the free market are to endure, and the self-evident *raison d'être* of films like *Southside* is not just to entertain, but also to inform and warn. Ordinary citizens, of course, cannot and need not do anything to support the systems underpinning every aspect of their daily lives. The *Why We Fight* films enlist viewers in the war against global tyranny. *Southside*'s demand is more modest. It is simply that we should all be cognizant of and grateful for the institutions that represent our collective will, once we are shown that they are equal to the vital tasks required of them. This is not much different from Hoover's admonition in *Street* that what the present "crisis" requires is an "alert and vigilant America."

The realist politics in *Stranger* are less strident, but, curiously enough, more open to the identification of large-scale problems that defy amelioration through well-established and carefully regulated procedures of surveillance, investigation, and prevention. What, after all, might be the "solution" beyond judicial retribution to the homicidal sociopathy of the "stranger," the secret sharer of law-abiding respectability whose actions resist any imputation of motive in the usual sense? Significantly, the film never brings this threatening creature to a court where questions of mental competence might problematize a desire for vengeance, which is instead enacted accidentally, without the need for judgment as such. And even though they are prone to error as a result, what are the courts to do but rely on the only evidence that they often dispose of, which is the eyewitness testimony whose truth value is perhaps most times problematic? The point of the film in some sense is to argue that appearances are deceiving and that "things" are not always what they seem. Hollywood's customary promotion of a moralizing that reduces all narratives to some uplifting message is hardly truthful, measured against a real world where virtue often does not triumph over vice. The debunking of this idealism is an inherently realistic project, providing noir with its most characteristic theme: the restoration to Hollywood's inherently socially conformist narrative style of some of the ambiguities, irresolutions, and uncomfortable immoralities of the world we actually live in. The semi-documentary form, in contrast, is thoroughly idealist and even chauvinist, with, as we have seen, even one filmmaker not too embarrassed to summon up the ghost of Daniel Webster to pass enthusiastic judgment on the state of the union, a message that plays out over the poignant image of one of the nation's most sacred *lieux de mémoire.*

Many of the noir films made during the classic period (conventionally said to end in 1958) follow *Stranger*'s critical attitude toward American institutions and further its engagement with the seemingly ineradicable discontents of modern life: psychopathology, anomie, political corruption, economic dissatisfaction, and, especially perhaps, the lack of coherent and fulfilling bonds that might but only seldom connect the millions of "strangers" who inhabit the modern city to one another. Noir protagonists are usually doomed by their moral failings: Joe Gillis's inability to end his unloving dependence on Norma while escape from the easy life she gave him is still possible, the disappointed actress's furor at her failure to cope with changing fashions and the inevitable decline of her physical beauty, Rose's untroubled willingness to murder her husband in order to escape a distressing marriage, and George's irresistible compulsion to strangle the woman who betrayed him even when through good fortune he is given the opportunity to begin a new life without her. Compared to these narratives in which self-destructive and antisocial energies burble up to the narrative surface, *Stranger* offers an even stronger critique of social conformism because it uncovers the powerful, if unacted-upon, murderous impulses in the main character with whom the viewer is asked to sympathize and, in the end, regard as innocent. Mike, so the film suggests, is to be understood as something of an everyman, seemingly—but not actually—far removed from unreasonable thoughts of violent retribution. Like all of us, in other words, he is a stranger to the terrible impulses that lie not buried deeply enough within his own mind, the revelation of which is one of the film's narrative goals, unrelated as it might be to the actual solution of the crime that constitutes the narrative focus. This is realism of a kind, and that's how it struck film noir's first admirers: French critics who saw that Hollywood had determined, for whatever reason, to start telling more of the truth about the human experience than it had previously done, hobbled by a Victorian aesthetic.

In *Southside* and other noirish semi-documentaries, a quite different form of cultural politics dominates, one that centers on the demonstration of the impressive, impersonal authority of state institutions to identify and resolve problems in the public sphere. These films reflect the unshakable faith in American exceptionalism of both Zanuck and de Rochemont, whose cultivation of a close friendship with Hoover provided a model to other filmmakers eager to partner with federal or state agencies and produce films in which the many supposed strengths of official America are foregrounded, while threats from within and without to domestic order are neatly blunted, thus avoiding lasting damage to the nation. The strident nationalism that had unsurprisingly emerged in American culture during the war years must have made the transparently propagandistic orientation of such themes acceptable to postwar filmgoers. In the semi-documentary more generally, governmental power manifests itself not only in these stories of surveillance and investigatory success that celebrate the irresistible, collective power of huge bureaucracies, but also in images of their impressive public edifices, which are deployed as a visual earnest of their scale, organization, and bureaucratic rather than individual intentionality. These institutions are notably absent in *Ramparts,* but de Rochemont, after helming cinematic tributes to the marines and navy during the war, cultivated a friendship with an admiring J. Edgar Hoover, and the result was the trend-establishing *House on 92nd Street.*

Authoritative Voices

Highlighted in documentary-style prologues, state power also finds a structural reflex in the deployment of an offscreen narrator, whose confident male voice metonymically represents the organization for which he stands in. In *Southside,* as in the genre more generally, the commentary provided by this unseen figure, though of contrasting kinds, bridges what might be a problematic formal divide. The narrator exercises near-complete semiotic power over the succession of images in the prologue, whose assembly and assigned meaning reflect his shaping purpose. But he never disappears as a presence once the story proper begins to unfold, driven by its own dynamics, and not so clearly responsive in its structure to whatever designs the narrator might have. His power at this point is epistemological; unlike the characters whose actions he surveils, he knows all. This figure will surrender his control no sooner than do the government agents who detect and dispose of threatening criminal conspiracies, never resting until public order is restored. Transformed into an extradiegetic commentator in the manner of classic literary realism, this unseen figure continues until the credits roll to marshal and interpret data like his diegetic counterparts, the investigators who actually solve the case and corral the criminals. He never allows viewers to forget his authoritative presence while transforming such seemingly composite texts into effectively unified, "authentic" fiction.

All the semi-documentaries deploy voiceover narration to solve, some more successfully than others, the problem of melding the documentary and story portions of the text. How this may be artfully accomplished is best demonstrated in *Southside*. As noted, the film's introductory section is in effect a cinematic essay that argues for the centrality of a stable currency to the survival of the democratic West. A hand spins a globe and lands on the Korean peninsula, as the narrator suggests that the struggle between totalitarianism and democracy, begun in 1914, may be entering its final phase with the outbreak of this proxy war between communism and the free world. A montage of battle scenes from World War II (generic images of huge naval task forces, aerial dogfights, and nighttime artillery fire) offers a catalogue of weapons that the narrator avers are not as powerful as a strong currency in maintaining a free society against threats from within and without. A short discourse on the nature of paper money follows ("essentially promissory notes" whose value, we are told, is maintained by the government that issues them, a position perfectly in line with the Bretton Woods system). Deploying a succession of images, the narrator then illustrates the importance of a reliable currency to all aspects of the functioning of society, from farms to vacation resorts, in the process providing an attractive catalogue of various aspects of "free society," though key areas of the postwar domestic economy (housing, kitchen appliances, automobiles) do not merit a mention. And it certainly is possible to take issue with the narrator's proclamation that "the strength of a nation depends on the value of its currency," a view that seems especially strange in the wake of a truly global war in which more than ten million Americans volunteered or were called upon to serve, and whose supposedly latest phase is then requiring a substantial sacrifice of American blood and treasure. In any event, the nation that emerges from these images is productive and prosperous, well fed and comfortable, seemingly safe from any threat, internal or external. But that appearance of an inviolable social order is deceptive, if only in the limited, and ultimately recuperable, sense that the film will go on to explore. There will always be threats, as the narrator explains, but the system we have created to deal with them will prove equal to the challenge of their total defeat.

In the manner of classic documentary, the individual shots in this essay are not readable in terms of their "point" without the narrator's explanation. Viewed without that commentary, they would make no coherent sense. Thus the juxtaposition of images of a small and then a large dairy farm means nothing until the narrator explains that a stable currency is as important to small enterprises as it

FIGURE 26 This process shot from the opening essay of *Southside 1–1000* suggests that a stable currency undergirds every social transaction (frame enlargement).

is to larger ones; a shot of a man on water skis is opaque without the narrator's comment that money is necessary for those eager to enjoy leisure-time sports. The images, we might say, are less important than the narrator's screed, which could be as easily and effectively illustrated by unlimited others. The essay ends with a direct borrowing from *House*: a panning shot that links the Washington Monument with the Treasury Department building, affirming by this visual demonstration of the proximity of the two structures and the easy passage between them, and in a manner that Hamilton and the Federalists would have endorsed, the centrality to American life of the printing of money and of its appropriate disbursement. Like the society it supports, the American dollar in its material form finds itself vulnerable to threats from within and without that would destroy its ability to function as necessary social glue. Once enunciated, this truth leads naturally to the exemplification of how Treasury agents prevent such a potentially disastrous debasement. Currency must assume a material form if it is to function as a medium of exchange, and the fact that bills and coins are generic makes them liable to unauthorized reproduction despite all reasonable precautions. This is especially problematic in the case of paper currency, whose forms are easier—and more profitable—to duplicate.

In this prologue, images serve as metonymies of the larger points made by the narrator; they illustrate and exemplify what he has to say even as they have no importance per se. They are established as pictures of things in general, not of things in particular. The rhetorical space occupied by the narrator is not extradiegetic as such since at this point there is no diegesis beyond a string of otherwise disconnected illustrations. The point from which he addresses us is the only place where meaning and truth can be made available. By contrast, in *Stranger,* voiceover narration appears at the moment when an exteriorly focused or dramatic approach to the depiction of character proves inadequate; such an audible articulation of private and uncommunicated thoughts affords access to the inner life of the *dramatis personae,* and it does not issue from a point of address outside the image track whose meaning it seeks to fix. Mike's meditations on his involvement in Briggs's conviction and subsequently Meng's murder are supplements to images that by themselves can no longer convey anything more than the grim and threatening mood established by the chiaroscuro lighting set-ups. Importantly, voiceover is abandoned once Mike begins to dream. The inner truths of his character then take shape dramatically, making it possible for the narrative to shift back from telling to showing, from the verbal expression of feelings and thoughts to their visualization in fully subjectified images and their attendant narrativization. Once Mike returns to consciousness, what has been revealed in the dream world assumes dramatic form, restarting the narrative of crime and punishment that had been briefly suspended and obviating the need for further interior monologue. With Mike reassuming his connection with the other characters, the story is propelled toward a closing exteriorization, exemplified by the "restorative" death of his secret sharer.

Southside, interestingly enough, manifests a similar kind of movement away from telling to showing. The primacy of the narrator's well-constructed diatribe yields focus to a story world that by its nature yields meanings that are readable without accompanying commentary. The cinematic essay proper ends and the exemplum begins, even as a hardly surprising rhetorical shift occurs. First lectured effectively on a central truth of modern social life, the viewer is now positioned to be entertained by a story illustrating important aspects of that truth. But this transition masks, if rather transparently, another move, as the film assumes a conventional identity as a Hollywood product designed to deliver the different pleasures of compelling narrative. In recognition of this delayed but inevitable move away from documentary rhetoric, *Southside* could turn completely from telling to showing, abandoning its direct address to the viewer, as other films in the semi-documentary cycle in fact do. Having discovered effective visual and dramatic ways to present exposition, the classic Hollywood story of this era had no need for extradiegetic voiceover commentary. Voiceover is available to filmmakers only as a stylistic option that is used rarely and then usually as character-focalized and associated with subjective flashbacks, often, if hardly exclusively, in film noir. But the complete abandonment of voiceover once the story begins in *Southside* would undermine the way in which the film has hitherto carefully constructed a connection between the narrating presence of the cinematic essayist and the powerful state institutions whose nature and purpose he explicates. He is their enthusiastic and omniscient spokesman, presenting the argument for their importance in the real world that exists beyond the exemplifying fictions (however generally true) that the narrative will trade in.

Given the industry's commitment to entertainment, these forms of "real" meaning more easily emerge from the film's story world when mediated by the voice of the non-character narrator. Becoming simply a source of narrative, representational, and dramatic pleasure, valued only for its well-done action sequences and the suspenseful twists and turns of the plot, the story might easily lose its value as an exemplum. The didacticism of the noir semi-documentary depends on an admittedly uneasy accommodation of contrasting rhetorics at which some of these films prove more adept than others. In *Southside,* the story world that is in some sense self-contained (the truth illustrated) must remain clearly subordinate to the framing set of ideas and values that calls it into being. The documentary framing of *T-Men,* developed more briefly and in less depth, soon slips from sight as the suspenseful and exciting narrative of crime and pursuit becomes the main focus. In his other semi-documentaries as well, such as *Border Incident* (1949), Mann slights the journalistic, informational aspects of the form, concentrating instead on staging gripping action sequences. A useful balance between facts and fiction, however, is more consistently maintained in *Southside* and in those other semi-documentaries that are invested in de Rochemont–style pictorial journalism, especially, and most spectacularly, *The Phenix City Story.*

Sin City, USA: A Cinematic Exposé

The semi-documentaries present an intriguing variety of ways in which this necessary formal accommodation is managed. Not all the films in this series are structured around the movement from general to specific truth. *The Phenix City Story* exemplifies an alternate pattern; the film was written and, as the credits proclaim in a unique gesture that emphasizes its particular truthfulness, "researched" by Crane Wilbur. The film lives up to this unusual billing; it is certainly the most journalistic entrant in the series. In the manner of reportage, *Phenix City* treats a series of real events, providing both information and also a narrative reenactment (with considerable but not distorting fabulation) of an intriguing civic history whose twists and turns had already been featured in numerous magazine and newspaper articles, as well as in a best-selling book. Here the Hollywood cinema positions itself as the latest in a series of media to take up a story that for at least a year had been enthralling the nation.

Phenix City is thus journalistic in the sense well established by *MOT* and de Rochemont's factual films for Fox, except that, compared to *House,* for example, it is a much more accurate reenactment of recent history, with no names changed and the satisfying conclusion to these events provided not by a screenwriter, but by the members of the community themselves. This urge for optimistically rendered truth in which the power of an outraged and engaged citizenry is emphasized can hardly be traced to director Phil Karlson, who spent the early years of his career stylishly directing low-budget actioners for both Monogram and Eagle-Lion, and his energetic, economical style is nicely exemplified in the fictionalized retelling of how the downfall of organized crime in Phenix City came to pass. Karlson's earlier noirish city portrait film, *Kansas City Confidential* (1952), follows the semi-documentary tradition in offering a detailed depiction of a complicated robbery, but otherwise it rejects the conventions of the series. Here is a film, an explanatory title proclaims, that is *not* drawn from the files of the Kansas City police, which are said to be filled with interesting cases; instead what the filmmakers pretend to offer is a dramatization of the proverbial "'perfect crime,' the true solution of which is not entered in any case history." The story, it is hardly surprising, is simple fabulation, its exciting twists and turns, and considerable violence, coming straight from the somewhat fevered imaginations of the screenwriters (George Bruce, Harry Essex, and Harold R. Greene).

Credit for the multilayered realism in *Phenix City* instead must be given to the versatile Wilbur, one of the silent screen's most notable actors (starring in the iconic serial *The Perils of Pauline,* among other substantial credits) and subsequently enjoying a career as a film and stage director, as well as a novelist and journalist. During the war, working for Warner Bros., he made for theatrical exhibition a number of propaganda shorts, including the sixteen-minute *I Am an American* (1944) that stands out for its artistry and sophistication in a genre whose entrants were normally hopelessly banal or laughably hyperbolic in their self-congratulatory nationalism. The film offers an extended homage to de Rochemont–style filmmaking, blending a socially typical story, its various points reinforced by authoritative voiceover, with clips of newsreel footage and a coda in which a Hollywood star delivers a closing homily directly to the viewer. *I Am an American* traces the experiences of an Eastern European immigrant family coming to America in the nineteenth century (the father loses an arm fighting for the Union in the Civil War) and, in succeeding generations, establishing itself as a pillar of the community in a rural Ohio town. As America enters World War I, the patriarch from his deathbed proclaims to his family: "We must fight with everything we have. Like all Americans, you are the sons and daughters of immigrants. You are the new blood that keeps fresh the lifestream. You are the hope of today and tomorrow and all of the tomorrows to come." Images of famous first-generation Americans (Joseph Pulitzer, Andrew Carnegie, Knute Rockne, and Arturo Toscanini chief among them) then fill the screen. In the de Rochemont manner, the film's final segment is a newsreel clip from the "I Am an American Day" celebration inaugurated by Congress in 1940 (later Citizenship Day) in which some of the industry's most popular stars, including Humphrey Bogart and Ava Gardner, take part. *I Am an American* closes with actor Dennis Morgan facing the camera directly to proclaim the pride he feels in being part of a diverse yet unified society. As historian Jeff Stafford observes, what Wilbur has designed is "both a valentine to a nation which has welcomed countless immigrants to its shores but also a call to arms to all immigrants who have become American citizens and created better lives for themselves in the U.S."[26]

Wilbur's script for *Phenix City* reflects the same kind of political and cultural engagement, as life for the decent and law-abiding in an army town threatened by a municipal administration held hostage to irresistible graft would have made an ideal subject for an *MOT* issue or, indeed, a short subject on the model of *I Am an American.* The facts that the filmmakers disposed of, however restaged, made unnecessary any further hyping. Working with Wilbur, Karlson here upholds a more stringent form of particular truth, with his hook being the then-ongoing investigation of a sensational case of political murder. Making allowance for some fictionalizing in a series of subplots, *Phenix City* certainly meets the journalistic standards set by the Columbus, Georgia, *Ledger,* which rose to national prominence for its accurate reporting on the evil twin city across the Chattahoochee River. The film presents a thoroughly true story with considerable realism, even if the main character's less than admirable connection with the Ku Klux Klan and his indefatigable support for segregation are elided, making him seem more socially progressive and fair-minded than he in fact was. Karlson and Wilbur devoted themselves to an extended period of local research, carefully scouting the city, which allowed filming to proceed in the precise locations where the various events occurred, including notorious 14th Street, where most of the city's vice emporia were still clustered and where the filmmakers, who could hardly be understood as other than scandal-mongers, confess they felt threatened as they surveyed locations and then set about shooting most of the film's exteriors.

Phenix City begins with not one but two nonfictional prologues that introduce its only lightly sensationalized reenactments of the murder of a public official, which has at last moved the local citizens to clean up their vice-ridden town. The truth value of the rather noirish narrative of crime and punishment that follows is vouched for by a sort of prologue, bearing no marks of production, that is entitled "A Report from Phenix City," a thirteen-minute series of unpolished, stand-up interviews that feature no actors, only real people appearing as themselves speaking to Clete Roberts, a nationally known correspondent for the local CBS television affiliate in Los Angeles. Roberts was noted for grabbing an 8 mm camera and traveling to some newsworthy location, there to research and shoot a feature story. His appearance in Phenix City attests to the national importance of the case and the subsequent trial of those accused of killing Albert L. Patterson, a local lawyer who had been nominated for the office of state attorney general. In the solidly Democratic South, Patterson had been certain to be elected on a platform whose main plank was rooting out the gambling and prostitution syndicates in what was then widely known as "Sin City, USA." He had been prevented from taking office by those in organized crime opposed to ending a hugely lucrative local business that for many decades had attracted, much like Las Vegas soon would, gamblers

FIGURE 27 A semi-documentary, *The Phenix City Story* begins with a television-style stand-up presentation by a journalist covering ongoing developments in America's sin city (frame enlargement).

from near and far, as well as continuing hordes of lonely soldiers from nearby Fort Benning eager for paid female companionship and cheap liquor. During the war, as Gen. George S. Patton discovered to his great dismay, these working girls were motored out to the gates of the base in trucks equipped with mattresses. Vice of the most traditional kind was very big business in Phenix City.

Working in a seemingly impromptu style with notes scribbled on a slip of paper, Roberts talks about the case with fellow reporter Ed Strickland, who, along with his colleague Gene Wortsman, had published a tell-all book about the town. Interviews, obviously uncanned, follow with a local, Hugh Bentley, and with Hugh Britton, the deputy sheriff who has courageously been a witness in the trial and who tells about the numerous death threats received. The segment ends with Roberts speaking to Patterson's widow, who is afraid for the life of her son John, now nominated by the Democratic Party to run for the same office because he has vowed to carry on his father's fight against the crime syndicates. Roberts then signs off from Phenix City, "where our camera and microphone have been," and sends viewers back to the cities where they live, with no indication that there is a fictional narrative to follow that will cover much of the same ground. Roberts's witnesses, however, only testify to the problems that John Patterson will face. The re-creation offered by Karlson goes much further with its detailed dramatization of the successful campaign to root out municipal corruption that precedes the eventual shuttering of the gambling dens, saloons, and brothels. The film's prologue, if that is what it is, begins and ends in precisely the form that on-scene reporting was then assuming in the still-emerging practice of television news. Apparently misdirected toward viewers who are not at the other end of a television screen, it seems very much a kind of celluloid *objet trouvé,* not produced for and connected only loosely to the other text. These two documents together constitute this notorious city's "story," with the first more journalistic than the second even though both are committed to relating the particular truths of the case.

When the film was distributed, exhibitors were advised that they could simply leave out the initial report from Clete Roberts and begin with the more traditional title sequence. It seems that in most theaters the entire film was screened in precisely the manner that Karlson envisioned, with the prologues offering different levels of affirmation of the story's truth value. The second one begins, in effect, with a title card: "There is no other place in the world as Phenix City, Alabama. For almost one hundred years it has been the modern Pompeii where vice and corruption were the order of the day. Unlike Pompeii it did not require a Vesuvius to destroy it, for Phenix City is now a model community—orderly—progressive—and a tribute to the freedom loving peoples everywhere." Introduced by a simple title and bearing no other marks of production, the report exists entirely apart from the story, only some of whose outlines it more or less anticipates, if in a somewhat offhand manner. The details that Roberts and company provide, supported by the undeniably real images of the several interviews, corroborate the truth of a story still to be told. As it turns out, the story's truth value is to be measured against the details of the Roberts report, from which it maintains a kind of independence. This disconnection, then, acts to affirm the story's claims to present the events as they happened. With its unattributed testimony to the story's true value and ideological meaning, the written preface justifies the film's prying into some of America's dirty secrets. In its orderliness and progressiveness, national exceptionalism has been preserved by the actions of an aroused citizenry, who have proven themselves more powerful than an erupting Vesuvius in destroying a pit of vice and corruption, with an image that perfectly suits the overheated and often puritanical moralizing of the genre.

Further proof of the filmmakers' bona fides follows immediately. *Phenix City* proper begins with a burst of stirring musical score as the title flashes across the screen, and images of magazine covers appear, one after the other (*Time, Newsweek, Look,* and *Life* chief among them), all featuring some version of the "story" of Phenix City. These covers frame a larger central image of the *Ledger,* whose banner headline proclaims that the paper has been awarded the Pulitzer for its investigative reporting on events in the wide-open town just across the Chattahoochee River and state line. Contrasting images of Columbus and Phenix City (the two main streets, similar residential neighborhoods, parks filled with children playing) are introduced by another narrator, this one offscreen (at least at the moment), who goes over much the same ground already covered by Roberts. His main point, however, emphasizes that Phenix City, in an irony that the film will refuse to explore further, has more churches than any other city of its size in the state. The narrator reveals that he is none other than the John Patterson whose incipient political campaign is the main subject of the Roberts interview. The Patterson who speaks here, however, is not one of the real-life participants in the story featured in the Roberts interviews, but a character (played by Richard Kiley) who will figure centrally in the lightly fictionalized narrative that follows.

Patterson's narration of what is now the recent past, however, is not abandoned when he enters the diegesis as a main character. He is heard in voiceover intermittently throughout, in much the same way as the extradiegetic narrator's commentary figures in *Southside*. But the difference is that Patterson's narration is subjectified. We must hear his commentary as shaped by his point of view on the reestablishment of law and order in the city and as restricted, if not consistently, to what he could reasonably be expected to know or have learned. The closing sequence rhymes interestingly with the opening report. With the narrative in which he has played a central role at an end, Patterson turns to face the camera, assuring viewers that Phenix City has now been utterly transformed, even as he promises that since he has now been elected state attorney general such corruption will never take root again either there or in any other Alabama town. In real life, Patterson was not long afterward elected governor of the state and served from 1959 to 1963 in a controversial term that saw him spend extraordinary energy resisting desegregation of the state's schools and otherwise supporting what were then euphemistically known as "local customs."

In *Southside*, the narrator is never personalized as a character and hence is positioned absolutely outside the world of the story, able for this reason to dispose of a presumed omniscience that lays to rest all doubts about the reliability of his observations and explanations. We don't ask to see what credentials he might have for attesting to the worth of what he has to say about the economy; that he is not a character allows his words in a formal sense to be understood as beyond argument or disagreement. Only the impossible emergence of a character bearing the full burden of institutional power could compensate completely for his withdrawal, and this move, as Ingster must have recognized, would have been aesthetically disruptive, allowing the film to collapse into two related but not coherently related sections. In the story world that *Southside* creates, the narrative voice is carefully calculated and never more than an occasional presence, its function no longer to be the sole source of determining information but to remind viewers of the presence of a space of meaning-making and surveilling power beyond those acted out in the story world. What emerges in the drama that the film stages is a place where unquestioned truth value might be proclaimed and the informational deficiencies of the characters made good. At times, the narrator intrudes to summarize the meaning of a scene or to effect a transition to the next stage of the action, functions that could be, and often are, just as readily performed by the narrative itself. But this redundancy serves a larger rhetorical purpose. In another instance, the narrator assumes something like his initial role as the assembler of images whose meaning must be fixed, as a complex montage shows how counterfeit money, once produced in large quantities, is laundered by criminals acting within the larger economy, especially through seedier institutions (horse racing and casinos) where, because of a high volume of cash, no close attention is paid to individual bills.

The retention of the narrator, however, depends on an interesting if hardly obvious transformation. The self-sufficient space of truth-telling first established as the only source of meaning-making for a succession of disparate images becomes an extradiegetic place for comment, forecasting, recapitulation, and summary, turning *Southside* into something very close, structurally speaking, to the nineteenth-century realist novel, which is characteristically dominated by its omniscient, non-character narrator, a voice that effects, as the critical commonplace has it, the attendant subordination of other voices as well as the reduction of the experiences of the characters proper to contingencies that require recuperation. This presence evidently stands outside and above the world inhabited by the characters, transforming a drama into more of a self-conscious telling. If *Southside* has a main character of sorts (investigator John Riggs, played by Don DeFore, who also goes undercover as a criminal named Nick Starnes), there is no doubt that the driving force of the narrative is, within the world of the story, the Treasury Department more generally and, for the film as a whole, the usefully disembodied and hence transindividual spokesman for that institution, who represents its importance, value, and ethos with unflagging enthusiasm. With its proof of the truths laid out in its documentary prologue, *Southside* pointedly does not end with the kind of repression that *Stranger* must muster in order to provide a conventionally happy ending, with questionable social structures left unreformed and difficult ethical issues unresolved. The narrator's omniscience (including the ability to penetrate the consciousness of the various characters) perfectly reflects the proven omnipotence of the Treasury to manage the nation's financial system, which cannot be threatened successfully by those eager to subvert it, no more than the pathetic Nazi spies in *House* can even come close to stealing America's nuclear secrets.

If displaying some of the jingoistic tone of wartime productions, the noir semi-documentary still in part discovers the dark underside of American culture and institutions in the manner of *Stranger*'s disturbing meditations on the justice system and the guilty, antisocial desires usually buried deep within the human heart. These films are truly semi-documentary in the sense that their fictional or fabulized elements, though set within an authentic, uniformly positive representation of contemporary American society, engage with questions of morality and psychology that a strictly documentary approach would hardly prove able to broach. In contrast to earlier noir entries such as *Stranger*, it is true enough in these films that the state and its various levers of power do show themselves capable of, indeed irresistibly successful in, surveilling, controlling, and usually eliminating any serious and organized threats to the common good, whether these are foreign or domestic. Criminality, to be sure, is rarely a matter of inexplicable turpitude or social disadvantage, seldom reflecting the pathological anomie that dominates in wartime noirs like *Double Indemnity* and *Murder, My Sweet* (both 1944).

Criminality, at least usually, figures in the semi-documentary as a powerful and well-structured opposition to the common good, a rational and calculated force dedicated to the extensive undermining of the public order, or even, in those semi-documentaries with Cold War themes, to the overthrow of society and the installation of a different form of civil order. This kind of criminality cannot be countered and defeated by that most prevalent of noir stock characters, the private detective; it requires instead the information-gathering, evidence-sifting, hypothesis-building procedures of a modern intelligence service backed, if necessary, by the fully armed power of the state. This intelligence service finds its formal reflex in the film's voice of God narrator, always patient in explaining what the presumably not very enlightened viewer might not understand about institutional practices and criminal behavior, which are thoroughly commented on as well as exemplified in the film's narrative. In the noir semi-documentary, to put this another way, narrative works to transcend individual circumstance and the inner life (which rarely if ever figures as a thematic or visual focus). Morality is a matter for the law to determine, not a mode of self-understanding or critique, not a sensibility whose unexpected contours reveal themselves in a crisis. *Phenix City* might seem an exception to this general rule since the point of the film's narrative is to identify the essential crookedness of municipal and, to an extent, state institutions. But in this film it is the fourth estate in its various forms (televisual, cinematic, and journalistic) that wields the irresistible power of surveillance and control, demonstrating its ability to arouse the reformative zeal of an exploited community.

Coda: The Sociopath as Protagonist

In the semi-documentary, the two forms of experience—impersonal institutional regulation and transgressive, but ultimately unknowable, individuality—are not always reconciled easily to the advantage of the collective good. Consider, for example, Alfred E. Werker's *He Walked by Night* (1947), with uncredited directorial assistance from Anthony Mann and produced for Eagle-Lion. Here is a film that, in the tradition of *House,* sets out to sing the praises of modern law enforcement, especially its dedication to the crime-fighting techniques promoted by Hoover, such as the mass collection of data, made accessible through advanced techniques of sorting, that can be used to interpret the evidence generated by individual cases. Law enforcement in the collective sense is undoubtedly the main character, and yet the villain (portrayed by the charismatic Richard Basehart) is set up by the script to steal every scene in which he appears, with his illicit derring-do providing most of the exciting action.

He Walked by Night is based on an actual case: the killing of two policemen by a fellow member of their own Pasadena, California, department, who worked in the fingerprint records division. In the hands of screenwriters John C. Higgins and Crane Wilbur, this story is reworked in a manner that Darryl Zanuck would certainly have approved. The rather mundane criminal becomes a self-taught and sociopathic genius, who is not only adept at designing innovative electronic equipment, but is also bold enough to steal what others have invented and pass it off as his own. Roy Martin (Basehart), unlike the pathetically inept German agents in *House,* is a cunning and quite intrepid adversary. After he somewhat rashly kills a policeman who spots him about to burglarize an electronics shop, Martin eludes capture because he proves amazingly knowledgeable about police technique. Moreover, he is brazen enough to shoot it out with detectives who have staked out the businessman to whom he sells his inventions and stolen property. Wounded in the encounter, Martin is even possessed of the necessary sangfroid to operate successfully on himself. The police discover his hideout, yet Martin this time escapes through the Los Angeles sewer system, whose intricate twists and turnings he has made not only a private path of attack and retreat, but a hideout as well. Only a lucky chance enables the police to corner and kill him. Having once again foiled his would-be pursuers, Martin is about to make his way to the dark city above when a car happens to park on the manhole cover he needs to lift up. The shotgun and stores of ammunition he had previously cached underground do him no good as he cannot triumph in a shootout against a force of determined policemen.

The film offers much of the same documentary stylization to be found in *House,* even though the "case" in this film is even more superficially based on actual events. A written title somewhat misleadingly proclaims: "This is a true story. It is known to the Police Department of one of our largest cities as the most difficult homicide case in its experience, principally because of the diabolical cleverness, intelligence and cunning of a completely unknown killer. . . . The record is set down here factually—as it happened. Only the names are changed, to protect the innocent." These words are echoed by those of the narrator, who, as shots of Los Angeles and its police department play on the screen, provides an overview of the nation's largest urban area, whose cosmopolitanism and mixed, transient population, so he avers, provide a challenge for law enforcement. Somewhat wryly, he concludes that "the work of the police like that of woman is never done. The facts are told here as they happened." Many of the sequences in the film that detail police work are in every sense documentary, having been filmed inside the headquarters (an imposing building shot from a low angle to emphasize its embodiment of well-organized power) and furnished with an appropriate voiceover commentary. The staged sequences are carefully stylized to match the reality footage. Producers Robert Kane and Bryan Foy were so eager for authenticity that they asked the Los Angeles Police Department for a technical advisor. Sergeant Marty Wynn, who was eager to have the film avoid the distorting clichés

FIGURE 28 "This is the city, Los Angeles, California," intones the film's narrator of this opening establishing shot in *He Walked by Night* (frame enlargement).

that had dominated Hollywood treatment of crime detection, provided much valuable information about police procedure. Under Wynn's tutelage, the screenwriters and performers learned the jargon of the trade, including the abbreviated code of police radio calls and the specialized vocabulary of evidence gathering and testing.

Yet it is important to note that the film, in detailing what it confesses is for the LAPD "the most difficult homicide case in its experience," commits itself to focusing on the extraordinary rather than on the everyday aspects of police work. Influenced by film noir's preoccupation with the bizarre and the perverse, Werker and the screenwriters not surprisingly developed Roy Martin, the "diabolical" genius, as a kind of monster who, in fact, cannot be identified and collared by ordinary police procedure. Instead, in a movement of the plot that intriguingly anticipates the spectacular finale of a more celebrated contemporary thriller, Carol Reed's *The Third Man* (1949), Martin must be hunted down and exterminated in his filthy underground lair in the city's sewer system (these sequences, like many in the film, were shot on location). Werker and cinematographer John Alton, famous for his Expressionistic set-ups and visual stylization in such noir classics as *The Big Combo* (1955), *Mystery Street* (1950), and *Hollow Triumph* (1948), put Martin in control of a shadowy alternative world, a place of darkness, anomie, and reckless self-assertion that the police enter only to their peril. Detective Sergeant Marty Brennan (Scott Brady) is foiled repeatedly by Martin, who seems to know police procedure better than the policeman themselves, while the criminal survives and prospers by his wits and considerable derring-do. Certainly the film's most striking scene shows the gunshot Martin removing a bullet himself without the benefit of either anesthetic or medical advice. An accurate and detailed account of a complex procedure requiring skill and determination, the operation rhymes with the film's several accounts of police practice, including the identification of a murder weapon by the matching up of bullets fired from it. But the scene of self-surgery creates a not inconsiderable bond between the sociopath and the viewer, who can hardly help admiring the man's courage and skill. Brennan is a colorless character in comparison, allowed no scenes of comparable physical accomplishment; he is instead the typical "organization man" soon to be analyzed and derided by sociologists in the next decade.[27] Scott Brady's low-key performance in the role makes him much less dashing, energetic, and resourceful than the man he seeks, played by the charismatic and attractive Richard Basehart. In fact, Brennan's failure to capture Martin after an abortive stakeout that results in the wounding of one of his partners earns him an early dismissal from the case. Only a sudden flash of inspiration persuades his chief to let him rejoin the investigation.

Martin confounds police procedure by changing what the narrator calls his "modus operandi," transforming himself from a burglar to a robber and, to some degree, making nonsense of the techniques of forensic investigation, which are predicated on the regularity and hence predictability of criminal behavior. In his new incarnation, Martin succeeds in terrorizing the city with a series of daring liquor store robberies. The man's intimate knowledge of how police work suggests that he is a rogue cop. His cunning duplicity revealed by police lab work (bullets fired from the cop killer's gun are shown to match one fired from the robber's), the killer is eventually, in a striking sequence, given a face by police artists who assemble the robbery victims to construct a group portrait. The patient and time-consuming check of leads provides yet another breakthrough. Martin is identified by Brennan, who wearily troops from one area police station to another looking for a match to the composite sketch. Surrounded a second time, however, the resourceful Martin manages to escape the police cordon into his sewer hideout. There he can only be stopped by his own bad luck (the blocked manhole cover) and the heroic—but group—action of the police.

The unfortunate criminal is gunned down in a shootout reminiscent of the western and the classic gangster film (such as *Public Enemy* [1931], *High Sierra* [1941], or *White Heat* [1949]). This climactic sequence provides Martin with a dramatic apotheosis, as his bullet-ridden body tumbles from a ladder into the sewage below; he suffers a literal "fall" from power and control. Significantly, there is no closing narration to fix the meaning of this event, no celebration of the successful pursuit of a dangerous felon. The law triumphs, but that victory is not "documented"; it is neither brought into the public realm to be adjudicated nor stylized as "real." In fact, bad luck is as responsible for Martin's capture as the patient police work that brings him into focus as a suspect. The surveilling and enforcement powers of the police may prove superior (if only barely) to Martin's resourceful monstrousness, but in the clash of representational traditions the expressionism of film noir, and not the naturalism of classic documentary, furnishes the film with its summative image.

As does the noir semi-documentary more generally, *He Walked* juxtaposes a city of light (populated by citizens going about their business and surveilled by the benevolent police) and a city of darkness (a criminal underworld that, metaphorized by the darkness and night that enfold it, does not easily admit the knowing, official gaze). Like the film's narrative and visual structure, the sound track is schizophrenic, split between the heavy, grim romantic theme that plays over Martin's lurking in the shadows and the upbeat, almost military air that accompanies the work of the police, the grinding routine according to the "book" that eventually identifies the criminal. The city is the focus of productive communal life (as the opening montage of shots depicting everyday activity emphasizes—an affecting survey of the ordinary), but its anonymous spaces shield those who, in their exceptionality, would live in defiance of officially imposed law and order. The two worlds found in the contemporary American metropolis seem utterly opposed, but they are actually strangely connected because Martin, as it turns out, is a former employee of a local police department.

And Martin is hardly, at least at the outset, a career criminal, nor is his lawbreaking to be explained sociologically. The underworld he inhabits is never figured in either economic or class terms. It seems, instead, the underside of bourgeois normality. Martin's thefts of electronic equipment are meant to further a career of invention and self-promotion for which his extraordinary mental abilities would certainly qualify him. Because he is never interrogated by the police, Martin's abandonment of a career in law enforcement remains a mystery. His former employer reveals that he left in 1942 for the military, refusing after his discharge any offer to rejoin the department. This much is clear. Eager to make a mark for himself in a postwar world driven by technological advance, inured to violence, and disposing of technical knowledge and skill gained from government service, Martin is yet another version of the returning soldier who cannot fit easily into a changed world despite his exceptional talents and energies.

The veteran mysteriously damaged by wartime service is a stock character of the film noir, an essential element of the nightmare vision of American life offered in this contrarian Hollywood series. *He Walked,* as its title suggests, is finally more interested in exploring, if not explaining, this enigmatic figure (Martin's moral nature is evoked but little through dialogue and mostly by visual style and mise-en-scène). Despite its opening avowal of truth-telling and the narrator's commitment to describing events "as they happened," the film is more than a straightforward chronicle of the infallible methods, the irresistible institutional power, and the quietly heroic dedication of the police to identifying and capturing criminals. The something else in this film, of course, is nothing less than the kind of dramatic interest Zanuck a few years earlier had correctly identified was necessary if these "films of fact" were to succeed with audiences, including making the criminal protagonist somewhat attractive and at least minimally sympathetic. As *He Walked* makes clear, however, filmmakers often found it difficult to balance properly a journalistic commitment to the particular truth and the perceived needs of audiences for the dramatization of the extraordinary, including the arousal and satisfaction of an emotional connection to the good/bad guy at the center of the narrative.

Werker's film exemplifies the complexities and compromises of American postwar cinematic realism, with the desire to open up filmmaking to the accurate, truthful representation of a world in seemingly perpetual crisis inevitably accommodated (and even thwarted) by the more pressing requirements of the national film industry to make films that would engage viewer interest and emotions. Journalism, as Louis de Rochemont had shown, was not incompatible with fiction filmmaking, but its commitment to inform and mold public opinion would inevitably find itself ultimately subordinated to accustomed forms of entertainment. As Darryl F. Zanuck clearly recognized, it was useful for some films of this period to convince the public that they were true to both particular events and life more generally; but it was even more important for them to be dramatic, creating imaginative worlds that engaged, excited, and satisfied those eager for well-established forms of diversion that, in spite of substantial changes in the postwar world, proved to be of enduring interest, however morally problematic and unmindful of civic virtue they might be.

Conclusion

Authentic Banality?

One of the most perspicacious observers of the cultural scene, critic Manny Farber could hardly have missed the development and emergence to some prominence in the immediate postwar era of that cinematic tradition we have termed pictorial journalism, with its deep connections to both *MOT* and Louis de Rochemont. The production cycle was still gathering steam when Farber made it clear that he did not much approve. It is impossible to read his commentary without realizing that what he called the semi-documentary, with its somber Middle American and WASPish populism, was pretentious enough in its own way to merit a thorough, if not quite dismissive, deflating. As always, Farber is worth quoting at length:

> A quietly dignified fame attaches to Producer Louis de Rochemont, who developed his pseudo-documentary style—real life stories reduced to streamlined banality—in March of Time and three fact-packed movies: *The House on 92nd Street, 13 Rue Madeleine,* and *Boomerang.* These are stuffed with sober, official hot air. The de Rochemont style is easily spotted: its sanitary realism is midway between Norman Corwin [famous at the time for being the so-called poet laureate of radio writers] and Walker Evans [the photographer who chronicled the effects of the Depression for the Farm Security Administration]. It avoids the problems of human relations and glories in objects, jobs-routines, and skills. Its Hero is an Institution like the FBI, and its trademark is the dignified, know-it-all narrator whose voice drips with confidence in an America that is like a Watson Business Machine. His terrain-conscious titles spotlight de Rochemont's managerial outlook in which the Post Office, Parish House dance, time-honored remark, are the determinants that shape, protect, and dominate Americans, lucky cogs in a golden social machine. Aiming at spontaneity, his writers dote on the actions, remarks, and facial expressions made most often by Americans;

in no movies do characters spend so many serious moments and such concentrated energy on pedestrian actions like parking a car and walking to a telephone, the implication being that a commonplace culture is full, rich living.[1]

This argument, of course, depends on a thoroughly dubious straw man: the notion that Hollywood filmmaking otherwise devotes itself to dramatizing the "problems of human relations" in ways that would avoid the hackneyed and superficial rather than obsessing over the glorifying depiction of realia, including everyday behaviors like "walking to a telephone." The fact that de Rochemont films are "terrain-conscious" does not seem a virtue to Farber, but the phrase is a truly revealing way of describing de Rochemont's cinematic vision, and one that serves well as a description of many of the films discussed in this book, productions that have gone outside the studio in search of places to film and ways of life to chronicle.

Of course, to accuse de Rochemont of avoiding seriousness (and, by implication, art) was simply to confirm that he was making films that Hollywood would produce and Americans would pay money to see. Though there were obvious exceptions, limited worldviews that could be easily spoofed were the dominant themes of Hollywoodian fabulizing of the era. These same themes were then to be found in the visions of the national life promoted by print journalism, with its strong strain of American exceptionalism. The voices of popular culture had undoubtedly grown shriller in singing the country's praises after total victory in the global war just concluded, while the growing rivalry with the Soviet Union encouraged a certain defensiveness about American values and institutions. In order to avoid alienating its audience, the national cinema could not accommodate much more negativity than the oblique critique of cultural pieties offered by the film noir, then gaining in popularity, but these films could be, and generally were, read in this country as either apolitical versions of contemporary experience or simple genre exercises. French journalists, of course, saw things otherwise, but then, viewing from the outside what Hollywood produced, they were more sensitive to the quite different values this innovatively dark cinema could be read as embodying. Unlike their U.S. counterparts, French critics were not reluctant to see how that most characteristic of noir narrative themes, the amoral surrender to desire that leads inevitably to violence and social breakdown, constituted a critique of the creed of self-fashioning so central to how Americans preferred to see themselves.

How different were the semi-documentaries, including the signature de Rochemont releases, from the ordinary studio product? Consider the dramatization of the "problems of life" in Fox's critically acclaimed attack on the reflexive antisemitism of American culture, *Gentleman's Agreement* (Elia Kazan, 1947). This story began life as a serialized feature in *Cosmopolitan* magazine, written by Laura Z. Hobson, earning such praise and popularity that she was encouraged to turn it into a novel, which soon topped the best-seller list. Here the main character, a journalist, Philip Green, played with proper liberal seriousness by Gregory Peck, is a Gentile pretending to be a Jew in order to write an essay on antisemitism from the inside, as it were. The main thrust of the narrative is his demonstration that what seems to be his fiancée's prejudice against Jews is an easily reformable cultural reflex. Occupied with the moral compass of the nation's *goyische* majority, who need to be shown the (largely unconscious) error of their ways, the film delves only superficially into the effects of discrimination on its actual victims, who are represented in the film by a thoroughly assimilated (and small) group, including one who is "passing." *Gentleman's Agreement* seems more concerned with demonstrating that even a Protestant divorcée, Kathy Lacey (Dorothy McGuire), from the residentially restrictive upscale town of Darien, Connecticut, can learn to reject casual defamation. With a bit of soul-searching, she finds herself willing to stand up against the public expression of such offensiveness after falling in love with Green and being recruited, if somewhat unwillingly, into his crusade for tolerance.

Bosley Crowther enthused: "To millions of people throughout the country, [the film] should bring an ugly and disturbing issue to light."[2] True enough, but the critic seems mostly concerned about the fact (actually quite remarkable) that Hollywood made any kind of film about antisemitism; there were many influential players in the industry who thought it a bad idea. In any case, Crowther shows himself oblivious to the representational emptiness at the heart of this desperately earnest story. He is untroubled by Kazan's palpable reluctance to solicit much in the way of audience empathy and interest for anyone but a faux Jew and a woman forced to face a social ill only because she has become his intended. Something of a Jewish flavor is provided to the tale by John Garfield, at the time perhaps Hollywood's best-known performer of that background, who plays a Jewish veteran, Green's best friend Dave. But trapped in a minor role (a comment in and of itself), Garfield breezes in and out of a story whose focus lies elsewhere. Green's most unpleasant experience is being refused accommodation at a swank hotel once he reveals who he really is, a scene in which his embarrassment and frustration are shown to be genuine enough. But of course, a Jew is what he really is not, and that makes all the difference. Green need not take the rejection personally; his experience is more in the subjunctive than the indicative mood.

There is a difference between sympathy and empathy, as Kazan, Hobson, and company certainly were conscious of and seem to be emphasizing. For it is precisely on the issue of Gentile privilege that the film's romantic (which is to say its main) plot turns. Kathy had earlier earned Phil's anger by telling his young son, who is harassed at school by boys who call him, among other things, "a dirty Jew," that he shouldn't feel bad since he isn't really Jewish, only going along with his father's undercover charade. Disgusted, and giving way to a self-righteous impulse, Green breaks up with her, even though the truth she articulates could be applied to his own "mistreatment" as well, directed only at the persona he has determined to adopt for journalistic reasons. Kathy is subsequently redeemed by putting herself in the line of prejudicial fire, if only after a fashion. She agrees to look after, and defend as needed, Dave and his family, who have determined to move into a rental in Darien and thus contest, though not intentionally, that community's exclusionary practices. In terms of moral stands, her expression of open-minded bona fides seems very small beer indeed, but it suffices to motor a rapprochement between the attractive Gentile lovers, whose restorative embrace provides the film with its happy ending. Tellingly, no closing shot shows the Jewish family now happily ensconced in the über-Christian precincts of Fairfield County, whose high-toned suburbanity is evoked with some detailed location shooting. There is no scene in which either of the two protagonists defies directly the force of the "gentleman's agreement," the notorious informal understanding about restrictive practices at the heart of the community's culture that gives the story its title.

Gentleman's Agreement is widely acknowledged to be among the Hollywood productions of the era that deal most courageously with contentious social issues. This film broke with industry practice in a way that Zanuck had advised a few years earlier in a Saturday Review think piece, an annotated copy of which de Rochemont thought important enough to save with his personal papers:

> Is it possible to make pictures which have purpose and significance and yet show a proper return at the box office? I believe it is. I believe the answer is entertainment. I am not now speaking of the purely escapist stuff which has no purpose than to entertain. I'm speaking of entertainment as a device to make the serious, worthwhile pictures palatable to mass movie audiences. I'm firmly convinced that the run of the mill movie patron is ready for such pictures—has been ready for them for years. We simply have failed to dress such pictures properly. It is a gap we must bridge in order to justify our place in the social, economic, and political scheme of things. . . . We must forge ahead. We're in danger of being left, like so many of our isolationists, with the ground out from under us. We've got to move into new ground, break new trails.[3]

Certainly, Gentleman's Agreement, like a number of the "problem" films made at Fox, does indeed "break new trails," and yet Kazan's film doubtless makes a plea for tolerance in a fashion that is carefully calculated to neither threaten nor offend most filmgoer sensitivities. Such films, however innovative, must remain "palatable" in order to show a "proper return" at the box office. Here is realism that is indeed as "sanitary" as what, according to Farber, de Rochemont characteristically practiced.

Beyond questioning the seriousness of pictorial journalism, Farber's objections otherwise seem mainly to have been to the de Rochemont focus on "streamlined banality," a getting down to brass tacks in terms of style and manner that distinguished his productions most obviously from the ordinary industry product, the "purely escapist stuff" that Zanuck advised the industry to get beyond if it was to justify its "place in the social, economic, and political scheme of things." Farber, of course, was correct in choosing to identify de Rochemont as an appropriate representative of that particular strain of cinematic realism he was in fact largely responsible for inaugurating, which, as has been argued here, is the most distinctive native contribution to the emergence and flourishing of various forms of cinematic realism in postwar Hollywood, including the so-called message pictures dealing with social problems. Pictorial journalism of the de Rochemont variety, let us admit with Farber, is unapologetically midcult in several of the senses identified by social critic Dwight Macdonald, most particularly by showing little interest in either urbanity or intellectual complexity. Perhaps, more accurately, such filmmaking is often downright disdainful of sophisticated attitudes and whatever smacked of highbrow pretentiousness, issuing a broad appeal to the anti-intellectualism then making itself prominently felt in the national culture.[4]

A carefully conceived plainness, after all, was the most notable feature of the midcult magazine that the producer both mined for material and furnished with stories he needed to be "pre-sold." *Reader's Digest*, it is important to remember, was his business partner in some of the key locative realist films of the first decade of the postwar era. With the magazine's founder, DeWitt Wallace, de Rochemont shared strongly anticommunist views, as well as more or less conservative opinions on most social issues.[5] An essential part of the magazine's incredible appeal, as Wallace correctly predicted, turned out to be streamlining; a good portion of the nation's reading public wanted only the gist of a story or argument, a simplification euphemized by the carefully chosen term "digest." The world of *Reader's Digest* was black and white, ideologically speaking, ideal for expressing and promoting a Cold War mentality that had little use for political or cultural nuance but was strongly chauvinist, as historian Joanne Sharp points out; the magazine, just to take one example, gives voice in its treatment of U.S./Soviet relations to the clear sense "that America is no longer respected as an international leader," a position of prominence whose restoration it advocates, aligning Wallace and company with the assertive interventionism that was increasingly dominating U.S. foreign policy.[6] It is easy enough to understand why J. Edgar Hoover was eager to work with both editor and filmmaker in order to promote the importance of the FBI. Wallace conceived and gave lasting global popularity to a magazine that provided readers with brief, apparently bipartisan (though essentially conservative), and eminently readable pieces that addressed various aspects of the current American scene. Wallace's vision of what constituted a good story was completely compatible with the journalistic mission that de Rochemont believed American filmmaking should pursue. The industry, he believed, reflecting Zanuck's view, should abandon frivolous entertainment and captivating spectacle for more nourishing fare. Writing in the *New York Times*,

drama critic Howard Barnes overflowed with praise for de Rochemont's alternative model:

> Louis de Rochemont is a master craftsman of the screen. Starting with
> elaborated newsreels, he has always paid unswerving attention to such
> simple and all-important qualities of film artistry as realism, simplicity,
> and action. Extravagant production trappings and stars have meant no
> more to him than theatrical illusion or bestseller novels. . . . He startled a
> complacent Hollywood to such an extent that he is now on his own. . . . He
> was always aware that the motion picture had its own peculiar vocabulary—
> that the camera was capable of immediate and absorbing communication
> with an audience.[7]

Farber simply doesn't see this more radical side of de Rochemont: the non-
conformist devoted to pointing his camera at the world outside the soundstage
and standing exterior, the puritan artist who embraces simplicity in contrast to
an industry obsessed with "extravagant production trappings" and the falsity of
"theatrical illusion." There is even a quite palpable neorealist feel to the notion of a
filmmaking approach "capable of immediate and absorbing communication with
an audience," an effect, ironically enough, due in large part to de Rochemont's
emphasis on a technique with no counterpart in Italian filmmaking of the
period: the stentorian narrator derided by Farber as having a voice that "drips
with confidence." In Farber's view, de Rochemont has been found mostly guilty
of high-minded piousness, of a blinkered patriotism that encourages him to
promote America as a "golden social machine," imagining it to be a well-ordered
culture in no need of thoroughgoing reform. Farber's de Rochemont is thoroughly
Coolidgean; he sees a country whose business truly is business. As if to confirm
this view, smooth-running commerce, with the interests of labor and management carefully aligned by win/win contracts, is imagined as the goal of community in one of de Rochemont's subsequent releases, *Whistle at Eaton Falls* (1951);
this project was developed not only with professional scriptwriters but with the
Harvard Business School, an approach to popular entertainment that Sinclair
Lewis's George F. Babbitt would certainly have endorsed. More on this below.

However, such sober Chamber of Commerce plain-dealing, with its low-
church distrust of "ornament" and make-believe, was in terms of social themes
and engagement not much different from what mainstream Hollywood ordinarily
purveyed after the bestseller lists were mined for presold material and projects
were assembled with A-list stars. Hobson wrote *Gentleman's Agreement* in easily
consumed installments for *Cosmopolitan*, while William L. White, supplied with a
lead by de Rochemont, researched and wrote up the story of the Albert C. Johnston
family for *Reader's Digest* that soon became the source for one of RD-DR's most
successful films, *Lost Boundaries* (1949). In both cases, book publication and out-
standing success in the vast midcult market soon followed. The magazines may

FIGURE 29 The trailer for *Gentleman's Agreement* reminds prospective viewers that this film, like many considered in this volume, was based on a story published in a national magazine (frame enlargement).

have appealed to somewhat different readerships, but the films shared much—if not everything—in common. The crucial difference was de Rochemont's terrain consciousness, which was achieved by the painstaking and careful incorporation into his productions of the real in its various forms, achieved most importantly through shooting on location.

Though thoroughly grounded in this approach as a result of his several locative realist projects (especially *Boomerang*), Kazan only gestures toward actual, living space and community in *Gentleman's Agreement*; the film is basically a talk-fest in the mainstream Hollywood tradition, with only a few exteriors filmed on location that break up the visual monotony of what is obviously a succession of soundstage set-ups. Zanuck, whose pet project this was, of course firmly believed that filmgoers needed only to be convinced initially of the real nature of the dramatic action they witnessed. A characteristically Zanuckian gesture toward real place undergirds the film's opening sequence, which is staged *en plein air* at a Rockefeller Plaza most Americans would have instantly recognized and whose distinctive architectural particularities Hollywood filmmakers would not have tried to reproduce. But with productions like *The House on 92nd Street* and *Call Northside 777*, Zanuck had given filmmakers the taste for a kind of extended exploration of the real that de Rochemont was more willing to provide.

Farber confessed to a certain admiration for *Lost Boundaries*: "Unlike his other films . . . it is mildly poignant, has a simple direct honesty . . . though it is over-populated by creamy people, friendly smiles, and least exciting real-life talk, it has a homespun, non-Hollywood plainness unmatched in current movies."[8] Farber, too, it seems, was not entirely unappreciative of a postwar realism that contested the conventions of cinematic entertainment as established by several decades of Hollywood success. *Lost Boundaries* is the tale of a determined-to-be-just-another-American "colored" doctor, Scott Carter (Mel Ferrer), who is forced to pass for white in order to establish himself in a practice that will support his wife and children, including adolescent son Howard (Richard Hylton); ironically enough, this crisis arises because Carter is not considered dark-skinned enough to serve on the staff of a Negro clinic, where he might be mistaken for white and thus make patients uncomfortable. Carter had previously, and unthinkingly, stayed on what contemporary social rules insisted was his own side of the color line; but to practice the profession for which he trained he is forced to pass himself off as exactly what many, including "his own people," think he is.

Lost Boundaries was not made in partnership with Zanuck and Fox, and a deal with MGM also fell through, freeing de Rochemont to make production decisions largely on his own and to arrange for an exhibition exploiting the growing national enthusiasm for art houses. De Rochemont was under no pressure to hype the story's drama or cast marquee players as had earlier been the case (cf. Dana Andrews in *Boomerang*, James Cagney in *13 Rue Madeleine*, or James Stewart in *Call Northside 777*). With design costs held to a minimum through the utilization of real locations for exteriors and interiors, *Lost Boundaries* does indeed have a "homespun" look, with the only somewhat recognizable player being Ferrer. Discarding Zanuck's formula for the "drama of fact," the film does not climax with suspenseful action, but with a community meeting whose high point is a far-from-fiery sermon from the local pastor. The man preaches earnestly, but it quickly becomes apparent that those gathered there are already converted, a demonstration of inherent American bona fides that seems to be one of the film's main ideological points. The congregation signals its post-racial solidarity when it enthusiastically sings New England poet James Russell Lowell's hymn for resolute tolerance, "Once to Ev'ry Man and Nation." And so, despite their deception, the Carters are welcome to stay. Scott will continue as the town physician, a position he has tellingly inherited from one of the community's most beloved and important figures, while his children will not be excluded from participating in the social life they have come to know, a key issue whose more vexing aspects are never even hinted at.

White's full-length chronicle of the near-white family's trials and triumph devotes considerable attention to Howard's exploration of what it means exactly to be a Negro who can, and often does, pass for white in turn-of-the-century America.[9] Going beyond the conventional simplifications of the *Reader's Digest* formula, White in fact draws a nuanced and affecting portrait of race relations that does not shy away from confronting the issue of what it means to show allegiance to one's own, whoever they might be understood as being. The screen version of the story, in contrast, is less invested in exploring the experiences of America's most justly dissatisfied minority and more in the dramatic trajectory on which the narrative is made to turn: how sober-minded New Hampshire townspeople accept with no demurral the revelation of their beloved physician's otherness, thereby demonstrating *in parvo* the racial fairness of the national body politic, who find themselves needing no persuasion to render judgments based on character content rather than skin color, especially, if this is not too cynical to observe, when "black" is just a label, not an impossible-to-ignore existential fact, disconnected from more vexing questions of social class.

With no struggle at all, the not-really-Negro Negroes are reaffirmed in their rights as citizens, among which is the opportunity to live untroubled among whites. A radical alteration in the cultural economy of the nation, if only in miniature, thus takes place without official intervention of any kind. A crisis is quickly averted when Howard, shaken to the core by the revelation that he is not who he thought he was, makes his way to Harlem in order to understand what it means to be a Negro. In a startlingly swift confirmation of then-current stereotypes, he immediately becomes involved in a violent incident, after which he is taken into police custody. Nothing he sees in what seems to strike him as a kind of foreign country pushes him over any brink, however; he is quickly retrieved from the lock-up by a friend and returned, with a sense of relief, to the small town he has always called home. Howard may be a Negro, but he does not have to live as one. This is, of course, a choice, but one that the film tellingly feels no need to dramatize.

However, this documentary evocation of the otherness of a ghettoized negritude is neither fleeting nor simplistic, and this is due almost entirely to de Rochemont's insistence on the exploration of real space both geographical and social. The Harlem sequences are deeply authentic, a troubling collection of images detailing urban blight, deprivation, perhaps even despair. Seen through the eyes of the bewildered Howard, who is and is not "one" with those he meets there, this rendering of Harlem reveals itself as deeply paradoxical, a place that is America and yet is all that America is not—and, in contradictory and distressing ways, should not be. De Rochemont's camera manages a through and carefully calculated survey of this upper Manhattan cityscape, as production records attest. But this alternative America, if in some sense unforgettably rendered, is soon abandoned for what is meant to be understood as the comforting familiarity of an all-white New England in which those who are said to be but do not seem to be Negroes are allowed to continue living despite the revelation that they are, in some sense, interlopers. Howard, so the implication runs, need not discover what it "really" means to be black, whatever that might mean. As the narrative makes clear, Howard is meant to live henceforth not as a stranger in a strange land, but as a stranger in his own home. More poignant, perhaps, is that the strange land he visits in search of his own roots only briefly endures after his anguished retreat from it. Harlem is separated by different forms of distance from de Rochemont's version of the city on the hill; it is, after all, a community that has taken shape in response to a quite distinct history that the filmmaker is hardly moved to evoke

FIGURE 30 *Lost Boundaries* offers striking and authentic images of a Harlem in which Howie (Richard Hylton) tries to come to an understanding of his racial inheritance (frame enlargement).

in detail. And yet, as de Rochemont must have sensed, because of the rich and complex cultural meanings it expresses, Harlem permits the concretization of a trans-subjective truth that could not otherwise be readily expressed in the film. Surely this is why the congenitally parsimonious producer insisted on shooting there, necessitating a move that was both time-consuming and expensive from the New England sites where the other sequences were filmed.

Because of its wish-fulfillment solution to the problem of segregation, viewers might have drawn from the film the incorrect lesson that the then-prominent campaign of the NAACP to overturn *Plessy v. Ferguson* and its support for Jim Crow legislation was hardly necessary. Walter White, the distinguished executive secretary of that organization, was moved to express his admiration for the film, whose progressivism, however limited, he could of course hardly reject. And yet White strains to draw from what de Rochemont has produced a ringing endorsement of activism where there is none, arguing in the *New York Times* that *Lost Boundaries* is "a unique and immensely moving story of what fanciful notions about race can do to human beings. . . . But the very extension of the line of battle is proof that the Negro will not be kept back. It proves, as well, that millions of white Americans respect his ability—and are willing to join in the battle against proscription."[10] With its somewhat compromised advocacy for social equality, *Lost Boundaries* differs very little from *Gentleman's Agreement. Pace* White, this film also stages no "battle" for social justice. It is true enough, as Crowther was moved to observe: "[The film's] statement of the anguish and the ironies of racial taboo is clear, eloquent and moving. There are tears and there is scripture in this film."[11] But, once again, as Farber says, the mode here is a "sanitary realism," the tears being few and far between, while "racial taboo" figures most centrally as a cultural force reflexively sidestepped by ordinary people of good will, especially when led in the properly moral direction by their pastor.

It's difficult to shake the impression that de Rochemont's film, having discovered Harlem as it were by accident, cannot escape fast enough to its Norman Rockwell version of what constitutes the center of the national life. Unthinkable is the notion that black culture might offer a community, comparable in its appeal to blood and shared history, that such a "voluntary Negro" (what the very light-skinned Walter White called himself) might wish to join. And yet, such is the power that flows from the authenticity provided by on-location shooting, that Harlem, its truths revealed by the camera, cannot be effaced from the viewer's consciousness by the retreat of the narrative. To be sure, in order to resolve the more limited issue it raises, *Lost Boundaries* returns to an equally real location (sequences shot in various New England locales) that provide an alternative version of how Americans live, a place where peace and goodwill prevail in addition to a nearly universal whiteness. But de Rochemont's terrain consciousness gives considerable representational weight to a more troubling reality as well.

Exemplifying in many ways the best that had yet been realized from this tradition of locative realism, *Lost Boundaries* seemed to Farber to be "an affecting, wholesome affair held down by De Rochemont's belief that the documentary should be safe, artless, and free of variety . . . a poster-like portrait to show the virtues of the Democratic Man of Tomorrow."[12] But de Rochemont's characteristically uncritical faith in the communal goodness of the country he obviously loves deeply deserves this put-down only in part. By abjuring studio interiors and depending on locations already replete with meanings that cannot be hijacked by even the most syrupy of feel-good stories, de Rochemont produces the kind of film that opens onto the real, which it inevitably thereby captures, reflecting the producer's realist sensibilities. As Irving Drutman observed in a focus on de Rochemont cameraman William J. Miller, shooting on location was also cost-effective, calling into question conventional wisdom about the business model Hollywood had long followed:

> Miller is a stanch advocate of on-the-spot filmmaking. "It's the only way to produce pictures . . . audiences get tired of dressed-up stuff. They want to see something real. There's never yet been a studio set that could give the same effect as an actual location." . . . When de Rochemont was scheduled to make *Lost Boundaries* for M-G-M, the studio estimates for the film were $1.5 million. The scenario aroused an inter-office controversy and de Rochemont decided to produce the film independently. Shooting on location, mostly in Portsmouth, NH, and Kittery, Me, he was able to complete the project for only $620,000. Miller: "We used thirty-five different interiors.

In Hollywood they would have had to build all of these in the studio and
the sets wouldn't have looked natural. We shot in old Colonial houses that
had been lived in for a couple of hundred years and you can't successfully
fake worn floors and torn wallpaper. Also it's an event in Hollywood when
they have ceiling interiors, as all thirty-five of ours have."[13]

Audiences at the time were indeed eager "to see something real," and *Lost Boundaries* catered to this desire in a cost-effective fashion, even if the film's politics
were then seen, especially by those less inclined to make excuses for America's
shortcomings, as reflecting a national reluctance to face up to what was arguably
the most destructive and difficult of social problems. Gunnar Myrdal's *An American
Dilemma: The Negro Problem and American Democracy* had been published some five
years previously, with financing from the Carnegie Foundation, giving a name to
the issue that *Lost Boundaries* takes on with a certain amount of unconvincing triumphalism.[14] Penning the festival notes at Cannes that year, where *Lost Boundaries*
was honored with a screening, Franck Jotterand noted: "An embarrassed America
tries to resolve the black problem by turning Negroes white."[15] A fair enough
comment, of course, but the Swiss critic surely overemphasizes the palpable wish
fulfillment of the film's narrative while underplaying the considerably disruptive
power of its authentic, unconventional representations.

De Rochemont, not surprisingly, understood very well this crucial distinction
between story and its visualization. To be sure, his theoretical understanding
of the medium he practiced did not approach the intellectual sophistication of
Kracauer, Bazin, or Zavattini, but he recognized that in thinking of the cinema
simply as a form of mass diversion Hollywood was ignoring its representational
power. In a speech delivered at Boston University just months before the release
of the film, de Rochemont gave public expression to his view that commercial
filmmaking should follow a journalistic model more directly connected to the
world beyond the studio soundstage:

> The tremendous emphasis on entertainment—which after all is Hollywood's
> primary and legitimate objective—has almost obscured in the public mind
> other important and necessary functions of the film. Just as the printing
> press was the invention which made possible a great new medium of mass
> communication, the motion picture camera is an instrument which poten-
> tially can be even more effective because instead of *requiring* a man to visu-
> alize scenes of people and places suggested by the printed word—the camera
> with its ability to capture experience visually and audibly—can record for
> all time not merely the imagery conjured by our great story tellers, but the
> day to day record of our lives and living. . . . Though we enjoy an entertain-
> ing drama or work of fiction—we cannot and must not limit the uses of
> so powerful a medium as the motion picture. Today there is a critical and
> appalling need for the motion picture in the field of public information.

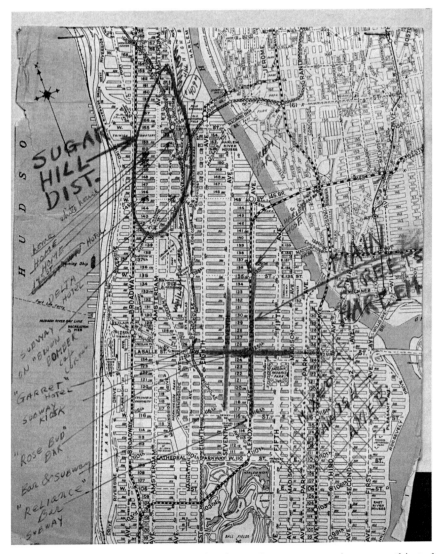

FIGURE 31 The location scout's report for the Harlem sequences shows something of the extensive work that went into preproduction planning for *Lost Boundaries* (courtesy of the Louis de Rochemont archive, Keene State).

No peaceful weapon has yet been devised that can be more effective in the defense of the American ideals of freedom than a film—journalistically conceived and produced, to show those who have been fed by untruths and malicious propaganda how we live and how we work. The motion picture has the power to show the people of the world that in a freedom unknown and unequalled anywhere on this earth, the American laboring man is the most prosperous and highly favored on earth.[16]

De Rochemont here promotes an aesthetic that most realists could endorse by advocating that the national cinema show audiences around the world "how we live and how we work . . . [providing] the day to day record of our lives and living." But, more troubling perhaps, this journalistic desire is linked to a political agenda: promoting American exceptionalism, demonstrating that the citizens of the United States enjoy a "freedom unknown and unequalled anywhere on this earth" and that the national "laboring man" is "the most prosperous and highly favored on earth." De Rochemont's form of cinematic journalism thus abandons, at least in part, the capacity for critical exploration that realism by its very nature makes available. At the same time, his deep engagement with place, as *Lost Boundaries* exemplifies, could through its own energies push hard against any jingoistic pressure toward distortingly self-congratulatory simplification.

De Rochemont, no doubt, was an enthusiastic Cold Warrior, and *Lost Boundaries* can, and should, be seen in part as a dismissal of Soviet attacks on American racism, which de Rochemont criticizes as "untruths" and "malicious propaganda." And yet it is only in a self-limiting sense that the film actually turns black people white, solving Myrdal's "Negro problem" by showing that its foundational "dilemma," the conflict between acknowledged values and actual practice, is an illusion easily contradicted by a "true story" whose authenticity was beyond question. And yet, let us be honest, the rather unique saga of the Johnston family appealed from the outset to de Rochemont because of its political value; it fit perfectly the formula firmly established by decades of *Reader's Digest* storytelling.[17] In a speech given at the Screen Directors Guild, probably in 1950, de Rochemont offered an impassioned defense of this approach to filmmaking:

> We call our pictures "dramas of real life." That term is used to differentiate them from routine fiction films. . . . I prefer to treat with stories in which the characters are people I know—real people whose problems are universal. Entertainment can be served up in many delightful and palatable ways. . . . Like millions of movie goers, I enjoy these films, but I prefer to make pictures which have what Mr. De Witt Wallace, editor of the *Reader's Digest*, terms "take-home value"—a little something to think about after the last scene has been flashed upon the screen.[18]

In that same speech, de Rochemont referred to a dialogue he had had with "a very able and astute movie producer in Hollywood," whom everyone present must have supposed, and probably correctly, was Darryl F. Zanuck. The producer said that Americans had no enduring interest in this type of film but were interested in formula entertainment: "Boy meets girl, boy loses girl, boy finds girl again." But just that week, de Rochemont says in response, "the nation sat glued to television sets watching the scenes played in the Kefauver committee room," as the Senate Special Committee to Investigate Interstate Crime grilled a number of notorious gangsters, including Meyer Lansky, Frank Costello, and Louis "Little New York"

Campagna.[19] This early success of what we would call "reality" television propelled the relatively unknown senator from Tennessee, Estes Kefauver, into national prominence (including the Democratic vice-presidential nomination in 1956), surely confirming in some sense de Rochemont's point, *contra* Zanuck, that the American people could be fascinated by "dramas of real life."

But Zanuck also had a point, and it was arguably more telling. Not all projects that seemed to Wallace and de Rochemont to have "take-home value" would in fact succeed with the national film audience; they had to be, as he said, "palatable," a quality most consistently and accurately judged by Hollywood professionals who knew something about what made for successful entertainment. The Kefauver hearings, we must remember, featured in-person testimony from some of the nation's most notorious crime bosses, all celebrities of a sort, and this provided a powerful reason for many to stay "glued" to the sets that were at the time still very much a novelty. The crime/investigation hooks that Zanuck helped de Rochemont either supply or fully exploit for all his projects of the early postwar era except *Lost Boundaries* surely contributed to the box office success these films generally enjoyed. Because it dealt, if obliquely, with racial inequality, then an issue very much in the headlines that Hollywood proved able to turn into a very successful cycle, RD-DR's purely social-themed entry also profited from a topic of current national interest that drew customers to the theater.[20]

However, one of the follow-ups to this success, *Whistle at Eaton Falls*, showed the weakness of the RD-DR approach, its tendency toward an authentic banality that needed to be counterbalanced by entertainment value of some kind. This particular project certainly was a case of a subject too far. *Whistle* is a picture as full of earnest conviction as *Lost Boundaries*. It provides no reason to doubt the producer's firm belief (proclaimed in publicity materials) in its theme, that the country was threatened deeply by the persistent labor unrest that had troubled the economy in the late 1940s as the transition to peacetime production proved more difficult than many had expected. This was a serious disruption in the body politic at a time of Cold War ideological confrontation that many found deeply disturbing.[21] But dramatizing effectively and with engaging suspense how disagreements between managers and employees might be resolved to the benefit of all parties posed a considerable problem. As Bosley Crowther observed about the film, "Louis de Rochemont's disposition to tackle vital contemporary themes . . . has lured him to take on a subject of staggering challenge and complexity." Not surprisingly, perhaps, this attempt to explore management/labor relations turned out to be resolutely undramatic because the filmmakers failed to contrive "a realistic showdown in which the two elements are validly joined, but have whipped up an illusory deadlock out of melodramatics and sentiment."[22] Here was a film that did not avoid the appeals to emotion of the typical Hollywood product, as well as the somewhat implausible plotting that might lead to the required happy end. *Lost Boundaries* had, arguably, suffered from much the same fundamental structural problem, but it proved more successful in addressing a social climate that disposed viewers to overlook its patent oversimplifications and distortions.

To be sure, *Whistle* might have been too ineptly produced to perform properly at the box office. It was quite "homespun," obviously limited to a "non-Hollywood plainness," just to borrow two of Farber's backhanded compliments; but the film might have been improved with the addition of the kind of storytelling interest that made *Gentleman's Agreement* attractive to filmgoers, particularly the connection that this film's screenwriters (Broadway whizz Moss Hart, aided by Kazan) established between the film's political theme and its romantic plot. In the case of *Whistle*, the talented and well-traveled Robert Siodmak did his best with a project that, because of its deglamorized approach to ordinary living, must have reminded him of one of his earliest productions, the justly famed *Menschen am Sonntag* (*People on Sunday*, 1930). Lloyd Bridges, a rugged actor with a good deal of experience in B-productions starred, while an interesting new face, Ernest Borgnine, played a major role. Dorothy Gish, long absent from the screen, was cast effectively as one of the townspeople. But Zanuck might have predicted that such minimal production values, absent a compelling subject and story, would not make for a solid box office performance. Union conflict with management just did not engage viewer interest with the same fervor (and partisanship) as race relations.

De Rochemont, of course, had little respect for Hollywood executives and institutions, as well as, especially, their (to him extravagantly expensive) approach to turning out a crowd-pleasing product. Yet bypassing the time-tested process for script development in this case proved to be a huge mistake. In this regard, the project provides valuable insight into de Rochemont's working methods. In an undated letter written to convince a potential investor, RD-DR executive Borden Mace provides this account of the project's unorthodox development:

> The original idea was the outgrowth of his meeting with a member of the faculty at the Harvard School of Business Administration, Dr. Sterling Livingston. Louis told him that he liked the idea, but could not put money into it until it had been explored to a greater degree. At a story conference in Portsmouth, Professor Livingston, Mr. and Mrs. De Rochemont, and myself developed the initial story outline after hearing about interesting case histories which Prof. Livingston and his staff had uncovered. We assigned a writer (Larry Dugan) to the project. Livingston brought in an associate of his at Harvard, Paul Ignatius, to assist in the project. After about twenty weeks of slow but steady progress we discovered that we could advance the story further by having Livingston and Ignatius prepare a version of the script from a sound business and economical point of view and Mrs. de Rochemont from a dramatic point of view. . . . Prof. Livingston had completed arrangements whereby a non-profit organization contracted with us to advance $15,000 to us to prepared a screenplay based on the original idea for *Whistle* [this is probably the Washington-based Committee

on Economic Development, founded in 1942]. We have a 12 month option to purchase the screenplay for the same sum. Livingston and Ignatius have been paid by Harvard, but Louis has verbally agreed that if the picture is made they will be compensated for their months of service. . . . We engaged a Yale professor of playwriting and former Fox screenwriter for one month as a consultant and have had various staff members work on parts of the script. Louis has found by experience that in the making of his kind of real life pictures it is too costly to give the basic idea to a Hollywood screen-writer . . . and prefers to do the preliminary work with less expensive (and less experienced) writers.[23]

The script that emerged from this process of bargain-basement development concluded with an improbable reconciliation between angry workers and a management able to persuade them that their best interest lies in moderating demands for changed working conditions so that the company can remain competitive in a difficult market. Innovation plays a key role as, after the installation of labor-saving devices results in layoffs, workers help develop a new product that proves popular enough to hire back the furloughed workers. This allows the filmmakers, as Crowther grumbles in his notice, to "bring the whole thing to a happy ending by an easy, issue-jumping device."

Of course, we might say that the much-praised *Gentleman's Agreement*, like many a Hollywood production, also offers a diversionary finale, neatly sidestepping the more intractable questions raised by the poisonous *mentalité* of antisemitism, whose capacity for unimaginable destruction few if any in the film's postwar audience would have been inclined to minimize. Taking on a less sensational subject, and lacking the crowd-pleasing appeal of a romantic plot involving major Hollywood stars, *Whistle at Eaton Falls* never found much of an audience. And yet it did not lack for admirers. Writing in the *Herald Tribune*, Otis L. Guernsey Jr. praised the film as "an industrial idyll based on realistic events but having a little touch of the fairy tale about it in its sweet, convenient triumph of public good over private evil. . . . [It] recreates and examines the very weave and texture of labor attitudes and business administration, doing so in an earnestly impartial manner and with a most constructive emphasis on the threads of good will and reason."[24] *Whistle* suffered from all the weaknesses that could mar a pictorial journalistic production. The film offered no action sequences and was as a result more than a little boring for long stretches. Not featuring a romance between two charismatic A-listers, it resolutely avoided the erotic in all its forms. Its setting was a gritty mill town lacking completely in glamor or exoticism. Its themes were developed in a fashion that was transparently didactic, with the Smithian invisible hand summoned up at film's end to provide a solution not dependent in the least on regulation or even negotiation. Reminiscent of *Reader's Digest* is, as Guernsey suggests, a "most constructive emphasis on the threads of good will and reason" as the two sides struggle to deal with one another and as the inevitable walk-out for a time severely stresses local households. But even this not especially entertaining entrant in the informal movement whose outlines have been traced in this volume manifests the principal virtue of locative realism: the authenticity for which studio exteriors and soundstages were never an adequate substitute. What appeared on the screen, as Alton Cook opined in the *New York Telegram and Sun*, showed that "this picture [had] moved right into a small town and was filmed in semi-documentary fashion, using the people of the town itself."[25] Eaton Falls was a fictional town, of course, but the images of the various New England sites of which it was composed were real enough, as were the outlines of the "actual case" upon which the script was based. Particularity here was rightly abandoned in search of the depiction of more general truths.

Perhaps one of the professors who worked on the project should have the last word on this project and on pictorial journalism more generally. Columbia, which had signed on for distribution, was eager to dump *Whistle* once its exhibition started to go badly; many theaters had passed on the release, in de Rochemont's opinion because it was promoted with inept and deceptive advertising (*Whistle* was the film, so one poster slug line mysteriously proclaimed, "that comes right out and says it"). De Rochemont used his considerable influence in a failed attempt to convince Columbia to do otherwise, even arranging for President Truman's chief of staff, John R. Steelman, one of the era's most powerful political operatives, to ask J. Raymond Bell, a vice president at Columbia, for his continuing support of the release: "The more I have thought about the picture, the more I am hopeful it can be seen all over the country. There are many scenes in the picture to stir the memory of almost any citizen of our country. While this is especially true of the average and small towns all over America, even in the largest cities, I am quite certain you will find a universal interest."[26] Among the many testimonial letters that he solicited and received, however, none more eloquently and even movingly captured the intentions of the filmmakers than the one penned by Harvard's Paul Ignatius:

> The picture is a story of the strength of our society, of our people, of our industrial system. In making the picture we believed its theme could be best expressed through the unfolding drama of a single individual. In the character of Brad Adams we hoped to show the qualities of forthright union leadership and responsible business management. Most of all, we wanted to make a picture that people would like—which told an honest story in human terms and stimulated thought about contemporary problems. We hoped to achieve that final goal of entertainment where the audience lives the events portrayed in the drama—where for an hour-and-half they would be citizens of the town we called Eaton Falls.[27]

NOTES

PREFACE

1. Robert Rosenstone, "Oliver Stone as Historian," in *Oliver Stone as Historian*, ed. Robert Brent Toplin (Lawrence: University Press of Kansas, 2000), 34.

2. Ibid.

3. Ibid.

4. Saverio Giovacchini, *Hollywood Modernism: Film and Politics in the Age of the New Deal* (Philadelphia: Temple University Press, 2001), 1–2, 5.

5. Nick Smedley, *A Divided World: Hollywood Cinema and Émigré Directors in the Era of Roosevelt and Hitler, 1933–48* (Bristol, UK: Intellect, 2011), 35, 80.

6. See William Graebner, *The Age of Doubt: American Thought and Culture in the 1940s* (New York: Waveland, 1998), and William O'Neill, *American High: The Years of Confidence, 1945–60* (New York: Free Press, 1989).

7. Drew Casper, *Postwar Hollywood 1946–1962* (London: Wiley-Blackwell, 2007), and Frank Krutnik, Steve Neale, Brian Neve, and Peter Stanfield, eds., *"Un-American Hollywood": Politics and Film in the Blacklist Era* (New Brunswick, NJ: Rutgers University Press, 2007).

8. Edward S. Casey, *The Fate of Place: A Philosophical Inquiry* (Berkeley: University of California Press, 1997), ix.

9. Erving Goffman, *Asylums: Essays on the Social Situation of Mental Patients and Other Inmates* (New York: Doubleday, 1961).

10. Ibid., 4.

11. Jean Baudrillard, *America* (London: Verso, 1988), 56.

12. David B. Clarke, ed., *The Cinematic City* (London: Routledge, 1997), 3.

13. Mark Shiel and Tony Fitzmaurice, eds., *Cinema and the City: Film and Urban Societies in a Global Context* (Oxford: Blackwell, 2001), 5.

14. Edward Dimendberg, *Film Noir and the Spaces of Modernity* (Cambridge, MA: Harvard University Press, 2004).

15. John Agnew, *Place and Politics: The Geographical Mediation of State and Society* (New York: Unwin Hyman, 1987), 28.

16. Deborah A. Carmichael, ed., *The Landscape of Hollywood Westerns* (Salt Lake City: University of Utah Press, 2007); John David Rhodes and Elena Gorfinkel, eds., *Taking Place: Location and the Moving Image* (Minneapolis: University of Minnesota Press, 2011); Graeme Harper and Jonathan Rayner, eds., *Cinema and Landscape* (Bristol, UK: Intellect, 2007); Martin LeFebvre, ed., *Landscape and Film* (New York: Routledge, 2006); Imogen Sara Smith, *In Lonely Places: Film Noir Beyond the City* (Jefferson, NC: McFarland, 2011); Jon Brinckerhoff Jackson, *A Sense of Place, A Sense of Time* (New Haven, CT: Yale University Press, 1994); and W.J.T. Mitchell, ed., *Landscape and Power* (Chicago: University of Chicago Press, 1994).

INTRODUCTION: REAL HISTORY, REAL CINEMA

1. Andrei Cherny, *The Candy Bombers: The Untold Story of the Berlin Airlift and America's Finest Hour* (New York: G. P. Putnam, 2008), 7.

2. Ibid., 8.

3. Bosley Crowther, "The Big Lift," *New York Times*, 17 April 1950, http://www.nytimes.com/movie/review?res=9C07E2DB1439E13BBC4F51DFB266838B649EDE (accessed 17 January 2015).

4. Some reshoots were done in the United States after the production team returned stateside at the Lockheed Aircraft facilities in California.

5. *Motion Picture Daily*, 1 April 1950, Production Code Administration (PCA) files, Academy of Motion Picture Arts and Sciences (AMPAS), Beverly Hills.

6. See further on Staudte's film in Robert Shandley, *Rubble Films: German Films in the Shadow of the Third Reich* (Philadelphia: Temple University Press, 2001).

7. A Fox production file at AMPAS contains a letter dated 10 June 1949 from Maj. Reade Tilley, USAF, to Commanding Officer at Lagens Air Field, Terceira Island, Azores, introducing Charles Clarke and Louis Kunkle of Fox: "They desire to shoot some footage of Air Lift plans landing and taking off from Lagens Field in order to portray one stage of the journey of an Air Lift plan from the United States to Europe."

8. Keith Lowe, *Savage Continent: Europe in the Aftermath of World War II* (New York: St. Martin's, 2012), 43–44.

9. Breen to Col. Jason S. Joy at Fox, 16 August 1949, PCA files, AMPAS.

10. For details, see Danny S. Parker, *Fatal Crossroads: The Untold Story of the Malmedy Massacre at the Battle of the Bulge* (New York: Da Capo, 2012). The issue of judicial retribution for war crimes dominated the first years of peace, with very uneven results, as chronicled by Lowe, who observes that "the new authorities in Europe were unable to establish themselves before first bringing the forces of vengeance under control. Revenge was a fundamental part of the bedrock upon which postwar Europe was built" (*Savage Continent*, 77).

11. For details see Johannes Morsink, *The Universal Declaration of Human Rights: Origins, Drafting, and Intent* (Philadelphia: University of Pennsylvania Press, 1999).

12. A less sympathetic reading of Gerda's developing independence, and of the presentation of the schatzies in general, is to be found in Annette Brauerhoch, *Fräuleins und GIs: Geschichte und Filmgeschichte* (Frankfurt am Main: Strömfeld, 2006).

13. Saverio Giovacchini, *Hollywood Modernism: Film and Politics in the Age of the New Deal* (Philadelphia: Temple University Press, 2001), 208.

14. Qtd. in Steven Jay Rubin, *Combat Films: American Realism, 1945–1970* (Jefferson, NC: McFarland, 1980), 27.

15. Ibid., 28.

16. Qtd. in ibid., 27.

17. Ibid., 36.

18. Ibid., 2.

19. Richard Overy, *The Bombers and the Bombed: Allied Air War Over Europe 1940–45* (New York: Penguin, 2013), 148–230.

20. "Twelve O'Clock High," *New York Times*, 28 January 1950, http://www.nytimes.com/movie/review?res=9E05E3DF173DE03BBC4051DFB766838B649EDE (accessed 6 February 2014).

21. http://www.imdb.com/title/tt0041996/business?ref_=ttfc_sa_3 and http://www.imdb .com/title/tt0041163/business?ref_=ttfc_ql_4 (both accessed 6 February 2015).

22. "Of Small Headaches," *New York Times*, 16 April 1950, X5.

CHAPTER 1   FILMING THE TRANSITORY WORLD WE LIVE IN

1. http://web.missouri.edu/~materert/mod/Conrad.htm (accessed 25 January 2014).

2. See, for example, Rhonda L. Flaxman, *Victorian Word Painting and Narrative: Toward the Blending of Genres* (Ann Arbor: University of Michigan Press, 1987).

3. Kazuo Ishiguro, *The Remains of the Day* (New York: Knopf, 1989), 3.

4. Andrew Higson, *English Heritage, English Cinema* (Oxford: Oxford University Press, 2003). See further the discussion of *The Remains of the Day* and related films in Higson's *Film England: Culturally English Filmmaking since the 1990s* (London: I. B. Tauris, 2011), 27.

5. For further details, see Earl G. Ingersoll, *Filming Forster* (Teaneck, NJ: Fairleigh Dickinson University Press, 2012), 195–249.

6. Higson, *English Heritage, English Cinema*, 39.

7. Cesare Zavattini, "A Thesis on Neo-Realism," in *Springtime in Italy: A Reader on Neo-Realism*, ed. and trans. David Overbey (Hamden CT: Archon Books, 1978), 68.

8. Ibid., 75.

9. E. M. Forster, *Aspects of the Novel* (London: Harcourt, 1927), 69, 78.

10. Zavattini, "A Thesis on Neo-Realism," 75–76.

11. Forster, *Aspects of the Novel*, 61.

12. See Keith Lowe, *Savage Continent: Europe in the Aftermath of World War II* (New York: St. Martin's, 2012), 44–47, for further discussion.

13. Siegfried Kracauer, *Theory of Film: The Redemption of Physical Reality*, ed. Miriam Hansen (1960; rpt., Princeton, NJ: Princeton University Press, 2007).

14. I discuss this issue at some length in *Joel and Ethan Coen* (Urbana: University of Illinois Press, 2005), 80–102.

15. Kracauer, *Theory of Film*, 34.

16. For further details see http://movielocationsplus.com/century.htm (accessed 27 January 2015).

17. John Pym, *Merchant Ivory's English Landscape: Rooms, Views, and Anglo-Saxon Attitudes* (New York: Harry Abrams, 1995),

18. See http://www.thelouisianawavestudio.com/about.html (accessed 6 February 2013).

19. For further details see http://www.bajafilmstudios.com/ (accessed 6 February 2013).

CHAPTER 2   THE POSTWAR TURN TOWARD THE REAL

1. See the classic study by anthropologist Hortense Powdermaker, *Hollywood: The Dream Factory* (New York: Little, Brown, 1950).

2. Robert Knopf, ed., *Theater and Film: A Comparative Anthology* (New Haven, CT: Yale University Press, 2005), 1.

3. Gilberto Perez, *The Material Ghost: Films and Their Medium* (Baltimore: Johns Hopkins University Press, 2000).

4. Siegfried Kracauer, *Theory of Film: The Redemption of Physical Reality*, ed. Miriam Hansen (1960; rpt., Princeton, NJ: Princeton University Press, 2007), xlix.

5. André Bazin, "The Ontology of the Photographic Image," in *What Is Cinema?* vol. 1, ed. and trans. Hugh Gray (Berkeley: University of California Press, 1967), 15.

6. Dudley Andrew, "Introduction," in *What Is Cinema?*, xvi.

7. Ibid., xvii.

8. http://www.moma.org/collection/theme.php?theme_id=10135 (accessed 23 April 2014). See further Matthew Gale, *Dada and Surrealism* (New York: Phaidon, 1997).

9. Qtd. in Julia Hallam and Margaret Marshment, *Realism and Popular Cinema* (Manchester: Manchester University Press, 2000), 5.

10. Kracauer, *Theory*, xlvii.

11. Aubrey Solomon, *Twentieth Century–Fox: A Corporate and Financial History* (Boston: Scarecrow Press, 1988), 68, 104.

12. Saverio Giovacchini, *Hollywood Modernism: Film and Politics in the Age of the New Deal* (Philadelphia: Temple University Press, 2001), 211.

13. Consider, for example, Howard Hawks, whose 1948 western *Red River* makes effective use of real locations in Louisiana, Mexico, and Arizona, in contrast to his 1959 exercise in the same genre, *Rio Bravo*, whose on-location "exteriors" were shot at the Old Tucson Studios in the city's suburbs.

14. For details see http://www.toursanfranciscobay.com/tours/hitchcocks-vertigo.html (accessed 12 May 2014).

15. Nathaniel Rich, *San Francisco Noir* (New York: Little Bookroom, 2005).

16. Frank Capra, *The Name above the Title* (New York: Macmillan, 1971), 375.

17. William S. Graebner, *The Age of Doubt: American Thought and Culture in the 1940s* (Boston: Twayne, 1991).

18. Ibid., 19–20.

19. Ibid., 17.

20. Reinhold Niebuhr, *The Irony of American History* (New York: Charles Scribner's Sons, 1952), 39.

21. Graebner, *The Age of Doubt*, 19–20.

22. Niebuhr, *Irony of American History*, 7.

23. Thomas Schatz, *Boom and Bust: American Cinema in the 1940s* (Berkeley: University of California Press, 1997), 382.

24. Cesare Zavattini, "A Thesis on Neo-Realism," in *Springtime in Italy: A Reader on Neo-Realism*, ed. and trans. David Overbey (Hamden CT: Archon Books, 1978), 72.

25. "Intruder in the Dust," *New York Times*, 23 November 1949, http://www.nytimes.com/ movie/review?res=EE05E7DF173FE76ABC4B51DFB7678382659EDE (accessed 12 May 2014).

26. Zavattini, "Neo-Realism," 73.

27. Ibid.

28. Arthur Miller, *Timebends: A Life* (New York: Grove Press, 1987), 184.

29. Ibid., 317–318.

30. Ibid., 184.

31. Zavattini, "Neo-Realism," 72.

32. http://www.filmsite.org/mart.html (accessed 4 March 2014).

33. http://www.imdb.com/title/tt0048356/business (accessed 4 March 2014).

34. Paddy Chayefsky, *The Collected Works of Paddy Chayefsky: The Television Plays* (New York: Applause Books, 2000), 183.

35. On the American enthusiasm for neorealism, see the excellent account in Tino Balio's *The Foreign Film Renaissance on American Screens, 1946–1973* (Madison: University of Wisconsin Press, 2010), 3–61.

36. Not many award-winning commercial films can be said to be important documents of the changing social currents of an American urban neighborhood, but *Marty*—again much in the manner of the Italian neorealist films—offers an in-depth portrait of the Italian American areas of Arthur Avenue. See Themis Chronopoulos, "'Marty' and Its Significance to the Social History of Arthur Avenue, the Bronx, in the 1950s," *Bronx County Historical Society Journal* 44 (Spring/Fall 2007): 50–59.

CHAPTER 3   OF BACKDROPS AND PLACE: *THE SEARCHERS* AND *SUNSET BLVD.*

1. Alan LeMay, *The Searchers* (New York: Curtis Publishing, 1954).

2. Ernest Renan, *Qu'est ce qu'une nation?* (Paris: Édition mille et une nuits, 1997). There Renan observes that "L'oubli, et je dirai meme l'erreur historique, sont un facteur essential de la creation d'une nation" (Forgetting, and I'd even say historical error, is an essential factor in the creation of a nation) (13).

3. Leo Braudy, *The World in a Frame: What We See in Films* (New York: Doubleday, 1976), 44, 46, and 48.

4. Ibid., 48.

5. Paul Rotha, *Documentary Film* (New York: Faber & Faber, 1935), 26.

6. Qtd. in Gene Frankel, *The Searchers: The Making of an American Legend* (New York: Bloomsbury, 2013), 268.

7. Qtd. in ibid., 3.

8. Qtd in ibid., 269 (emphasis added).

9. Ibid., 284, (emphasis added).

10. Elizabeth McKinsey, *Niagara Falls: Icon of the American Sublime* (Cambridge: Cambridge University Press, 1985), 28.

11. See Edmund Burke, *A Philosophical Inquiry into the Origin of Our Ideas of the Sublime and Beautiful,* trans. Abraham Mills (New York: Harper & Brothers, 1856).

12. McKinsey, *Niagara Falls,* 33.

13. Ibid., 32–33.

14. Frankel, *The Searchers,* 268.

15. Jonathan M. Smith, "The Place of Nature," in *American Space/American Place: Geographies of the Contemporary United States,* by John Agnew and Jonathan M. Smith (New York: Routledge, 2002), 29; and Agnew and Smith, "Introduction," in *American Space/American Place,* 9.

16. These affinities are discussed in some detail by William Howze, "The Influence of Western Painting and Genre Painting on the Films of John Ford," but without much attention paid to the notion of landscape as such, especially as it figures in *The Searchers. Connexions,* 2 September 2011, http://cnx.org/content/co111357/1.1/, (accessed 15 April 2014).

17. See Henry Nash Smith, *Virgin Land: the American West as Symbol and Myth* (Cambridge, MA: Harvard University Press, 1970).

18. R.W.B. Lewis, *The American Adam* (Chicago: University of Chicago Press, 1959), 5.

19. Tag Gallagher, *John Ford: The Man and His Films* (Berkeley: University of California Press, 1986), 385.

20. For further details, see http://www.comanchelodge.com/quanahpg.html (accessed 15 May 2014) and Frankel, *The Searchers,* chapter 3.

21. Agnew and Smith, *American Space/American Place,* 8.

22. Qtd. in Frankel, *The Searchers,* 294.

23. "Stagecoach," *New York Times,* 3 March 1939, http://www.nytimes.com/movie/review?res=EE05E7DF173FE170BC4B53DFB5668382629EDE (accessed 14 April 2014)

24. Frankel, *The Searchers,* 271.

25. Ibid., 267.

26. For a fascinating account of how Hollywood filmmakers utilized Los Angeles locations to limn one portrait after another of the modern urban built environment, see Mark Shiel, *Hollywood Cinema and the Real Los Angeles* (London: Reaktion, 2012).

27. For more details, see Homer Pettey and R. Barton Palmer, eds., *International Noir* (Edinburgh: Edinburgh University Press, 2014).

28. Braudy, *World in a Frame,* 49.

29. Ibid., 51.

30. Fox's interest in realist projects is explored fully in subsequent chapters of this book. For some interesting comments on Columbia and this postwar movement, see J. P. Telotte, "*Film Noir* at Columbia: Fashion and Innovation," in *Columbia Pictures: Portrait of a Studio,* ed. Bernard F. Dick (Lexington: University Press of Kentucky, 1992), 106–117.

31. From the so-called "Wilder Memorandum," which was the director's report to his military superiors, subsequently made public and printed in full in Ralph Willett, *The Americanization of Germany, 1946–1949* (New York: Routledge, 1989), 40–44. The quotation is from page 40.

32. A full accounting, making use of information made available for researchers following the fall of the Soviet Union, is offered in Timothy Snyder's groundbreaking study *Bloodlands: Europe between Hitler and Stalin* (New York: Basic Books, 2012).

33. Wilder Memorandum, 40.

34. Ibid., 40–41.

35. Ibid., 40.

36. Qtd. in Willett, *Americanization of Germany,* 33. Crowther's review of the film emphasizes the talent of screenwriters Wilder and Brackett in making palatable its biting denunciation of cherished American values (especially the national creed of exceptionalism, which at times is given a pronounced Hitlerian spin): "indeed, there are moments when the picture becomes down-right cynical in tone, but it is always artfully salvaged by a hasty nip-up of the yarn." *New York Times,* 1 July 1948, 19.

37. Bosley Crowther, "A Foreign Affair," *New York Times,* 1 July 1948, http://www.nytimes.com/movie/review?res=EE05E7DF1739E565BC4953DFB1668383659EDE (accessed 21 May 2014)

38. Ed Sikov, *On Sunset Boulevard: The Life and Times of Billy Wilder* (New York: Hyperion, 1988), 291.

39. Ibid., 292.

40. On the history of Perino's see http://www.paulrwilliamsproject.org/gallery/1960s-restaurants/ (accessed 19 February 2014). On Schwab's see http://www.nytimes.com/1983/10/25/arts/schwab-s-hollywood-drugstore-shut.html (accessed 26 March 2014).

On Hollywood and Vine, where the Walk of Fame is located, see http://articles.latimes
.com/2008/may/04/local/me-thenandnow4 (accessed 15 March 2014). On the Bel-Air
Country Club, founded in 1927, see http://web.archive.org/web/20080619014630/.
http://www.latimes.com/classified/realestate/printedition/la-re-guide6mar06,0,448797,
full.story?coll=la-class-realestate (accessed 15 March 2014). Much useful information
about the various ways in which Wilder's film is about Hollywood can be found in Gregory
Paul Williams, *The Story of Hollywood: An Illustrated History* (Lebanon, TN: Greenleaf,
2005), and Sam Staggs, *Close-Up on Sunset Boulevard: Billy Wilder, Norma Desmond, and the
Dark Hollywood Dream* (New York: St. Martin's, 2003).

41. Staggs, *Close-Up*, 89, 87.

42. See ibid., 110–117, for a useful discussion of the careers of these famous former stars.

43. For further details about the Alto Nido see http://www.altonidoapts.com/ (accessed
4 June 2014).

CHAPTER 4   AN AMERICAN NEOREALISM?

1. Mark Shiel, *Italian Neorealism: Rebuilding the Cinematic City* (London: Wallflower, 2006), 1.

2. For a survey of the latest scholarly views on these issues, see the thorough and perspica-
cious discussions in Torunn Haaland, *Italian Neorealist Cinema* (Edinburgh: Edinburgh
University Press, 2012), and Luca Barattoni, *Italian Post-Neorealist Cinema* (Edinburgh:
Edinburgh University Press, 2012).

3. Shiel, *Italian Neorealism*, 1.

4. Hence the outlaw nature of much modernist fiction. In *The End of Obscenity* (New York:
Harper & Row, 1968), Charles Rembar provides a fascinating discussion of the legal and
artistic issues involved in the several famous cases of the era that made for a victory of
the modernist impulse toward truth-telling.

5. Julia Hallam and Margaret Marshment, *Realism and Popular Cinema* (Manchester:
Manchester University Press, 2000), 24.

6. Shiel, *Italian Neorealism*, 1.

7. Bosley Crowther, review of *Paisan, New York Times*, 30 March 1948.

8. An easily searchable version of the Code, including all amendments and deletions
effected during its history, can be found at http://productioncode.dhwritings.com/
multipleframes_productioncode.php.

9. The contingency of European recovery is exhaustively and effectively chronicled in Tony
Judt, *Postwar* (London: Penguin Press, 2005).

10. See Joseph Tuman, "Miller v. California," in *Free Speech on Trial: Communication
Perspectives on Landmark Supreme Court Decisions*, ed. Richard A. Parker (Tuscaloosa:
University of Alabama Press, 2003), 187–202; and the discussion of its implications for
the film industry in Jon Lewis, *Hollywood vs. Hard Core* (New York: NYU Press, 2000).

11. Qtd. from the 1930 version. See http://productioncode.dhwritings.com/multipleframes_
productioncode.php (accessed 20 September 2013).

12. These developments are chronicled in Gregory D. Black, *Hollywood Censored: Morality
Codes, Catholics, and the Movies* (Cambridge: Cambridge University Press, 1996), and
Thomas Doherty, *Pre-Code Hollywood: Sex, Immorality, and Insurrection in American Cinema:
1930–1934* (New York: Columbia University Press, 1999).

13. See Thomas Doherty, *Hollywood's Censor: Joseph I. Breen and the Production Code
Administration* (New York: Columbia University Press, 2009).

14. From Zavattini's "A Thesis on Neorealism" (actually a compilation of three polemical journal articles published in the early fifties), reprinted in *Springtime in Italy: A Reader on Neorealism*, ed. and trans. David Overbey (Hamden, CT: Archon Books, 1978), 67–69.

15. Overbey, *Springtime in Italy*, 10.

16. Shiel, *Italian Neorealism*, 2.

17. Zavattini, "A Thesis on Neorealism," 70, 71.

18. A notable exception of sorts is *Amore in Città* (1953), an anthology film in which the leading directors of the era each contributed a segment in different cinematic modalities. Carlo Lizzani's "Paid Love" is documentary reportage, while Zavattini and Umberto Maselli's "Story of Caterina" is a straightforward re-creation of a true story.

19. See Tino Balio, *The Foreign Film Renaissance on American Screens, 1947–1973* (Madison: University of Wisconsin Press, 1941), 16–18.

20. Zavattini, "A Thesis on Neorealism," 67.

21. Ibid., 75.

22. Ibid., 72.

23. Ibid., 68.

24. Bosley Crowther, review of *Bicycle Thieves* [as *Bicycle Thief*], *New York Times*, 18 December 1949.

25. Bosley Crowther, review of *Bitter Rice*, *New York Times*, 19 September 1950.

26. Robert Sklar, "James Agee and the U.S. Response to Neorealism," in *Global Neorealism: The Transnational History of a Film Style*, ed. Saverio Giovacchini and Robert Sklar (Jackson: University Press of Mississippi, 2012), 71.

27. Balio, *Foreign Film Renaissance*, 3.

28. See ibid. for a full and richly informative account of how this area of film exhibition developed in the postwar United States.

29. Shiel, *Italian Neorealism*, 5.

30. "Rome's New Empire," *Time*, 14 July 1952, http://www.time.com/time/magdazine/archives (accessed 6 February 2013).

31. Sklar, "James Agee and the U.S. Response to Neorealism," 72.

32. Patrick Gilligan, *Alfred Hitchcock: A Life in Darkness and in Light* (New York: HarperCollins, 2003), 533.

33. François Truffaut, *Hitchcock*, trans. Helen Scott (New York: Simon & Schuster, 1966), 171.

34. Barattoni, *Italian Post-Neorealist Cinema*.

35. Shiel, *Italian Neorealism*, 15.

36. Giovacchini and Sklar, *Global Neorealism*, 12.

37. See http://www.imdb.com/title/tt0046126/business (accessed 5 February 2015).

38. W.J.T. Mitchell, ed., *Landscape and Power* (Chicago: University of Chicago Press, 1994), 2.

39. See http://www.tcm.com/tcmdb/title/88977/Samson-and-Delilah/notes.html (accessed 9 June 2014).

40. Figures cited from http://www.boxofficemojo.com/movies/?id=80days56.htm (accessed 4 March 2014).

41. Raymond Fielding, *The March of Time: 1935–1951* (New York: Oxford University Press, 1978), 4.

42. Ibid., 5.

43. Ibid., 73.

44. Qtd in ibid., 30.

45. Ibid., 7.

46. For details, see ibid., 68–242, on which the account offered here is based.

47. Otis Ferguson, "Time Steals a March," *New Republic*, 9 February 1938, 19.

48. See Wayne S. Cole, *Charles A. Lindbergh and the Battle against US Intervention in World War II* (New York: Harcourt Brace Jovanovich, 1974), for further details.

49. Broadside produced for premiere of *The Ramparts We Watch*, de Rochemont archive, AHRC.

50. Charles Peters, *Five Days in Philadelphia: 1940, Wendell Willkie, FDR, and the Political Convention That Freed FDR to Win World War II* (New York: Public Affairs, 2006), 5.

51. Peter Lev, *Twentieth-Century Fox: The Zanuck-Skouras Years, 1935–1965* (Austin: University Press of Texas, 2013), 71–72.

52. Thomas M. Pryor, "Down the Homestretch," *New York Times*, 30 June 1940, 103.

53. Bosley Crowther, "Time Marches On to the Ramparts," *New York Times*, 22 October 1939, 133. See also the brief discussion of a change in production plans for the project, involving some reshoots, in "Concerning Certain Cinematic Chat," *New York Times*, 24 March 1940.

54. George Fielding Eliot, *The Ramparts We Watch: A Study of the Problems of American National Defense* (New York: Reynal & Hitchcock, 1938).

55. This is a best guess on how de Rochemont obtained his copy of the film. See the different account in Fielding, *The March of Time*, 248–249.

56. See "Censors Stand Pat on 'Ramparts' Film," *New York Times*, 20 September 1941, 23.

57. Qtd in ibid.

58. Bosley Crowther, "'The Ramparts We Watch,' a Stirring Document," *New York Times*, 20 September 1940, 27.

59. Ibid.

60. For full details see http://www.fbi.gov/news/stories/2007/december/espionage_120307 (accessed 21 February 2013). For a self-congratulatory and not very accurate account, see Turrou's *Nazi Spies in America* (New York: Random House, 1938).

61. Bosley Crowther, "The Myth of the Trend," *New York Times*, 3 March 1940, X5.

62. Bosley Crowther, "Lost Opportunity; or, Where Was Hollywood When the Lights in Germany Went Out?" *New York Times*, 23 June 1940, X3.

63. Ibid.

64. Ibid.

65. Crowther, "Time Marches On."

66. Ibid.

67. Pryor, "Down the Homestretch."

68. Ibid.

69. See for further discussion R. Barton Palmer, "'The Story You Are About to See Is True: *Dragnet*, Film Noir, and Postwar Realism," in *Philosophy and TV Noir*, ed. Steven M. Sanders and Aeon J. Skoble (Lexington: University Press of Kentucky, 2008), 33–47.

70. Pryor, "Down the Homestretch."

71. Zavattini, "A Thesis on Neorealism," 68–69.

72. Ibid., 69, 67.

73. Crowther, "Time Marches On."

74. Broadside produced for premiere of *The Ramparts We Watch*, de Rochemont archive, AHRC.

75. Qtd. in Fielding, *The March of Time*, 251 (from a review of the film for the British journal *The Spectator*, 11 April 1941).

76. Qtd. in Fielding, *The March of Time*, 246.

77. Crowther, "The Ramparts We Watch."

78. Ibid.

79. Raymond Williams, *Marxism and Literature* (Oxford: Oxford University Press, 1977); Anstey qtd. in Fielding, *The March of Time*, 251.

CHAPTER 5   NOIR ON LOCATION

1. For an account of this critical tradition, along with relevant texts, see R. Barton Palmer, trans. and ed., *Perspectives on Film Noir* (New York: G. K. Hall, 1996).

2. A. W., "Niagara Vies with Marilyn Monroe," *New York Times*, 22 January 1953, 20. Further references noted in the text. See also the review in *Variety*, 31 December 1952, which concludes that "Niagara is a morbid, clichéd expedition into lust and murder."

3. *Variety*, 20 January 1953, Production Code Administration (PCA) files, Academy of Motion Picture Arts and Sciences (AMPAS), Beverly Hills.

4. http://www.tcm.com/tcmdb/title/70092/Call-Northside-777/full-credits.html (accessed 15 May 2014).

5. *Call Northside 777*, PCA files, AMPAS.

6. Most notably in Thomas Cripps, *Making Movies Black: The Hollywood Message Movie from World War II to the Civil Rights Era* (New York: Oxford University Press, 1993), esp. chapter 6.

7. *Hollywood Reporter*, 21 January 1948, PCA files, AMPAS.

8. Breen to Col. Jason Joy at Fox, 5 December 1945: "We have read the story from the December issue of READERS DIGEST, carrying the title, THE PERFECT CASE, and I am pleased to say that this story, as it is written now, seems to us to be acceptable under the provisions of the Production Code, and to contain little, if anything, that suggests any real danger from the standpoint of political censorship." PCA files, AMPAS.

9. *Variety*, 24 January 1947, reports that the crew decamped to Stamford (and to nearby White Plains, New York, for the courtroom sequences) "because the authorities proved a bit sensitive over having the long unsolved murder put on the screen." PCA files, AMPAS.

10. *Hollywood Reporter*, 24 January 1947, PCA files, AMPAS.

11. Fox publicity sheet, n.d., PCA files, AMPAS.

12. Telegram from Zanuck to de Rochemont, 5 September 1946, de Rochemont Archive, American Humanities Research Center (AHRC).

13. Telegram from de Rochemont to Zanuck, 5 September 1946, de Rochemont Archive, AHRC.

14. "13 Rue Madeleine," *New York Times*, 16 January 1947, PCA files, AMPAS.

15. Rudy Behlmer, ed., *Henry Hathaway* (Lanham, MD: Scarecrow Press, 2001), 209.

16. *Variety*, 12 September 1945, PCA files, AMPAS. The film's revised first draft continuity, 14 February 1945, offers this ending, which is oddly reminiscent of the so-called "death ray" research associated with inventor Nikola Tesla, known to the scientific community more formally as "directed-energy weapons." Project 97 is, according to the narrator, an individual weapon: "This is the new device . . . small . . . held easily in a man's hands."

The narrator's next three lines are "withheld for security reasons." The next shot was to have shown a man with the device destroying a concrete blockhouse. The film's final shot was to be of planes to have been destroyed by a ray coming from "Robot planes . . . remainder of speech withheld for security reasons." Narrator: "This is our new weapon . . . which the enemy tried to steal and turn against us. He spent years . . . and expended many of his agents. But he has failed in this, as he has failed in other ways." The film ends with a shot of the FBI seal. Wartime research did focus to some degree on directed-energy weapons, continuing after the war and culminating in some sense with the invention of laser technology.

17. Telegram from J. Edgar Hoover to Louis de Rochemont, 7 March 1945, de Rochemont archive, AHRC.

18. Philippe de Lacey at MGM to LDR, report on treatment of NOW IT CAN BE TOLD (later HOUSE), 16 December 1944, de Rochemont archive, AHRC.

19. Igor Gouzenko, *The Iron Curtain: Inside Stalin's Spy Ring* (New York: E. P. Dutton, 1948).

20. "The Iron Curtain," *Variety*, 31 December 1947, PCA files, AMPAS.

21. See Behlmer, *Henry Hathaway*, 210.

22. Ibid., 211.

23. Thomas M. Pryor, "The House on 92nd Street," *New York Times*, 27 September 1945, http://www.nytimes.com/movie/review?res=EE05E7DF1739E26BBC4F51DFBF66838E659 EDE (accessed 19 May 2015).

24. Telegram from Spyros Skouras to Darryl F. Zanuck, 31 August 1945, de Rochemont archive, AHRC.

25. *Variety*, 31 December 1945, PCA files, AMPAS.

26. Qtd. in Peter Lev, *Twentieth Century–Fox: The Zanuck-Skouras Years, 1935–1965* (Austin: University of Texas Press, 2013), 138.

27. Ibid., 17–18.

28. Ibid., 159.

29. Philip Dunne Oral History, American Film Institute Library, Los Angeles.

30. Raymond Fielding, *The March of Time: 1935–1951* (New York: Oxford University Press, 1978), 36.

31. "Escape," *New York Times*, 16 August 1948, http://www.nytimes.com/movie/review?res=9 D02E2DD133EE03BBC4E52DFBE668383659EDE (accessed 9 April 2014).

32. See Robert Shandley, *Rubble Films: German Cinema in the Shadow of the Third Reich* (Philadelphia: Temple University Press, 2001).

33. Qtd. in Lev, *Twentieth Century–Fox*, 287.

34. All quotations from Zanuck are from his 4 March 1947 memo, reprinted in Rudy Behlmer, ed., *Memo from Darryl F. Zanuck: The Golden Years at Twentieth Century–Fox* (New York: Grove Press, 1993), 121–122.

35. Letter from Zanuck to de Rochemont, 6 January 1945, de Rochemont archive, AHRC.

36. "Five Fingers," *New York Times*, 23 February 1952, http://www.nytimes.com/movie/review ?res=9905E3DC103FE43ABC4B51DFB4668389649EDE (accessed 7 April 2014).

37. Behlmer, *Golden Years*, 194.

38. What he saw as gross inaccuracies in the film prompted the villain in question, Eleyza Basna, then still at large, to correct this "miscarriage" of justice. See his *I Was Cicero* (New York: Harper & Row, 1962).

39. Behlmer, *Golden Years,* 193.

40. Rick Lyman, "Stanley Kramer Filmmaker," *New York Times,* 21 February 2001, http://www
.nytimes.com/2001/02/21/movies/stanley-kramer-filmmaker-with-social-bent-dies-
at-87.html?scp=2&sq=stanley%20kramer&st=cse (accessed 15 May 2014).

41. Bosley Crowther, "The Juggler," *New York Times,* 6 May 1953, http://www.nytimes.com/
movie/review?res=9D00E1DC163FE23BBC4E53DFB3668388649EDE (accessed 15 May 2014).

42. "Umberto D," *New York Times,* 8 November 1955, http://www.nytimes.com/movie/review
?res=EE05E7DF173AA076BC4053DFB767838E649EDE (accessed 7 April 2014).

43. "The Top Box Office Hits of 1953," *Variety,* 13 January 1954.

44. Brackett to Harry Brand, interoffice memo, 19 January 1953, *Niagara* Production File, AMPAS.

45. Bosley Crowther, "Second Chance," *New York Times,* 23 July 1953, http://www.nytimes
.com/movie/review?res=9907E7D81231E53BBC4B51DFB1668388649EDE (accessed 23
March 2014).

46. Crowther writes, "Obviously Mr. Marshman [the screenwriter] was inspired to this melodramatic show by the incident of an aerial tramway accident in Rio de Janeiro some two
years ago. The locale of his story is a city in South America and the nature of his near-
disaster is much like that of the real-life happening. Except for one man being killed in
an attempt to go for help via a rope and the slugging melee on the platform, this could
almost be the Rio episode."

47. For an interesting account of notable voluntary trips into the gorge see http://www
.niagarafallslive.com/daredevils_of_niagara_falls.htm (accessed 19 March 2014).

48. http://www.niagarafallsstatepark.com/cave-of-the-winds.aspx (accessed 22 March 2014).

49. Raymond Borde and Étienne Chaumeton, *A Panorama of the American Film Noir, 1941–53,*
trans. Paul Hammond (1955; San Francisco: City Lights, 2002), 13; Susan Hayward, *Cinema
Studies: The Key Concepts* (New York: Routledge, 2000), 78.

50. Vivian Sobchack, "Lounge Time: Postwar Crises and the Chronotope of Film Noir," in
Reconfiguring American Film Genres, ed. Nick Browne (Berkeley: University of California
Press, 1998), 131.

51. Ibid., 130.

52. See Lynda Schneekloth et al., eds., *Olmsted in Buffalo and Niagara* (Buffalo: WNY Wares,
2011), for further details.

53. Ginger Strand, *Inventing Niagara: Beauty, Power, and Lies* (New York: Simon & Schuster,
2009), 207.

54. Ibid., 213.

55. Qtd. in ibid., 70.

56. Philip Shaw, *The Sublime* (London: Routledge, 2006), 2, 9.

57. Ibid., 5.

58. Cesare Zavattini, "A Thesis on Neo-Realism," in *Springtime in Italy: A Reader on
Neo-Realism,* ed. and trans. David Overbey (Hamden, CT: Archon Books, 1978), 67.

CHAPTER 6   THE LEGACIES OF *THE RAMPARTS WE WATCH*

1. *Hollywood Reporter,* 11 January 1944, Production Code Administration (PCA) files,
Academy of Motion Picture Arts and Sciences (AMPAS), Beverly Hills.

2. Michaela H. Moore, *Know Your Enemy: The American Debate on Nazism, 1933–45*
(Cambridge: Cambridge University Press, 2014), 217.

3. "The Hitler Gang," *New York Times*, 8 May 1944, http://www.nytimes.com/movie/review?
res=990DE5DC1331E03BBC4053DFB366838F659EDE (accessed 9 July 2014).

4. Richard M. Brickner, *Is Germany Incurable?* (New York: J. P. Lippincott, 1943).

5. Ibid.

6. In his sequel to *Escape, Man for Himself* (published in 1947 in the wake of the Nuremberg trials), Fromm explores these ethical questions in greater depth, relating them to Freud's theory of the binary forces at work in human nature, the life and the death instincts.

7. Full text at http://www.ibiblio.org/pha/policy/1943/431000a.html (accessed 26 June 2014).

8. For a detailed, balanced discussion see Moore, *Know Your Enemy*, 293–350. Much of the discussion of the Morgenthau plan is antisemitic to one degree or another; see, e.g., David Irving, *The Morgenthau Plan* (New York: Focal Point, 1986). Interestingly, there are unfortunate parallels between what Morgenthau argued should be the course followed for a defeated Germany and the German plan for conquered Poland, which was to be reduced to something like a premodern agricultural state.

9. See the full text of his remarks at http://usa.usembassy.de/etexts/ga4–460906.htm (accessed 26 June 14).

10. http://www.refworld.org/cgi-bin/texis/vtx/rwmain?docid=3ae6b39614 (accessed 26 June 14).

11. Qtd. in Donald Spoto, *Stanley Kramer: Filmmaker* (New York: Samuel French, 1978), 229.

12. See, for example, the brief discussion in Annette Insdorf, *Indelible Shadows: Film and the Holocaust* (Cambridge: Cambridge University Press, 2003), 252–254, which pays little attention to the first half of the film and its nuanced portrayal of postwar Poland.

13. Bosley Crowther, "None Shall Escape," *New York Times*, 7 April 1944, http://www.nytimes .com/movie/review?res=9900E7DD1331E03BBC4F53DFB266838F659EDE (accessed 15 September 2014).

14. Bosley Crowther, "Border Incident," *New York Times*, 21 November 1949, http:// www.nytimes.com/movie/review?res=9A0CEED8113DE03ABC4951DFB7678382659EDE (accessed 22 June 2014).

15. Joy to Breen, 4 June 1947, PCA files, AMPAS.

16. Breen to Joy, 6 June 1947, PCA files, AMPAS.

17. Telegram from Johnston to Zanuck, 9 June 1947, PCA files, AMPAS.

18. Telegram from Zanuck to Johnston, 13 June 1947, PCA files, AMPAS.

19. Breen to Joy, 13 November 1947, PCA files, AMPAS.

20. Letter from Hoover to de Rochemont, 19 March 1952, de Rochemont archive, American Humanities Research Center (AHRC).

21. Richard Nixon in the *Congressional Record*, 26 June 1952, de Rochemont archive, AHRC.

22. Bosley Crowther, "Stranger on the Third Floor," *New York Times*, 2 September 1940, http://www.nytimes.com/movie/review?res=9A01E6D6133EE432A25751C0A96F9C946193 D6CF (accessed 16 May 2014).

23. Matthew Potolsky, *Mimesis* (New York: Routledge, 2006), 4.

24. Margaret Hallam and Elizabeth Marshment, *Realism in Popular Cinema* (Manchester: Manchester University Press, 2000), 4.

25. Ibid., 6.

26. http://www.tcm.com/tcmdb/title/730264/I-Am-An-American/articles.html (accessed 25 June 2014).

27. Most notably discussed by William H. Whyte Jr., *The Organization Man* (New York: Doubleday, 1957).

CONCLUSION: AUTHENTIC BANALITY?

1. Robert Polito, ed., *Farber on Film: The Complete Film Writings of Manny Farber* (New York: Library of America, 2009), 325–326.

2. "Gentleman's Agreement," *New York Times*, 11 November 1947 http://www.nytimes .com/movie/review?res=9E0DE7DE113AE233A25751C1A9679D946693D6CF (accessed 22 February 2015).

3. Darryl F. Zanuck, untitled article in the *Saturday Review*, 10 October 1943, de Rochemont archive, American Humanities Research Center (AHRC).

4. Dwight Macdonald, *Masscult and Midcult* (New York: Random House, 1962).

5. See Larry Ceplair, *Anti-Communism in Twentieth-Century America* (New York: Praeger, 2011), for further discussion, and Joanne P. Sharp, *Condensing the Cold War: Reader's Digest and American Identity* (Minneapolis: University of Minnesota Press, 2000).

6. Sharp, *Condensing the Cold War*, xix. A point made by de Rochemont as well in *Man on a String*, a story of double agents and international intrigue that position America in an offensive mode, as opposed to the fight against domestic subversion dramatized in the earlier *Walk East on Beacon*.

7. Howard Barnes, "Lost Boundaries Illustrates the Use of Understatement," *New York Times*, n.d. (presumably summer 1949), de Rochemont archive, AHRC.

8. Farber, *Farber on Film*, 327.

9. William L. White, *Lost Boundaries* (New York: Harcourt, 1948).

10. Walter White, "Lost Boundaries," *New York Times*, 28 March 1949, de Rochemont archive, Keene State.

11. "Lost Boundaries," *New York Times*, 1 July 1949, http://www.nytimes.com/movie/review? res=9B05E1DB123FE33BBC4953DFB1668382659EDE (accessed 24 February 15).

12. Farber, *Farber on Film*.

13. Irving Drutman, "The East Is His Camera Preserve," *New York Times*, 29 May 1949, de Rochemont archive, Keene State.

14. Gunnar Myrdal, *An American Dilemma: The Negro Problem and American Democracy* (New York: Harper & Brothers, 1944).

15. Festival notes, Cannes 1949, "La pudique Amerique essaie de resoudre le problem noir en rendant les negres blancs" (translation mine), de Rochemont archive, Keene State.

16. Talk given at the BU Founders' Day Institute, 13 March 1948. Original typescript in the de Rochemont archive, AHRC.

17. Albert Johnston Jr. met de Rochemont when he was visiting the University of New Hampshire, where he was a student. Two young men tried to sell him a story that he did not like, but then Johnston offered him this one, and he immediately recognized its value. Though the magazine piece and the book-length forms of the story were essentially sources for the film, they only came into existence because de Rochemont recognized from the outset that this was excellent material for semi-documentary treatment.

18. Speech delivered at the Screen Directors Guild annual meeting, n.d. (probably 1950), de Rochemont archive, AHRC.

19. For further discussion and a text of the final committee report, see Estes Kefauver, *Crime in America* (New York: Doubleday, 1951).

20. See Thomas Cripps, *Making Movies Black* (New York: Oxford University Press, 1993), chapter 6.

21. De Rochemont himself observed to Leo Jaffe at Columbia Pictures: "Although Columbia (and Al Cole of *The Reader's Digest*) counseled against a story dealing with labor-management relations, I proceeded with 'Whistle' because of my conviction that the American industrial system, which affects the lives and living of all the people in this country—and at the present time is a subject uppermost in the minds of the majority of the world's people, was a proper subject for motion picture treatment. . . . You wanted me to . . . deliver you pictures that are out of the ordinary." De Rochemont to Leo Jaffe, 5 December 1951, de Rochemont archive, Keene State.

22. "Whistle at Eaton Falls," *New York Times*, 11 October 1951, Production Code Administration (PCA) files, Academy of Motion Picture Arts and Sciences (AMPAS), Beverly Hills.

23. Borden Mace to B. Birnbaum, n.d. (probably 1950), de Rochemont archive, Keene State.

24. "Whistle at Eaton Falls," *New York Herald Tribune*, n.d. (probably July 1951), de Rochemont archive, Keene State.

25. Alton Cook, "Whistle at Eaton Falls," *New York World and Telegram*, n.d. (probably July 1951), de Rochemont archive, Keene State.

26. John R. Steelman to J. Raymond Bell, 17 May 1951, de Rochemont archive, Keene State.

27. Paul Ignatius to Louis de Rochemont, 15 May 1951, de Rochemont archive, Keene State.

INDEX

ABOUT THE AUTHOR

R. BARTON PALMER is Calhoun Lemon Professor of Literature and director of Film Studies at Clemson University. He is the author or editor of nearly forty volumes on various cinematic and literary subjects, and the general or series editor of more than thirty additional books. His recent coedited volumes (both with Murray Pomerance) include: *"A Little Solitaire": John Frankenheimer and American Film* and *Thinking in the Dark: Cinema, Theory, Practice* (both Rutgers University Press).